Language and Power in the Creation of the USSR, 1917–1953

by
Michael G. Smith

Mouton de Gruyter
Berlin · New York   1998

Mouton de Gruyter (formerly Mouton, The Hague)
is a Division of Walter de Gruyter & Co., Berlin

∞ Printed on acid-free paper which falls within the guidelines of
the ANSI to ensure permanence and durability.

Library of Congress Cataloging-in-Publication Data

Smith, Michael G., 1960—
    Language and power in the creation of the USSR, 1917—1953 / by Michael G. Smith.
      p. cm. − (Contributions to the sociology of language ; 80)
    Includes bibliographical references and index.
    ISBN 3-11-016197-4 (cloth : alk. paper)
    1. Soviet Union—Languages—Political aspects. 2. Language policy—Soviet Union. 3. Soviet Union—Politics and government—1917-1936. 4. Soviet Union—Politics and government—1936-1953. I. Title. II. Series.
P95.82.S65S64 1998
306.44'947'0904—dc21
                                        98-37960
                                              CIP

Die Deutsche Bibliothek — Cataloging-in-Publication Data

Smith, Michael G.:
Language and power in the creation of the USSR, 1917—1953 / by Michael G. Smith. — Berlin ; New York : Mouton de Gruyter, 1998
    (Contributions to the sociology of language ; 80)
    ISBN 3-11-016197-4

© Copyright 1998 by Walter de Gruyter GmbH & Co., D-10785 Berlin
All rights reserved, including those of translation into foreign languages. No part of this book may be reproduced or transmitted in any form or by any means, electronic or mechanical, including photocopy, recording or any information storage and retrieval system, without permission in writing from the publisher.
Printing: Druckerei Hildebrand, Berlin. —
Binding: Lüderitz & Bauer GmbH, Berlin. —
Printed in Germany.

Preface

This book tells a story about the national frontiers of the early Soviet era, where people from a myriad of social, cultural and ethnic backgrounds met to discover what they shared in common, and what they held apart. Language intersected their worlds, sometimes as a sign of communal identity, sometimes as a mark of social difference. Language was also intimately bound up with the Soviet government's enterprise of nation-making and state-building. The Bolsheviks employed language, embodied in the distinct codes of spoken and written speech, to communicate to the peoples of the former Russian Empire, to reshape their values and behaviors, and to craft new national and class categories for them. The "word" had a special mystique for the Bolsheviks. According to V.I. Lenin's "reflection theory", words were like mirror images of objects in the real world. Language both reflected and refracted back upon objective reality. To name was to know.

Representatives of the Russian and non-Russian nationalities play a central part in this story; theirs were the literary cultures made anew. Linguists also play a crucial role; their formal and "structural" methods made language reform possible. In part because of the nature of the early Soviet political system, in part because of the sources that I used, my emphasis is on the agents and policies of the center, Moscow. Sometimes the voices of the periphery speak, as in the case of my archival findings from Iaroslavl, Baku and Tashkent. But they are voices almost always in dialogue with Moscow: it established the parameters of policy and conduct within which both the nationalities and the professionals operated. This meant a dual policy of russification and nativization weaving through the Soviet experience; what became in practice a most precarious negotiation between coercion and compromise.

The story unfolds in four parts. Part I covers the divided speech communities of the late imperial and early Soviet eras, along with the challenges of governing a society rent by dozens of varieties of Russian dialects, and over a hundred non-Russian languages. The Bolsheviks spoke to these communities in a "proclamation" style: the word as command. But they soon found that their commands broke down without efforts to democratize and nativize their messages, to speak to people on their own terms. Part II explores how linguists contributed to Soviet cultural and national policies during the 1920s and early 1930s. The formal linguistic classifications of the "structural" school locked the nationalities of the complex, multiethnic USSR into a manageable hierarchical space. The linguistic "paleontology" of N.Ia.Marr's school bound them into a submissive historical time. The struggle between these two schools illuminates the authority of academic elites to shape state agendas through new knowledge, as well as their vulnerability before the awesome power of the state.

Part III surveys the successes and failures of the major language reform projects during the 1920s. The campaigns to simplify Russian spelling, to teach language according to class and social dialects, and to "latinize" the Arabic alphabets of the Muslim peoples - all represent forgotten chapters of the Stalinist cultural revolution. In each case, the government exploited the mass literacy campaigns to intervene in people's daily lives, to demarcate and manage them through the medium of language. Part IV examines the decades between 1932 and 1953, when the party state imposed new standards of russification on the country as a whole; and, after a few years of uncertain and noisy debate between 1948 and 1950, cemented these standards through Iosef Stalin's famous little book, *Marxism and the problems of linguistics*, our point of arrival in chapter eight.

Many good people have helped me to complete this work. I owe special thanks to Melinda S. Zook, my loyal friend; and to Richard Stites, Susan G. Solomon, and David Goldfrank, mentors and friends. I am also grateful to Hans Aarsleff, Ralph Dumain, Jerry Easter, William Fierman, Joshua Fishman, Lawrence Flockerzie, Jerry Hough, George Liber, E. James Lieberman, Ulrich Lins, Kathryn Olesko, David Rich, and Elizabeth Zelensky. My Russian, Tatar, Azerbaijani and Uzbek colleagues were always generous with help and advice, especially A.S. Khodnev, A.B. Sokolov, A.I. Zevelev and A.R. Atadzhanov.

I would also like to recognize the archivists of Russia, Azerbaijan, and Uzbekistan, who labor day after day to preserve and renew the historical record, with special appreciation to Bakhtiar Rafiev, director of the State Archive of Political Parties and Social Movements of the Azerbaijani Republic; and A.A. Pashaev, director of the State Archival Administration of the Azerbaijani Republic.

Several institutions provided valuable research support and consultations: the Provost's Office, History Department and Research Institute at the University of Dayton; the East-West Center at Duke University; the University of Toronto Workshop of the Social Science Research Council; the Esperanto League for North America; the History Department and Graduate School of Georgetown University; and the History Department at Purdue University. Travel funds were provided by the International Research and Exchanges Board. Archival research and writing support for this book was made possible by a generous postdoctoral fellowship from the Social Science Research Council and the Joint Committee on Soviet Studies of the American Council of Learned Societies.

Except for a few cases, I have used the Library of Congress system for the transcription of Russian-Cyrillic characters.

Contents

Introduction   1

Part I. Historical challenges

1. Democracy and language in late imperial Russia   15
2. Divided speech communities of the Soviet Union   35

Part II. Theoretical approaches

3. G.G. Shpet, linguistic structure, and the Eurasian imperative in Soviet language reform   59
4. N.Ia. Marr, language history, and the Stalin cultural revolution   81

Part III. Practical experiments

5. Mass mobilizing for Russian literacy: scripts, grammar and style   103
6. "A revolution for the east": Latin alphabets and their polemics   121

Part IV. Statist solutions

7. The official campaign for Russian language culture   143
8. Stalin's linguistic theories as cultural conquest   161

Conclusion   175

Abbreviations and acronyms   181
Notes   185
Archival sources   225
References   229
Index   287

Introduction

*My loyal friend, my treacherous foe,
My tsar, my slave, my native tongue.*
Valerii Briusov[1]

At the end of the Russian civil war in 1921, the ruling Bolshevik party surveyed its conquests and found a disturbing canvas of cultural and ethnic realities. Comprised largely of urban and Russian speaking members, it now presided over a poorly developed Russian nation, with entrenched pockets of local identity; and a divided multiethnic state, layered with movements for national autonomy and independence. To their war weary relief, and perhaps nagging misfortune, the Bolsheviks had inherited the imperial national frontiers of old.

Most of the population of the Russian Socialist Federated Soviet Republic (RSFSR) and its allied states consisted of peasants or workers, a considerable portion of which were illiterate or poorly literate; and over half of the population was not Russian at all. As in many other parts of Europe, the formal attributes of language, custom, and homeland were functions of local rather than of an overarching national identity.[2] Elite notions of great Russian nationalism were far removed from the realities of most Russians, who lived in provincial villages and towns far from St. Petersburg and Moscow, where they maintained local communities and spoke a variety of mutually intelligible but distinct dialects. Tsarist schemes for russification of the peripheries were equally removed from the realities of empire. National identity was growing strong among the elites of the major nationalities. The distinctions of communal identity (kinship, language, and religion) predominated among the people at large. "The special features of the different nationalities have survived" the "crude russification policies" of late Tsarism, wrote one observer after the 1917 revolution. "The native language prevails in family and daily life."[3]

The Bolsheviks had won the war, but they realized that a difficult struggle remained to recreate both rural and peripheral Russia in a new image. This was especially true since the disruptions of war had left the country ever more "ruralized", more "easternized" than before. "The question of the nationalities", wrote S.M. Dimanshtein in 1927, remains "a question of civil war." This was a person speaking not from certain strength but from fearful dominion, from the realization that the center still had to employ great "care and tact", still had to compromise with its new subjects so as to avoid the resistance and revolt of the civil war period.[4] These forces of confidence and fear, conquest and compromise, blended into a diffuse anxiety, the anxiety which all colonial overlords share. The Bolshevik ideal of a unitary Soviet proletarian state was imperiled by the variety of peoples over whom they ruled and did not understand. When the victorious party looked out upon the rural and non-Russian countryside, it saw not identity but difference, not itself but the "other".

The Soviet government was besieged. "Center" and "periphery", together with all of the vast cultural and ethnic gaps between them, were everyday terms of discourse during its first years. A variety of government leaders recognized the divisions between the "civilized" cities and the "backward", "wild" villages of Russia. They positioned the "representatives of the republics" against those of the "center"; or wrote of Turkestan on "the outer limits" of the Russian federation; or warned with trepidation that "the revolution, having begun in the center, has spread into the peripheries, especially the eastern ones, with something of a delay".[5] From their perches in Moscow, politicians and linguists looked out upon the rural countryside and non-Russian regions of their new state and faced the same mass of 'backward' (*otstalyi*) humanity. The national question meant to them that the Russian peasant was as alien a quantity as any of the dozens of non-Slavic peoples who inhabited historical Russia. A.V. Lunacharskii, Commissar of Education, once compared the illiterate Russian with the illiterate Kalmyk; both were equally ignorant of the great Russian literary language. G.K. Danilov designed his book, *The Russian language for the non-Russian*, as much for the poorly literate adult Russian reader as for the poorly literate Uzbek.[6]

This unease was made all the worse since the "western" or "European" provinces of the empire (Finland, the Baltic states, and Poland) had achieved their independence; and the Slavic homelands of the "great Russian state", Ukraine and Belorussia, became distinct national republics within the new Soviet Union. The Russian federation was left to gather unto itself the Asian parts of empire, the lands of "Russia-Eurasia", what the Bolsheviks grandiosely named their "Soviet east", or more modestly their "non-Russian" peripheries of the Muslim Caucasus, Volga-Urals, Central Asia, Siberia and Far East. These were territories of incredible ethnic and linguistic diversity, a mosaic of Turkic, Iranic, Japhetic, Finno-Ugric, Buriat-Mongol and Paleo-Asiatic speakers.[7] They will serve as my primary points of comparison in this book. For Russians struggled with their self-identity, their place and purpose in the world, through the prism of the east. By reconstructing how Russians understood their own language, as well as these languages of the east, we can open a new window onto the national frontiers of the past. By surveying the attitudes and designs of people towards their own and other languages, we can reconstitute the web of self-perceptions, shared communities, and mutual antagonisms which at one time informed Soviet state policies, and may yet speak to us today about their mixed legacies.

The Bolsheviks were trapped in the bind of space and time, a bit too far ahead of the historical curve, new masters of the subject peoples of the old empire. What could they do? As veteran dialectical thinkers, they believed that history was still on their side, if moving forward at too slow a pace. Their duty as its benefactors was to give the "backward" nationalities of the east Europe's most precious gifts: class consciousness and nationhood. In a defensive "fortress mentality", forged during the years of civil war, they legitimized new types of unitary communist party rule and police powers to ensure a regime of order and loyalty. (Joravsky 1985: 94-113) This fortress mentality translated into an equally defensive frontier mentality, by which the Bolsheviks maintained Moscow's interests from behind their fortress state, the RSFSR, and through the main urban centers of the republics and regions of the Union of Soviet Socialist Republics (USSR). They fused their ideological preferences for unitary Marxian state-building with the practical necessities of nation-making, designing a federal structure based upon their peace with the villages and their recognition of ethnic pluralism.

The USSR system, built upon the national territorial principle, was more than just a handsome edifice of formal republics and regions; it was an effective means of managing a poorly developed, multiethnic country. The party's deliberate policy of 'nativization' (*korenizatsiia*), an effort to "root" itself in the life of the ethnic peripheries, was unenviable yet unavoidable. Ideologues invented this term to highlight their predicament. Having established a new state of national territorial units, the Bolsheviks now needed to legitimize Soviet rule through the definition, promotion, and management of native cadres and their formal attributes of language and custom. Once all of these structures and policies were in place, the greater historical process of the 'convergence' (*sblizhenie*) and 'mergence' (*sliianie*) of nationalities would proceed toward one world proletarian culture.[8]

Soon after creating their new federal state, Soviet leaders marshaled the forces of linguistic agents and diverse citizens to conquer two specific national frontiers. One was between the standard, urban Moscow literary language and the provincial and rural Russian dialects. Linguists and policy makers now began to reshape historical, literary Russian into a living, popular Russian; what had once been appropriate for an elite now had to serve the masses of workers and peasants as well. They dreamed of an epic linguistic 'union' (*smychka*) between city and village. Another frontier was between the Russian language center and the non-Russian national peripheries. As one observer noted by applying a clever analogy: if the infusion of the Russian language into the government, the press and education during the imperial period had turned it into a "powerful all-national state language", then the non-Russian languages had been relegated to nothing more than a "series of separate, uncoordinated peasant dialects", now requiring renewal and reform.[9]

Language occupied such a central place at these national frontiers because it was a traditional and accepted component of nationhood. Most leading Bolsheviks concurred that the nation was, first and foremost, a "speech community"; or in Iosef Stalin's definition, "a historically evolving, stable community of people, rising upon the foundations of language, territory, economic life, and psychological makeup, manifested in a community of culture". Nations were rooted in the objective, historical realities of language. Indeed, there was a widespread mentality within the party which held that the native language was the necessary and proper stamp of "national culture", an objective means of expressing one's national identity without succumbing to such partisan deviations as "national pride" or territorial separatism. Of all the "foundations" of nationhood, then, language was the least offensive to the Marxist mindset.[10] It was one of the most fundamental public signs of difference, by which the common people identified their friends and strangers, or by which a government might measure loyalty to itself. But the Bolsheviks also appreciated its plasticity, how language was a register of what we now call the "imagined community" of the nation, which people created on the basis of common native tongues, and all the legends, folklore, and literatures spoken or written in them. Nations, in essence, were comprised of irrevocable facts and all too pliant fictions.[11] Working within the tension between these principles, the Soviet government sanctioned a broad initiative in language reform, what it eventually called, with characteristic certainty, 'language construction' (*iazykovoe stroitel'stvo*). The term betrays an image of the government excavating the USSR's national sites, linguists drawing up the architectural plans, and the nationalities themselves placing the bricks.

To build this new edifice of state power, the Soviet government carefully legislated the principle of equality between the peoples and languages of the new state. It was a principle at the core of early Bolshevik pronouncements on the national question. It was a principle embodied in the official constitutions, commissariat charters, and party resolutions of the 1920s and 1930s. (Pipes 1964: chapter 1) But this abstract principle takes us only so far in understanding the complex realities of the age. We students of the national question in the USSR have too often cast ourselves about the history by relying on the policy statements of the Soviet state at face value. Such exercises have always been useful; pronouncements and policies do count. But they too often leave us with surface readings, filled with all the stops and starts of this crisis or that policy shift. By turning to language issues, a particular but crucial dimension of the larger national question, we might discover some deeper continuities of Soviet history.

By turning to actual linguistic practice, for example, we will explore how, regardless of its high sounding egalitarian propositions, the government also crafted a very unequal "ABCD" hierarchy of ethnolinguistic privileges. This hierarchy ranked the eastern nationalities into one of four developmental categories, roughly corresponding to a 'people' (*narod*), a 'nationality' (*natsional'nost'*), or a 'nation' (*natsiia*). Each of these formal "nationality" groups was to enjoy a specific degree of cultural autonomy, depending on its assigned attributes of civilization. Russian, the "first among equals", remained the prestige language of the USSR. This hierarchy institutionalized, in formal and legal terms, the Soviet government's explicit and local commitment to the development of native, non-Russian languages, and its implicit and universal commitment to the status and prestige of Russian. It represents, in a tangible piece of historical evidence, V.I. Lenin's wish for a flexible "codex" within which national representatives might develop their own literary languages, yet appreciate the abiding civic value of Russian.[12] It also represents a central piece of evidence in recent debates about the character of Soviet national policies. Were they basically egalitarian and pluralistic? Or were they hierarchical and unitary? No doubt they were a combination of both, but as the above hierarchy shows, a combination structured nonetheless by the imperative for state order and central power.[13]

This ethnolinguistic hierarchy helps to prove that language reform was of no less strategic value to the Soviets than the definition of ethnic groupings or the demarcation of national territorial borders. Language was even more important as a territory of the mind, the most original source of communal identity, and thereby a handy means by which to define the peripheries and govern them. For the USSR, as for most other governments in the modern age, language had a purely instrumental value.[14] Its ABCD language hierarchy transformed the Marxian logic of history into the Soviet structure of nationality; the hierarchy translated the horizontal progress of people through time into the vertical relationships of people in space. When it ranked the Soviet nationalities as either civilized or primitive, it locked them into both the historical logic and the spatial structure, and therefore into positions of dominance or submission.

As a functional representation of USSR state forms, in particular Stalin's preference for strong central authority and limited local autonomy, the language hierarchy may even reveal something of a cynical disregard for the national territorial rights of the non-Russian peoples. In a sweeping act of metaphorical thinking, the Bolsheviks took the part (the Russian federation) for the whole (the Soviet Union) maintaining the primacy of Russian language and culture for both. They looked out at the peripheries of their fledgling state from the fortress RSFSR, their federation of closest neighbors. To them, the USSR was often nothing more than a political fiction. They did not always think in union terms of juridical entities. They also thought in broader terms of Russia and its eastern frontiers, peopled by dozens of language and ethnic groups, which by political force were obliged to respect the most prestigious ethnic group and its language, Russian.

The ABCD hierarchy also reveals something of the reciprocal nature of language, a measure of how the Soviet regime - much like the British and French in Europe, or the British in India, or the postcolonial states in Africa - needed to create a "repertoire of linguistic competencies" for their subjects and citizens.[15] It could no more fashion a new integral Russian speech community to help modernize the country than it could an integral state system. So rather than engage in a blanket, maximal attempt at "russification", transforming the non-Russian peoples "objectively and psychologically into Russians", it engaged in a minimalist russification program of "internationalizing the Russian language and culture within the Soviet Union". (Aspaturian 1968: 159-160) This policy was a fateful choice for Soviet leaders because it was impossible without nativization. They found themselves solving the burdens of language development, which forced them to first promote the provincial Russian dialects and the native non-Russian languages so as to later exploit them as mediums for state communication. They also faced the burdens of language dependence, which meant that they should rely on those same dialects and languages as mediums by which to enforce the greater dissemination and use of modern, standard Russian. In terms of language reform, they had to negotiate between the conflicting needs to standardize literary cultures and at the same time democratize them. From the moment of its greatest victory in the civil war, to the most difficult days under the Stalin purges, the government was unable to break out of the historical and ethnolinguistic particularisms of the former Russian empire. It was forced to deal with the non-Russian peoples on their own as well as on Bolshevik terms. It was locked into a hegemonic imperative which required a measure of dependence upon the rural Russian and peripheral non-Russian peoples as much as domination over them.

There is nothing dramatically new about such play between central power and local resistance. The political theories of Antonio Gramsci, who by no coincidence was also a linguist, first clearly defined the nature of state hegemony in these terms. He argued that the dominance of one standard dialect over other dialects of the same language, or of one language over its neighbors, may serve as a model for the hegemony of city over rural, or of "civilized" over "backward" culture. Hegemony is based not on the simple unidirectional power of state governments, but on a more "reciprocal" conversation of power, on a subtle combination of coercion and consensus, pressure and participation. A group attains hegemony in society not by force alone but by a subtle process of force and counterforce, using language, newspapers, civic associations, clubs, the schools, religion and ideology to convince the people of the legitimacy of its rule. (Gramsci 1975, 3: 2341-2351)

We can find similar insights at work in the literature on Soviet national and language issues. One traditional approach has suggested that government policies swung alternately like a "pendulum" or "see-saw"; from centrifugal "nativization" tendencies during the 1920s, a constructive moment in the development of the non-Russian nationalities and languages; to centripetal "russification" tendencies during the 1930s and beyond, a destructive moment which subdued the nationalities to the conformity of Russian national values. But even within this rather dualistic approach there has always been much room to explore the intricacies and varieties of Soviet national policies, how they intertwined and caused reciprocal effects, how they were subject to the many demographic, geographic and political variables of the peripheries.[16] There was no sudden, irrevocable turn between "nativization" of the 1920s and "russification" of the 1930s. Elements of each coexisted in these decades and beyond. As state policies from above and social processes from below, they existed in a delicate symbiotic relationship, much in the way that apparently contradictory cultural and political trends coexisted through these times. The government's national policies, no matter how manipulative in intent or effect, still yet had to succumb at times to the resilience of people, and to the wondrous and reckless power of their languages.

We can see the principle of hegemony and its dialectic of power and resistance at work in yet other dimensions of Russian and Soviet history. It has become a standard of broad interpretation.[17] Historians have argued its relevance within a range of case studies. Russian peasants were not the unwitting pawns of modernization; they assimilated national educational principles and methods in their own interests and at their own paces. Through songs, jokes and anecdotes, Soviet citizens were able to retain some locus of identity and autonomy of action even under the worst repression of the Stalin era. Writers maintained their expressive power within the constraints of the communist party's official idiom and genre of socialist realism. The history of Russian popular culture in the twentieth century offers us compelling evidence as to the reciprocal dialectic between the coercive power of the state and the creative life of the people.[18]

My work offers yet another, even more essential proof, of this very human condition: the tension between power and resistance. We should not underestimate the dynamism and treacherousness of language. It was conductive and valent in ways which Soviet leaders were able to control, and in ways that they never could. Their policies had the power to determine language use, to subsume peoples within the sphere of influence of the Russian or any of a dozen other languages. But language also empowered people to move rather freely within their political and cultural spaces; just as they freely conversed within the formal structures and meaningful words of their spoken languages. "At the buried roots of language", J.G.A. Pocock has written, "there is a rich field of ambiguities, absurdities, and contradictions awaiting our exploitation." People will always misunderstand and be misunderstood. Even the language of authority is more a discourse open to play and interpretation rather than an unambiguous signal of control and obedience. (Pocock 1984: 25-43). The nature of language, defined most suggestively by Wilhelm von Humboldt as a medium for both conservative communication and creative expression, offers us perhaps the best model as to why power and resistance happen. For the conventionality and arbitrariness of the linguistic sign are precisely what makes it so slippery and variable, the perfect vessel of "linguistic subjectivity" and "linguistic relativity". (Aarsleff 1982: 345-347). By no coincidence, in language issues we see power and resistance happening all the time; and in the patrons and agents of language reform, we see the drama of hegemony played out in full relief.

The Soviet government promoted language construction with great fanfare as an extension of its strategic political agenda to dominate and develop the peoples within and around Russia. Its leaders were well aware of the power of language to mold and manipulate class and national identities. Words, they believed, had consequences. Be they Marx's social and economic analyses, or Lenin's agitational slogans, words were the Bolsheviks' stock in trade. Language, especially the nomenclature of Marxism-Leninism, was their fundamental tool of political power, economic production, and social management. By no coincidence, it was the 'Organizational Bureau' (*Orgbiuro*) of the 'Central Committee of the Russian Communist Party' (TsK RKPb) which took attentive charge over several language reform issues in the 1920s and 1930s. Iosef Stalin, with little more than a secondary education, but with broad experience in the multilingual Bolshevik underground, even fancied himself something of a linguist. In his early years as Commissar of the Nationalities, he became a patron for Latinization of alphabets during Central Committee (TsK) meetings; later joining with the ethnographer, N.Ia. Marr, in promoting the international language, Esperanto. In the last few years of his life, he wrote one of his most perplexing and fascinating treatises, the celebrated *Marxism and the problems of linguistics*, our point of arrival in chapter eight.[19]

Soviet leaders understood that classes assimilate into one national culture through a mixed process of social mobilization and language change. But that which had come gradually and chaotically to Western Europe over many centuries had to be managed with haste in the Soviet Union. The state recognized its "class" responsibility to promote these reform processes between the cities and villages of Russia in order to reshape a Soviet Russian nation. It also recognized a class dimension in its relations with the non-Russians, appealing to the languages and dialects of the peasant masses in an effort to promote native literacy most effectively, as well as to maneuver power over national 'elites' (*verkhi*) who had their own language reform designs in mind. Thus to the communist party, the peasant question in Russia was a national question; and "the national question" in the non-Russian territories "was also a peasant question". Stalin taught the party that these issues were inextricably linked. The real challenge was to forge an alliance between the proletariat of a "once powerful" nation, Russia, and the peasants of the "once oppressed" nations of non-Russia.[20] In either case, this emphasis on mass action required that the ruling communist party focus its attention on raising up the vulgar, vernacular linguistic forms of the 'common people' (*nizy*). That these forms were relatively undeveloped, and large numbers of people still illiterate, made this program all the more achievable. In many cases, the Bolsheviks were starting from scratch. Illiteracy was less a curse than a rare political advantage.

Research work in the newly opened Soviet archives confirms the fullness of the party's controls in these years. It defined the limits of debate and policy within which its selected agents worked. True enough, far from the sensational discoveries which have been reported in the newspapers, the "open" archives more often deliver only clues about major policy debates and decisions, whose facts may still remain hidden in secreted layers of documents. Or they reveal that the work of top party leaders, conducted by word of mouth without benefit of stenographers, still subject to underground rules of conduct, may be forever lost from the historical record. In one cinematic episode, during a meeting of the communist fraction which helped to organize and choreograph the Baku Turkological Congress of 1926, M.P. Pavlovich-Vel'tman told his comrades to "immediately burn and destroy upon reading" the guiding documents from the 'Political Bureau' (*Politburo* TsK) that he had passed along to them.[21]

We can almost picture the participants, sitting around a conference table, lighting their cigarettes from the burning Politburo papers. Only shadowy traces remain as to what those documents really said. But my research also confirms the rough contours of a participatory politics at work in these years. To fulfill its language reform initiatives, the party had to work with autonomous "strategists" - linguists, cultural professionals, and national representatives - to shape language into a foundation of national identity and into a "symbol for new community frontiers". (Weinstein 1979: 345) The archives are filled with the voices of people fighting courageously for their right to disagree or compromise, with patterns of policy and behavior, embodied in statistics or turns of a phrase, which put to shame the boasts of political leaders. To these autonomous actors of the early Soviet period, words did indeed matter; and they took care to weigh them well as a private currency in the public marketplace of ideas.

The expertise of linguists provided crucial support to the Soviet system and its peculiar style of cultural dominion. Inspired by G.G. Shpet's innovative phenomenology and semiotics of language, by F.F. Fortunatov's empirical studies of synchronic language forms, and by Jan Baudouin de Courtenay's insights into structural phonology, they came to fancy themselves as new scientists of the human word. Together they crafted a tentative but visionary "structural" approach to language - as an integral system of sound (phonological), word (morphological) and sentence (syntactical) subsystems, open to verifiable analysis and conscious manipulation.[22] I emphasize the word "approach" here and throughout the text, for early Soviet structural methods appear not as the pristine theories of West European structuralism but as awkward and unfinished forays into applied linguistics and language reform.

The government depended on these formalist and structural linguistic insights, unavailable just a few decades earlier, for practical successes on its state-building and nation-making-fronts. They were especially useful in the process of defining the national linguistic forms of the new Soviet republics and regions. Linguistic principles also matched well with the philosophical rationalism and scientism that underlay Bolshevik political thought. Lenin and his comrades believed that they could know the world objectively and apply scientific truths to reform it, especially by way of the material power of language. In order to ensure state hegemony over the Russian peasants and non-Russian nationalities, they recognized the need to define their dialects and languages within a comprehensive encyclopedia of knowledge. In marking and distinguishing the linguistic attributes of their scholarly "speaking" subjects, linguists thereby marked and distinguished the new "divided" national subjects of Soviet rule.[23]

Linguists also invented new paradigms about the ethnic dynamics of the USSR. A small school of structural linguists not only identified the language forms of the Russian and non-Russian peoples, but also placed them in a new geographic grid, "Eurasia". A rival school of historical paleontologists, under the leadership of N.Ia. Marr, studied the origins of sounds and words in order to set these same languages within a novel historical timeline of material development, centered around a new language group, the "Japhetic". These two schools coexisted in an often peaceful, sometimes agitated rivalry between the 1920s and 1940s. Each enjoyed its own institutional and ideological power base. Each contributed its own principled scholarly defense of the Soviet state system and its nation-making projects. In creating such vast new knowledge about the peoples of the Russian east, linguists of the structural and Japhetic schools practiced "colonial ethnography" or "orientalism" in the simplest sense of the term. They studied, described and classified the non-Russian peoples by academic standards for political purposes. (Said 1979: 2-3) But in an interesting turn on the conventional meaning of "orientalism", these schools, like the Soviet state, were sometimes anti-European in inspiration and design. Straddling both Europe and Asia, west and east, Soviet scholars and politicians could not help but see themselves as victims of European orientalism, and as patrons of a more judicious Soviet orientalist style.

Linguists became the government's primary agents in language reform, applying their rudimentary structural principles to codify new national literary standards: alphabets, spelling systems, grammars, as well as scientific-technical and literary languages. For the government repeated time and again that a highly literate intelligentsia was useless if its messages were not communicable to society at large. Any one person is only as literate as their entire speech community allows based on these formidable linguistic standards and their broader print cultures - encompassing bureaucracies, advertisements, newspapers, books, or popular fiction. But government leaders also appreciated how languages could only be planned to the extent that they were controlled. This meant placing each of the non-Russian languages within its proper place in the ABCD hierarchy: defined and ennobled within the structure, but also limited by its inherent constraints. They seemed to realize a crucial principle of language planning: that it either succeeds or fails based largely on the prestige of the language being planned. True to their insights and intentions, several languages of the USSR, Russian first among them, remained or became more "equal" (prestigious) than others.[24]

In calling forth the service of linguists in its grand projects, and in using them to fortify its own cultural authority, the government took a calculated risk. It had to depend on their expertise for the "production of public knowledge". But linguists also maintained a degree of professional autonomy and their own scholarly claims on the truth. They also tended to translate the overarching social and political ideologies of the day into their own idiosyncratic terms. As members of a scholarly profession and as active participants in national life, they were not always and everywhere pliable and obedient agents of state power. They often applied their values, theories and methods to broader political needs so as to fulfill their own agendas.[25]

These balancing acts between professional identity and public service were not always easy to maintain. Linguists sometimes faltered and let their loyalty to state patrons or ideals subvert their professional standards. The state sometimes actively intervened in linguistic disputes and suppressed one school or another, depending on its contributions to the official cultural and national policies of the day. This was the case first in 1929 and later in1949, when the communist party used the Japhetic school as its point of leverage to demand loyalty and conformity in linguistic science. In both episodes, it was merely fulfilling the dictates of its state-building and nation-making functions. Linguistic principles never rose or fell based on theory alone. Cognitive issues became a ground for power politics, but practicality was the rule. The government patronized either structural or Japhetic theories at one time or another based on their practical results.

Russian and Soviet structural theories were remarkably free from pedantry, disdainful of overarching generalizations and categorical schemes. They were distinct from all of those celebrated "structuralisms" which have graced Western academia with such names as Saussure, Levi-Strauss, Althusser, or Foucault - monuments to grandiose achievements in the social sciences and philosophy, punctuating history with all of their "epistemological breaks" and "scientific revolutions".[26] Western scholars have, nonetheless, elevated several Russian intellectuals - Roman Jakobson, Mikhail Bakhtin, and Lev Vygotskii - into this pantheon. These privileged personalities too often speak for the whole literary and linguistic establishment of twentieth-century Russia, too often in terms that are colored by Western perspectives and concerns. Writings about them verge on hagiography.[27]

This is strange stuff in a day when the leading literary theories of "deconstruction" proclaim the death of the author and intent. Stranger still that Bakhtin is often praised as the champion of the multiplicity of voices ("polyphony") and of dialects and styles ("heteroglossia"), or as the sentinel of the expressive "utterance" and "discourse". For it is precisely his voice that so often drowns out those of his equally talented contemporaries, including the much-maligned V.N. Voloshinov.[28] These latter figures are present in my work largely by their silence. Rather than stitch their insights into every few pages, and only highlight the notoriety that they have already achieved, I will try to let the world around them speak. In the process, I hope we will discover that they were ordinary products of an exceptional age: unique perhaps in our time, but not in their own. For what we need to do is jettison the "'heroic' theory of science", and instead uncover the full range of debate about language in the early Soviet era, explore the rich and complex fabric of intellectual history, what V.V. Ivanov appropriately calls the "circle of ideas" which animated the times.[29]

During the interwar years, in the relative comforts of the West, Roman Jakobson and his colleagues in the Prague Linguistic Circle had the luxury to theorize about "an ascending scale of freedom", by which people use the distinct levels of speech - strict phonology (meaningful sounds), open-ended morphology (meaningful forms), and free syntax (combined meanings) - not simply to communicate but also to express themselves more creatively.[30] But what may be true for language in the abstract is not necessarily true for language in society. When faced with the harsh demands of language reform and politics, the ascending scale of freedom turns on its head. Neat concepts suddenly give way to difficult choices. The self-evident sounds and forms of a language give way to political conflict. Linguists are confronted by the demands of the government for political control, but also face the newly articulated rights and freedoms of the nationalities - who presume to know better what to do with the sounds and signs of their own languages. When the Soviet government set into motion a pattern of continuous native language development, it admitted its dependence on national leaders to help implement cultural and language reforms.

Like the linguists with their various ideologies of service, national leaders had their own agendas in mind with regard to the creation of national language cultures. Their challenge was "to fix a group identity in which both intellectuals and illiterates could recognize themselves". (Allworth 1990: 192) For many cultural leaders in the Soviet east, such a challenge meant that they should either maintain their traditional elite Arabic scripts, or revise them in the interests of mass literacy. In the first years after the revolution and civil war, the major debates pitted the advocates of creating modified Arabic scripts against the advocates of wholly new Latin alphabets.

From the North Caucasus and Central Asia, to the Volga-Urals and Siberian North, national representatives struggled to recreate group identities within the constraints of power politics imposed from Moscow. A few, like Galimdzhan Ibragimov of Kazan or Bekir Chobanzade of Baku, promoted their own distinct maximalist programs for pan-Turkic unification and development. Dozens of others served Moscow's interests more directly by working on minimalist programs of nation-making or by serving state sponsored russification policies. Each national region of the Soviet Union endured its own unique struggles to recreate and maintain new literary cultures. Each had its own strengths and weaknesses. But to one extent or another, what we also find is that national representatives not only served Soviet power but also redefined it, working on native terms, according to native interests. They were not always the passive receptacles of Bolshevik experiments.

In academies and laboratories, the sounds and forms of language were reducible to their unproblematic and verifiable component parts. Language reform and the creation of national literary cultures always depended on the "narrowly technical acts" of linguists to ensure effective spelling and grammar systems. But their success depended perhaps even more on the broader political and social revolutions within which they operated. (Fishman 1977: xv) In public forums language remained a very creative and problematic means of expression, open to several layers of political, scholarly, and national complexity. Once written down and learned by people already sharing a common homeland, kinship or religion, language became a powerful means of self-representation and a symbol of national consciousness.

Linguistic theories and methods, so neatly designed for "practice", were thus often rent apart by its whirlwind. Applied linguistics, in the presumptuous form of "language construction", became charged with all the hopes and fears and passions of the early Soviet era. The struggle to build a communist language community, like the struggle to build a communist labor community, was weighed down by the competition of group interests and by chronic backwardness. As millions of men, women and children became the focus of education and propaganda efforts, linguists and national representatives tried to accomplish in a few years of central planning in the USSR what had taken centuries of spontaneity and sporadic creation in other parts of Europe. The difficulties of creating a new speech community were compounded by the scores of languages of the new Soviet Union, most of which were much less developed than Russian.

I will not exaggerate the power and performance of the Soviet state; there was no center without its agents in the professions or on the rural and non-Russian peripheries. Success depended on the constraints and freedoms that the Bolsheviks defined for the country, on the scholarly and disciplinary facts of linguistics, and on the social and cultural realities of the peripheries. All of these factors combined to create a patchwork of state management rather than a monolithic structure of Soviet power. Language issues help us better understand how the USSR was a machine of centrifugal as well as centripetal force. How the national frontier was a place of opportunity as well as submission. How language was a ground upon which people could both build and destroy, change and protect themselves from change, exercise their freedom and sense its limitations.

[handwritten note: Language — the double-edged sword]

Part I
Historical challenges

Chapter 1

Democracy and language in late imperial Russia

By the late nineteenth century, Tsarist Russia found itself in a troublesome but hardly unique set of historical circumstances. It had formed as an autocratic, imperial state centuries before it consolidated Russia's own national identity on a mass scale.[1] Only a small minority of aristocratic and middling elites had begun to shape a Russian national consciousness, as reflected in their appreciation for the native tongue that bound them together. They had been educated during a century of "scholarly interest" in the Russian language and understood its potential for "active patriotic agitation". They discovered a stable, common literary standard in Alexander Pushkin's "terse, elliptical syntax" and "conversational manner". The Pushkin celebration of 1880 peaked the growth of a national consciousness for the new "western-style reading public". His writings became a "validator of its national self-worth" as the "carrier of both the moral and political interests of the nation".[2]

But such an elite consciousness was hardly enough anymore to fulfill the latest demands of the evolving nation state. The governments of Western Europe had set a new pace in international relations: to modernize and unify their state systems by promoting national consciousness for the masses, by collecting their diverse subjects and citizens into one, by assimilating "peasants into Frenchmen", or into Germans, or Italians. Language reform was at the heart of this political imperative because politicians understood language as one of the most fundamental markers of group consciousness and identity. In the spoken and written languages of their peoples, governments recognized the dangers of difference and the potential for unity. The public sounds and signs of language became an economical means to measure political loyalties, and to gather the forces of difference under political control. So the European states became patrons of new, vernacular literary languages, for use in the public schools and armed forces as the foundations for mass national consciousness.

In order to compete, the Tsarist state had to make its own peasants and workers over into Russians. Social transformations in the villages, cities and armed forces, spurred on by the great reforms of the 1860s, now revealed a great divide, what G.O. Vinokur called that "deep breach" between the elite literary language and the local dialects of the illiterate or semiliterate masses. The linguistic standards of Russian remained poorly developed for use in the mass schools, newspapers and popular fiction. Now more than ever the populist intelligentsia of teachers, journalists and linguists began to see the gap between themselves and the broad public. (Vinokur 1929a) Beginning with the great reforms, they challenged the government to institute a series of radical reforms in spelling and grammar, essential to promote mass literacy and learning. Their populist agenda entailed one part of democratization with another part of standardization, bringing the established literary language to the people, and bringing the people halfway to it.[3]

A similar dynamic played out within the greater boundaries of the multiethnic empire, where Tsarist administrators engaged in a delicate balancing act between russification and nativization. Russia was trapped in a unique double bind: as the world's largest contiguous land empire, it needed to turn both its Russian peasants and non-Russian peoples into loyal imperial subjects. From the center, language strategists now upheld Russian as the official standard, while dispensing a benign multiculturalism and linguistic nativism to the nationalities beyond. From that beyond, native leaders fought consistently for their rights to native language use and self-determination; yet even they never relinquished the role of Russian as a practical language of state.

Linguists were valuable allies to Tsarist administrators in their projects to create a new nation state and multiethnic empire. Only their science could effectively discover the multifaceted parts of ethnic reality, the dialects and languages, through which the state might reach the people and ready them for political assimilation. To accomplish these tasks, linguists fit the dialects and languages of the people into several new temporal and spatial paradigms: Indo-Europeanism, formalist and structural linguistics, and Eurasianism. But these paradigms also became enduring forms of power, for linguistics and for the state, by staking scientific and political claims onto reality, even conjoining with it by their very acts of definition. As linguistic paradigms that explained social reality, they appeared even more objective, more authoritative. Such was the power and fame of comparative philology in the public discourse of the times. (Said 1979: 202-203) When the Soviet regime inherited the national frontiers of old, by default it inherited these definitive scientific paradigms as well.

1.1. A populist nationalism: linguistics as a social art

By 1880, linguistics had risen to prominence in academia with its own credentialed posts in the Academy of Sciences, state universities and professional societies. "Indo-Europeanism", centerpiece of the new historical-comparative philology, dominated the field. Its proponents assumed that all of the Indo-European languages, including Russian, developed from one common stock, one primeval 'protolanguage' (*Ursprache*), characterized by its inflective grammatical system, a mark of civilized superiority. According to August Schleicher's famed "organicist" paradigm, sometimes represented in the shape of a tree, the agglutinative systems of the Turkic languages and the isolative systems of Chinese were imperfect, inferior language forms. Languages were like organisms in the natural world, some stronger, others weak, but all developing according to an evolutionary path of growth and decay. In the excitement of the times, some scholars set out to prove the racial superiority of the Indo-European or "Aryan" peoples using comparative philology as their guide. The "Aryan nations", wrote the ever popular Max Müller, "have become the rulers of history, and it seems to be their mission to link all parts of the world together by the chain of civilisation, commerce, and religion". Their superior language system was but an emblem of the more civilized "soul" of the Aryan peoples.[4] More mindful of science for its own sake, other scholars took the name "neogrammarians", applying the historical-comparative method to analyze how sound laws and word formations developed and decayed in the Indo-European languages over time. Russian academics, not wanting to be left behind, became linguistic racialists and neogrammarians too. Schleicher's and Müller's works, among others like them, became obligatory readings in a country so eager to join Europe's superior language system and march to progress.[5]

German dialectical idealism and English empiricism provided Russian linguists with a healthy antidote to the inbred naturalism and historicism of many Western Indo-Europeanists, positioning them within that semiotic tradition in language thought "from Locke to Saussure", and preparing them for a novel "structural" approach to language.[6] G.W.F. Hegel taught them that the linguistic sign system, governed by formal grammatical rules, was the primary medium of human communication in the present. He defined language as both a referential and an expressive activity. Words are not just material signs that point to things in the world; they are also the creative and conductive mediums of human consciousness. The process by which language moves from its referential activity to its expressive activity, and returns again, became for Hegel a model for the unity of the person with the community. People communicate to each other through social dialogue, yet understand each other upon the ground of their own individual consciousness, as speakers and listeners. Language is always reality both objectively received and subjectively recapitulated.[7]

Wilhelm von Humboldt's works (translated into Russian in 1858) stated this principle even more precisely, in a formula which later became a rallying cry of early Soviet linguistics, when he wrote that, "we must look upon language, not as a dead product, but far more as a producing . . . . [It] is an enduring thing, and at every moment a transitory one." For Russian intellectuals, then, Humboldt conceived of language as both *ergon* (referential sign system) and *energeia* (expression or activity). "People surround themselves with a world of sounds", he wrote, "so as to assimilate and process within themselves the world of objects." Language operates in the world between people of the same speech community as a means of communication and expression precisely because each person within that community shares the language code by force of birth and habit. The very rules and representations of language make utterances and expressions possible.[8] These insights, centered around Humboldt's distinction between *ergon* and *energeia*, very nearly became the clichés of the 1920s and 1930s. We find them repeated again and again in the scholarly literature. They were first popularized, in the terms I outlined above, by the philosopher G.G. Shpet, in his classic but forgotten work, *The internal form of the word* (1927). They are the genesis of Mikhail Bakhtin's notion of "discourse", language as both a "product" (*dan*) and "reproduction" (*zadan*).[9]

Hegel and Humboldt, who by no coincidence were also political philosophers, viewed language as the ultimate building block of personal consciousness, national identity, and the modern state. They shared the essential insight that language was one of the most reliable media and linguistics one of the most precise methods, by which to understand different ethnic cultures as they exist in the world. To infiltrate the linguistic code, be it in the sounds, words, or grammar of a language, meant to grasp the essential features of any given cultural community. Language embodied the reason and order at work in a nation's history. John Locke's *Essay on human understanding* (translated into Russian in 1898) provided similar insights to the Russian reading public. One of Locke's popular biographers in Russia reserved special praise for his Third Book, "On words or on language in general", an early modern study of language as a semiotic system. The author argued that Locke's simple and complex ideas, woven together to form "reason", were modeled upon the even more basic building blocks of the different "combinations of sounds and words" that "create language". The Russian intelligentsia thus learned that the relationships between the sounds and words of language were a perfect paradigm for the relationships between the simple and complex ideas in human thought.[10]

These principles further reached Russian academic circles and the educated reading public through Alexander Potebnia's popular *Thought and language*. He and his students were especially keen on developing the associations between the outer linguistic form (sign) and the inner psychological form (sense); or between the "word" (*slovo*) as an "extraneous and arbitrary sign" and as the "symbol of a known content". Their path breaking studies of Russian grammar drew from the Humboldtian assumption that grammatical categories were the framework for the mastery of thought and for the promotion of national literary development. The Potebnians elaborated on the power of language as *energeia*, stressing that any word, or "image" (*obraz*), or work of art, will necessarily "act differently on different people" by the very energy it activates in them. Potebnia called this the "paradox that every understanding, even the fullest one, is at the same time a misunderstanding". As creatures of an optimistic age, the Potebnians held that linguistics, for all of its weaknesses, was both a social science and a liberal art, a means to better understand the powers of the human intellect and apply them to the betterment of national life.[11] In an age of ever-hegemonic nationalist and imperialist states, Potebnia took some comfort in knowing that the dialects and languages of the common people were very nearly indestructible. They were the grammatical and lexical mediums which formed a person's "circle of thoughts", the inescapable foundations of one's "worldview" (*mirosozertsanie*) and "national identity" (*narodnost'*). As language makes each human being uniquely individual, he declared, so it also makes different peoples uniquely local or national.[12]

Jan Baudouin de Courtenay and F.F. Fortunatov, founders of the Petersburg and Moscow schools of linguistics, were most responsible for applying these dialectical principles to new language theories and reforms. Both were traditional Indo-Europeanists. But the idealism of Hegel and Humboldt enabled them to escape, if not always consistently, the naturalist preoccupations of many of their German and French colleagues with the growth or decay of sound laws in history, or with the psychological functions of individual speakers. They reconceived of language "not as an organism, but as a system". For them, "the vehicle of language" was "no longer the soul of a people but an intersubjective communication".[13] As founders of uniquely structural and formal approaches along with Ferdinand de Saussure, they rededicated linguistics to the study of the "rules and representations" between sounds and words, along with their social implications.[14] In philosophical terms, they explored how the subject uses language as an object of discourse. This was an essential pathway to structural and applied linguistics at the turn of the century, and became quite provocative during the crude Soviet polemics of the 1930s and 1940s. Baudouin and Saussure both came to some of the first definitions of the phoneme, the letter sign in languages which carries and distinguishes meaning, apart from the many distinctive features of sounds. They delineated language into its abstracted parts: as a system of interdependent elements (*langue*), and as the actual speech of individuals and groups (*parole*); as well as a system which remains static (synchrony), and as a system which changes over time (diachrony).

Yet Baudouin and his students in the Petersburg school were less preoccupied than Saussure with these distinctions, more intrigued by the relationships between them, by the functions of their elements, and by their values between speaking persons. In the Potebnian tradition, they refashioned linguistics from a natural science into a social art. Baudouin studied how languages were splintered, how they had "different social values", how they were used "according to age, mental state, time of day, season, and recollection". He recognized "an everyday language, an official language, a language of church sermons, of university lectures". He also affirmed the human capacity to control and perfect language, which "is neither a self-contained organism nor an untouchable fetish" but "a tool and an activity". People have the "social duty to improve their tools in accordance with their purpose, and even to replace the existing tools with better ones". We create grammars for languages. We teach them. We correct mistakes in them. We simplify their alphabets and create new scientific and technical terms within them. In the case of argots and Esperanto, we even invent them. All of this paints a "picture of the interference of people's consciousness upon language", he wrote, "which at a certain point of development introduces true artificiality into language". Baudouin had a special interest in the principle of linguistic economy. He described language change as a "striving for convenience", the tendency toward ease and simplicity in everyday speech habits. Sometimes this principle took on very practical, politicized forms. As a member of the left wing of the Constitutional Democrats, he taught his students the possibilities of applied linguistics in building a new democracy for Russia. Reformed spelling and grammar systems, he argued, would lead to "a single, more or less standardized, and educated language", serving to "unify members of the nation" and to provide "a link between successive generations".[15]

At other times, Baudouin's linguistic "economics" took some rather eccentric forms. With his colleague, R.F. Brandt, Baudouin was one of Russia's leading Esperantists. An obscure Polish optician, Ludwig Zamenhof, had invented this language of eternal 'hope' (*espero*) in 1887. He was a Polish Jew living in the western borderlands of the Russian empire, a region of intense language diversity where the Tsarist regime had begun to forcefully impose Russian as a state language. Baudouin, like Zamenhof, looked to Esperanto as a neutral and rational alternative. As the most successful international language of its day, it was comprised of a European lexical base and Latin alphabet, easy structure and rules, and therefore practical accessibility for the masses. Baudouin supposedly learned Esperanto in twenty-five hours.[16] Neither Baudouin's nor Brandt's attraction to Esperanto was coincidental; it was but a logical, if extreme, function of their dedication to language reform, which was becoming all the more critical with the social transformations in Russia at the turn of the century.

F.F. Fortunatov, more the traditional Indo-Europeanist, devoted his Moscow school of linguistics to *russistika*, the study of the diverse layers of sounds, meanings, and literary styles in the Russian language. He was most famous for discovering a "formal" or "pseudo-structural" approach to morphology, the study of "language forms" and the "search for objective criteria of differentiation" between them. His students were known as the "armoured Muscovites" for the severity of their scientific methods. Not a grand theoretician in the manner of Saussure or Baudouin, Fortunatov's teaching still discussed many of their insights about the systematic and synchronic nature of language. With his students, the linguists and literary theorists alike, he proclaimed as the "primary object of linguistics the discovery of general laws of language" and thought.[17]

Fortunatov's school, which shared Baudouin's sense of linguistics as a social art, created its own unique kind of populism. Between the 1890s and 1910s, through the Moscow Dialectological Commission and the leading publications of the Imperial Academy of Sciences and Ministry of Education, the "armoured Muscovites" canvassed the dialect variations of the Russian heartland and the provinces beyond. Through their essays, maps and atlases, they described and compared the minute linguistic distinctions between Russian dialect territories. They also turned to the study of local traditions, customs, and ethnographic characteristics so as to better understand the broader contexts within which these dialects existed. Also a representative of the left wing of the Constitutional Democrat Party, and a member of its Central Committee in 1917, A.A. Shakhmatov brought his political leanings to this enterprise, much like the populist ethnographers and "itinerant" painters before him. He and his students became "dialectologist travelers", studying and collecting samples of "living speech". In an interesting combination of chauvinism and multiculturalism, several of these dialectologists began their studies from the assumption that Russian was one of the world's leading Indo-European languages, and therefore worthy of such detailed study. They even considered Ukrainian and Belorussian as component dialects of the singular "great Russian language". At the same time, they delineated the wonderful plurality and variety of local Russian dialects and regional cultures.[18] In setting out to discover the one Russian nation, they came to know the plural Russian people.

By their provocative theories, these linguists and their students participated in a Europe wide "crisis of the sign". With sympathetic artists and scientists, they discarded the traditional explanation about the origins of languages and the positivistic "preoccupation with genesis", focusing instead on teleology, the study of "the purposes of human endeavor". Revolutionary broadsides, from Einstein's theory of relativity to Saussure's theory of language structure, helped to fuel the crisis. Cubism in art and sculpture, and modernism in music, reflected its new departures. The students of the Petersburg and Moscow schools contributed as well, crafting the two main avant-garde literary movements of the war and revolutionary eras: formalism and futurism. Viktor Shklovskii, E.D. Polivanov and L.P. Iakubinskii founded the Petrograd Society for the Study of Poetic Language; with R.O. Jakobson, N.S. Trubetskoi, N.F. Iakovlev and G.O. Vinokur, they also helped to launch the innovative Moscow Linguistic Circle. As literary formalists, these classmates searched for semiotic forms in texts rather than for aesthetic imagery. Their quest, to revive all that was pure, universal and elementary in the human literary experience. With futurist writers, they applied some of the same techniques and methods to language reform that cubist painters worked on their canvasses by way of geometric shapes, and that futurist poets applied to the creation of 'nonsense poetry' (*zaum*) by way of disjointed sounds. This meant breaking down painting and language into their component parts in order to rebuild them in artistically creative and socially useful ways.[19]

By the turn of the century, with these principles and achievements at their disposal, educated Russians began to patronize language reforms with greater urgency and vision. Scholarship converged with social consciousness. These years saw the appearance of hundreds of professional, charitable and leisure societies - autonomous associations intent on managing social change in the interests of "civic consciousness" and "public duty". Teachers, united by their own associations and unions, and driven by their own sense of vocation, looked to the linguists as cultural authorities and joined with them in a populist alliance for the reform of scripts, language teaching, and school grammars. Debates spilled over out of the academies and ministries into public forums. The educated elite was overcome, perhaps for the first time in Russian history, by what Patrick Alston calls an "adventurous, empirical spirit".[20]

Profound social transformations compelled these developments. The great reforms of the 1860s had deigned to turn members of the lower social estates into able agricultural and industrial workers, civil servants and soldiers. The result was a broad campaign to teach reading, writing and arithmetic, an unparalleled expansion of educational opportunities and literacy drives.[21] Through the schools, books and newspapers, readership expanded in ever wider circles: beyond the relatively small numbers of the middle classes to the lower middle class artisans and civil servants of the cities and towns, even to the more enterprising peasants of the villages. They not only learned to read, but entertained themselves with the stories of adventure, mystery, upward mobility, and national pride in chapbooks; or with the melodramatic reports of crime and scandal in the penny press. Books and newspapers performed a critical nation-making function. They provided readers with a common sense of place, time and language. Mass readers, if only through the printed word, could travel beyond the horizons of their locale and beyond the confines of their traditional mentalities.[22]

These strides in education and publishing only brought the need for more specific language reforms into greater relief. Teachers and linguists alike complained that the schools had become places of torture rather than learning. According to the archaic "alphabet method", children recited the names of letters by rote memorization, rather than assimilate and apply their actual sounds to everyday speech. Instead of learning they just made a lot of noise. These noises were not their own, but the pronunciations of those past generations which had first codified their speech into written form. The letters and spelling rules of the Russian alphabet system were based on the historical principle, "write today as others spoke and wrote in the past". The Ministry of National Education codified this principle in Iakov Karlovich Grot's spelling primers, which reduced words to historical hieroglyphs of a kind, mismatched with the living spoken language of most Russians. Grammar lessons were equally archaic. Thanks to the writings of F.F. Buslaev and his students, Russian school grammars were based on the logical method, which defined the sentence as a "'thought' or logical judgment expressed by words". Grammar lessons meant studying the logical meanings of subjects and predicates, clauses and phrases. Students learned how sentences made "sense", but not how and why their grammatical elements and parts functioned in complex and creative ways. Potebnia was one of the first linguists to confront such traditionalism by proposing a new system for the schools based on the "semantics of grammatical categories". His ideas were seen as too innovative, but they did set the pace for the future critiques of Fortunatov's school.[23]

Teachers were the most enthusiastic supporters of radical language reform. They advocated the democratization of spelling through the sound (phonetic) principle. The rules governing Grot's system, they argued, had become so complex and difficult to learn that they prevented the masses of common folk from attaining full and productive literacy. Through their formula, "write as you hear", they claimed to speak for the masses of imperial Russia. This spelling rule was the fastest and simplest way to teach literacy to the vast numbers of Russian illiterates and semiliterates, whom they considered a national disgrace. Everyday, with their own eyes, they saw the many errors of their students, who were spelling words according to their own dialect patterns, not the official Grot standard. Children had yet to "assimilate the national language of civilized discourse". They were not being brought to the national language; it was being dragged to their village or city streets. Many teachers and state administrators saw language teaching as a means to cultivate a standardized and disciplined Russian national identity, a way to repress the dialects and slang speech in favor of correct usage.[24] But in order to succeed, they also understood the need to compromise with their students through a more phonetic alphabet system, which would be easier for them to learn and use, thereby reducing their many spelling errors.

Professors Baudouin and Fortunatov, already well known among the educated public for their new schools of linguistics, became the champions of spelling reform. They led a group of like-minded colleagues who believed in the need for a "democratization" of the Russian writing system. Like the teachers, they wanted to free it from ornamentalism and historicism, make it more accessible to the millions of new learners. But they did not want pure democracy on the people's terms. Their sound-form (morphological) principle, a corrective to radical phoneticism, proposed "to write according to the living associations between different forms of related words". This rather obtuse formula limited the size of alphabets to single phonemes, the letter signs that distinguish meaning rather than bloat it with many phonetic distinctive features. Some words and word parts with related meanings were also to be spelled the same, regardless of their phonetic differences, in order to facilitate reading, writing and comprehension. This principle, based on recent linguistic insights, was designed to streamline spelling for readers, promote a script which was more adaptable to the new technologies of print culture, and to guarantee the systematic unity of the

Russian language. Between 1901 and 1917, Baudouin and Fortunatov, along with many of their colleagues and students, lobbied for such a new spelling through the "Commission on the Problem of Russian Spelling" of the Academy of Sciences. Voices in favor of its reform projects ranged from progressive newspapers, to independent scholars and members of the intelligentsia, to leading members of the Academy. Elementary school teachers supported it as a device to help them teach literacy to the youngest and most impressionable of students.[25]

At the same time, Fortunatov's Moscow school targeted logical grammar as a backward pedagogical method, a remnant of medieval scholasticism. In its place, his students offered grammatical analyses that projected into new, more "scientific" directions. Within morphology they recognized a whole series of formal categories (declensions, conjugations, case affixes and the like), which functioned in contrastive ways and which made language learning easier and more efficient.[26] The formal method taught spelling and grammar not as rote skills but as processes of self-discovery. A.M. Peshkovskii's popular school textbook discredited traditional "logical" grammars in favor of studying the syntax of "intonation and speech rhythm" in the voices of the students themselves. He organized grammatical facts under formalist rubrics, what he called "tags" (*iarlyks*) designed to help students avoid the "boring cases, moods, and voices" of logical grammar and thereby promote their own self-taught insights. P.O. Afanasiev caused a similar sensation for his attacks on the elitist teaching of a strict Russian literary standard. He preferred to teach formalist grammar as a function of the diversity of the living Russian language, and as a product of the self-creativity of students.[27]

As government debates about script and grammar reform efforts stalled, public support mounted. The Tver "parent-teacher circle", the Teachers' Association of the Iaroslavl Region, and the All-Russian Congress on Public Education (Petrograd 1913-1914) - were but a few of the groups to demand their final consideration and implementation, resolute in their arguments that teaching the old spelling was a waste of time and energy which taxed the minds and hearts of innocent young students.[28] Even the Russian military establishment allied with reforming teachers and linguists. It needed to teach the Russian language more efficiently to new village recruits, enlisted men and petty officers. The Main Directorate of Military Educational Institutions lobbied for state consideration of script reform, and established formal grammar as the guiding standard in its schools throughout the country. Its officers appreciated the practical power of language to consolidate national identity and create a fully literate, organized, effective fighting force.[29]

However impressive in terms of their diverse support, these reform projects failed to succeed before the Russian revolution. Powerful forces were pitted against them in what Joshua Fishman has called the "gatekeepers of written tradition, the poets, priests, principals, and professors", as well as "the institutions and symbols" which these gatekeepers served. Opposition to spelling reform ranged from the president of the Academy of Sciences and most of its members, through members of the Tsar's court, the Ministry of National Education and its Scholars Committee, the Orthodox Church hierarchy, to the conservative press. Teachers from the middle and upper schools opposed the script reform because it meant that they would be forced to teach the new system to students who were already fluent in the old script. Together they defended the historical principle of spelling as patriots would a national flag, applying pressure on the government and using press intimidation to defeat the spelling reform project. The Ministry of Internal Affairs even attempted to prohibit the publication of any text that did not use all of the traditional letters of the Grot system. At stake was the Russian national memory, in script and spoken form, as a legacy for future generations. One opponent argued more honestly that the newly spelled words simply hurt his eyes.[30]

Maintaining the old spelling was, for the opposition, a first line of defense against the encroaching decadence of the lower classes. For it, mass education was less about promoting enlightenment and social change, more about consolidating national discipline and productivity by way of "sobriety and industriousness". Traditional curriculums highlighted the role of the Russian language in the "moral education" of students and the inculcation of "patriotic feelings". Schooling and literacy in the villages were centered around the cultivation of Orthodox values and the archaic alphabet method because children were supposed to be taught how to pray and recite, and thereby appreciate the limits of their caste.[31] The social changes that Russia experienced at the turn of the century only heightened the resolve of the conservatives. Russia was now suffering a severe "social and moral crisis", a general breakdown of civilized values and behavior. High culture had begun to mix with low. With the widespread growth of literacy and a mass reading public at the turn of the century, the standard literary language was fusing with the dialects, idioms and slang of the lower classes. Nowhere was this more evident than in the printed word. In the penny press and pulp fiction, elites were now able to read about scandals and crimes and general street life in the very low-culture language of the street.[32] Such a corruption of the great Russian literary language, along with all of the misspellings and grammatical mistakes which accompanied the rise of lower class personnel to new positions of authority in schools and business, had to be stopped.

During World War I, these debates intensified, taking on more xenophobic and colorful tones. In such rare moments of patriotism and militarism, Russians admitted that their literary language was not really their own. One publicist painted the Grot code as the "Molokh" of the twentieth century, alluding to the heathen divinity to whom the early Hebrews sacrificed their children for salvation. Another labeled Grot's spelling as the "brutal scourge" of the schools, claiming that it was based on the pronunciation of Petersburg Germans, and hence was fully anti-Russian. The time had come for the Russian intelligentsia to design a script on its own terms! A half hearted project also attempted to reform the teaching of grammar, but it made few changes except to highlight the importance of Potebnia's grammatical principles in opposition to the "dishonorable" and "unpatriotic" attachment of many Russian pedagogues to "Germano-Buslaevist pseudosyntactical systems".[33]

On the eve of the Russian Revolution, the First All-Russian Congress of Teachers of Russian in the Middle Schools (December 1916-January 1917) voted resoundingly to reform the Russian spelling and grammar systems as Baudouin and Fortunatov had advised. During the reading of the reform resolution on the last day of the congress, storms of applause broke out, hampering a full and fair vote count. Participants shouted the conservatives down, demanding that the congress "fully discredit the pseudoscientific orthography of Academician Grot". Their aim, to develop free and creative individuals, a new kind of "person-citizen".[34] Visionaries expected a new renaissance for the Russian language, a new age of revolutionary writers to bury once and for all the old order of censorship and bureaucratic verbosity. They even called for new courses in general linguistics for the primary and secondary schools - to teach the young about the creative wealth of their own spoken dialects in comparison with the Moscow standard; and to inculcate in them a respect for language, the ultimate system of signs.[35]

On 11 May 1917, already several months after the fall of Tsarism and the advent of the Russian Republic, Shakhmatov led a meeting of the Academy of Sciences on the question of the "simplification of Russian spelling". It resolved to accept the Baudouin-Fortunatov project, with modifications. The Ministry of Education and the State Committee on Education of the Provisional Government soberly accepted the resolution and prepared for its implementation in the schools. Texts, primers and teachers' aids now flooded the market to teach people about the new spelling which, as linguists boasted, was more "'scientific', more regulated, more Russian".[36]

1.2. Language and empire: the origins of Eurasianism

Under the last Tsars, Russians inhabited and administered the largest cities of the troublesome imperial frontiers, where the Russian language and script were the mediums of official state communication. During the era of limited reform between the 1860s and 1910s, the "gatekeepers" of written tradition elevated the Russian language and Russian national values as the central standards by which to govern the empire in cultural terms. Their plan for the non-Russians was to "disseminate the mastery of the Russian language among them and align them with the Russian nation on the basis of a common love for the fatherland". State functionaries proclaimed Russian as the "single cement" and "state language" of the empire, especially for the western borderlands of the Baltics, Poland, Belorussia, and Ukraine.[37] But russification was not a one-dimensional dictate from St. Petersburg. Several of the empire's leading intellectuals and administrators appreciated the variety of peoples and cultures in the east. They recognized the unique nature of Russia's hegemony, driven by a strategy for imperial assimilation, yet checked by the need for cultural adaptation. In response, they fashioned a differential strategy that mixed domination (russification and pan-Slavism) with dependence (nativization and pan-Eurasianism).

Several popular philosophical treatises from the middle and late 1800s argued for just such a unique imperial mission. Nikolai Danilevskii's *Russia and Europe* (1869) created a comparative timeline and morphology of "historico-cultural types", positioning Russia within it as a superior manifestation of world cultures. Russia's historical and organic development made it the most vital and powerful state between continents. With several like-minded publicists, Danilevskii argued that the Russian people and their language were the foundations for a new Slavic-based empire, a geographical entity linking the West and East. They entertained "the image of a multinational *Rossiia* springing up on the ruins of the Hunnic, Khazar, and Tartar empires", in strategic command of both Europe and Asia.[38] At the turn of the century, the writers Vladimir Soloviev, Andrei Belyi and Aleksandr Blok popularized this image of "Russia-Eurasia" (*Rossiia-Evraziia*), inspired partly from their disgust with the decadent West, partly from their attraction to Asian cultures, and partly from their own crisis of national identity. As Russia expanded eastwards, they believed, it created a unique union of peoples by being conquered as much as conquering, by becoming Asian as much as expanding European influence. These designs, Nicholas Riasanovsky has argued, were a creative but most "determined defense of the Russian empire".[39]

This "Eurasian" mentality had its manifestations in government policy as well. One of the most notorious promoters of Russian national values, Count Sergei Uvarov, crafted a differentiated policy toward the non-Russian subjects of the empire. Author of the infamous formula for statist rule, "Autocracy, Orthodoxy, and Nationality," he promoted the Russian national language and values to ensure loyalty to the Tsarist state. But he sincerely believed that these goals could be achieved more by cooperation than coercion. He therefore contributed to a tradition in Russian imperial administration that respected local non-Russian cultures and languages.[40] Uvarov was the forerunner of a whole generation of orientalists and ethnographers who mixed the charge to civilize and russify the peoples of the east with their own romantic longings to understand

and tolerate them. They inherited one of the prejudices of historical-comparative philology - that universal conclusions about the human experience were only possible through the formal classification of human differences. They came to understand that Europe's civilizing mission was unachievable without the proper appreciation for non-European forms. From their posts in the missionary academies, oriental departments, and foreign language institutes of Kazan, Moscow, and St. Petersburg, these scholars helped to classify and standardize the poorly known languages of the eastern peoples in preparation for civilizing them. In this way, they created new, objective linguistic and ethnographic knowledge. To the extent that the non-Russian languages at the peripheries of the state were lesser, alien tongues, they were thereby worthy of respect, study, codification, and comprehension.[41]

This perspective found its most complete and successful application in the practices of two late imperial linguists. P.K. Uslar promoted Russian Orthodox influence, at the expense of clerical Islam, by creating Russian-based scripts for several Northern Caucasus languages (Chechen, Avar and Lak). An early architect of russification policy in the east, he was also a patron of the native languages, taking great care to craft Russian scripts that were delicately modified to their sound and grammar structures. N.I. Il'minskii, an Orthodox missionary and linguist, applied this formula with even greater success and scope at Kazan, less so throughout the Volga-Urals, Central Asia, Siberia, and Far North. With the patronage of ideologues at the Tsar's court, he and his followers set out to fortify a Russian orthodox "community of believers". Their Russian-based alphabets for the "small peoples" of the east (the Gagauz, Ossetians, Christianized Volga Tatars, Chuvash, Kazakh, Kirgiz, Iakuts, Mari, Komi and Udmurts) were designed to obstruct any Tatar efforts at pan-Turkism and pan-Islamism, but always through the creative manipulation of vernacular, non-Russian linguistic forms.[42] In marshaling the forces of Uslar and Il'minskii, imperial administrators did not set out to blindly impose a unitary cultural hegemony. They appreciated the necessities of accepting and promoting cultural heterogeneity. Their dual strategy of russification and nativization became an abiding strategy for both the late imperial and early Soviet eras.[43]

The linguists of the Petersburg and Moscow schools also contributed to this nascent "Eurasian" paradigm. Although Russianists and Indo-Europeanists by training and methodology, they appreciated the variety and significance of the many non-Russian languages of the empire. Baudouin criticized traditional philology for its pretentious study of only the noble languages of Sanskrit, Greek, Latin and Old Church Slavonic. He referred to the conventional Indo-European historical classification of inflective, agglutinative, and isolative languages as "eternal thinking in waltz time," an example of "Indo-Germanic megalomania and contempt for 'inferior nations'". At Kazan University, he promoted the study and teaching of the Turkic and Finno-Ugric sub-languages of the area as part of his project for the "democratization of linguistic thought".[44] Baudouin helped to convert comparative philology from the study of history to the discovery of the spatial convergences and divergences between languages. He and his students experimented with new ideas about language mixing, how they interacted with each other in space. L.V. Shcherba explored the "reciprocal influences" of language borrowing, modeling, creolization and bilingualism. V.A. Bogoroditskii compared the sound characteristics between the Russian and Tatar languages. E.D. Polivanov theorized about the connections between the sound systems of the Germanic and Ural-Altaic, Chinese and Korean, and Japanese and Malay-Polynesian language groups.[45]

These "Eurasian" language issues were woven in a tight knot with politics. They compelled the Polish Baudouin, a victim several times over of Tsarist russification policies, to campaign for the full language and cultural rights of all the minority peoples of the empire within a restructured Russian federation. To this end, he was a founder and chair of the Union of Autonomist-Federalists in 1905, whose platform called for a "decentralization and autonomization of Russian power". For his proposals, later published in a booklet, *The territorial and national mark in autonomy*, and exacerbated by his protests against Russian chauvinism and "Black Hundredism", he was sentenced to a two-year jail term, of which he spent several months in a Russian prison in 1914. "Things here", he wrote to Shakhmatov, "are the same as in that big prison called the modern state". Still, the prison's air, so he was quoted as saying, was easier to breathe than the air of Russian freedom.[46]

Baudouin was punished for calling the Russian empire a "prison house" of captive peoples, bereft of rights. But he did not advise separatist nationalism as a panacea. The national principle was dehumanizing and reductive, he argued, subject to the cold rationalism of science, which "looks upon people simply as subjects of scientific investigation and classification, as impersonal creatures, as plants or animals". It was merely another weapon at the disposal of politicians to force the masses into a pliable herd mentality, to set one group against another. "People are not raw material or cattle to be arbitrarily classified by either natural or artificial markings", he wrote. "Citizens are not weak-willed slaves or soldiers who may be willfully divided into separate detachments or regiments." (Baudouin de Courtenay 1913: 16-17, 27-31, 56-58) Instead he favored a federal system based on the principle of "territorial, economic and political interests" shared between all ethnic and religious groups inhabiting the same political and administrative space. Rather than divide peoples into historical homelands, he sought to build democratic communities, to unite them in a "federal merging". These communities would be free to choose the languages of instruction in their schools; yet Russian was to remain the most practical and essential means of communication between them. (Baudouin de Courtenay 1913: 16-37, 40-48, 63-77)

This "proletarian intellectual", as Baudouin once referred to himself, passed some of these militant perspectives on to his students. He provoked them to go out into the world and help to define language systems, to build language bridges between peoples; but always in deference to their native cultures and popular aspirations. E.D. Polivanov, who became one of his most influential students in the early Soviet period, immersed himself in the culture of the east with a unique gusto. A specialist in the languages of the Pacific rim and Central Asia, he traveled to Japan and China before the outbreak of the First World War, and was equally at home in some of the more exotic ethnic ghettoes of Moscow and St. Petersburg, where he was able to speak fluently in the dialects of a dozen or more Asian tongues. Polivanov was an infamous personality in the Petrograd underground, known for his unorthodox social habits, including an addiction to opium that he had acquired in his youth, and kept replenished during his travels in Central Asia and the Far East. A Bohemian poet by temperament, his scholarly friends unanimously testified to his "eccentricities and extravagances". Shklovskii called him "a man of broad linguistic knowledge and a reckless life". As Polivanov wrote in later years, "from the second year of my studies, my world outlook was conditioned by the very comprehensive influence on me by my teacher, Baudouin de Courtenay - by conviction an internationalist-radical". Baudouin's political tract of 1912 and subsequent imprisonment inspired Polivanov's own call to action. At the beginning of World War I, he wrote a short oppositionist piece of his own, was arrested and jailed for a week. "My international platform became clear for me", he later wrote, "I was a pacifist; I then came to internationalism."[47] By 1917, Polivanov was a Bolshevik.

Fortunatov's students (R.O. Jakobson, N.S. Trubetskoi, N.F. Iakovlev) also began to explore the languages of the Russian East after 1915 through the Moscow Dialectological Commission, one of whose tasks was to survey the "interaction between the Russian language and its neighbors". Trubetskoi first enrolled at Moscow University to study ethnography, but relented given that it was taught "strictly in accordance with the principles of natural history", fully outdated in his mind. He eventually chose linguistics because it was, in his words, "the only branch of 'anthropology' that had a truly scientific method". The ethnolinguistic studies of Trubetskoi and his classmates helped them to conceptualize the structural rules of language. They came to see the "linguistic code" as a function of the "collective creation" of speech communities. They began to search for proof of their insights in the intricacies of the Russian and non-Russian languages of the empire.[48]

These interests were more than passing academic fads. In the last decade of the Russian empire educators and teachers were just beginning to recognize the vast potential of language teaching in the non-Russian schools of the empire. Their major conferences in 1914 and 1917 affirmed the right of every citizen of the empire, regardless of birth, "to think, feel, speak, and learn in the native language". Educators also sought to establish new methods of teaching Russian in the national schools according to the comparative principle. It meant the structural diagramming of the specific features of the native languages, in comparison with Russian, so as to better teach and disseminate both. These humanist educators thereby announced a new "language union" of the "veracious Russian language in fraternal commonwealth with the languages of other nationalities".[49] Such was the "Eurasian" perspective from Moscow looking outward to the peripheries.

The view from those peripheries looking back to Moscow was quite different. Among the Muslim communities of the Russian empire, from the Caucasus, to the Volga-Urals and Central Asia, the Russian language and alphabet were superficial products of imperial expansion. They never moved beyond the bureaucracies and schools of Russian colonial conquest. Several Turkic sub-languages (Osman, Crimean, Azerbaijani, Volga-Tatar, Chagatai) and Tajik-Farsi were the native means of elite communication, all written in the sacred Arabic script of the *Qu'ran*. They enjoyed a revival in the last half of the nineteenth century as their literate elites shaped new vernacular literatures for their peoples, through journalistic prose and light fiction, and discussed the means for pan-Turkic cultural unification. This meant removing Arabic and Persian words from their common vocabularies and creating purer Turkic terms and phrases for popular communication. The revival had several sources. Only recently conquered by the Russians, the Turks hoped that the empire might also become a vehicle for their own unification. As more and more of them began to travel and study abroad, they assimilated various forms of European and Muslim nationalism, including Russian Slavophilism and populism. Political revolutions in Russia, Persia, and Turkey between 1905 and 1910 heightened their sense of purpose. Language was often at the center of their concerns because Turkic leaders understood it as the matrix of traditional communal identity and the perfect ground upon which to begin their project for cultural renewal.[50]

The Volga and Crimean Tatars, who by no coincidence enjoyed the most developed commerce, industry and literacy of all Russian Turks, first shaped these stirrings into an organized movement. It began in the 1880s and spanned their cities of Kazan, Ufa, Orenburg, and Bakchiserai. Drawing from earlier Muslim scholars and reformists for support, they created a program for cultural and educational modernization, "Jadidism". Not unlike Russian populism, it revolved around a series of linguistic reforms designed to purge the Muslim primary and secondary schools of "medieval scholasticism and traditionalism". Jadidism took its name from Ismail Bey Gasprinskii's "new method" of teaching the Arabic script and the Turkic language by way of the phonetic or "sound method". Under the old educational system, students learned the Arabic script and vocabulary by rote as "religious symbols," so as to read the *Qu'ran* better, not to learn their own languages. Much like the alphabet schools of Russia, the old

Muslim religious schools were recitation chambers, where students "shouted their lessons at the top of their lungs" rather than learned. Instead, Gasprinskii's method gave special local value to the sounds of the Turkic languages, especially the vowels, which were not adequately represented in Arabic script.[51]

Although willing to use the Jadid method to teach the Arabic alphabet in popular, phonetic ways, Gasprinskii opposed revising the structure and form of this universal alphabet to fit the different sound systems of the Turkic sub-languages. He sought to maintain the unifying power of the Arabic script, even entertaining a vision to construct a united literary culture for the Turkic peoples, based on "Turki", the Istanbul vernacular of Ottoman Turkish. This design matched with the popularity of one "Turkestan" among native elites in Central Asia and their loyalty to the supranational values of Islam. Yet Gasprinskii's vision was premature. The Turks of Russian Central Asia lived dispersed from one another. Their societies and cultures had begun to develop in different places by different historical timelines: from the Kazakh and Kirgiz nomads of the north; to the Uzbeks (Sarts) of the settled oasis towns and valleys of the south; to the Tatars and Azeri Turks of the thriving cities of Kazan and Baku. They had no single great urban center like Paris or St. Petersburg whose dialect might serve as a literary standard. Too much "linguistic differentiation" was already in place to avoid infighting and disputes over a common pan-Turkic tongue. The momentum turned against Gasprinskii's assimilation project. Nationalists applied his very own Jadid sound principle to defend their separate causes.[52]

National consciousness and linguistic development were taking root among the distinct peoples of the region. Gasprinskii's own Tatars tried to write in his artificial Turki but were forced to 'Tataricize' (*otatarit'sia*) their language in order to be understood by their readers. Leading modernizers opposed Gasprinskii's attempts to impose an artificial base dialect, without regard for local particularisms. They preferred to experiment with the creation of vernacular Kazakh and Uzbek literatures. The Azerbaidzhani Turks were drawn to the unifying potential of Ottoman Turkish, especially given its similarities to their own sub-language. But many among them also appreciated the literary potential of their own vernacular.[53] These stirrings to protect and develop the native language translated into the Muslim national political programs of the Russian revolutionary era. At the First All-Russian Muslim Congress and the First North Caucasus People's Congress of 1917, delegates recognized their shared cultural and linguistic attributes, but also made provisions for native language development in the schools and for national and territorial autonomy in politics.[54]

None of these separatist tendencies meant a resounding defeat for integration and pan-Turkism. The majority of Turkic and Northern Caucasus intellectuals recognized the need to develop both the native sub-languages and a common Turkic communicable between all. Pan-Turkism, in fact, was less about an integral political union of peoples, more about a federal system of cultural cooperation. The need for a tiered cultural universe was accepted by most intellectuals within the Turkic world. It mirrored the simple facts of local identities and dialects, as well as the overarching realities of the Turkic speech community and Muslim faith community. The Turks and Northern Caucasians had an even greater handicap than the divisions within their own ranks. They had no powerful state system to protect them. They were forming territorial and national identities at a risky historical moment, the last years of the Russian and British empires, which either contained or surrounded them. Without a viable state system of their own, they were trapped in a geographical vise which history was closing all the tighter. At this moment, Russia and the emirs of the oasis khanates of Central Asia sought to maintain their statist power at all costs. The Tsar's secret police even considered something as innocent as the Jadidist "new method" of literacy teaching to be a threat, "a serious crisis", the grounds for a resurgent Turkic nationalism. So they maintained a strict surveillance and control over the "new method" schools.[55] These external pressures kept the process of Turkic national formation slow and clumsy.

Thus, on the eve of the revolution, the patterns of scholarship and state policy were already in place to shape language reform for years to come. Advances in linguistics translated into language reform projects with political overtones. Linguists and educators positioned themselves as arbiters over the detailed scientific and pedagogical questions of literary culture. Challenged to regularize language in new written and spoken forms for broader social use, they played a delicate balancing game between democratization and standardization, nativization and russification. The new Soviet regime inherited these challenges, and the scientific paradigms fashioned to resolve them, with an even more pressing and serious sense of purpose.

Chapter 2

Divided speech communities of the Soviet Union

> *I believe that you have two state languages:*
> *Russian, since you are part of the federation;*
> *and Turkic, since it is your local language.*
> Iosef Stalin (1920)[1]

As professional journalists and agitators, many leading Bolsheviks valued both the organizing and the liberating power of language. Through Lenin's forceful newspaper articles, Lev Trotskii's radical speeches, and the popular slogans of the party, words transformed into fulcrums of political authority. Anatoli Lunacharskii once called 1917 a "season of mass rallies," a moment when the common people were enthralled by "the new revolutionary words". Futurist poets, first among them Vladimir Maiakovskii, were thrilled by the possibilities. "I want the pen to become the bayonet, forged of steel and iron", he wrote; "the work of poetry to become like Stalin's Politburo reports."[2] In the Red Army, a school for literacy as much as for socialism, words were nearly as equal to the best new military technology. Through vast literacy campaigns and newspaper networks, Bolshevik activists set out to reach a stunning variety of Russian dialects and non-Russian languages. Native literacy became a precondition for mass politics. The Bolshevik propaganda-state, as Peter Kenez has argued, had to educate people with basic skills before it could ever hope to persuade or indoctrinate them. Alphabetical literacy was but the first step toward Lenin's greater vision of political literacy. (Von Hagen 1990: 98; Kenez 1985: 8, 146)

The literacy campaigns were all the more important because the traumas of war and revolution had shattered the slow and stabilizing development of the Russian literary language, reinforcing the divisive "bilingualism" between high brow literary styles and low brow speech. What contemporaries and historians have called the "dual power" in politics, between the elites of the Provisional Government and the masses of the Soviets, had its manifestations in language too. Events also shifted the non-Russian peoples into a whole new Soviet state orbit, one in which they enjoyed more formal native language privileges, but also felt a sustained pressure to master Russian. The gaps between city Russian and rural Russian, and between the Russian language and the scores of non-Russian languages of the peripheries, were most unsettling to rank and file Bolsheviks. In their own councils, or even when they ventured out into the factories and offices of Russia's largest cities, they took some comfort in being able to understand each other and the general public around them. But beyond these confines, they became strangers in their own land. In the distant villages of Russia, or in the reconquered cities of the periphery, they met the most basic of psychological barriers, the discordant sounds and words of unintelligible tongues. The Bolsheviks did not retreat from these national frontiers but set out to negotiate them, to demarcate them, and eventually to conquer them. To achieve some measure of a unified state, they relied on established strategies from imperial days, balancing democratization with standardization for Russians at home, and nativization with russification for the non-Russians beyond.

2.1. The crisis of Russian 'bilingualism'

"What language is this written in? Some kind of gibberish?", wrote Lenin shortly after the Bolshevik victory in the civil war. "This is Volapük, and not the language of Tolstoy and Turgenev!" He was protesting the vulgar literary standards in Soviet newspapers of the early 1920s. Leading comrades in the party shared his concerns. Nikolai Bukharin rallied journalists to improve their written Russian and their language "hygiene". Trotskii cautioned that crude speech and poor grammar were putting the established literary language at risk.[3] Emigre linguists predicted doom for Russian, claiming that the godless Bolsheviks threatened the national language more than the orthodox faith. The masses remained believers, but the vast social changes of the revolution had left Russia linguistically impoverished. (Volkonskii 1928).

The Tsarist regime had bequeathed the Bolsheviks with pockets of literacy and cultured speech in a population of millions who were either illiterate, or poorly literate, or spoke and wrote in substandard dialects of sounds and words. The years of war and revolution made matters worse; now the language crisis reflected a broader crisis in class identities. The Bolsheviks had overthrown, exiled, and disenfranchised the former aristocratic and middle class elites along with their speech patterns. The peasants reverted to the traditional village community, undoing decades of progress in literacy, the dissemination of printed materials, and the refinement of popular reading tastes. (Brooks 1985a: 164-165; Fitzpatrick 1991: 12-24) The Bolsheviks may have engineered a political revolution, but they were also riding a wave of social upheaval. Workers and peasants now enjoyed official promotion, but they did not understand the mighty Russian literary language like the privileged castes before them.

Memoirs of these years recalled the depths of the crisis, Russia's "talking revolution". The explosion of mass democracy in 1917, in the form of workers', peasants' and soldiers' committees, shattered the fragile standards of elite public speech. From the podiums of the first and last Constituent Assembly of revolutionary Russia, politicians lectured on the need for gradual reform. They were met by the catcalls and vulgarisms of the Red Guard soldiers in the galleries above. As one old professional reminisced, from impressions gathered during a train journey through central Russia in 1918, accompanied by all kinds of sights, smells and discourtesies: "they talked loud and long; the Bolshevik was the first to give up; but God, what horrors occur in the heads of gorillas! What a mixture of memorized phrases, adopted or drummed-in 'slogans', stupidity of a sort that knows neither bounds, restraint, nor criticism." (Mstislavskii 1988; Got'e 1988: 160-161)

Ideological interests complicated this revolution in public speech. Party journalists had became accustomed to precise methods of communicating to a small elite of Russian speaking Bolsheviks, mostly by way of illegal papers. During their underground days, these writers had developed skills in literary simplicity and clarity given the shortage of resources and print space. They wrote in a "proclamation" style; they developed "expressiveness" to captivate their readers and move them to action, to "fire the heart by a word". Yet by the early 1920s, with more and more diverse audiences being readied for Bolshevik ideology, these methods were no longer as effective or appropriate.[4] At stake was mutual understanding between social groups within Russia and the communicability of Bolshevik political messages to the country at large. As the renowned linguist, A.M. Selishchev put it, the "revolutionary waves" which hit the "center" with the new foreign words, acronyms, neologisms, and phraseology of urban socialism did not reach the rural peripheries with the same effect.[5]

The city had begun to speak a different Russian idiom than the village. Various studies confirmed these linguistic gaps between elites and masses. In compiling data about the abilities and preferences of urban, peasant, and military newspaper readers, researchers found that they were all poorly versed in the new government lexicon. Words from the Marxist lexicon like *communism* and *bourgeois*, comprehensible to the average Bolshevik intellectual, confused novices. Philosophical terms like *dialectic* and *materialism* may as well have been ancient hieroglyphs to the average Russian reader. New Soviet acronyms - like *RSFSR* (the Russian federation), *Orgbiuro* (Organizational Bureau), *Narkompros* (the People's Commissariat of Education), *RKK* or *erkaka* (Wage Rate and Dispute Commission), *Persimfans* (First Symphonic Ensemble), and *Vserabotzemles* (All-Union Council of Land and Forest Workers) - became words unto themselves, alien to the ears of most Russians who first heard them. Such linguistic creativity even reached proper nouns, some enthusiasts naming their children in honor of the new communist epoch in world history with "magical" words like *Rebel*, *Barrikada*, or *Elektrifikatsiia*.[6]

This new idiom reached its extreme in the secretive speech of "Young Communist" (*Komsomol*) cells. The linguist E.D. Polivanov even believed that their incomprehensible jargon amounted to a whole new language. He argued that such phrases as - "in the name of the Komsomol bureau of cells" (*ot imeni biuro iacheiki RKCM*), "march over here" (*shagai siuda*), "blatherers will not be tolerated" (*trepachei ne poterpit*), "you will be judged in the RKK" (*okhlopochesh' v Rakake*), and "don't f--k with me" (*mudistiku ne razvodi*) - were completely meaningless, foreign jumbles to the ears of the genteel high society people from before the war and revolution. But this jargon was also becoming increasingly intolerable to urban Soviet society. No longer necessary for underground work, it turned into simple "street slang," a vile corruption of Russian. (Polivanov 1928b: 168; Markovskii 1926: 15-16)

The Bolsheviks needed to speak to all varieties of workers and peasants, and to all shapes and sizes of Russian dialect communities. But they realized the brutal truth that not all Russians fully understood each other even when speaking in Russian. They termed this a kind of "bilingualism" within their speech community. Lunacharskii spoke of a "language barrier" which prevented the working masses from attaining high culture and the "mastery over the literary language" which it entailed. He applauded language change "under the pressure of the street, of the meeting, of the proletarian masses". But with other leading educators he also feared that such mass creativity might imprison the people in ignorance and "muddy" the great Russian language.[7]

Lenin and his commissars searched with care for ways to stem the tide of bilingualism, to "draw the several languages back together". They developed innovative means of speaking to the mostly illiterate or semiliterate general public after 1917: revolutionary agitation and propaganda trains and posters; the silent cinema; the "talking" propaganda statues and monuments erected in Moscow in the first months after 1917; and the "telegraphic" windows of the state news agency. "Our cultural front", wrote one observer, needs such a "clear, visually graphic poster language . . . the concrete language which is understandable for all dialects and tribes", for all peasant and national groups.[8] To reinvigorate the mass readership from before the revolution, state censors also allowed certain forms of the old pulp fiction to return to the market: entertaining detective novels and adventure stories refitted for propaganda purposes.[9]

The Soviet press became the privileged medium of mass communication in the 1920s, a ground for mass democracy and regime legitimacy, a field of discourse between the party center and its agents, surrogates, and affiliates beyond. Through the press, the Bolsheviks began to develop a communist language for optimal communication between the vanguard and the people. In the earliest years of the civil war, they debated whether to standardize newspapers for elite readership alone, or to differentiate them for both elite and mass readers. They chose decisively for the latter, understanding very well their own hegemonic imperative, and the cultural gaps that separated them from the people. "Differentiation of the press must be introduced severely and decisively", wrote the editors of *Zhurnalist* (*Journalist*) in 1923. "Our press must turn to every stratum of the population using different formats, but in one communist language." In practice, this basic innovation of the 1920s meant that the mass newspaper had to be communist by content, so as to serve party ideological demands, but bourgeois by form, so as to appeal to average tastes and expectations.[10]

Editors created newspapers to appeal to different groups of people, high society and low, especially after the Bolsheviks closed down all specialized, independent papers. The free market may have disappeared, but the party still needed newspapers that sold well. According to their new reading hierarchy, they targeted *Pravda* (*Truth*) for the party worker, *Izvestiia* (*News*) for elite readers, *Rabochaia gazeta* (*Workers' Gazette*) for the average worker, *Bednota* (*Villager*) for the elite rural peasant, and *Krestianskaia gazeta* (*Peasants' Gazette*) for the mass rural reader. Hundreds of varied provincial newspapers and subsets of professional, trade, and party newspapers reached yet more specific audiences.[11] Party journalists advised readers to turn to specific newspapers for quick and easy news in order to rationalize their time and energy. Rural teachers were supposed to read *Krestianskaia gazeta* rather than other national dailies because it contained the best balance of local and national news, moving from in-depth treatments of one to measured doses of the other, at a slow and readable pace. In turn, party editors called on journalists to shape their messages and styles to better reach the mentalities of different readers. They cautioned journalists to be sensitive to the "physiognomy of the listener", for the young communist from the city was of one mindset, the rural youth of another. The latter simpleton, so declared a Bolshevik journalist, required a textual flow from simple to general facts, or from local to national news, without complex words of any kind.[12]

All of this meant, in practice, that the Soviet regime had to begin to translate its alien communist party idiom into the everyday language of the average Russian. In Mark Von Hagen's terms, the Soviet state needed to "nativize" its ideas and visions within the particularisms and localisms of the average Red Army recruit. So journalists began to expunge difficult foreign words from their articles and books, simplifying their meanings by using the religious and naturalistic terms of traditional village life. To circumvent the intelligentsia altogether, and provide for better social communication between center and peripheries, the party even promoted "worker and peasant correspondents", journalists who could navigate between the higher and lower idioms of state and society. The message of Bolshevism was to remain the same; only the style changed for popular consumption.[13]

These innovative approaches to journalism were also informed by a new philosophy and linguistics of readership. N.A. Rubakin's and Ia. Shafir's theory of "functional dependence" held that there were as many contents of a book as there were readers: "content exists only insofar as it influences the reader". In their view, based on the "law of Humboldt-Potebnia", the word was not merely a transmitter of information but also a "stimulus" which provoked different reactions in different readers. It was not simply a means of plural communication, but also a field for individual expression.[14] Great care, they cautioned, had to be taken in order not to confuse or misinform readers. If the Bolshevik party wanted to reach the people, it first had to make the effort to understand their patterns of thought and speech.

M.S. Gus elaborated on this principle to define the Soviet press as "one of the foundations of the Soviet state" and "one of the ties between Soviet institutions and the masses". The press was a medium for mass mobilization, a "collective agitator, propagandist, and organizer". It was also a forum for the masses to understand and critique the practical questions of state business. "The newspaper as it is written today", wrote Gus, "is the result of the influence of the language culture of millions of people. We have influence over worker and peasant correspondents, they strongly influence us in turn, and here arises the general reciprocal action." Gus believed that the proletariat was both the subject and the object of party newspapers, as vanguard in the communist party and as mass readership, as both speaker and listener in shared dialogue. Or as he wrote in more Hegelian philosophical terms, "the newspaper transforms the reader, the object transformed by the newspaper; the newspaper is transformed by the reader, the subject who transforms the newspaper. The proletariat thus influences itself through the newspaper by a process of constant self-change, continually transforming the newspaper and continually being transformed by it."[15]

These idealistic principles were a far cry from Soviet realities. Most press readers were bored with the printed product. Newspaper language was often vague in style, sometimes even incomprehensible because of poor grammar. Lack of spacing between words, badly constructed headlines, and poor graphics and typesetting made newspapers difficult to read. Party observers criticized the newspaper, *Bednota*, as being altogether unreadable on all counts. Ia. Shafir's opinion surveys discovered that readers bought and enjoyed *Rabochaia gazeta* because its language was "simple and clear"; unlike *Izvestiia*, whose language was complex and confusing.[16] In his provocative book, *Newspaper language*, which studied the linguistic standards and literary styles of several leading newspapers, Gus found that the improper use of syntax made reading boring and difficult. Instead of applying active verbal constructions, most authors imitated bureaucratic and cliche speech by using passive forms. These resulted in more complicated genetive case endings that disturbed the flow of speech. Gus's findings caused a minor scandal. Leading journalists called for immediate action to correct these literary abuses.[17]

Lunacharskii even scolded some journalists for unwittingly creating an "imaginary peasant language" in an effort to reach their rural readers. He called it a kind of "falsetto" or "lisping speech" (*siusiukanie*), a patronizing style which only alienated the serious reader. "To him [the peasant] it seems as though he is being spoken to as a child, and so in vexation he turns away from the printed word." Lunacharskii also warned journalists about speaking to their readers in condescending academic and intellectual terms or in incomprehensible foreign words. He advocated patiently educating readers about the new Soviet Russian literary language so as not to offend them. Yet these conditions remained troublesome throughout the first decades of Soviet power. Most linguists offered little help beyond esoteric theories and explanations, which usually turned the newspaper professionals against them.[18] Publishers and editors continued to advise writers to studiously avoid "lisping language", bureaucratic and scientific technical terms, abbreviations and acronyms, borrowed international words, vulgarisms, slang, complex sentences, passive constructions, and even sophisticated literary tropes. Simple words from the literary language were also forbidden if they seemed difficult or incomprehensible in any way.[19] For the moment, struggling editors had little to rely on besides these literary prohibitions.

Linguists and educators did offer some idealistic solutions to the crisis of Russian bilingualism. Through the Institute of the Living Word (1918-1923), they sought to raise the lower classes of Russia out of their previous silence or out of their existing jargons and dialects, transforming them into integral members of a new speech community. Lunacharskii proclaimed at the opening session of the Institute that "the person who is silent in an epoch of political crises is only half a person. He is obliged to speak. He is obliged to speak even when to fully speak his mind is to put his life at risk." Bolshevik visionaries founded the Institute in the first months of the revolution, before the exertions of the civil war, when they were awe-inspired by the euphoric power of Lenin's words to move party members to action. Its noble tasks were to fortify the new Soviet democracy with the "living word". Scholars traced the concept back to democratic Athens and republican Rome, with the hopes that Soviet communism would become an heir to their humanism. Applying the lessons of the Greek *polis* to contemporary needs, to build the "proletarian" city, O.D. Kameneva demanded that the living word be marshaled for communist tasks. It "fires the hearts of people", she said, "reaches over across oceans, through huge spaces; it unites peoples, transforming them into brothers and sisters."[20]

A dialectical philosophy of language informed the work of the Institute, which sponsored lectures on Hegel's "theory of the symbol" and the dialectic, and on the "harmony of human dualism (von Humboldt)". But now their philosophies were directed to the fulfillment of idealistic communist aims. Lunacharskii articulated this vision best when he declared that speech was a "path between the internal human world and its word expressions", albeit a tortuous and complex one. For "the word, after it has been pronounced, enters into a general world, into the psyche of another person through the sense organs, transforming into the emotions and ideas of that person's own internal world." Yet the "word, as an objective phenomenon in the subjective life of people", offered no guarantee of correct translation, imperiling both communication and community. Lunacharskii called on the Institute's founders to help people communicate more effectively by way of the word, to help them translate it from a "psychological" into a "social" phenomenon. This task was especially important in Russia, beset as it was by so many rural and provincial Russian dialects and by so many different languages. He asked its directors to create no less than a new united speech community for socialist Russia.[21]

Institute linguists helped to fulfill Lunacharskii's aims. They taught their science as the "study of a given system of symbols and their meanings", lecturing on phonetics and the phoneme, on the formal bases of syntax, on language in all its variety as an "individualistic-psychological" as well as "social phenomenon". They surveyed the regional patterns of Russian dialectology and fashioned new methods of teaching the correct Moscow pronunciation and articulation. This work was not meant for a few select actors and announcers. The Institute set out to master the intricacies of agitational speech, the stuff of the revolution. Its aims included an educational "program maximum" to help party members, judges, lawyers, teachers, and bureaucrats to master the spoken word for better social use. The Institute set a pattern of excellence in declamation and pronunciation studies for the next few decades designed to help people speak correctly on the stage, in the schools, at the podiums, and on the radio. For nothing in life was greater than to live "in the world of ideas, 'live in the word', to think by way of words".[22] For the rather liberal years of the 1920s, the remaking of language culture was an enterprise filled with promise and creative potential.

Linguists offered yet other practical solutions to the crisis. They cooperated on the project for the *Dictionary of the Russian language* (from Pushkin to Gorkii, in four volumes), designed to modernize and standardize the Russian language. Lenin sponsored the work during the civil war, believing that the social changes brought about by the revolution demanded immediate action on the language front. It was to be a dictionary of the contemporary language designed for the general public, with extensive lexical contributions from the classical writers, populists, and revolutionaries of the nineteenth and twentieth centuries. The dictionary project was but one part of a wider campaign by the early Soviet government to promote conservative values and tastes among mass readers. Between 1918 and 1923, the works of the great Russian writers from the late nineteenth century were published in millions of "people's editions". The regime promoted the new "thick journal", *Red virgin soil* (*Krasnaya nov'*), in an attempt to fashion a periodical combining belles-lettres, history and politics; as well as to shape the styles and language of a new generation of Soviet writers.[23]

On Lenin's death, linguists wrote panegyrics to his avid purism and conservatism. The corpus of his writings and speeches became a standard for imitation, both as literary style and as political command, a central pillar in what was fast becoming the cult of personality. "For Lenin", wrote the futurist poet A. Kruchenykh, "the word is one of the greatest, if not the greatest of human values, as a signal to action." In characteristically Leninist words and phrases like 'commune' (*kommuna*), 'union' (*smychka*), 'purge' (*chistka*), and 'to sum up'(*podytozhivat'*), the party inherited a direct, declarative political style. From Moscow State University, one of Fortunatov's best students, D.N. Ushakov, even began an ambitious project to study these characteristics of Lenin's speech, and ultimately to compile a dictionary of his words and phrases, the most sacred heritage of the revolution besides his corpse.[24]

2.2. The challenge of the multiethnic state

If the Russian speech community was beset by dozens of provincial and social dialects, the speech community in the USSR was fractured by scores of languages and sub-languages, many poorly diagrammed or studied, others still not developed into alphabets or written literatures. The languages of the Soviet east were most problematic. Time and again in the early 1920s, policy makers spoke in confusion and ignorance about its many "Muslim languages" (*muziazyki*). In the legal and binding documents of state, they referred to the Azerbaijanis as "Tatars", the Kazakh as "Kirgiz", the Uzbek as "Sarts", and the Tajiks as "Uzbeks".[25] Ethnic naming was a difficult business; sometimes simply wrong, at other times just plain insulting. Even linguists and native cultural leaders could not agree about the ethnic and linguistic identities of the various Northern Caucasus and Central Asian peoples. Was there one or were there many? They endlessly bickered about the definitions of languages and dialects within the Turkic family, sometimes speaking of the "Osman-Turkish" and "Sart" dialects, both broader and even derogatory appellations for Caucasian and Central Asian Turkic.[26]

The Bolsheviks were perplexed and disturbed that they could not even communicate with their new subjects in the east. Tens of thousands of "extremely savage and backward" Muslims in Kazan and Tiumen spoke hardly a word of Russian, warned one report. The party could call on only a handful of native speaking members to reach them. Agitation and propaganda were failing miserably because "political-cultural education" was privileged by the Russian language and "European thinking", alienating the native peoples from participating in party and state work. Military leaders even blamed a murderous uprising in a Muslim reserve battalion during the civil war on the illiteracy rate among its angry members, who were unreachable by conventional means of agitation and propaganda. The mob had reportedly searched for "Europeans" chanting the slogan "Death to Jews and Communists". From Red Army encampments in the Caucasus to the small villages of the Arctic North, the

Bolsheviks were in urgent need of Russian speaking activists, literate in the native languages and attuned to national customs, able to engage such disaffected masses and convert them to the Soviet cause.[27]

This communication gap was all the more troubling given certain residues of great-Russian chauvinism in the party ranks. It was a chauvinism reinforced in the first years of Soviet power as party members, dizzied from the variety and numbers of ethnic peoples of the new state, retreated into the familiarity of Russian-ness. Many Bolsheviks were intent on assimilating these peoples and their languages under Russian communist domination, preferring a unitary proletarian state without much regard for the distinct ethnic and social groups that populated it. Lenin legitimized this ideal in his theoretical arguments before World War I. He was unwilling to surrender central Russian control of state and economic policy to the non-Russian peripheries. In a 1913 essay on "Marxism and the National Question", written in support of Lenin's position, Stalin even called for the "merging of the backward nations and nationalities" of the Caucasus "within the general stream of superior" culture - presumably Russian. Harboring many suspicions against the rural and national peripheries, he considered them to be inherently disloyal, a clear and present danger to the proletarian heartland. (Stalin 1951, 2: 351; Blank 1988: 72-90)

Party members shared these attitudes, airing them openly in official gatherings and unofficial conversations. In Central Asia, they were inclined to retain the former "privileges" of empire and displayed the "colonial attitudes" of "communist imperialism". One party activist openly termed the North Caucasus a conglomeration of "half-barbaric" people, whose one saving grace was that literate "westerners" or "Europeans" (Balts, Ukrainians, Russians, Jews, Georgians and Armenians) lived among them. As late as 1924, Russian administrators in the People's Commissariat of Internal Affairs were still applying the Tsarist term 'alien' (*inorodets*) to the Soviet nationalities. Party ideologues reprimanded them for such outdated colonialism. The proper substitute was 'native' (*rodnoi*) or 'non-Russian' (*nerusskii*), hardly any more affirmative.[28]

The most recalcitrant Bolshevik chauvinists settled into the People's Commissariat of Education (Narkompros) of the RSFSR. By early 1919, it had displaced its competitor, the People's Commissariat of the Nationalities (Narkomnats), for the right to craft a new school system for the non-Russian peoples. Narkomnats lost partly because of its internal disorganization and weaknesses, partly because of the political errors of its Muslim communists from Tatarstan, under the direction of Mir Said Sultangaliev. Besides blazing their own anticolonial, nationalist revolution in Asia, they had also planned to promote autonomous control and native language teaching in education. The party purged Sultangaliev and his Tatar supporters from power on both counts. In their place, Narkompros raised a different vision of school reform, governed by a take all or give nothing mentality, meaning either complete domination with the help of the Russian language, or effective negligence of national needs. An educational conference in early 1919 offered the non-Russians just such a choice: integration by way of Russian domination or educational apartheid.[29]

This very dynamic played out between 1919 and 1924. Narkompros educators were notorious for their attempts to "artificially fuse children of different nationalities" by way of the Russian language, if under the rubric of proletarian "internationalism". They did not see the need to "derussify" the schools at first, believing that Russian would always take center stage in them, and that some of the smaller nationalities did not really need to formally learn their own languages. M.N. Pokrovskii's speech at the First All-Russian Congress on Education promoted this attitude in a chauvinistically "Russian" rather than federative "all-Russian character", according to one participant. Representatives of the Kirgiz Autonomous Soviet Socialist Republic (ASSR) and Turkestan ASSR Education Commissariats reported that the "European" administrators of Narkompros were harassing them with attempts to "russify" their language cultures and to play the "old Imperial politics" once again, forgetting that they were autonomous republics.[30]

The government tried to avoid such abuses by creating one of the very first institutions to promote nativization policy, the Council of National Minorities (Sovnatsmen) within Narkompros in 1919. Its charge, to devolve more authority to local administrators and promote native language needs. "The diverse conditions and complexities of nationality interrelations in the provinces" demanded it, proclaimed one report.[31] Russian educators responded with a policy of benign neglect. Pokrovskii counseled the need for "tact and moderation" in relations between Russian and non-Russians, sending an implicit message that the latter should not expect too much aid from Moscow but should depend on their own resources for development. Narkompros now devoted its attention to Russian children in the cities and ignored the non-Russian countryside. In what one observer referred to as the "remnants of Tsarist colonial policy", the Turkestan Narkompros channeled seventy-five percent of its resources and energies to the European schools, even though Europeans amounted to just less than ten percent of the total regional population.[32]

Narkompros circulars spoke in high and mighty terms about education of the nationalities, but its "Russian Soviet functionaries" carelessly proceeded with their "negative", "conceited", "scornful attitudes". Meanwhile, Sovnatsmen fell into an administrative limbo as a third rate department without any consistent funding or real power. It instituted few native language curriculums, textbooks, or teaching courses. Its communist fraction, in a desperate plea sent off to Iosef Stalin for redress, described its position as simply "catastrophic".[33] These troubles lingered into the later 1920s as long as Russian Narkompros educators were in charge and not the nationalities themselves.

Burdened by these unforeseen consequences of colonial domination, and by the pressing need to engage the non-Russian masses in party and state work, the Soviet leadership postponed its immediate dream of a unitary state. By 1922, it sanctioned the USSR system, a hierarchy of national territorial units with formal rights to administrative and linguistic sovereignty. At its center was the Russian Federation (RSFSR); on its peripheries were lesser Soviet republics, those closer to Moscow with limited autonomous or republic status, those farther away with full. To breathe life into these national units, the government devised a program for ethnic and linguistic nativization. It bowed to the *status quo antebellum*, recognizing the long standing yet modest demands of every major national group for linguistic self-government in a new federal state.

With the experience of Sovnatsmen as an early model, the government now met national needs halfway, fulfilling their central platforms from the late imperial era, yet also quieting the sting of nationalism from the civil war years. Nativization promised equality of rights for all of the non-Russian peoples of the Soviet Union through local economic initiatives and the promotion of native cadres. It provided them with formal rights to language use and with financial and administrative patronage for the development of their press and publications, cultural organizations and educational establishments. In the tempered words of one supporter, no less than "Comrade Dzhugashvili" (Iosef Stalin), the Georgian-born commissar of Narkomnats and "leader of the small, all-Russian nationalities", was charged with implementing the program.[34]

Bolshevik propagandists boasted proudly about the national territorial rights and nativization programs of the USSR system. In decree after decree, the distinct ethnic governments of the USSR and RSFSR - from Azerbaijan to Turkestan - elevated their native languages to official status.[35] They now commanded their administrative offices to translate their documents and communications from Russian into the language of the majority native population. Slogans proclaimed the "acclimatization of the bureaucracy to daily life" and the "attraction of the people to active Soviet construction". They declared that the "language of state and the language of the population are one and the same". In those regions where national communists shared some power with Moscow and where literary cultures were already developed, the native language began to compete with Russian as the main language of party and state. This was especially true in Tatarstan, whose cultural leaders understood language reform as the central foundation for further national development. They even created an acronym for it, *RTI* or the "realization of the Tatar language", what very nearly became a slogan for Tatar national independence.[36]

In the most liberal moments during the peak of nativization, certain non-Russian languages took precedence over Russian as the primary languages of a region or republic. Thanks to the efforts of N. Samurskii, a Lezgin national and First Secretary of the Dagestan Regional Committee of the RKPb, Dagestan chose Azeri Turkic as its primary language of state between 1923 and 1928. In his view, to learn such Dagestani languages as Lezgin, Avar, Dargin, Lak, and Kumyk was sufficient only for work in the provinces. Otherwise people needed to learn a "real language of civilization".[37] Impressive gains in language nativization were also made in the western Slavic republics, Ukraine and Belorussia. Through the 1920s and 1930s, linguists standardized their native languages into new grammars, dictionaries and terminologies. The Soviet state raised them to new status in print culture (newspapers and books), in the schools, and in government office work. Linguistic nativization took hold, redoubling the popular "national identity" in turn.[38]

The seriousness with which the government promoted federalism and nativization was a measure of its willingness to compromise with the non-Russian nationalities. Soviet policies became measured, informed responses to ethnic and linguistic realities, and even to the needs of the separate ethnic groupings themselves. The government acquiesced on the national and language fronts because it knew that the peoples of the Soviet east needed to develop culturally and linguistically, according to native terms, before they could ever develop politically and economically, according to a European pace. It could no more work from the model of a literate society heading toward language unification than it could from the model of a developed capitalist economy converting to socialism and communism.

Nativization was indeed a serious business. Its initiatives did not come cheap. Newspapers and other printed materials for the non-Russian languages were costly to publish, sometimes two or three times more than similar Russian materials. Native personnel who were proficient both in their own language and in Russian could similarly extract high salaries from all too willing employers. In the Transcaucasus, the guidelines for the use of the Russian, Georgian, Armenian, and Azerbaijani languages on the railroads (everything from office documentation to the printed matter on tickets) alone amounted to a staggering sixteen pages. Local governments even sacrificed efficiency and profits for nativization. "Uzbekification" commissions decreed that the nativization policies should take precedence over various management and organizational "rationalization" projects then in place, promising better salaries for those who complied, and harsh penalties for those who were careless in any way.[39]

The Soviet government even promoted a policy of reciprocal bilingualism, decreeing that all "European" public officials working in the peripheries should learn the primary native language of their regions. Or, in the idealistic words of one participant, "since we all live together we should understand each other". Azerbaijanis and Tatars published language textbooks for the benefit of the average European transplant who did not know Turkic. Central Asians and North Caucasians established courses in the native languages for civil servants and students. In 1927, the Uzbek Communist Party even required European workers in state and party executive organs to leave urbane and comfortable Tashkent and travel to dusty and tradition-bound Samarkand for a three-month course in Uzbek. "Going to Samarkand" was likely not very easy for them. But such was the price of nativization.[40]

For all of these accommodations, we must not forget that the national territorial principle and nativization programs were also functions of Bolshevik power politics, of its "divide and conquer" strategy, an abiding reality of these years. From the Volga-Urals and Central Asia to the Northern Caucasus, the established native elites had favored broad territorial, ethnic and religious unity rather than national separatism. In opposition, by displacing the Tatars and Uzbeks from their pretensions to govern over large pan-ethnic territories either within or adjoining the borders of historical Russia, and by dividing their ethnic groups into homelands with poorly formed national identities, the Bolsheviks ensured that they alone would rule. It is often difficult to measure this strategy with any precision, especially by subtracting intentions from results. But Stalin likely maneuvered it in place through his "autonomization" program, meant to provide the nationalities with the most limited local autonomy, set within the artifice of national rights and state federalism. Or as he spoke in a revealing moment in November of 1920: "at present, it merely serves our interest to demonstrate the independence of Azerbaijan. In truth, it is impossible for communists to be independent from each other."[41]

Let us examine for a moment several examples of the "divide and conquer" and "autonomization" policies. By no means do they imply a concerted and efficient campaign imposed by the center upon the peripheries. Although they sometimes appear quite methodical, at other times just plain messy, these policies were usually a function of the tense, improvised moment. But they nonetheless do provide a meaningful political backdrop to the language issues at hand.

In the Volga-Urals, Tatarstan was the first of the new states of the civil war period to suffer division and conquest by the Red Army. The Tatars has hoped to establish an "Idel-Ural" state, referring to the territories of the Tatar-Turkic and Finno-Ugric peoples along the broad expanses of the Volga (Idel) river and Ural Mountains. It was to become, in the scenario of the Muslim communist, Mir Said Sultangaliev, the base for a Tatar-led anticolonial revolution in the east. His well-defined pretenses threatened the Bolsheviks with a "dual power" fiasco similar to the one they experienced during the 1917 revolution. The conflicts between Soviet power and the Provisional Government back then were now replaced by the conflicts between Moscow and Kazan in the present. So, with each step the Tatars took to realize their state vision between 1918 and 1923, the Bolsheviks countered decisively with superior armies and successful power politics. They abolished the first Tatar inspired Idel-Ural state in 1918. They suppressed Sultangaliev's communist nationalism. They abolished the Tatar-Bashkir Soviet Republic and put in its place a rump Tatar ASSR in May of 1920, part of the RSFSR; it unified no Turkic or Finno-Ugric peoples, nor even a homogenous Tatar population.[42]

In Central Asia, the native course of political development (between 1914 and 1924) favored a regional Turkestanian state: providing for internal autonomy between the Tatar, Kazakh, Kirgiz, Turkmen, Uzbek and Tajik peoples, yet also for their "organic mixture" into a common "Turkic" and Muslim ethnoreligious grouping. But the Bolsheviks held that the "compactness" of nations was more progressive than the "dispersion" of tribes and clans within larger territorial units. Their solution was the 'national demarcation' (*natsional'noe razmezhivanie*) of 1924, which transformed the Turkestan ASSR (and the adjoining Bukhara and Khiva People's Republics) into the Uzbek and Turkmen union republics; as well as the Tajik ASSR within Uzbekistan, and the Kazakh and Kirgiz ASSRs within the RSFSR. The traditional interpretation holds that the Bolsheviks most feared the threat of "pan-Turkism", and so took recourse to this policy of political manipulation and "divide and conquer". Archival testimonies substantiate this view, albeit with some nuances. Stalin initiated the 'demarcation', it seems, in order to subdue the tenacious national 'frictions' (*treniia*) over land and water rights, mostly between Uzbek and Kazakh party members. He and his comrades on the Central Asian Bureau of the RKPb were less preoccupied with pan-Turkism, more with the frustrating realities of governing such a large and varied territory. Their solution was a practical one: rewarding Uzbek party members for their political loyalties with a prestigious nation-state of their own; punishing Kazakh party members for their pan-Turkic pretensions by redrawing the borders against their favor; and conveniently displacing Tatar elites from their influential roles throughout Turkestan.[43]

Soviet national policies in the Transcaucasus were even more complex. In the Northern Caucasus, national leaders originally envisioned a broad regional state rather than separate nations. Even Stalin's Commissariat of the Nationalities (Narkomnats) concurred by establishing two large autonomous republics here in early 1921: the Gorskii (Mountain Region) and Dagestan ASSRs (within the RSFSR). But by 1922, in a classic example of the "divide and conquer" strategy at work, Stalin's "autonomization" program created new autonomous 'regions' (*oblasts*) out of the Gorskii ASSR: the Karachai-Cherkess and Kabardin-Balkar Autonomous Oblasts (AOs); the Chechen and Adygei AOs (winter 1922); and the South Ossetian and Ingush AOs (November 1924). These peoples were no longer united by ethnicity and language. Common "nationalities" (the Karachai-Balkar Turks and the Cherkess-Kabardin Circassians) were now rent from each other. They were no longer wed to a separate territory outside of Russia, but were now subsumed within the "North Caucasus Region" of the RSFSR. These artful creations had their reverse application in the rest of the Transcaucasus, where the ethnic and national divisions between the separate Georgian, Armenian and Azerbaijani peoples were so well established as to allow for their integration into a regional state, the Transcaucasus Republic of 1922. The identities and interests of each nation were so distinct that the Bolsheviks had little to fear from such a construct. For them, especially among the Turks of Azerbaijan, pan-Turkism was less of a threat than individual nationalism. (Wixman 1980; Pipes 1964)

To demarcate the peoples of the east in these ways meant to define and control them according to the modern, objective standards of scientific description and classification. Baudouin de Courtenay's worst fears, articulated in *The national and territorial mark in autonomy*, were realized. With state patronage, Soviet ethnographers and geographers now "mapped" these peoples, as Eileen Consey has argued, in the interests of "spatial ordering" and "optimal observation". (Consey 1995) A series of linguistic demarcations now followed the national demarcations, driven by the political interest of detaching native populations from prerevolutionary elites. As I discuss with more care in chapter six, nativization strategy was designed to speed the process of literacy and literary development, a political task of the first degree. The mass literacy campaigns dictated that languages should follow local and native rather than pan-Turkic or pan-Caucasian development. Separate peoples needed fully native "mass" scripts and literary languages, fitted to their unique sound systems, in order to help them better come to literacy. In the words of one leading party activist from Central Asia, the government set out to create literacy for the "broad masses" rather than the leading "elites".[44] The promotion of local politicians and their dialects from below offered the government a convenient mechanism to reinforce its own statist policies from above. By developing mass languages, with the assistance of local linguists and "sympathetic" Russians, it attempted to displace other native elites who had their own designs for national literary languages. Language became a weapon by which to subdue any pan-Caucasian and pan-Turkic threats, and to heighten the value of Russian as a language of international communication.

The Soviet government did not thereby impose whole new native languages upon the eastern peoples. They did not artificially fashion out of the common Circassian language group several new sub-languages in Adygei, Kabardian, Abkhaz, and Abazin. Nor did it shape out of a common "Turkic" the new sub-languages of Tatar, Bashkir, Uzbek, Kazakh, Kirgiz, Turkmen and Azerbaijani.[45] Such an interpretation would comically exaggerate the power of the Soviet government to resolutely plan languages and manipulate the subtle questions of language reform, or to spontaneously shape the characters and destinies of whole Caucasian and Central Asian peoples. Rather, the government simply chose to promote selected patterns of linguistic and ethnic separation already in place. In William Fierman's balanced formula, "language was a fundamental element of the social and political environment in which the Bolsheviks carried out their revolutionary policy. At the same time, language itself was also an instrument and object of Bolshevik policy". (Fierman 1991: 46-51) In other words, the national territorial principle and nativization programs were unavoidable means to a greater end, Soviet Russian rule, not ends in themselves.

To fulfill these means and ends, policy makers in the Council of National Minorities (Sovnatsmen) devised the "ABCD hierarchy", a new ethnolinguistic union for the reconquered peoples of the east. It formally plotted Soviet nationality frontiers into a hierarchical grid, ostensibly for the RSFSR alone, but unofficially for the USSR as a whole, along with all of its distinct parts: national 'regions' (*raiony*), 'districts' (*okrugi*), and 'provinces' (*oblasti*); autonomous republics; and union republics. The variables of the hierarchy expressed the government's appreciation for its diverse eastern frontiers. But its constant was Russian, the "language of the federation".

> A. Small nationalities without scripts, which are generally bilingual, live in compact groups surrounded by larger nationalities, and are territorially 'scattered', will conduct all education and create all literature in the 'language of the federation'.
>
> B. Small and medium-sized monolingual nationalities without scripts, which live as compact masses, are agricultural and not united territorially, will create primary schools, educational literature and mass political propaganda in the native language. Secondary schools, middle professional education and higher education will be conducted in the 'language of the federation'.
>
> C. Medium or large-sized monolingual nationalities, using a traditional script and having a proletariat, intelligentsia and bourgeoisie, which live in compact groups or are territorially united, will create primary, secondary and middle professional education, together with political-educational literature and other scholarly and educational literature, in the native language. The 'language of the federation' will be introduced no later than the third grade and is to continue into higher education.
>
> D. Economically and culturally developed nationalities that have traditional scripts and are territorially united, will create all education from primary schools to universities, and all literature (including technical texts), in the native language. The 'language of the federation' will be introduced no later than the third grade.[46]

The bureaucratic style in this hierarchy is striking in its simplicity. Its political model seems to have been Stalin's report on the national question to the Twelfth Congress of the RKPb in 1923, which justified the formation of the new USSR by way of the principle, "from multiplicity to unity", with an emphasis on "unity". He dictated that autonomy in the new USSR would be much like autonomy within the RSFSR: formal and conditional. S.M. Dimanshtein, one of Stalin's deputies in the making of national policy, gave even more revealing testimony to this principle. During the constitutional debates of the later 1920s, he offered that "we are headed along the path of the 'dying away' of the federation and the strengthening of the union". The whole point of the USSR state system was its unitary function rather than its federal form. If you "want to call its governments separate and distinct, you are wrong", said Dimanshtein. "We can never agree to this. We need to aim for one union government. To speak of a federation of governments is just empty talk".[47] In the ABCD hierarchy itself, we do not read of sovereign regions or republics, but simply of undeveloped and developed nationalities in relation to the guiding standard, Russia. This verbal style reveals the extent to which federalism and autonomy were sometimes little more than fictions for early Bolshevik leaders. Territorial units remained artificial constructs. Moscow and its state language were the centerpieces of Bolshevik power.

Fulfilling even the minimal standards of the ABCD hierarchy was not easy. Narkompros was bewildered by the poverty of human and material resources inherited from the Tsarist system. In the first few years after the civil war, the vast majority of children in the Muslim Caucasus, Volga-Urals, and Central Asia did not have the opportunity to attend school, except for religious or Russian language schools, both of which were politically incorrect.[48] Narkompros made a valiant effort during the early 1920s to correct this imbalance. It eventually trained enough native language teachers for the first grade classrooms of most nationalities. But without any more such teachers to spare, not to speak of textbooks and writing materials, Russian became the language of instruction in most higher grades, by default. This was especially the case with the small peoples of the North Caucasus and Volga-Urals. Narkompros established new "native language" schools for them, but many in name only. Even in developed Baku, capital of the Azerbaijani Soviet Republic, only three out of twenty one native language secondary schools in 1923 actually operated with full Turkic language instruction.[49]

The documents of the 1920s are filled with complaints and protests about these troubles. Educators grew frustrated and exhausted with the lack of funds and attention to their pleas. The Russians among them, sitting in city administrative buildings far from the classrooms, were unsure how to apply the nativizing standards of the ABCD hierarchy to the complex circumstances and different stages of national literary development among the non-Russians. They knew little about the very people they were supposed to serve. So they turned the ABCD hierarchy on its head. For them, the crucial question was when and how to introduce Russian into the schools, either as a subject for study or as a language of instruction. They now implemented the hierarchy according to the following adaptations. For the minority peoples living in large industrial cities (Jews, Ukrainians, Belorussians, Estonians and Latvians); and for the small nationalities living within the RSFSR (Iakut, Shor, Karelians, Veps and Izhor); Russian was to be introduced as a subject during the first grade and most classes thereafter were to be conducted in Russian. The minority peoples with their own autonomous regions and republics (the Adygei, Cherkess, Chechen, Kabardin, Ossetian, Ingush, Mordvinians, Chuvash, Udmurt-Votiaks, Komi-Zyrian, Komi-Permiaks and Mari) and the "Turko-Tatar" peoples were to enjoy degrees of nativized schools in the earliest primary grades. But for them Russian was to be introduced as a subject anywhere from the second to the fifth grade, and most classes were to be conducted in Russian after the fifth, when the native language thereafter became an elective. (Mansurov & Epshtein 1927).

Ostensibly designed for nativization, the hierarchy became an excuse for a public campaign to promote Russian. In Azerbaijan, the TsK AKPb directed an effort in the media and schools to improve and broaden its teaching. Without much fear of being labeled "great-Russian chauvinists", policy makers and educators openly proclaimed that Russian was an "obligatory" subject in every school in the USSR and the language of instruction in many. The reasoning was simple. It was no longer the language of colonial exploitation but the "language of the proletarian revolution". People had to learn it to become properly class conscious. Students had to be sufficiently literate in it - to show mastery of basic grammar and spelling skills, and the "ability to read deliberately and speak expressively" in Russian - if they ever hoped to move up to the secondary and higher schools.[50]

The ABCD hierarchy reminds us that the Russian language remained a constant and heavy handed imperative in Soviet life. If the non-Russians were encouraged to speak out and act locally, they were also required to think and relate to each other internationally. The government could not deny the fundamental right to native language development. But the standard of a unitary socialist culture defined before the revolution ensured its right to intervene in nationality affairs. Nativization of language did not mean nationalization of power nor an end to the dominance of Soviet values and the Russian language.[51]

It is relevant to note that both Lenin and Stalin embodied the duality of this state policy in their own personal histories. Lenin, the son of an imperial educator with nativist sympathies, disapproved of an official, coerced state language. By dismantling imperial russification policies, he hoped to make peace with the nationalities, helping them to develop their own languages and cultures, and in this circuitous way convince them of the value of the Russian language in Soviet life. (Kreindler 1982: 130) As a young man in the Tiflis seminary, Stalin entertained a passionate local nationalism for a time, reading the epics of Georgian literature and writing some successful poetry of his own.

Several of his pieces even reached the leading literary journal of the day, *Iveria* (1894), and made their way into compilations of Georgian national verse. Yet in later years, as a rising member of the Bolshevik party, he moved beyond this nativism to forge a new identity as a Russian speaking "proletarian". (Suny 1991: 56-57) Although he never fully mastered his adopted tongue, speaking with a thick Georgian accent and writing in an elementary style, his Russian words nonetheless became the stuff of poetic admiration and political command. In a sense, Stalin's voice became the master voice of the ABCD hierarchy and its mixed bilingualism.

Thus, drawn from a page in his own biography, Stalin's concise formula of 1925, "national in form but socialist in content", summarized both the liberality and the severity of Bolshevik language policy. National communists had room to interpret and operate within the realm of "national in form", but were constrained by Moscow's right to determine the kind and extent of "socialist in content". "National in form" implied compromises on the native language front in education and culture. "Socialist in content" meant party control in politics and economics, whose language was Russian. This logic meant that the native language, although a necessary course of study, was inherently inferior or substandard to Russian. In Stalin's pointed terms, Russian was that great "zonal language" of the USSR driving the historical dialectic "from multiplicity to uniformity". By no coincidence, it was at this very same time that Stalin promoted the statist slogan, "socialism in one country", for the USSR at large. These concepts eventually translated into his, later the party's, general formula about the "convergence" and "mergence" of peoples into one great proletarian world culture.[52]

Leading Bolsheviks, of all persuasions and nationalities, completed this litany. Lunacharskii, who ultimately approved the ABCD directives as Commissar of Education, held that the "backward" peoples of the USSR could not hope for much progress through nativization. "We are obliged", said Lunacharskii, "altogether obliged to promote them to the Russian language", the bearer of democracy and civilization. Anastasi Mikoian, party leader in the North Caucasus and a patron of nativization, termed the non-Russian language as a "domestic" language at best. Nadezhda Krupskaia, Lenin's wife and a leading voice in Narkompros, joined with M.P. Pavlovich-Vel'tman, a Bolshevik propagandist, in proclaiming that civilization must first come to the small peoples through the native language, the "greatest means of revolutionary propaganda and enlightenment"; second through Russian, the "great language" of the USSR.[53] The natives had to begin with the small corners of their provincial lives, and only then proceed to the big, universal tasks of Soviet power. The native languages may have grounded the non-Russians in their own local lives, but it was Russian that made them truly mobile. Such was the hubris of the patrons of the Russian language.

The documents of everyday life were filled with these prejudices. Administrators referred to Russian as the "state language" of the RSFSR. They termed it a "general language", the "first among equals" for the USSR as a whole. It was not a foreign language for the non-Russians but the cement that held them together, "the language of all-union state institutions" and of "relations between all peoples". Russian was the "language of Bolshevism" and of "the October Revolution". It was the language, without exception, of the secret police and all "secret" or "top-secret" documents. Few in this chorus, however, could match the chilling words of A. Enukidze, who described Russian as "the fixed axis around which all the nationalities of the Soviet Union must develop".[54]

The nativization decrees may have required that some Europeans learn the native languages, but they exempted no one from learning Russian. Many people understood this simple calculus of Soviet power, even welcomed it. As long as their children were learning Russian in "native language" schools and not the russified schools of the past, parents in the North Caucasus, Bashkir and Kirgiz ASSRs were not afraid to demand more attention to Russian. Adult learners voiced the same concerns, realizing that no matter how literate they were at a native "literacy station" in their hometown, they would always become illiterate at the Russian station down the road.[55] Ossetins from the North Caucasus, Kalmyks from Astrakhan, Jews from Saratov, and Tatars from Kazan - all spoke with apparent spontaneity and sincerity about Russian as the language of state discourse and upward mobility.[56] Within the statewide school system, educators never promoted the native languages at the expense of Russian; they appreciated the need to study, teach, and develop both. They always required that the native languages be taught in the primary schools, but they also retained Russian as the standard language of instruction in secondary and higher education. "This is the demand of surrounding life," wrote one educator, "the total sum of contemporary existence". (Gasilov 1929: 38)

Still, all was not well on the national frontiers. The new kinds of multiethnic contact encouraged by Soviet power, backed by the dual commitment to nativization and russification, only highlighted the differences between Russians and non-Russians and the tenacity of ethnic prejudice. As more and more of the non-Russians came to speak and write the Russian language, it appeared more truly as something of their own: not the language of Pushkin or Gorkii, but an awkwardly colloquial Russian *koine*, a tattered and worn currency of the new Soviet Union. As soon as the Russian language campaign started in 1925, educators publicly voiced their alarm over the poor mastery of the Russian language by non-Russians. Narkompros reported that seventy-five percent of national schools in the RSFSR were teaching the Russian language without success. Where it was offered as a subject, wrote one critic, students "recite beautifully like parrots, but do not understand a word of what they have read".

Observers spoke of mixed success with native language teaching in the Turko-Tatar and Finno-Ugric schools, but of disturbing problems with Russian in most grades in most other national schools. They were still operating without specific standards and timetables as to the required language of instruction, be it Russian or the native tongue. The campaign for Russian in the schools often resulted in a "Chinese literacy", which suffocated "the thrill of learning" in children and imperiled the legitimacy of Soviet power. In the North Caucasus, the Russian of most native teachers and students was atrocious, leaving them to communicate in a mixed "mountaineer-Russian speech", neither native nor Russian but "something in between, a kind of jargon, cutting to the ear". The schools used it all the way from the first grade to the last years of university education, which meant that native students learned neither their own languages nor Russian well, holding them back in their schooling and careers. This was deeply troubling to administrators in Moscow and to the Russian teachers manning the outposts on the peripheries.[57]

In official state business, the dual imperative of nativization and russification sent confusing, frustrating signals. On the one hand, the government needed nativization to create a new multiethnic civic community. On the other, it also needed to function properly in office and business settings, and in this latter enterprise Russian was the only language that really counted. The highest organs of the communist party and the Soviet state sent out nativization decrees time and time again. They reorganized the Committee for Uzbekification every few years and read report after report as to how their decrees were either implemented poorly or not at all. They warned the guilty parties of punishment "by the full extent of the law" and saw these warnings ignored with impunity. But they were partly to blame for this sad state of affairs given their own countermanding actions and orders. Government authorities exempted the main banks, health commissariat, statistical directorate, internal police (GPU), and commercial institutions of Uzbekistan from their nativization decrees in 1927. Every few years they extended the deadlines for European postal and telegraph employees to learn Uzbek. After all, they reasoned, the mail had to get through.

The attempts to promote the native non-Russian languages in the official discourse of Central Asia often turned out to be miserable failures. Financial and commercial institutions were especially obstructionist. They simply did not have enough native language study courses, materials, translators and typists to implement the policy. Plus, during the relatively liberal years of the "New Economic Policy" (NEP), too many profits were to be made. The commissariats for education, land, labor and internal affairs consistently refused to allocate money for nativization. The Textile Syndicate predicted "chaos" if it converted office work to Uzbek. The Water Services Administration warned Moscow that it would not nativize for fear of endangering the water supply, a viable threat since the cotton fields of arid Uzbekistan would wither away without irrigation.[58]

Divided speech communities of the Soviet Union 57

Some native 'promoted ones' (*vydvyzhentsy*) also took the dependence of state institutions on Russian a bit too seriously. Those with a mastery of both their native language and Russian were often at a premium for employers in Moscow. Consequently, they tended to refuse to leave the center for their distant homelands, where their skills were also needed to implement nativization policy at the grass roots level. The practice was so widespread that Dimanshtein once had to remind national politicians that Russian was not simply a language of social mobility. It should never become a ticket out of one's "backward" surroundings, he noted, otherwise we would find the Kalmyk in the Russian capitol saying, "I want to stay here. Why do I need to go out to the Kalmyk steppe and drink tea when I can sit here in Moscow and sip cocoa".[59] The Soviet Union, engaged in the serious pursuit of building communism, could ill afford to tolerate such luxuries.

Perhaps most telling was the nearly complete failure of the project for reciprocal bilingualism, largely because of an undercurrent of Russian ethnic prejudice. Native language courses for Russians in Central Asia failed over and over on account of poor attendance and weak "social consciousness". In 1927, of 25,000 Europeans working in state and party institutions in Uzbekistan, only 1,700 of them were enrolled in Uzbek language courses. Many simply refused to learn; others rationalized that, in the interests of state business, they could not afford to lose even a day of work in Uzbek language classes. In the pointed terms of one observer, people still harbored a disrespectful and "contemptuous" attitude toward Uzbek, a mark of continuing "Russian autocratic chauvinism". Dimanshtein certainly exacerbated the problem when he expressed what was likely a majority view among ethnically Russian members of the communist party. We cannot force the native language on the Russian worker, he explained. In fact, "we cannot nativize [*korenizirovat'*] the proletariat".[60] In the schools, Russian literacy teachers often showed disrespect toward the native language and refused to teach in it. Narkompros even encouraged Russian students to leave native language classes and join their "own kind". When asked what benefits he might receive by learning Tatar, one Russian student responded that it would only help him to "end up in some hut to chat about the devil knows what, like how to knife some poor fellow".[61]

Such overt racism was grounded in family life. Children learned it from their parents at a young age: how to identify differences in speech, or custom, or religion as something to be avoided and suspected. The government's very own initiatives in "international education" and multiculturalism were not so much a step into the utopian future as a reaction to racial and ethnic hatreds in the present - hatreds that so often took the form of scorn among Russian school children for the study of the native non-Russian languages. Thus, "great-Russian chauvinism" was not simply a function of elite politics. It was rooted in the mass mentality. Or in the words of one observer, while the Soviet government was promoting class solidarity with the world proletariat abroad, citizens at home were engaging in all kinds of ethnic antagonisms. "Love for far away lands" did not, he wrote, "guarantee a love for one's neighbors" next door.[62]

Faced with a series of glaring practical problems of state management, the Soviet government had crafted a precarious balance between compromise and coercion. It had accepted the need to speak to the Russian masses in their own terms, and to develop the native languages of the peripheries; but it also raised the standard for a disciplined Russian language culture to bring the provincial Russian dialects and non-Russian languages all the closer to Moscow. The basic dynamic was now in place to define the character and scope of all other language reforms to come. The historical trajectory was clear: forward and up.

Part II
Theoretical approaches

Chapter 3

G.G. Shpet, linguistic structure, and the Eurasian imperative in Soviet language reform

> *People surround themselves within a world of sounds in order to apprehend and cultivate the world of objects. At the very same moment that they elicit language from within themselves, so also they draw themselves back into it. In a sense, each language fills its own people within a kind of circle, which they can only depart by entering into another one.*
>
> G.G. Shpet[1]

Once the national frontiers had been defined and slated for conquest, linguistics became an indispensable part of state business. At the creation of the USSR, politicians and linguists shared a common fascination with the relationship of parts and wholes. The Bolsheviks knew that they had to define the parts, the national territorial republics and regions, before they could define the whole, the USSR. Linguists performed the vital function of defining the formal properties of the parts. They set out to study, describe, and classify the speech patterns of the Russian and non-Russian peoples. They explored the territorial and "class" dialect variations within Russian. They positioned the non-Russian peoples in new, definitive spaces of knowledge and control. These new partners, politicians and linguists, temporarily joined in the business of state-building and nation-making, understood that social demarcation began with language. But they also understood it as a means to envision a larger whole, of which Russia and non-Russia were but parts, a Soviet Eurasia. This is not to say that all was agreeable between Soviet power and structural linguistics. The 1920s were a decade of extraordinary possibilities and remarkable fluidity.

Amid the revolution and civil war, Russia's prestigious community of linguists broke into bits and pieces. N.S. Trubetskoi fled to Bulgaria and later Austria. Roman Jakobson eventually settled in Czechoslovakia. Baudouin de Courtenay and V.K. Porzhezinskii, a leading Moscow formalist, immigrated to Poland. For those who remained behind, life was both bleak and exhilarating. Left to congregate in the cold lecture halls and apartments of Petrograd and Moscow, they scraped together just enough food and fuel to survive. Yet their commitment to ideas did not flag. They continued to discuss their novel approaches to language and their fascination with its power to organize human experience, to shape people's worlds and provoke them to action. Shklovskii applauded their self-styled "concept of structure" and described them as "constructors of a new life". This "was a time of great tasks", he wrote, "which gave rise to a great self-confidence in us. We thought that even language would give way to conscious changes and, in any case, supposed that the very expression 'literary language' already designated the possibility of a willful relationship to language." (Shklovskii 1966: 373-375) To these young scholars, linguistics was less an abstract science than a practical discipline to serve the developmental plans of the Soviet regime. Their fortunes soon improved. If the 1920s was a decade of crises in language culture, it was also a decade of much promise. Formalist and structural linguists unfolded the precise diagrams of correct speech for all to see and hear, be it through Russian, or the non-Russian languages, or even the international language, Esperanto. The new thoughts and words of communism deserved nothing less.

3.1. Recasting the Russian speech community

To realize the tasks at hand, the Soviet government quickly established a network of scholarly research centers designed to retain as much of the old, prerevolutionary professoriat as possible, albeit under loose Marxian theoretical direction. At the top were the Main Scientific Directorate (Glavnauk), the State Academic Council (GUS), and the Russian Association of Scientific Research Institutes of the Social Sciences (RANION).[2] Members of the Petersburg and Moscow schools took first place in them. Moscow State University remained their stronghold, where M.N. Peterson and D.N. Ushakov taught the intricacies of the Russian language to new generations of linguists and schoolteachers. The Institute of Language and Literature of RANION, directed and staffed largely by Baudouin's and Fortunatov's students, continued to develop and apply their methods. At closed meetings of the Moscow Linguistic Society and the RANION Language Institute in 1922, they raised the traditional Indo-European languages (Latin, Sanskrit, Greek and Old Church Slavonic) and the latest linguistic methodologies (comparative phonetics, morphology and syntax) as the leading standards for the country at large.[3]

In these difficult years, ever isolated from the European academic community beyond, Russian linguists suffered from a crisis of identity. They tended to believe that the writings of Ferdinand de Saussure and his students, centered on the *Course in general linguistics*, were the most innovative and important in the field. "The leitmotif of all their works may be formulated thusly", wrote M.N. Peterson, "'language is a social phenomenon', 'language is a system of linguistic signs with multifaceted social functions'". In Moscow's discussion circles, linguists anxiously debated the merits of the Saussurian "synchronic" method, exploring its applications to language, literature, the arts, and culture.[4] Sergei

Kartsevskii, "an apostle of the Saussurian school" in Roman Jakobson's words, briefly returned to Soviet Russia from abroad in 1918 and "fired the young generation of Moscow linguists" with structural insights. Thanks to Baudouin's and Fortunatov's preparatory teachings, he found a ready if somewhat disappointing audience. As a true believer, Kartsevskii resented the propensity of his colleagues to take Saussure on their own terms, complaining that they were unable to achieve a true "philosophy of language", instead wallowing in the empirical research of the Fortunatov school, which examined language not as a structured whole but as the mere "sum of its concrete facts".[5] Two Moscow formalists took this criticism to heart. A.M. Peshkovskii, the leading theoretician of the new formal grammars, eventually integrated his work more fully with Saussure's and Kartsevskii's methods. M.N. Peterson did likewise in his *Introduction to linguistics*. Louis Hjelmslev, founder of the Copenhagen structural school, even celebrated it as an excellent and "beau travail" for its "radicalism", "energy", and "clarity" in breaking away from the traditional study of phonetics and semantics and in exploring the novel realms of linguistic signs and forms.[6]

Both Peterson's praises and Kartsevskii's disappointments were overstated. For at this moment of transmission, Russian linguists read and understood Saussure largely in light of G.G. Shpet's remarkable phenomenology of language. A onetime revolutionary socialist and Marxist, Shpet became professor of philosophy at Moscow State University (1918-1923) and founder of its Psychology Institute; editor of the journal, *Thought and word* (1918-1921); and later vice-president of the State Academy of Artistic Studies (GAKhN) and head of its Philosophy Section. Although he had tempered his radical leanings by then, Shpet was still one of the few leading philosophers of the day upon whom the new Soviet regime could place some trust. So, as many of his colleagues were expelled from the country in the great academic purge of 1922, Shpet stayed on, at the express invitation of the Marxist historian and Bolshevik administrator, M.N. Pokrovskii. As others bemoaned the revolution and the catastrophes that it had heaped upon Russia, Shpet went to work for the new regime, proud to serve the revolution in broad terms, regardless of his political disagreements with the Bolsheviks. He framed these sentiments in a quote from the Latin poet, Ovid. "I leave for others to recollect upon ancient, better times. I for one am content to live in the present."[7]

Shpet was one of the most important and influential philosophers of his day. He popularized Hegelian philosophy, reinterpreted Humboldt's linguistic theories, and introduced Husserl's thought to the country. His lectures at Moscow University, according to his students, were truly "events". Impeccably dressed in his finely tailored suits and beaming with confidence, he would fly through his "highly refined, elegant, and profound generalizations", much to the dismay of his young, unprepared students. Perhaps more than any other person he helped to engineer Russia's "linguistic turn" in philosophy, the humanities, and fine arts; what the philosopher V.F. Asmus called that "new 'repartition'" (*novyi razdel*) of the social sciences toward the "principled analysis of the structures of language".[8] The young linguists of the Petersburg and Moscow schools, reported Roman Jakobson, maintained "close and effective connections with phenomenology in its Husserlian and Hegelian versions". But it was Shpet who conducted "continuous and ardent debates" on Husserl's *Logical investigations* with them. Their discussions about the phonology, morphology, sociology and phenomenology of language crystallized what Roman Jakobson called the idea of "structural laws", which soon "became the catchword of linguistics". Shpet's ideas were so influential, a veritable phenomenological movement, that some Moscow linguists even began to call themselves Shpetians rather than Saussurians.[9]

Why all of this excitement? Husserl, Shpet's mentor, had posed the existence of a "pure, a priori grammar" in the human mind. Its ideal structures of meaning allegedly translated into the formal sound and meaning structures of language, and eventually into the intentional and signifying utterances of individuals. A priori grammar enabled people to create objects of thought through language, thereby shaping experience and allowing for reflection back upon it through sound and word sequences. Husserl thereby defined language as a very special kind of sign system: pointing to real things in the world, but also allowing people to create abstract thoughts and signify multiple meanings about them. He believed that we humans enjoy the power to discover and share ideal meanings independent from the experiences, sounds and signs that give them external form. We can, after all, communicate the same meaning by way of different sounds, words and languages, to different people, in different places, at different times. Although they exist in diverse syntactic and semantic contexts, ideal meanings are universal. In their complex and varied manifestations, Husserl concluded, language codes are the best ways for people to understand what makes world cultures all so very different, and yet all so very human.[10]

Consummate student of Husserl's phenomenology, Shpet defied the fashionable urge to explain the world by way of psychological, genetic, or naturalistic hypotheses. They were nothing more than metaphors, tropes of scientific consciousness. The phenomenological method preferred to observe the world in its self-evident actuality and through human intuition and interpretation come to understand it on its own terms. Language was just such a self-evident "thing" (*veshch'*). In his best-known work, *Aesthetic fragments* (1922-1923), Shpet defined "the word" or "speech" (*slovo*) as the organizing "principle", the "archetype of culture". As he later wrote, "in its formal structure, the word is the ontological prototype of every social-cultural thing". Like language, culture was a system of signs, codes and messages open to analysis and interpretation, both for their surface, formal expressions, and their deeper, more ideal meanings.

And like language, culture was a dynamic social phenomenon which people expressed and reinvented as the subjects and objects of discourse. "The life of consciousness is the play of word upon word, dialogue". (Shpet 1922: 12; Shpet 1927a: 140)

For Shpet, language was not an innate talent in humankind, a fact of nature; rather it was a gift of culture, given from generations long passed away, eternally renewable in generations yet to come. Speech was the ultimate cultural act, the ultimate human act: part unconscious and given, part willful and refined. Language speaks through us as an "alien object" (*chuzhdy ob'iekt*), and we speak through it as the subjects of discourse. But neither speaks just as it might please. For language has a free floating, "independent internal life". It "reproduces not actual objects, but ideas (*poniatiia*) about them", and is thus never irrevocably bound to the objects it names in the world, nor to the established meanings it conveys. (Shpet 1923, 3: 96-97; Shpet 1927a: 11-12, 17-26)

In perhaps his most important and rigorous work, *The internal form of the word* (1927), Shpet combined a reading of Hegelian and Humboldtian philosophy with his own analysis of the dialectical unity of language and thought, individual and society, form and content. For "language is the generative organ of thought", the condition of our lives. "People understand themselves only because they understand others, only because language develops in society". "Language consciousness" is a "dialectical consciousness"; the play between "objectified subjectivity" and "subjectified objectivity". With all its dense references and philosophical style, this is not an easy book to read. But it is well worth the effort for its penetrating phenomenological insights, as when Shpet portrayed language, every human language, as a system of sound and word parts that empower people with the deep structures of meaningful expressions. "Thought demands the synthesis of multiplicity into unity", he wrote. This meant that the wonderful infinity of sounds, meanings, and expressions which were possible in human speech were by necessity contained in its universal structure of rules and representations, or all those "threads, necessary for understanding and for sowing relations of ideas", necessary for "freedom and mobility".[11]

Reluctant though he was to break out of his sometimes obtuse philosophical style, Shpet nonetheless did make sense of these insights in concrete terms. He returned Husserl's "a priori foundations" of pure consciousness back to the more practical study of language, as embedded in history, literature, society, and even political economy. "The word is the real material carrier", said Shpet in counterpoint to his teacher. "There can be no such analysis of consciousness in which there is no material, articulate carrier". At GAKhN, as he once admitted in his autobiography, he "centered all work around the examination of the problem of the word". This meant everything from studies of "the metaphor and artistic consciousness" to the "semantics of literary styles"; from the "musical syntax of children's speech" to the study of "Caucasian folk tales". It was here at

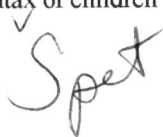

GAKhN that the Institute of the Living Word found a worthy successor in a new commission by the same name, dedicated to declamation studies and experiments with script graphics - the practical means to create better speakers and readers in the Russian speech community.[12]

Shpet also showed an affinity for Marx's "structural" analysis of economic exchange in *Capital*, as when he equated the "word" to Marx's commodity: also a material thing, a product of creative human labor applied to nature; and also a sign, which on the open market "changes into a thing which transcends sensuousness". Both phenomena were "sensuous-supra-sensuous" (*chuvstvenno-sverkhchuvstvennoe*). The market commodity, like the word in discourse, was a "social thing" charged with creative power, and was a "meaningful sign" charged with collective value. (Shpet 1927a: 178-189; Marx 1977: 163)

This dialectical philosophy into the practical study of ethnic psychology, which Shpet defined as a "descriptive typological science", one which searched for all of those "common types" of behavior as represented in the "social facts" of language, art, customs, and the law. It studied the "signs" (*znaki*) of collective life, along with their multiple "meanings" (*znacheniia*) and "expressions" (*vyrazheniia*). "Language is not simply an example or illustration, but a methodological model", one applicable "to the study of all other forms of 'expression'".[13] Like Baudouin and Fortunatov before him, Shpet undermined the popular definition of ethnic psychology as the study of the "spirit of a people" or its etymological inventory. Instead he called for this new "semasiological" approach, the study of ethnicity and culture as sign systems all their own, based on language as the matrix of individual and group consciousness. There was nothing radically new here. Humboldt and Potebnia had said it before: language was the primary "expression" and "mark" (*priznak*) of national identity. Shpet merely grounded the insight in more rigorous phenomenological and hermeneutic distinctions. Languages were not fortified bastions of the national "spirit", eternal by content and form and impermeable to change, but were universal structures of meaning open to comparison and reciprocal influence no matter how different in lexicon and grammar. People are bound to each other not by obtuse psychic impressions, but by the material signs of collective life and by the experiences which individuals live and share together through them.

It was precisely this binding of sign and experience, Shpet believed, which made nations so tenacious through time. For national "peculiarities" (*osobennosti*) are those "social things" rooted in language and in the values people associate with them. "A person's spiritual wealth is the national past to which they reckon their self." Granted, nations are not permanent and immutable. Like everything else they are subject to the fluidity of time. In fact, Shpet was prepared to argue that, if "present day nations somehow divided themselves up into classes which, transfusing between this nation and that, created new, never before seen collectives, then we would be correct to say that they had merely given birth to new nations [*narodilis' novye narody*]." (Shpet 1927a: 23; Shpet 1927b [1989]: 574) Like so many of Shpet's constructions, the words are puzzling at first, but only at first. For all their mutability through time, he seemed to say that nations are complex and tightly bound structures and relationships of meaning. The circles they occupy may meet and converge, but the circles never go away. They are the very conditions of our lives. One of Shpet's closest collaborators, G.O. Vinokur, perhaps said it best when he dismissed Husserl's vain search for a "utopian" universal grammar, applicable to all peoples, times and places. For Shpet and his students (like Vinokur) had strayed long and far from their teacher. Their conclusion, that we cannot escape our own syntax, the "ontological condition of our existence". The nation, like the language that speaks through it, is already the inner form of the word.[14]

Posterity has not been kind to Shpet; from the point of view of the communist party bosses, for good reason. He may have bowed to the dialectic in history, and even to the materialist ethic. But he played too fast and loose between "subjective" and "objective idealism". And he callously celebrated the permanence of form over content.[15] Still, it is hard to overestimate his contributions to early Soviet intellectual history. His ideas captivated the young generation of Soviet linguists. At the boisterous meetings of the Moscow Linguistic Circle, they defied Saussure's abstract dichotomies between *langue* and *parole*, between synchrony and diachrony, instead seeking out the points of tension between them. L.I. Zhirkov complained that Saussure exaggerated the "arbitrariness of the linguistic sign", calling instead for the study of the "problem of meaning, which is an issue about boundaries". "The phoneme is at the center of things, but boundaries are important too." G.O. Vinokur wrote not of pure theory or abstract structure, but of the "meaningful and multifaceted arbitrariness of the intelligent being". In their works, especially those of L.P. Iakubinskii, we even find a "teleological" insight about language (the study of the "goals of a speech utterance"), that it was purposeful within itself as a sign system and without as social communication.[16]

N.F. Iakovlev similarly analyzed the phoneme not simply as an individual or psychological phenomenon but as a transparent carrier of social meaning, embedded in the contrastive system of signs. N.M. Karinskii's university lectures between 1923 and 1928 reveal just how widespread these ideas were in the academic communities of the day. He defined language, the totality of associations between its physiological signs and its psycho-social meanings, as communicative and social only to the extent that it was composed of a structure of interrelated, contrastive elements (phonemes, morphemes and lexemes).[17] Together these innovative linguists recognized language as a semiotic system of signals and codes which makes communication between human beings possible. They understood that language functions, the combined acts of individuals in a speech community, both depend on and determine language structure.[18]

But most significantly of all, these linguists translated their proto-structural principles into a practical, applied linguistics. They set out to confront the most immediate dilemma of language reform, how to stitch back together the broken remnants of the Russian speech community. They devoted such time and energy to the deficiencies of Russian "language culture" because the stakes were high, both for illiterate and poorly literate Russian at home, and for the "backward" non-Russian peoples beyond. For they too had to begin to master the language of Lenin. Inspired by Saussure's "theory of synchronic linguistics", the Moscow formalist Vinokur began the "construction of a practical stylistics" or "linguistic technics". He regarded language as a "social fact", an object of analysis; but also as a kind of "societal norm", a standard of social conduct in the crucial fields of agitation, propaganda, and education. Readers must be taught, nurtured and prepared for literacy over time, Vinokur asserted. For all their nuances and varieties of interpretation, words have definite meanings which need to be standardized to promote healthy social communication. Words also take their meanings from their contrastive relations with other words as parts of greater texts.

R.O. Shor later defined all of this into what she called a "structural analysis" of formal meanings: between the word as a "name", as a "sign of a certain objective meaning, communicated by the speaker to the listener"; and "the word as a sign indicator of the mental attitude of a speaker" - a formula which she based on the corresponding relationship between the standard phonemes and distinctive features of structural phonology. Vinokur's and Shor's excursions into philology and stylistics promoted a standard literary language to help people express themselves in more creative and complex ways.[19]

M.S. Gus popularized these notions from his post in the Central Union of Press Workers. Gus's "Commission on the Language of the Press" applied formalist and structural insights to remedy the heavy and boring bureaucratic style of most newspapers. The structural dialectic between system and expression, *langue* and *parole*, form and content was at the center of one of his popular textbooks, designed to promote a "conscious orientation to language" among Soviet journalists and worker and peasant correspondents. In a creative twist on Humboldt's formula, it contrasted the basic 'informational article' (*stat'ia*) as a "means of communication of one or another content" governed by "comprehension and expediency;" and the light 'literary satire' (*fel'eton*) as artistic speech, "content, an end-in-itself". The book also promoted a new grammatical stylistics for Russian based on the crucial role of grammar forms "as factors of intelligibility". Gus effectively translated the insights of Baudouin, Fortunatov and Saussure into practical lessons for the people.[20]

Linguists also turned to the study of the standard Russian language and its many social and class dialects. L.P. Iakubinskii and his colleagues identified the distinct forms and functions of language (the nominative, interrogative, informational, aesthetical and imperative) in their different social settings, based on a new sense of the "social functions of speech (oratorical and practical)". They classified the idioms of metal, textile and chemical workers, as well as various other class groups, into new terminological dictionaries, hoping to promote better social communication between them. They then set out to bring "applied linguistics" to aid in the education of "lower worker-agitators", using the speech patterns of famous revolutionary orators (Marat, Robespierre, Volodarskii and Lenin) and the recordings of famous poets and actors as their standards. Between 1927 and 1930, they took dozens of expeditions to the provinces and offered hands-on teaching with dictaphones, reaching over 4,000 communist activists and workers with the new sounds and furies of Bolshevism. Recordings of Lenin's voice were a popular favorite.[21]

Polivanov's Institute of Language and Literature (RANION) was similarly dedicated to the study of "collective dialects" based on their speakers' economic conditions. He established a new school of "sociological linguistics" there in the middle 1920s to study social dialects, language theory, and Marxist ideology - and their triple impact on contemporary Russian. With M.N. Peterson's help, Polivanov marshaled formal grammar for these tasks by publishing a descriptive study of Russian phonetics, morphology and syntax. He planned to "revise linguistic methodology for all aspects of descriptive and historical linguistic research on the premises of Marxist linguistics".[22]

Vinokur also challenged linguists and activists to perfect the "look" of the new Soviet press and literature. The outer form of a text, he argued following Shpet, was inextricably linked to its inner content. If traditional linguistics focused on sounds and their historical development, modern linguistics should study the intricacies of printed speech and their present significance. His new science of "graphics" explored letters and words as signifying forms, a self-contained "language" or sign system all their own, as well as an independent field for "aesthetic" representation.[23] Vinokur's comparisons of the different scripts and layouts of newspaper articles and headlines revealed the advantages of larger, streamlined scripts, balanced headlines, "telegraphic syntax" and summary quotes. Such improved formats allowed for better communication between the writer and reader.

One of Vinokur's students, A.A. Reformatskii, pursued these approaches with even more vigor. In celebration of Husserl's and Saussure's "study of language as a synchronic sign system", he argued that even the simple letter was "a structural element of written speech". Vowels and consonants, like grammar and syntax, functioned as unique linguistic sub-systems that transformed their structural elements to meet the needs of different speech "genres". Notwithstanding its rather specialized title, Reformatskii's *The technical editing of books* applied these principles to improve print layouts and formats. He advised editors how to make books more readable, based on Vinokur's theory of the "unity of form and content". By examining the "correlative system of signs", he showed how different types of script were better suited for different types of texts, be they for business purposes intent on "designating" or poetic works intent on "expressing".[24]

These were, as we have already seen, no idle concerns. The "Down with Illiteracy" movement and Organizational Bureau of the TsK RKPb recognized that rationalized technical formats helped beginning readers to master literacy. Books needed to be written in a popular language, designed with easy-to-read scripts and layouts. Worker correspondents and journalists demanded this into the 1930s. One editor from the Iaroslavl region even complained that the print face of local newspapers appeared to be "suffering from tuberculosis". In its place, he pleaded, we need a "living, beaming, communicable print".[25] Structural principles had proven their value, and would prove it yet again, in restoring the sick patient back to health.

3.2. Language reform for the Soviet east

After the civil war, linguists also perfected their phenomenological and structural approaches, and their ideas about language contact and mixing, into a "Eurasian" imperative in language reform. I use this term in a broad sense: it includes the theories of the Russian emigres, N.S. Trubetskoi and Roman Jakobson; and those of the leading cadre of Soviet structural linguists, E.D. Polivanov, N.F. Iakovlev, L.I. Zhirkov and D.V. Bubrikh. These former classmates from the university seminars and discussion circles of Petersburg and Moscow maintained rather close contacts and research agendas into the 1920s. Trubetskoi and Jakobson even considered the latter as honorary members of their own Prague Linguistic Circle.[26]

Together these linguists shared the Shpetian insight that language was a paradigm for the unity of human thought and action in the world. If language consisted of an integral system of referential signs and expressive styles, then cultural development similarly depended upon the realities of linguistic space and national self-determination. Yet these "Eurasianists", by setting out to study the linguistic and ethnic forms of Shpet's "circles", ultimately showed how they were not so separate, but already intertwined, concentric circles, and seemingly intertwining more and more all the time.

Emigre Eurasianism had its eccentric manifestations. In their first published salvos of 1920 and 1921, N.S. Trubetskoi and his colleagues fashioned a classic Russian polemic against Western imperialism and chauvinist orientalism, which they believed had arrogantly defined civilization and progress by exclusively European standards. The Eurasianists developed the theory that the Slavs, Caucasians, Turks, Mongols, and Finno-Ugrians shared such geographic, climactic, and ethnolinguistic attributes as to manifest their own unique pocket of world culture. Mixing a Russian exceptionalism with a Eurasian multiculturalism, they believed that "Russia-Eurasia constituted an independent, self-contained, organic entity". Trubetskoi even coined the term, "speech union" (*sprachbund*), to liberate the great Russian language from the stale model of Indo-European genetics and place it in the freer orbit of "Eurasia", where Russian was already converging with the languages of Asia.

Krystyna Pomorska has called this enthusiasm for spatial over temporal study as a peculiarly futurist characteristic of modern linguistics whereby, as in the case of Einstein's relativity and European cubism, "time and space are discussed as structure determinants". Trubetskoi explored such determinants in the quintessentially "Eurasian" Turkic languages. The Turkic or Turanian "linguistic type", he theorized, "is characterized by schematic regularity and a consequent realization of a small number of simple and clear principles which mold the language into a single whole". Fascinated by such symmetry and balance, he studied their traces in Russian, translating his appreciation for the geographical space of Eurasia into a novel approach about the structural geography of language.[27]

Jakobson developed the theory of "Eurasian language union" along these lines. But he was doubly inspired by Shpet's theories, which he credited several times (in private correspondence) for forcing him to rethink linguistics and ethnography with more "radicalism". In Shpetian terms, Jakobson exchanged the traditional genetic relations within language families for the modern spatial relationships or existing geographic, cultural and linguistic interconnections between the Russians and their eastern neighbors. Trubetskoi and Jakobson cultivated this theory, in tandem with their excursions into structural phonology, through the Prague Linguistic Circle. Their ethos was a sincere multiculturalism and scholarly objectivity. But their theories also fed back into the russophilism of past and present Eurasianists.

P.N. Savitskii, a founder of the Eurasian movement and a member of the Prague Linguistic Circle, took Jakobson's theories as his own, reading them with a clear bias for Russia. "The Russian people is creating a new Eurasia", he wrote to Jakobson. "Eurasianization is fast approaching russification, not in the violent but in the organic sense of this word." Russian, what he called "the typical Eurasian language", has covered the whole continent as the dominant language, and is now even subject to a process of "asianization" and the creation of whole new dialects as it mixes with the peripheral languages of the USSR.[28] Savitskii was merely stating in a moment of candor what Trubetskoi and Jakobson had implied all along.

Soviet linguists and policy makers shared some of these "Eurasianist" tendencies during the 1920s. Scholarship now merged with state policy in a marriage of historical convenience. The "Eurasian" image of Russia, one of several available in the Soviet inventory, became a dominant pillar of state identity. Altogether isolated from Europe as a pariah state after the years of civil war, the government had to turn east; its Russian communist leaders even spoke of a world revolution beginning in Asia and ending with an "Easternization of Europe". At this moment, the new Soviet political federation - centered in Moscow with Russian as the dominant language of communication, and bounded by the native languages of the peripheries with substantial privileges - embodied the best merits of Trubetskoi's and Jakobson's fraternal union.

The emigre Eurasianists may have despised Bolshevik internationalism, but they nonetheless welcomed the new federal forms of the USSR, what they called a progressive "supranational" state and "Eurasian nation". In words reminiscent of Stalin's own, Trubetskoi heralded this new "zone" of "symphonic" relations between the elder and younger brothers of Russia-Eurasia. Soviet leaders appreciated such rare measures of public support from the West, and went so far as to provide funds to emigre Eurasian publications abroad. Under the strict controls of the secret police, they even promoted a network of "Eurasian" clubs at home that in 1926 gathered for their own special congress in Moscow.[29]

In this spirit of Eurasianism, the special charge of Soviet linguists was to spread out into the "east" (the Caucasus, Central Asia, Volga-Urals and Siberia) and standardize the non-Russian languages for better social communication. Most of these languages were still in their formative stages, requiring several levels and phases of linguistic study and corpus planning to determine base dialects; to codify sound and sign systems, grammars and lexicons; and to implement these new standards in real life along with any needed revisions.

The Soviet government legitimized the role of structural principles in this project through N.F. Iakovlev's manifesto in the journal, *Life of the nationalities*, and later in his famous "mathematical formula" for the creation of alphabets. He proudly recognized that his methods were based on the linguistic theories of two innovators, Saussure and Baudouin. Their "synchronic" approach to the study of language, especially phonology, enabled him to delineate the necessary graphemes and spelling rules of the non-Russian languages of the North Caucasus. They also empowered him with the methods to translate morphology and grammar into school texts, as against the misdirected and unsystematic methods of "traditional scholasticism". The "historical-geneological point of view" was dead, he proclaimed; now superseded by the unity of theory and practice in synchronic linguistics.[30]

Iakovlev institutionalized the Soviet project for language reform in the Moscow Linguistic Circle, where he was chair beginning in 1923; and the Scientific Research Institute for the Study of the Ethnic and National Cultures of the Peoples of the East, which he was instrumental in creating between 1923 and 1926. In each, he taught and promoted structural and sociological linguistics, folklore studies, and applied linguistics for the non-Russian nationalities of the

USSR. With his closest colleagues - D.V. Bubrikh, E.D. Polivanov, L.I. Zhirkov, R.O. Shor, N. Tiuriakulov, and B. Chobanzade - he diagrammed and codified alphabets, grammars and vocabularies for the whole range of Northern Caucasus, Turkic and Finno-Ugric peoples.[31]

When E.D. Polivanov returned to Russia in 1926 from his research expeditions in Central Asia, he expanded this work through the RANION Institute of Linguistics. Here he planned a series of books, *The languages of the national minorities of the USSR*, to study the social and territorial dialects of these peoples; and published his classic, *Introduction to linguistics for the eastern universities*, which established the contours of structural linguistics for their languages. The Narkompros RSFSR, in its turn, created even more institutions for the same purpose, under the logic that linguistics was the scientific base upon which the whole policy of nativization depended. Narkompros retooled dozens of academic institutes and created new ones (the Central Institute of Living Eastern Languages, the Institute of Orientology, the All-Union Association of Orientology, the Communist University of the Workers of the East) in order to prepare linguistic studies, alphabets, dictionaries, school texts, and native language cadres for work in the east.[32]

These linguists and their Narkompros patrons became quite bold and colorful in their rationales for further government funding and support. When nativization initiatives faltered, I. Davydov, a director of the Council of National Minorities and an architect of the ABCD hierarchy, lobbied time and again for a "competent", "powerful", and "authoritative" office within Narkompros to deal with the primary scientific questions of language reform. The linguist D.V. Bubrikh joined this call with a most creative and potentially heretical twist on the current party formula, noting that work in the realm of "proletarian content" was far less important than work in the realm of "national form", for only such a new office dedicated to the nationalities could strengthen the base for the introduction of proletarian ideology in the future.

Few, however, could match Iakovlev's gift for maneuver and hyperbole. At a major conference on language reform in 1929, he painted the literacy and nativization drives in the Soviet east as a welcome "yellow peril", a new Mongol invasion of Genghis Khans and Tamerlanes, this time of Asians armed with Soviet native language books, the new weapons with which to conquer the technology and culture of Europe. With perfect timing, his words were greeted by loud applause and an orchestral flourish.[33]

These achievements in the study, diagramming and propagandizing of the native languages (Shpet's "circles") were only one side of the Eurasian coin. Linguists mixed respect and toleration for cultural diversity, inherited directly through Baudouin and Shpet, with a missionary zeal to bring the benefits of European scientific and cultural values to the eastern peoples. Polivanov did not hide his Eurocentric visions of modernizing the Turkic languages. At the

Orientology Institute in Tashkent, he campaigned to teach the fundamentals of "European science" to future public officials of the region, if always in their native languages. As a member of the Scientific Council of the State Academic Council of Turkestan, he applied the "full resources of European science" to promote "cultural development among the indigenous peoples", this against the backdrop of the "backwardness" and "poverty" in the region.[34] "European science" and "cultural development" were little more than polite code words for a new Soviet speech community with the Russian language at its center. Either by assumption or design, Soviet linguists framed nativization as a means not so much for the creation of truly viable national print cultures as for preparatory work in the dissemination of Russian.

Policy makers and linguists embodied this mixed imperative for nativization and russification in the so-called "comparative method" of language teaching. Egalitarian and objective in theory, the method became quite insidious and obtrusive in fact. The native languages of the east were now open to the "rational" and "scientific" investigation of their distinct forms and structures. But these studies were only valuable if the school system could apply them, dialectically of course, to better teach and disseminate Russian. The comparative method was the linguistic heart and soul of the ABCD hierarchy. Narkompros educators never propagandized one without the other, lobbying for both from the highest reaches of the government (the Central Executive Committee of the USSR), to the lowest reaches of the school classroom. Every national school of the RSFSR was obliged to base its teaching methodologies and textbooks on the specific internal "peculiarities" of the national languages in comparison with Russian. This method was applied to all national schools in the outer Soviet republics, but by advisement only. G.G. Mansurov perhaps put it best when he called on teachers and students in every corner of the Soviet Union to avoid the "contrapositioning of one language against the other", reaffirming that the native languages remained the primary mediums by which to spread the use of Russian. The better they would be taught, the better Russian would be taught.[35]

All of this proved that Shpet was right when he said that any person could move, albeit with great effort, from one national circle to another; and that circles based on the idea of the nation might indeed become circles based on the idea of class or some other animating principle. But Shpet never elaborated as to the dynamics of moving between the circles or as to their relative value. What he had said with some balance and caution, these linguists and administrators were now implementing in reality with haste and impatience. Whereas Shpet had been quietly at work in his office at GAKhN, they were now busy at work on the noisy and messy frontiers of national politics and culture. After all, a new state of nations was being built. Its organizational principle demanded that the circles interconnect according to the ABCD hierarchy, that they be mutually penetrable, and that the Russian language hold them together.

The comparative method was impossible without the spadework of linguists, based upon formal and structural studies, in detailing the sound, word, and grammar forms of the native languages - together with their Russian "analogies". Bubrikh, Iakovlev, and Zhirkov wrote new "comparative" terminologies and grammars for the eastern languages, which they published in ever increasing scope and numbers between the 1920s and 1950s. Their works quickly became classics in the genre of "language union" studies. They heralded their contributions to the making of new Soviet nations; in quieter tones they admitted that they were merely readying the native languages for easier adaptation to Russian, "the leading and richest language" of the USSR".[36]

Polivanov wrote groundbreaking Russian language primers for Turkic children, adult Uzbek speakers, and non-Russian party members, all based on what he called "differential grammar", "descriptive linguistics", and the principle of "self-control over language". G.K. Danilov, his best doctoral student, wrote one of the first books designed expressly to train non-Russian adult natives in Russian, filled with sophomoric essays on the Spartacists of ancient Rome, on peasant jacqueries and the Paris Commune, and on the structural elements of language. With the express sponsorship of the RKPb, Polivanov and Danilov disseminated the comparative method all the way from the highest party schools to the lowest courses for political education. The problem, as they saw it, was in teaching the new national cadres in the party to think like proper communists in their native languages as much as in Russian. This was crucial in order to reach the masses with Moscow's propaganda. But it was something most party workers were not always able to do, given the difficulty of expressing Russian concepts in their "backward" languages, which lacked comparable words and syntax.[37]

These initiatives highlighted once again just how limited nativization policy was in the Soviet project of nation making. Polivanov extolled, if always with respect for native non-Russian languages, the "all-union" and "international" role of Russian, the "language of Soviet culture". Danilov shared his mentor's perspective that "the great Russian literary language" was the "most vital", progressive and international of all languages of the union. He even wrote a graduate thesis for Polivanov on the "Class physiognomy of language", a controversial piece which argued, in precise Marxist terms, that "every social class, every social group", creates its own separate language based on its distinct economic position. One of his disputed conclusions maintained that Ukrainian was a peasant language; Russian a proletarian one. According to Danilov's reading of the party formula of "convergence-mergence", Ukrainian was therefore slated to eventual extinction.[38] Such a blatant violation of the official policy of nativization was not tolerated. No less a dignitary than S.K. Kaganovich, the party boss of Ukraine, chastised Danilov for his improper views, although he then continued in his work unhindered. (Kaganovich 1931: 88-95).

3.3. Experiments in speech rationalization: from *zaum* to Esperanto

These prejudices for the Russian language may seem contradictory given the service of Soviet linguists to the native peoples. But we need to remember that most of them respected the "progressive" historical development of Russian culture, as well as the political and geographic realities of Russian Soviet hegemony. They received the world around them in hierarchical terms. History was moving all peoples toward a united world culture. The Soviet government contributed to this progressive timeline by collecting and assimilating them into one united political space. Linguists were naturally inspired to define and classify the languages of the east in preparation for this grand project. They were also naturally prone to recognize the historical and political rights of Russian as one of the mightiest of world languages. But they also realized that it was not the most integral of world languages. As rationalists, they looked beyond their very mundane work and entertained visions of fully economized human speech patterns, namely through 'nonsense poetry' (*zaum*) and Esperanto, fusion languages which they fantasized might even surpass Russian in the long but quickening march toward a global culture.

Inspired by Marx's writings on the inevitable revolution in industrial society, Russian Bolsheviks were faced with the question of how to hasten this transformation given their own backward and impoverished country. So they turned to what they called the 'scientific organization of labor' (NOT) as a catalyst for quick change. The Soviet NOT movement was based in part on F.W. Taylor's time-motion studies and theories of scientific management, originally intended for use in the capitalist workplace to maximize profits, now applied to the socialist workplace and bureaucracy to rationalize work movements, standards and procedures in the interests of improved production. Taylor had argued that a new standardized language for internal communication was at the center of his scientific management techniques. Without special codes and an official language, neither technical functions nor administrative work could proceed effectively. Communication (the formal instructions between the manager and the worker) underlay Taylor's whole theoretical system. His quest was to overcome "word-of-mouth" and "rule-of-thumb" work patterns through their systematic rearrangement: by "classifying, tabulating, and reducing this knowledge to rules, laws, and formulae" in the interests of productive labor.

The Bolsheviks appreciated Taylor's attempts to rationalize speech patterns. They took the learning of literacy and the "ABCs" as one of the most fundamental models for rational human conduct. The better organized the model, the better organized the mind. The "ABCs" meant more than just the ability to read, but referred to the written word as a means of control over nature, science, and technology - indeed one's very self. P.M. Kerzhentsev, director of the Taylorist "Time League", even spoke of "organizational illiteracy" and the need to eradicate it. For him, "precision in execution, accuracy, economy of time - these are our ABCs". Other writers discussed aviation, technical, military or any of a dozen other kinds of "ABC literacy".[39]

As Taylorism spread throughout Soviet cultural discourse in the 1920s, so too did the imperative to master language in the interest of more efficient production and administration. Alexei Gastev, one of the leaders of the Soviet NOT movement and a proletarian poet, shared Lenin's appreciation for Taylorism, and its potential applications to language reform. "Although there is not yet an international language", he wrote in 1924, "there are international gestures, there are international psychological formulas", both applicable in the workplace. An early systems thinker and Lenin's comrade in the young Bolshevik party, Aleksandr Bogdanov developed these principles in his 'general science of organization' (tectology). In the tradition of Humboldt and Potebnia, he defined "thought as internal speech", as "speech minus sound".[40]

But Bogdanov also identified language as the "first instrument of organization" and the storehouse for natural knowledge. An auxiliary international language was a prerequisite for any attempt at a universal science of organization. "It is necessary", he wrote, "to aspire towards the elimination of that uncoordinated 'science', which has resulted from the introduction of specialization; to aspire towards the unity of scientific language ...towards the elaboration of an absolute monism." Bogdanov held that language was a function of production, originally taking shape in primitive humans from the sound "reflexes" of their labor acts. But language was also an organizer of production, a tool in the form of the independent "word-ideas" by which we in the modern world are consciously transforming our economies and societies. "The concept of organizing action is hidden in the term *production*", he wrote, for at the basis of production was "the word" as "command".[41]

Publications and commentaries of the early Soviet period shared such insights. Through their posts as university teachers of the Russian language, the young G.K. Danilov and his compatriots taught future communist elites that speech was a "complex symbolic reflex", uniting language and thought in creative acts of communication and expression. Language and thought were two dimensions of the same process of reflexive understanding. Thought was "internal speech" (*vnutrenniaia rech'*) or a "hidden language" (*skrytyi iazyk*) and language nothing more than "revealed thought" (*obnaruzhenaia mysl'*), our calling card in the real world of life and labor. (Nikiforov & Danilov 1928: 6-15)

In their popular science booklets and journals of these years, people learned that the recent advances of factory production, the telegraph, radio, and telephone demanded a more rationalized language to serve them properly. As the pedagogue M.A. Rybnikov recognized, such a language was essential in the workplace. Norms were needed to prevent wastefulness and misunderstanding, to ensure that business began with the proper "conditions" (*usloviia*, from the root 'word'), with the necessary "agreements" (*dogovor*, from the root 'speech'), and with the "elaboration of word formulated rules". Only the "precision" of the word could "save the labor collective from verbosity and loss of time". Linguists appreciated the power of these arguments; economic modernization and language reform needed to be governed by the same "principle of least effort". They referred to language as a machine, an "industrialization" process, and to linguists as engineers of a kind. They looked at the ways in which engineers applied the principles of the 'scientific organization of labor' (NOT) to the means of production as a model for their own project to apply the structural method to language reform.[42]

Linguists even experimented with *zaum* or "nonsense" language as a new, more rational medium for public communication. Poets and literary futurists, inspired by structural insights into sound patterns, created *zaum* in the years just before World War I. They believed that poetry was most powerful when its rich "texture" captivated the reader's attention, "defamiliarized" their normal, everyday meanings, and reached their senses with new feelings and images. The futurist writer Velemir Khlebnikov wrote *zaum* poetry based on nonsense sound formations rather than conventional semantic units. He understood language as a primal force to be rediscovered beneath all the layers of style and speech habits accrued since the first act of speech. Once rediscovered, it might become a new currency for international communication.

Yet other language professionals, inspired by constructivist designs for worker housing and clothing, understood *zaum* as the prototype for a new practical street language. It could reunite different social groups and professions, otherwise fractured by their own unique social dialects, with new forms of communication and expression. "*Zaum* is the language of loud, compact and clear signals, the language of maximal dynamism", they wrote. It was the new "language of public activity". Polivanov even considered it a first step toward the rationalization of speech in practical life, since with *zaum* "the whole creative energy of the author and all the attention of the perceiver (reader or listener) are directed at the formal (phonic) side of speech". Although lacking conventional meanings, it was "saturated" with sound repetitions containing a maximum of rationality in form, analogous to the "principle of symmetry in the graphic arts (architecture, sculpture, and painting)".[43]

Interest in a future international language also captivated several Marxist political theorists. The socialist visions of Karl Kautsky and August Bebel defined a future society united by a productivist economics, a proletarian ethos, and a common world language. During his lonely days of imprisonment in Azerbaijan and exile in Siberia between 1907 and 1914, even Iosef Stalin began to learn the most famous of international languages, Esperanto. For him, a new language community was to follow and fortify the new labor community. He predicted that the world language of the future would not be a victor language (like English or Russian), but a fusion of all or some of the world languages, including Esperanto.[44]

These Marxian thinkers shared a vision of social and linguistic harmony with Bogdanov, whose famous science fiction novel, *Red star*, projected a socialist society onto Mars, governed by a planetary language. At his most idealistic, Bogdanov saw a marked tendency in history toward an international language, even grudgingly accepting the successes of Esperanto. Yet to him it would be based on real economic and social unification and the resulting development of unitary collective life. Bogdanov the realist understood artificial languages as "utopian" in comparison with natural international languages, his favorite of which was English. (Bogdanov 1925a: 328-332; Bogdanov 1924: 83-86, 99-101)

Several leading structural linguists recognized the power of Esperanto as a means of rationalizing speech and unifying and modernizing the Soviet peoples. Although they were not fanatics for the language, Polivanov and Jakobson respected its elegance. They sometimes referred to each other as *samideonoj* ('comrades') and opened their institutes to Esperantists for discussion and research.[45] Their colleague, N.V. Iushmanov, was an avid Esperantist, enthralled with the nascent science of 'artificial international languages' (*kosmoglottika*). Unsatisfied with the lack of rational planning in Esperanto, he became a militant advocate of Ido, a new and even more vigorous prototype. The militant slogan of the Idoists was, by no coincidence, "always perfectible". This mania propelled Iushmanov to construct his own planned language, *etem* (an acronym for *ekonomi, tempor, energi, medi*), an attempt to combine neutral word roots with a maximal logic and simplicity. Iushmanov, who worked as a Kremlin radio translator and interpreter during the revolution and civil war (1917-1921), claimed to have engaged in lively debates over these issues with Lenin and Trotskii, no less.[46]

Shortly after the Bolshevik Revolution, members of the Academy of Sciences and Narkompros began to patronize Esperanto. A special government commission, in cooperation with leading Esperantists, even called for its elective teaching in the public schools. Visionary communists proposed that the TsK RKPb and all major party and Soviet organs use Esperanto in their work. Eager party regional committees offered their help in the popularization of Esperanto; enthusiasts in the Central Asian republics proposed to teach obligatory Esperanto classes in the secondary schools. A group of Soviet Zionists even established the *Nova Vivo* collective farm in the Crimea where Esperanto, not Hebrew, was the language of choice. Their unique experiment thrived into the 1930s.[47]

With state patronage, Esperantists founded the Soviet Esperanto Union (SEU) in 1921 at their Third All-Russian Congress in Petrograd. Their charge was to forge contacts with Esperantists and internationalists at home and abroad through pen pal and radio clubs. They soon aligned with the World Non-Nationalist Association (SAT, or Sennacieco Asocio Tutmonda), founded in 1919 by the French anarcho-syndicalist, Eugene Lanti, devoted to the promotion of non-nationalism (*sennaciismo*) through cultivation of the Esperanto language. At the height of its popularity in the middle 1920s, SAT claimed tens of thousands of supporters in hundreds of laborist Esperanto circles across Europe and the USSR. The Soviet government sought to exploit them as conspiratorial cells for world revolution. (Lanti 1925: 10-11; Forster 1982)

Among the Soviet Esperantists, none were more visionary than the writers and poets, most of whom were closely allied with SAT. Esperanto expressed their deeply felt sentiments for a new world order of liberty and justice. It was ready made, lyrical and free from bourgeois fetters, a perfect way to reinforce new ways of thinking in people's minds. With the Russian futurists, the Esperanto writers shared the insight that poetry was a medium in which "texture" was all important. Richness, not rationality, was at the core of meaning. The poetry of Evgenii Mikhal'ski (1897-1937) was renowned for its repetition of vowels and consonants, playful arrangements of sentence structures and compound nouns, and creation of words to "sound like they mean", not unlike Khlebnikov's *zaum*.[48]

Soviet Esperantists celebrated what they held to be an achievable future, a universal speech community. In his 1922 Esperanto essay, *The path of future science*, academician A.E. Fersman noted that his own reflections were not utopian imaginings in the manner of Jules Verne or H.G. Wells, but measures of what was possible on earth given the scientific and technological advances, human ingenuity, and perseverance to make them work. The main character of V. Varankin's successful Esperanto novel, *Metropoliteno*, even imagined himself "an invisible observer in a novel by Wells", such were the strange and magnificent sights of the novel's setting, twentieth-century Berlin. Varankin idolized Germans for their technical genius, and German communists for their collective spirit. The Soviet Esperantists even published a celebratory Esperanto translation of Bogdanov's Martian chronicle, *Red star*, in 1929. Yet in their preface to the work, they did not hesitate to fault the anglophile Bogdanov for underestimating the value of their work and the rationality of Esperanto. To them, the novel was less an exercise in utopian freethinking than a statement of impending reality, which the Esperantists took all too seriously.[49]

The first and last president of the SEU, Ernst Drezen, translated this constructivist utopianism into the everyday life of the movement. An Esperantist from his youth, and president of the Petersburg Esperanto Society before the war, he played a significant role in the Russian revolution and in the establishment of Soviet power: first as a member of the War Revolutionary Committee and Central Executive Committee of the Petrograd Soviet; then as deputy commander of the Tauride Palace and Smolny Institute (Bolshevik headquarters) during the October Revolution; later as secretary to President M.I. Kalinin and an administrator on the Central Executive Committee (TsIk) of the USSR. Quite a resume!

During the 1920s and 1930s, as deputy director of the All-Union Society for Cultural Relations Abroad, Drezen actively promoted the use of Esperanto in international communication. The problems facing postal, telegraph and telephone ties within the multilingual Soviet Union were but a microcosm of the dilemmas facing international relations, especially between Europe and Asia. With supporters in the media and industry, Drezen advocated Esperanto for the translation of documents, for instruction in technical schools, and for use by international operators, correspondents, and union officials. It was, after all, "neutral for all peoples"; its "structure" (*stroi*) combined the word roots of European with the "agglutinative" grammar of the Asian languages. Its sixteen rules, without exceptions, and twelve verbal endings made it faster to learn than even the easiest "natural" language.[50]

Drezen and his collaborators were a radical fringe of the Taylorist and Bogdanovite movements. Russia's leading publicist on the scientific organization of labor, he wrote treatises on the science of office management and record keeping, and even on the rearrangement and "rationalization" of the whole state apparatus.[51] Drezen appreciated the relevance of Bogdanov's theories, time and again referring to language as an "organizational device" to help master and direct production collectives. He also made the striking parallel between Taylor's theories of scientific management, as aids for rational production in the workplace, and Esperanto, as an auxiliary international language for more rational human communication. Its simplicity and utility had proven that language, an instrument of production, was "liable to a certain rationalization, NOTisization". In the words of one of his comrades, "the scientific organization of labor is impossible on a world scale without a universal language" - in essence, without Esperanto.[52]

During the first decade of Soviet power, such utopian imaginings were often tolerated, sometimes entertained, but only rarely put into action. There came a point in the late 1920s when the machine metaphors and Taylorist rationality of linguists, *zaum*ists, and Esperantists became outdated and unpopular. V.A. Kaverin's novel, *Skandalist*, poked fun at these visionaries. A friend of Polivanov's in the early 1920s, Kaverin mocked the futurism and rationalism of his onetime colleague through the main character, a Leningrad linguist and fan of the "scientific organization of speech". A parody of Polivanov's own insights into the economy of speech production, this character revealed the bankruptcy of futurism and formalism, presaging Polivanov's own coming humiliation (Kaverin 1980).

As the utopian rationalism of linguists became passe, their very own structural insights and reform initiatives for the Russian and non-Russian languages became outdated as well. The communist party now labeled structural linguists as "bourgeois formalists". In part this was a reference to their participation in the public forums of the literary formalist movements. But it was also a veiled attack on the party's ideological concept of "national in form", because the linguists named in the party indictments had participated in the language reform campaigns of the 1920s. The structural linguists, in effect, had begun to out serve their initial usefulness. They had helped to lock the national languages in place, and to promote the Russian language through the ABCD hierarchy and comparative method. They even fancied language a great tool of production. But their principles tended to be too static, too intellectual, too whimsical. And in the case of their "Eurasian" leanings, too closely aligned with "reactionary" emigre groups in Prague.

In its realignment of policy toward the non-Russians, the Soviet state took recourse to an alternative method, N.Ia. Marr's Japhetidology, which cared even less for Soviet Eurasia and its national forms, and much more for the Soviet Union and its proletarian content, an engine of change at work in world history, in the Russian language. For if, according to Shpet's phenomenology, we as speaking human beings occupy a space in language as much as in the world around us, the Soviet state now deemed that very space worthy of its conquest.

Chapter 4

N.Ia. Marr, language history, and the Stalin cultural revolution

"We believe that in the beginning was the deed. The word followed, as its phonetic shadow." (Trotskii 1971: 183) Strange words from Lev Trotskii, one of the great wordsmiths of the revolution. But then neither he nor other leading Bolsheviks ever pretended to write simply for the sake of writing. Practice was their rule; words always served political tasks. The philologist and ethnographer N.Ia. Marr shared the insight. As the leading rivals of the formalist and structural linguists, Marr and his students in the "Japhetite" school practiced what they called "historical paleontology". Before the revolution, they busied themselves with the word etymologies of the Caucasus languages, collecting and analyzing literary relics, myths, numerical and geographical terms, and proper names in order to discern their shared relations and patterns. Afterward, they shaped these findings into a pyramid of language development, inspired by Marx's laws of the productive base, matched by the tenets of Lenin's dialectical materialism. Marr's Japhetidology became the "new theory of language". If the structural school served the regime by creating a spatial linguistic grid for the Soviet nationalities, Japhetidology positioned them within a progressive historical timeline, moving from disorder and division to global order and unity.

Through the relatively liberal 1920s, structural linguists and Marr's Japhetites worked with each other in a delicate balance of power. Both claimed to be the patrons of Marxist methods; both presumed to know what was best for the non-Russian nationalities. They erupted into noisy polemic with the cultural revolution between 1928 and 1932, when E.D. Polivanov and the young "Language Front" linguists tried to displace Marr's ideological paradigm of historical paleontology with their own action paradigm for language reform. Their conflict represents a lost chapter in the saga of Stalin's cultural revolution. Once the battleground had cleared, the party rewarded the Marr school for its ideological conformity. But the stakes were even higher. For the Japhetites provided several convenient formulas for the party's initiatives in nation-making and state-building. In theory, they espoused ethnic relativism and linguistic equality; in effect, they legitimized Russian as the most developed language of the USSR.[1] True, the structural linguists had already staked such a claim, but they were now about to relinquish it to Marr. The Soviet government repudiated the "Eurasian imperative" for Marr's principles of "crossbreeding" and stadialism, exchanging the metaphor of static linguistic space for a metaphor of dynamic language time.

4.1. From Japhetidology to the new theory of language

To introduce Marr properly, we need digress to the turn of the century. His theories, like those of the structural school, bridged the late imperial and early Soviet eras. As a young Georgian scholar, filled with a romantic nationalism which only the study of linguistics could fill, Marr shared some of Baudouin de Courtenay's resentments against great-Russian chauvinism and Indo-European traditionalism. He acted on them by studying the "backward" languages of the Russian empire, rather than the more "civilized" languages of Europe. Marr's first claim to fame was an article in the leading Georgian journal, *Iveria* (1888) that argued that his native tongue shared word and grammar similarities with the noble language of the Old Testament, ancient Hebrew. Marr's quest was nothing new. For centuries, hosts of etymologists had been attempting to discover, largely through conjecture and dubious theories, the patrimony between the original language of the *Bible* and their own native tongues.[2] We can only wonder if the young Stalin, who sent his own poetic verses to the same journal a few years later, admired Marr's handiwork. I have never found any evidence that the two met in their lifetimes. But their shared interests in a literary nationalism, tinged with social democratic leanings, may have partly accounted for Marr's eventual successes under Stalin's regime.

For the next three decades, nearly obsessed with this biblical quest, Marr focused his work on the ancient manuscripts and archeological sources of Armenian and its neighboring languages, mounting sixteen expeditions to the Caucasus, all with the aim of proving his original hypothesis. Largely in recognition of these accomplishments, state academic boards appointed him chair of Armenian at the University of St. Petersburg in 1901 and elected him to the Imperial Academy of Sciences in 1912. The very name Marr chose for his formulas, "the Japhetic Theory", betrayed his preference for language history rather than linguistic structure. The term came from the biblical account of the dispersion of the descendant's of Noah's sons: Ham, Shem and Japhet. The favored nation of the Japhetites allegedly lived on the shores of the Black and Caspian seas, not far from where Noah's ark is said to have landed in the southern part of historic Armenia, on Mount Ararat. Marr chose the term as a metaphor for the Caucasus as a genesis point for a new primal language, as yet unexplored by linguists, so focused had they been on the languages of Europe. He even created a transcription system, later called the Abkhazian Analytical Alphabet (AAA), by which to represent the newly christened Japhetic languages - Georgian, Mingrelian, Chan, Svan, Armenian, Abkhaz and Avar - in their pre-Indo-European prototypes.[3]

For all their novelty in divulging the relationships between these little known languages of the Caucasus, Marr's theories were still very much captive within the tradition of historical-comparative philology. His work was all about diagramming the origins and patterns of language through prehistorical and historical time; mapping interethnic word comparisons, what he called language "crossbreeding" (*skreshchenie*), into long and cumbersome "semantic" lists; and surmising a general principle of linguistic and ethnic development. These inquiries matched best with what Baudouin defined as "philology", neither truly linguistics nor a "homogeneous science", but a "conglomerate of parts of different sciences (linguistics, mythology, history of literature, cultural history, etc.)". Marr did not study language in the abstract, but the languages of a set of peoples, together with their varied textual and material artifacts. If the structural linguists studied the contrastive rules and functions of sounds at the basis of meaning, Marr studied word etymologies and language stages as hypothetical, ostensible meanings. He pieced together fragments of literary culture and lost letter-signs from history old and new, but without regard for established sound laws, leading to all those "queer etymologies" and attempts to trace the development of human speech to its origins in "one or several consonantal groups".[4]

At first, Marr was not publicly ill disposed to Indo-Europeanism. He never denied the authority of its methods, and even sought to write a comparative grammar of the Japhetic languages. Yet he became ever more intransigent, shaping his career in opposition to those critics who snubbed his eccentric theories. His vendetta against them weaves through the following story. Marr did not so much construct a concise theoretical system as a "series of *ad hoc* formulations" which continually responded to his critics and to the political demands of the moment. After his first contacts with Western linguists in 1894, he degraded "their ignorance of Armenian and other Caucasian languages", and their "purely formal techniques". They rejected his Japhetic theory. Even Marr's elder colleagues in Russia despaired of his tendentious methods, referring to his "stupefying fantasies", appropriate perhaps for philology, but totally irrelevant for linguistics.[5]

In answer to these embarrassing criticisms, Marr fashioned a peculiar kind of "anti-orientalism", a means of studying, conquering and "restructuring" the east, but with the aim of chastizing Europe and Russia for their exclusivism and chauvinism. The Bolshevik Revolution empowered him to begin this ambitious project. Marr was the only member of the Academy of Sciences to openly profess his allegiance to Marxian principles, serving the new regime as one of its first "materialist" scholars, along with the venerables M.N. Pokrovskii, V.M. Friche and V.F. Pereverzev. Leading Bolsheviks recognized him in their ranks. Marr collaborated with them in establishing the first All-Russian Conference of Scientific Workers. Originally designed as a base for cooperation between the scientists and professionals of the old regime and the new, it eventually became more "bellicose and doctrinaire" in its attacks on the "bourgeois specialists" of Soviet academia. He became more bellicose with it.[6] In the early 1920s, Marr engineered an administrative gathering of power to defend his school from mainstream Indo-European linguistics, remaking the landscape of oriental studies in his own image. He helped to create the Japhetic Institute of the Academy of Sciences, where he was director; the Institute for the Comparative Study of the Literatures and Languages of the West and East (ILIaZV), where he was chair of its section on General Linguistics; and the State Academy of the History of Material Culture (GAIMK), where he was chair and director of its Groups on the Archeology of the Caucasus, the Japhetic World, and Primitive Culture. Proud to call himself a "linguist and historian of material culture", at one time or another he was also director of the Caucasus Section of the Committee for the Study of the Population of the USSR; director of the Caucasus Historical Archeological Institute; chair of the Committee for the Study of the Languages and Ethnic Cultures of the Peoples of the East of the USSR; director of the Public Library in Leningrad; and chair of the Central Bureau of Regional Studies.[7]

Propped up by all of this state patronage, Marr translated his prerevolutionary formulas into a rough, Marxian dialectical materialism, what he soon called his "new theory of language". He refashioned his research to appeal to the historicism, utilitarianism and transformism of Soviet leaders, assuaging their hopes that the objective world could be known, and therefore better controlled, by its natural causes and laws. Ever conscious of the ideological pressures in place after the revolution, he ensured that Japhetidology served two central "epistemological postulates" of Leninism.[8]

Marr's formulas of language origins and "crossbreeding" fulfilled the first Leninist epistemological postulate: on science as the study of the historical "causes in nature and society". In a series of academic reports between 1920 and 1926, he crafted a new theory of genetic language relations, pairing the surface "morphology of language" with the deep "morphology of social structure". He set out to discover linguistic "crossbreeding" between the Japhetic and Indo-European languages in order to prove his hypothesis that they were moving along a path from multiplicity to unity, like socioeconomic structures in general.[9] He now placed the sign language of shamans and priests, not sound, at the source of human language. As work gestures of a kind, these signs proved that creative labor propelled human history. The social person was not so much a speaker as a worker, whose consciousness and communication developed based on labor (hand) skills, and who was therefore always beholden to the weight of productive forces through history.

Marr claimed that four basic speech elements, *sal-ber-yon-rosh*, the "magical sound complexes" or "totems" originally used in primitive rituals, were the root sources of all words. His paleontological method identified these elements in the history of human speech by discovering etymologies or "semantic clusters" in different languages at different times. One of his more accessible hypotheses held that the Slavic word 'speech' (*rech*') had its root in the word 'hand' (*ruka*). The neat conclusion was that in advanced capitalist or socialist societies the word had become a tool of production and speech in the same way that the hand had been such a primary tool in earlier stages of economic development. This was an obvious appeal to the authority of Friedrich Engels and his meditations on "the role played by labor in the transformation from ape to man".[10] It was also quite a bold apology for the communist party's nascent political and economic idiom. Just as the ape had once used simple tools in the conquest of nature, so now the communist party would exploit language to modernize the Soviet Union.

By further appealing to Engels' theories on the objective, material "laws of nature", Marr verified the second Leninist epistemological postulate: that knowledge and science were "reflections of a reality existing independently of the human mind". Lenin had used this postulate in his polemical tract, *Materialism and empirio-criticism*, to undermine V. Plekhanov's semiotic insight that human sensations do not mirror events or things in the world, but communicate them by way of hieroglyphs or symbols. Plekhanov had argued that sensations and perceptions, like concepts and ideas, are not reflections of the real world but human hieroglyphs and "conventional signs", interpretive fragments of culture rather than of nature. Using Engels' theories as support, Lenin accused Plekhanov of detaching consciousness from nature. Instead, he posited that "the materialist regards sensation, perception, idea, and the mind of man generally, as an image of objective reality". With Engels, Lenin preferred to speak "neither of symbols nor of hieroglyphs, but of copies, photographs, images, mirror-reflections of things".

Marr simply adapted this reflection theory to his own purposes. If language were but a reflection of worldly things in the present, his etymologies would uncover the selfsame linguistic reflections of reality from the historical past. The Japhetites read Lenin's statements on this issue as unequivocal support for Marr's own thesis on the unity of language and thought, on language as semantic substance reflecting the real world.[11] Marr may have claimed a very modern Marxian provenance. But his Japhetic theory was little more than an eccentric twentieth-century manifestation of what Hans Aarsleff has called the "Adamic doctrine", that well-worn "doctrine of divine origin - with its postulates that words somehow refer directly to things, like a nomenclature that constitutes an inventory". Marr merely resurrected, albeit in new wrappings, that age-old search for the natural origins and essences of language, those fragments of sound and meaning which perfectly reflected the physical world. (Aarsleff 1982: 35-36, 87, 346)

But reflection was not quite enough. Embedded in the material laws of the physical world, such a theory was far too passive for such revolutionary times. Thus, perhaps the most ambitious of all Japhetite projects was to integrate these principles with Ivan Pavlov's reflexology, especially his concept of language as a "second signal system". Famous for his ubiquitous dog, Pavlov had studied conditional reflexes and signal systems in animals. In the neural processes of the subcortical and cortical areas of the central nervous system, he theorized, connections are made between external stimuli and internal responses that determine and influence behavior. Late in his career, Pavlov decided that human language was not reducible to such a primary "signal system", but was part of a "second signal system" which operated in the area of the frontal lobes, where connections were made not between stimuli and responses but between experiences and speech. He presumed that human behavior was not reducible to biological or physiological processes, but involved more complex relations between social influences and human thought, whereby material and psychic signals were themselves "signalized" by way of words.

Joining Pavlov's physiology with Marr's sociology, the Japhetites now analyzed language as a higher order of gestures and sounds, one step above the primary signal system in animals, yet still a "conditional reflex" in response to social conditions and stimuli. Marr's Speech Physiology Laboratory, headed by the medical doctor and speech pathologist, S.M. Dobrogaev, and staffed by "linguist-biomechanists", studied the physical and psychic qualities of human sound with these purposes in mind. They were some of the most loyal and vocal propagandists of both Pavlov's and Marr's theories.[12]

Besides Marr, the speech laboratory had even bigger patrons. After Lenin's debilitating stroke and aphasia in the spring and summer of 1923, Dobrogaev instructed Nadezhda Krupskaia in the latest methods of speech therapy, which she applied to her husband's sickness, unfortunately with little result. With the help of cue cards, Lenin learned and memorized the basic vocabulary of Bolshevik speech: such words as 'peasant', 'revolution', and 'congress'. But he was never able to put them into any consistent, meaningful order. The best he could say was, 'that's right' (*vot-vot*), as a universal response to any given stimulus. The signal words of the revolution had turned into incomprehensible jumbles in the voice of the great leader. All the more reason, then, for top party leaders to promote the speech laboratory in the 1920s. Its work was avowedly materialist. It promised to identify the means by which human speech and thought might be better controlled with the right stimuli and signals. It stressed the plasticity and transformability of people through behavior and language conditioning. It promised an idiom of state communication by which political signals might be reliably sent and obediently received.[13]

The reflection thesis and reflexology, which locked human beings within the objective laws of epistemology and physiology, provided Marr with the ideological backing to uncover the equally objective laws of language in history.[14] He argued that the meanings of utterances (semantics) were the most direct reflections of the economic base, and therefore the most important objects of linguistic study. The Indo-Europeanists were automatically guilty of reductive formalism, divorcing sounds (phonetics) and forms (morphology) from meanings (semantics). The structural linguists, in turn, were guilty of corrupting the progressive and meaningful logic of history with the formal arbitrariness of the linguistic sign. In contrast, Marr now equated language with thought - not because of their mutual reciprocity and interaction, in the manner of Humboldt's or Potebnia's or Bogdanov's or Plekhanov's semiotics - but as "reflections of labor activity", in the manner of a simple Engelsian historical materialism. Language was a superstructure created by human consciousness, both of which were determined by the productive base.[15]

To name, Marr implied, was to know. Words, as reflections of things in the real world, were thereby convenient instruments of industrial power, levers of political control. They served not merely a nominative but also an imperative function. His theories moved far beyond mere etymology into the realm of behavioral psychology. The word, especially in the form of the precise ideological meanings of Marxism-Leninism, became part external stimulus, part internal reflex. Marr voiced these ideas with great success at a conference of Marxist historians in 1929. Using Greek, Latin, Etruscan, Slavic, Georgian and Ossetian words, he showed the eager audience how "language was tied to production, how the terms related to production are the commanding factors in language".[16]

From these building blocks, Marr constructed an elaborate "stadial" theory that incorporated his language data into evolutionary stages in the development of human speech. These stages fused the developmental chronologies of Karl Marx with the language typologies of August Schleicher. Political economics married historical-comparative philology. Marx had plotted human progress in history from backward tribalism, through early modern feudalism, to modern capitalism and socialism. Marr now paired these stages with Schleicher's model of backward (isolative), developing (agglutinative), and perfected (inflective) stages in the growth of human grammatical systems. Thanks to Marr's insight, the "differences and complexities of the economic organism" were now graced with these ascending stages of sound "signalization". In an instant, Marr created an etymology of economics that divided history into epochs revealing the connections between the material base (production and labor) and the superstructure (language and thought). He packaged these notions into a most attractive shape, the pyramid, whereby languages developed from many to one, guided by the gradual but progressive processes of "crossbreeding", but sometimes propelled by sudden "leaps" (*skachki*) in economics as well.[17]

Marr's notions of language "crossbreeding" and stadial development were not without their practical implications. They readily served as metaphors for the conjoining of languages already under way in the USSR. His pyramid recognized and elevated the various minority languages of the USSR, including those of the forgotten peoples of the Caucasus and Central Asia. His ideas fueled the Bolshevik "rebellion against 'great power' philological theories" and the "liberation" of the Soviet minority peoples from the legacies of Tsarist repression. (Bukharin 1927: 12-13) A patron of language nativization, Marr joined with N.F. Iakovlev, one of his most admiring of colleagues, in establishing the Institute for the Study of the Ethnic and National Cultures of the Peoples of the East. As I noted in chapter three, it devised language reforms for the eastern languages and trained native linguists and ethnographers. For at least a few years in the middle 1920s, Marr and Iakovlev joined forces to create a balanced curriculum that was Japhetite by ideology and structural by method, what Iakovlev called a united school of "evolutionary linguistics".[18]

Marr's own language reform designs centered on Abkhazia, which he treated like his own personal research fiefdom, largely because of the role of its language in the Japhetic theory. The beach and mountain resorts of the country were no doubt appealing as well, for Marr often vacationed there after 1923, ostensibly to collect materials for a bilingual Russian dictionary, establish cultural and scientific institutions, and train native linguists. These trips began just after his celebrated conversion to Marxian historical materialism, part of a calculated plan to enliven and legitimize the Japhetic theories as sources for Soviet nation-making. In speaking engagements during the trips, he lambasted Orientology and Indo-Europeanism for their neglect of the "periphery" and for their great-Russian chauvinist attitudes. He fancied himself, in contrast, as the one true champion of the emerging nationalities. "The native tongue is a powerful lever for cultural upsurge", he proclaimed, an "irreplaceable weapon of class warfare."[19]

Although they championed the native peoples, Marr's theories were also inspired by Stalin's russifying historical dialectic. Together Marr and Stalin promoted the thesis that the national languages of the Soviet Union, indeed of the whole world, were developing according to the slow, spiraling formula of convergence and mergence toward proletarian 'unity' (*edinstvo*). This thesis locked the native peoples within the upward stream of historical time. In principle, no matter what their stage of development, Marr considered the Soviet languages equal; in practice, one language (Russian) was more equal than others. In his theory - "crossbreeding," the reflection theory, and stadialism - all guaranteed the importance of Russian terms for the present stage of economic development. If the "nativizing" non-Russian languages of the east were to participate in the Stalin revolution and the march of progress, by necessity they had to adopt its Russian concepts and terms.

Japhetite school curriculums conveniently demanded that Russian, the "great language of the revolutionary epoch", always be taught according to its 'ties' (*sviazi*), 'convergences' (*skhozhdeniia*), and 'divergences' (*raskhozhdeniia*) with the other languages of the union. All were part of the "single world sociolingual [*glottogonic*] process".[20] In other words, in Marr's view there was no such thing as the abstraction of 'language' (Saussure's *langue*), nor even the plurality of languages (Shpet's circles). The struggle against Plekhanov's "arbitrary" semiotics had turned, in essence, into a struggle against the arbitrariness and randomness of nations. And the Russian language was the catalyst that ensured unity and purpose out of multiplicity and disorder.[21]

By narrating these processes at work in the distant pages of history, the Japhetites legitimized the dialectic at work in the Stalinist present. Led by the enterprising S.N. Bykovskii, they explored the remnants of ancient material culture in order to divulge the varying patterns of social and economic relationships between historical epochs. Marr's linguists analyzed terms associated with the economic base and social superstructure. In 1931, amid the "great transformation" in Soviet agriculture and industry, they proudly compiled a terminological dictionary for metallurgical production in the ancient Caucasus and Egypt. Marr proclaimed that this work was invaluable for the grand economic and social changes under way in the USSR. Language development was not only determined by class based revolutions from the past, but also by collectivization and industrialization in the present, driven by Russian proletarians in their native language.[22] That the Japhetites grounded these apologies for russification within a "class" analysis must have made them all the more palatable to party authorities.

With all of their attention on language origins and etymology, on the past rather than the present, Marr and the Japhetites helped to turn Soviet national languages into pure ethnographic material, not self-sustaining literary cultures. They were always ready to analyze them, but they were ill prepared to reform them. Japhetidology had the political virtue of sounding radical and revolutionary. Its militancy against alleged Indo-European linguistic racism and its promotion of the native non-Russian languages matched well with Soviet national policies. But it also had the political value of not being associated with any problematic language reforms. Such a superficial militancy proved useful to a regime intent on placating the non-Russian nationalities, but always within strict limits.

Marr's theories gave a powerful voluntaristic edge to Stalin's vast modernization campaigns of the 1930s. They promised state expansion and control over productive forces through the human word. By no coincidence, Marr renamed the inflective Indo-European language types, the most advanced in world history, as the "promethean" languages, which included Russian. In a curious way, in spite of the fanfare for the Japhetic languages, the "promethean" Indo-European tongues often took center stage in Marr's classification schemes. As the Greek god Prometheus had conquered fire, so the "promethean" peoples had conquered the great technology of the modern era, the industrial machine.

Fit with the propaganda and the reality of Soviet policy

4.2. Towards the cultural revolution in linguistics

How did other scholars initially react to Marr's theories? Most linguists at least entertained their validity. The Moscow Linguistic Society debated them. Ethnographers reorganized the classification of the Caucasus peoples according to them. Secondary schools and universities taught them. For a time, the futurists were fascinated by Marr's semantic series and etymological charts, playfully comparing them to their own initiatives with 'nonsense language' (*zaum*). As experiments with alien sounds and forms, Marr's creations seemed as fantastic and colorful as theirs. But the futurists also understood that Japhetidology, like *zaum*, was art rather than science. Marr's inability to distinguish between the two equated, in their minds, with a mild form of madness.[23] Some of the most pointed criticisms of his methods can be found in the works of G.G. Shpet, who brooked no patience for the newfangled "social sciences" and their dependence on "explanation" (*obiasnenie*), which all too often collapsed into "psychologistic", or "mechanistic", or "genetic" theories. In a barely veiled assault on Marr, he complained about all those "theories which brag about 'explaining' the 'origin' of the meaningful word out of the meaningless cry, the 'origin' of understanding and intellect out of the frightened trembling and teeth-clenched spasms of prehistoric man". (Shpet 1927b: 558-559; Shpet 1923: 22)

Such impressions were rarely spoken in public, and if so, never in direct reference to Marr himself. Cooperation was usually the order of the day. At the Marrist Institute for the Comparative Study of the Languages and Literatures of the West and East (ILIaZV), scholars crafted a balanced curriculum of General Linguistics, Indo-Europeanism, and Japhetidology. Its traditionalists quietly applied comparative methods to the study of Mordvinian phonetics, Latvian and Russian dialectology, and the Finno-Ugric and Turkic language systems. Its Japhetites studied Marxian language theories, word "crossbreeding," and the history of production terms in Russian.[24] Several linguists even exploited Marr's materialist credentials to legitimate their own semiotic approaches to language. R.O. Shor wrote a highly charged article attacking scholars for their Humboldtian notions of language psychology. Using ideas from Baudouin, Saussure, and Marr, she countered that language was not dynamic *energeia* but stable *ergon*, a communicative system of signs and a cultural historical product. (Shor 1927: 32-71)

Structural linguistics and Japhetidology were by no means incompatible. Several leading students of the Moscow and Petersburg schools - N.F. Iakovlev and L.P. Iakubinskii - were perhaps the closest to Marr, and the most compromised by his dubious methods. Iakubinskii began teaching Marr's paleontology, in unison with his structural principles, as early as 1918 in the Institute of the Living Word. He later joined Marr's project, centered at ILIaZV, to create the world's greatest semantic list of numerical terms, with the logic that numbers best reflected the development of productive forces through history. Iakubinskii's contribution was to search the Indo-European languages to discover the etymological linkages between the words "one-half" and "hand". Both he and Iakovlev seemed to genuinely believe that the union of structural and Japhetite principles was both possible and desirable. To them, Marr represented the legitimacy of the sociological approach, and not a little institutional authority. (Vinogradov 1953; *Iazykovednye problemy po chislitelnym* 1927)

L.S. Vygotskii offers another interesting case study in collaboration. He has become, in his own right, one of the most celebrated developmental psychologists of the twentieth century. On the one hand, I would argue that an essential theme in his work stems from an incidental remark made by Shpet, in his *Aesthetic fragments*, when he pointed out that children may begin to "talk" a lot at a certain age, but only develop true speech when they join the social collective, when language as a "social thing" becomes the "inner form of the word". This is a topic which, through his own experiments and insights, has helped to make Vygotskii so famous. He called it the "internalization of social speech". In broader terms, Shpet and Vygotskii also shared the same central, organizing principles to their work: that language and thought are inseparable, that they are social historical products, received by all and remade by all, and that they are mediated in human consciousness by way of signs. I do not mean to diminish Vygotskii's work, or to unfairly highlight Shpet's, but simply to point out the intersection between the two. Surely their intellectual paths must have crossed, given Vygotskii's studies of philology and literature at Moscow University after 1914 (where Shpet was already teaching); given his lifelong interest in the aesthetic and language theories of Humboldt and Potebnia; and given his placement at the Institute of Psychology, which Shpet had helped to establish.

On the other hand, there also seem to be some interesting points of conversion between Vygotskii's and Marr's theories, functions not merely of their shared sources (Friedrich Engels, for one), but also of their reportedly close collaboration. With Marr, Vygotskii posited that the tool and the hand gesture were the first human means of labor and communication, the first sign systems. Together they believed that words not only name, but also enforce actions. Speech not only reflects established patterns of social behavior; it also regulates them. Some of Vygotskii's behavioral experiments with children, centered on word associations, were essentially stimulus-response exercises with words. Was he intent on discovering the workings of the "second signal system", the signalizing functions of consciousness? Did Vygotskii, in essence, give Marr's reflective and reflexological approach a firm grounding in behavioral psychology? The questions can only be raised, not yet fully answered. But given Vygotskii's criticisms of Pavlovian reflex theory, and its gross mutations in the USSR, it seems that he was closer to Shpet rather than to Marr. For his abiding concerns were in the semiotics of human speech and child development, with an accent on "signification" as a most creative, fluid act of human consciousness. David Joravsky is right when he argues that, for all of Vygotskii's equivocations, he was most likely too open minded a thinker for the conformist and orthodox fashions of the day - a judgement validated by contemporary sources.[25]

Perhaps the most famous clients of the Marr school were the members of the so-called "Bakhtin circle" - V.N. Voloshinov, P.N. Medvedev, and Mikhail Bakhtin - the former two of whom were members of the Subsection on Methodology of ILIaZV. Under the patronage of Marr and Iakovlev, they advertised themselves as subscribers to new "materialist" and "sociological" methods. Voloshinov's *Marxism and the philosophy of language* (1929), written while he was an administrator on the staff of the Subsection and published in its Linguistics series, was a curious piece. It was well versed in the leading linguistic and aesthetic theories of the day, and centered around a semiotic appreciation for language, albeit a semiotics grounded in social and economic realities and expressing their ideological meanings.

Voloshinov's "word as sign" was a kind of neutral, third reality floating between the material world which it "reflected" and the ideological meanings it "refracted". Sometimes his work even reads as an attempt to legitimate Humboldt's dialectics, Husserl's phenomenology, and Shpet's cultural semiotics - charges which Marr's polemicists would eventually aim against him. Time and again Voloshinov's words echo Shpet's. *"Consciousness itself can arise and become a viable fact only in the material embodiment of signs."* "The word is not only the purest, most indicatory sign, but is, in addition, *a neutral sign.*" The word is *"the semiotic material of inner life - of consciousness* (inner speech)." "Social psychology in fact is not located anywhere within (in the 'souls' of communicating subjects) but entirely and completely *without* - in the word, the gesture, the act."[26]

Yet Voloshinov's work was also very much a polemic in the Marrist style: filled with fawning quotations from the great master; blanket condemnations of linguistics as a sterile, abstract discipline; and a rash intolerance for any and all philosophical rivals. Voloshinov perfected the categorical dismissal to a high art, relegating the whole linguistics establishment to one of two suspect radical fringes, either the "individualistic subjectivism" of Humboldt and Shpet, or the "abstract objectivism" of Saussure and Shor. He developed what later became the hallmark of the Bakhtin circle, its self-styled power to explore the social dimensions of language as the "whole sentence", as utterance or 'dialogue' (*parole*). What Marr had done for Caucasian philology in the distant historical past - to draw out "living speech in its limitlessly free, creative ebb and flow" - the Bakhtin circle would now do for literary criticism in the Soviet present.[27]

None of these arguments and trends lasted long within the orbit of Japhetidology. With the advent of the cultural revolution in 1928, Marr and his students tolerated no such aberrations. Their materialist theories outgrew scholarly cooperation, instead becoming political standards by which to measure loyalty to the regime. Shortly after he was appointed rector of Moscow State University, A.Ia. Vyshinskii gave Marr's ideas yet another stamp of ideological purity when he demanded subservience to them from several leading Indo-European linguists. "Military measures" were necessary, he advised, to purge bourgeois elements from academia.[28] Linguists were now forced to declare their loyalty to one of two camps, the Japhetite or the Indo-Europeanist. The former was a medium for professional advancement, especially for linguists who studied any one of the several languages deemed worthy by Marr. Many scholars joined it willingly; many in the general public happily celebrated its achievements.

Marr's theories appealed to party youth who were eager for a cult of science. He brought the distant Academy of Sciences into touch with the masses by way of his pitch and oratory. As he declared to an extraordinary session of the Academy in 1931, "How happy am I to be a scholar in such a country where one may, in his own language, in the language of science, speak with the worker, where the language of science turns into the language of politics, into the language of the masses, and where politics calls on science to join in the struggle for socialism." (*Literaturnaia gazeta* 34: 25 June 1931) With calm and confidence, his ideas convinced people that they could conquer the many developmental tasks facing the USSR, even with such poor and undeveloped resources at their disposal. The very defilement of Marr's theories in the West became proof of their revolutionary character. Like Marxism, wrote M.N. Pokrovskii, Marr's theories were "already hated everywhere". This was a "very good sign", a "badge of honor". The struggles of one man came to be seen as the struggles of a whole country. They were no longer driven by his petty resentments from years past but by political intrigues bigger than Marr himself.[29]

Marr did not craft this cult of personality alone. Several Japhetite loyalists, V.B. Aptekar' foremost among them, defended his theories before the reading public. From his post in the Society of Marxist Historians, Aptekar' led a campaign against "bourgeois" influences in history, archeology, and ethnography, demanding their assimilation into a new Marrist orientology. In 1928 he took this fight to language studies, Marr naming him one of his best "linguistics" students, an honor which Aptekar' ridiculed in private, proud to admit that he had never read Saussure. In the fashion of Voloshinov, he was also fond of saying that linguistics, divided into such disparate and "unsettled" parts as phonetics, morphology and syntax, was less a science than an empirical and "scholastic aid" at the service of historians. Japhetidology, in contrast, was an integrative, materialist linguistics; and Aptekar's popularization of it was a healthy antidote to the rarified and "aristocratic" terms of "university science".[30]

To be an Indo-Europeanist did not mean automatic recrimination. Linguists survived by accepting Japhetidology implicitly or by not attacking it openly. From most accounts, much of both went on. There was much less toleration for those who actively opposed Marr and his school. As the cultural revolution worked its chaos on the liberal arts and natural sciences, frontline polemicists derided linguistics as one of the most backward of fields, hardly touched by Marxian methods and personnel. Yet the coming battles in linguistics pitted two of its most famous "Marxist" members against each other: Polivanov and Marr. Polivanov set the confrontation between the structural and paleontological (Japhetidological) schools into motion when he returned to Moscow from Central Asia in 1926. Administrators of the RANION, likely aware of Polivanov's militant Bolshevism, appointed him chair of its Linguistics Section in order to establish a Marxian circle within it, with Marr's cooperation, and lead an assault on the traditional linguists of the Fortunatov school entrenched there. Instead, Polivanov began to work closely with them in a joint effort to create a curriculum uniting Marxist sociolinguistics with formalist and structural methods.[31] But first Polivanov had to displace Japhetidology, what he considered a charlatan science, from its rising eminence in the field.

In a series of reports and essays, later republished in *For a Marxist linguistics*, Polivanov pleaded for a return to sanity and professional conduct in linguistics. He answered the major assertions and slanders of Japhetidology - "pressed in recent times by the light hand of N.Ia. Marr" and repeated by his "obedient but completely ignorant admirers of choral singing" - with his own collection of sarcastic and pithy arguments. In lighthearted moments he poked fun at Marr's fetish with the protolanguage elements, "*sal-ber-yon-rosh*". For the Japhetite consonant *b* in the Latin word *urbs* stood as much a chance linguistically of deriving from *ber* as a "white church wall" stood of having a genetic relationship with a "white rose petal", simply by virtue of their same color. In more serious moments he defended traditional Indo-European methods, bourgeois or not, as irreplaceable tools in the massive Soviet project for language reform. "We are studying the present", Polivanov wrote, "not as a circus trampoline for jumping into the sociolingual [*glottogonic*] epochs" of the past, but as a means of creating a more democratic literary culture for the future."[32]

These harsh words provoked a series of debates within the Institute of Language and Literature of the Communist Academy. In September of 1928, Marr's forces organized a Subsection for Materialist Linguistics in it to purge the science of its bourgeois theories and practitioners, among whom they now counted Polivanov, and to elevate once and for all a new standard of dialectical materialism. But the Subsection was also open to anti-Japhetite forces. What began as a glorification of Marr soon devolved into an argument over the very definition of a "Marxian linguistics". Marr elaborated on the basis of nineteenth-century materialist trends; Polivanov constructed his brand of Marxist linguistics based on the achievements of modern linguistics. The Marr school dominated the first series of reports delivered to the Communist Academy Subsection between October of 1928 and May of 1929.

Polivanov answered with a harangue against Japhetidology for using "concrete material which contradicts the facts". He criticized its followers who used it as a paradigm to study other disciplines, namely ethnography, folklore and archeology. He argued for a new Marxian linguistics based on structural and sociological principles. But the Japhetites counterattacked, shouting Polivanov down, condemning him in public. Communist ideologists dismissed him from Moscow as a pseudo-Marxist and anti-Japhetite, exiling him to Samarkand (Uzbekistan). With Marr's and Aptekar's participation, a purge committee then turned on Polivanov's Institute of Language and Literature for inquisition and reorganization under the standard of "communist ideological leadership". In the tally of its members, there was only one communist (G.K. Danilov) and only one scholar "becoming Marxist" (R.O. Shor). Purgists labeled all others, including M.N. Peterson, as "idealist-formalists". They disbanded the Institute in April of 1930.[33]

Polivanov's RANION Institute was not alone. A party commission purged and reorganized G.G. Shpet's State Academy of Artistic Studies (GAKhN) under the same standards and purposes. In addition to some trumped up charges of financial misconduct, it accused Shpet of poisoning philosophy with his "arch-reactionary, objective-idealistic, mystical perspectives", labeling him a Husserlian idealist and "pseudo-specialist". These charges represented nothing more or less than communist party fears about Polivanov's structural theories and its philosophical foundations in Shpet's thought. Both men had lobbied against the crass materialism then popular in most party circles. "If you want to know what kind of materialist I confess to be, you would need to call on Feuerbach", said Shpet at the purge hearings. He denied the notion that Soviet dialectical materialism had in large part developed from the simple materialism of the 1700s and 1800s. Dialectical materialism, countered Shpet, "arose out of idealism alone, as Feuerbach expressed this and later Marx. This idealism was placed from its head back onto its feet. It did not arise, of course, from my philosophy; it arose earlier. But I do believe that it may be useful in our general work."

Shpet's tragic fate had trapped him between two epochs, one of Bolshevik toleration for the "specialists" from the old regime (1921-1928), the other a wave of persecution against them (1928-1932), at which point he became a target of attack and recrimination. He recognized this turn of events as patently unjust, even before his accusers. The Soviet government had supported him in 1925, yet now "marked" him "as objectively harmful" to Soviet society. Purgists called Shpet a "finished man", tracing a series of prefabricated charges that he was "cunning, hypocritical and vulgar". All of these "estimations of my activities are proceeding here outside of every historical circumstance", he responded to the purge committee. "People are offering only finished slogans. This is the wrong perspective. A slogan is the end of something. To judge something from the end (a priori) means not to give the real history. The purge brigade is not interested in giving the history but in getting results."[34] Shpet's choice of words was intentional. They might as well serve as his epitaph, for they were emblematic of his whole philosophy of language. Shpet spoke a language of freedom and possibilities (a posteriori) in stark contrast to the party language of "finished slogans" (a priori).

The party did indeed get results. Both of these institutional purges accompanied the even more newsworthy inquisition within the Academy of Sciences. In each case, the party removed persons of questionable loyalty and service, be they renegade Marxists, or non-Marxists, or former political opponents of the Bolsheviks. Amid the campaigns for collectivization and industrialization, the party favored scholars and scientists not for their own sake, but for the sake of rebuilding the Soviet economy and society. "Scientific utilitarianism" took priority over traditional theories or methods.[35] In this new atmosphere, Polivanov's work with national linguistic forms and Shpet's phenomenological theories paled in comparison with Marr's emphasis on the relevance of language history for Soviet state-building.

Polivanov may have been unique for his intransigent and tactless attacks; Shpet for his brave defense of philosophical idealism. But neither was alone in their opposition to the Marr school. Still other linguists mounted a broad campaign of criticism against it. R.O. Shor leveled charges against Marr's "dogmatism" and self-proclaimed novelty, arguing that scholars in the West had been exploring the semantic and sociological dimensions of world languages for some time. Iakovlev set out to study language as a "social form of thought and therefore as a system of definite (material) signs of social communication". He meant the study of the word as content and as form, both of which evolve and develop thanks to mutually reciprocal influences over time, which follow material changes in human life. This formula elaborated on some of Marr's own themes; yet it was also an attempt to salvage a proper semiotic and structural base of study for linguistics. G.K. Danilov challenged the primacy of the Japhetic school with an interesting attempt to amalgamate structural insights with historical materialism, fusing formal (phonetic, morphological, syntactical) and semantic (psychological and sociological) analyses into a dialectical whole. He also combined the Humboldtian sense of language as product and activity with a Pavlovian concept of language as a sign system of "conditional reflexes", more specifically language as a "collection of sound, hand, and facial movements which are the signals of a given act of reflexive understanding".[36]

Two other independent linguists skillfully undermined Marr's contentions about language origins and the second signal system. A.I. Dobrovolskii criticized his futile search for origins in the murky, prehistoric past, arguing that language was an "organic part of social life", subject to "eternal re-creation" in people. Bubrikh wrote that the processes of "sound signalization" and "sound speech" irrevocably separated animal from human communication. He trashed the Japhetite "method of collecting different speech phenomena" in favor of the new structural method of defining "grammatical and phonetical articulation", and of "fixing the living interconnected flow of speech".[37] According to reliable testimony, such structural theories were "on the move" among Soviet linguists even at the height of the cultural revolution. Older scholars were unrelenting in their criticisms. P.A. Chernykh openly referred to Saussure's structural insights as the real "new theory of language". Younger structural thinkers like P.S. Kuznetsov were originally attracted to Marr's militancy, but eventually recognized the "arbitrary and baseless nature of many of his positions".[38] Cut off from career advancement and patronage by the Japhetites, they now joined forces to revive linguistics where Polivanov had failed.

4.3. The 'Language Front' challenge

These debates intensified between September and December of 1930 when scholars from Moscow and Leningrad united in the 'Language Front' (*Iazykfront*) to overhaul theoretical and practical linguistics and align them with "socialist construction". We have met some of these scholars before. M.S. Gus and Ernst Drezen were already active in language reform projects. G.K. Danilov, T.D. Lomtev, P.S. Kuznetsov, and A.M. Sukhotin were Polivanov's and Iakovlev's best students, shaped in the mold of the structural school.[39] These Frontists matched their own struggles in linguistics with the fierce debates of the cultural revolution in politics, the liberal arts and natural sciences. Their model was the Russian Association of Proletarian Writers (RAPP), which promised to use literature for the "radical transformation of human beings" rather than for the sake of art or entertainment. RAPP promoted a whole new proletarian genre for the new reading masses. M. Bochacher, one of its most radical voices and a member of its rebel splinter group, the "Literary Front", inspired the young linguists to raise a similar challenge.[40]

Compelled by the excitement of the cultural revolution, and the hubris of youth, the Frontists spared no enemies, right or left. They criticized the Indo-Europeanism of the Fortunatov school as a "metaphysic that isolates sounds from forms, forms from meanings, and language from society". In step with the party's dictates against formalism in the arts and sciences, they attacked their very own "Saussurian" teachers (Polivanov, Iakovlev, Vinokur and Voloshinov) for defining language as the "totality of associations" between the elements of speech and the objects of the real world. This had violated Lenin's arguments against Plekhanov's concept of the hieroglyphic, and the party's current understanding of language as a superstructural reflection of the productive base. Not especially known for their loyalty, the Frontists threw some of their hardest blows against their once favorite teacher, Polivanov, for having tried to make a pseudo-Marxism out of bourgeois Indo-Europeanism.[41] Marr, they seemed to say, was right.

But the Frontists saved their most persistent and sharp criticisms for the Japhetites, nastily mocking them as children who could "not make a move without Marr". They openly paraded his sloppy concept of class and "mechanistic" methodology for the Soviet public to see and hear. They teased that Marr, so preoccupied with language origins and primitive history, was nothing more than a "traditional eighteenth-century materialist". They targeted his vain "patent and monopoly on Marxism" as unjust, noting that bourgeois heritage did have a role to play in the making of a materialist linguistics. Without relief, they attacked Marrism's "divorce from practice", its total lack of contributions to any language reform efforts.[42]

These arguments were fraught with contradictions. At one time or another, Marr or Polivanov or Shpet had raised the same arguments too. The Frontists tried to take the best from each of them, using Marr to vilify the positions of traditional and structural linguistics, then reviving those positions to vilify Marr's Japhetidology. They understood that the ideological momentum had turned against mainstream linguistics, what Lunacharskii called "all those bourgeois recidivisms", personified by the "notorious Polivanov".[43] So they turned too. But the Frontists could not deny who they were, the academic children of Baudouin, Fortunatov, Polivanov and Shpet. Their double punch was an effort to appropriate mainstream principles on their own idiosyncratic terms, simply as a matter of political survival. But they were also true believers, members of the governing elite. They believed that language was power, that the words of the ruling Marxist-Leninist ideology could indeed change the world.

For this was not simply a great debate about ideology. It was also a struggle about changing society, about shaping language reform for the future. The young Frontists were filled with vast potential, new ideas, and energies - just waiting to break free and be put to work. Their struggle helps to prove that Stalin's political system did not always rely on instrumental controls and totalitarian orders to rule the country. The Language Front raised an alternate model, centered on praxis or interaction, in which power was based on dialogue and communication. The Frontists understood that new relations of production, a new labor community, was necessary to make alienated people whole again; but they also appreciated the need for new discursive relations between people, a new language community as a means to complement labor relations. Their ideology teaches us that Soviet communism could bring such a philosophy of praxis to life and nurture it, at least for a few years between 1928 and 1932, decades before similar pronouncements by Western European Marxist thinkers.[44] The myth that Soviet Marxism only developed in its orthodox, oppressive version should be finally put to rest.[45]

What were the sources of this novel approach? Many of the Frontists had attended seminars at Polivanov's RANION Institute directed by the renowned philosophers M.A. Dynik and V.F. Asmus. These courses covered a wide range of issues from historical materialism, to dialectical and formal logic, to aesthetics and poetics - all the elements of Europe's twentieth-century "linguistic turn" in philosophy. Asmus was especially influential in teaching, as his syllabi attest, the idealistic and voluntaristic principles of Hegel, Humboldt, Potebnia, Bogdanov, Shpet and Voloshinov. He took special care to weave Hegelian dialectical philosophy, Humboldtian linguistics, and Marxian theory into a novel (rather very Shpetian) understanding of linguistic and social praxis.[46] Humboldt's ideas were already in wide, favorable circulation.[47]

But the unlikely centerpiece in this project was the Italian Marxist philosopher, Antonio Labriola, who first invented the term, "philosophy of praxis", by which he meant a historical materialism with a focus on the creative human powers at work in history. Marxism as a philosophy of praxis challenged people not so much to think about the world as change it. Labriola, whose main work, *Historical materialism*, was published in Russian in 1926, had shaped this voluntarism from his own recipe of Hegelian idealism and Humboldtian language theory. He had once defined human thought as both a fixed entity and a function or process; grammar as a "genesis", "not a mere fact" but a "process of work and production". From the journal of the Communist Academy, Asmus now raised Labriola's insight - that "language is a condition and an instrument, a cause and consequence of society" - as the new banner for linguistics. (Asmus 1927: 250; Labriola 1926)

With this learning in mind, the Frontists were well placed to craft their own unique brand of Marxism-Leninism. From the recently published *Philosophical notebooks*, they quoted Lenin's dictum that "a wise idealism" was closer to Marxism than a "vulgar materialism"; that the process dialectic and reciprocal interaction between subject and object were the engines that moved history, not some simple reflective materialism.[48] Upon this authoritative foundation the Frontists named Humboldt's philosophy of language as the departure point for modern structural and sociological linguistics. His understanding of language as both a 'product' (*delo* or *ergon*) and an 'activity' (*deiatel'nost* or *energeia*), became the central premise for their work.

In a stinging indictment of the Bakhtin circle, the Frontists argued that language was not simply dialogue, "a continual formative process brought to life by the social interaction of speakers". That approach may have been well suited to literary criticism, but it left language reformers in the revolutionary present at a complete impasse. Language, countered the Frontists, was at once "something stable" and "something mobile", at once something "already said" as well as "something being said". Dialectical philosophy, joining Humboldt with Lenin, was thereby a model to help people become more active participants in society through their mastery of language, as both an expressive (subjective) and communicative (objective) civic activity.[49]

To fulfill their philosophy of praxis, the Language Front took its disputes "into the streets", posing a direct challenge to party authority by demanding revolutionary language reforms based on mass participatory action. Since several of the leading Frontists had already been teaching the Russian language in pedagogical colleges, worker faculties and party schools for the last few years, many of their former students and colleagues joined their campaign. Twenty-five new members subscribed to their ranks; cells were organized in Leningrad and Smolensk. Teacher collectives in Moscow, Kiev, Tashkent, and Voronezh declared support for the program. Leading Esperantists joined too. Disgruntled moderate linguists, caught between their approval of structural theories and their loyalty to Marr, hastily supported the Front's cause. It established strongholds in the Subsection of Materialist Linguistics of the Communist Academy; the Scientific Research Association for the Study of National and Colonial Problems; the Russian Language Section of the Moscow Pedagogical Institute; the Linguistic Section of the Russian Association of Scientific Research Institutes of Material, Artistic and Speech Culture; the All-Union Committee for the New Alphabet; and the Society to End Illiteracy. It commanded loyalists in scores of factories, schools, collective farms, editorial boards, unions and party cells. It created a central power base in the Scientific Research Institute of Linguistics (NIIaz).[50]

The Frontists hoped to "make a linguist out of every teacher" and proposed to establish a Linguistics University for Workers. They conducted readings of Hegel and Humboldt, mounting a "bourgeois heritage brigade" in which R.O. Shor studied the classics of Western linguistics in critical appreciation. They organized brigades for "language construction", designed to create new spelling systems, grammars and literary standards for the Russian language; as well as new Latin alphabets, dictionaries and grammars for all of the non-Russian languages of the USSR. The Front's journal, *Revolution and language*, was devoted to rationalizing language for better social use, focusing on such timely topics as telephone audibility and terminological standardization.[51]

All of these noisy presentations were not without their calmer moments. Some linguists reconciled the Language Frontists and Marr's Japhetites by defining the common principles between them. Others sought to educate the public about the importance of language reform, as a movement for cultural change, by drawing freely from Polivanov's and Marr's theories, without any concern for the conflicts between them. In a few cases, the Japhetites acceded to the Front's criticisms. Marr publicly recognized that his readings of Marxism were weak and undeveloped; his students reorganized into brigades in order to better serve language construction.[52]

But the Japhetites saved most of their attention for a powerful counterattack. In staged debates and publications from the Communist Academy they responded to the Front's accusations, point by detailed point. They reaffirmed the worth of Marr's stadialism in the Soviet project for nation-making and state-building. They characterized the Front as beholden to "conservative" forces, what they termed "Humboldtianism" and "Saussurianism" in linguistics. Aptekar', the most pugnacious voice among the Japhetites, labeled the Frontists and their sympathizers as idealists for their fetishization of "sound language" at the expense of the more truly Engelsian "gesture language". Only a fool would argue against the latter, he believed, which was a function of Charles Darwin's theory of evolution and humankind's descent from the apes, who were the first "social animals" to speak with their hands. Marr's students spoke with certainty and dedication that the Japhetic theory had given a "new ideological weapon not only to research linguists but also to revolutionaries in the struggle for communism". They recognized Japhetidology as the vanguard theoretical system in linguistics; allegiance to it, they argued, meant allegiance to the party.[53]

In May of 1932, the Cultural Propaganda Office of the TsK RKPb took a definitive stand towards the controversy by disbanding the Language Front. It placed NIIaz on probation and dismantled it about a year later. The leading Frontists promptly recanted. In its rationale, the party cited their weak criticisms of Indo-Europeanism, their disrespect for Marr, and their pretensions to a monopoly over language theory. They were most guilty - given their vision, self-determination, and popularity - of overstepping the bounds of the party line and trying to create a radical Marxist linguistics, an ideology "more left" than the party's own. Like the formalist and futurist movements in the 1920s, and the most militant proletarianists in the recent cultural revolution, the Front could not survive such an affront to party authority.[54]

One of the accusations leveled against the Frontists carried a special weight, with implications far beyond ideology. To be accused of "formalism" meant that they had joined their teachers in the Petersburg and Moscow schools as "bourgeois", "subjective-idealist" Indo-Europeanists. In Marr's logic, their methods differentiated languages according to the historical-comparative, formalist and structural methods, thereby isolating them into disparate and haphazard racial families and national groups, in violation of Soviet internationalism From the authority of history, he and his Japhetites argued that such methods were static and divisive. Marr's dedication to a reductive dialectical materialism, as well as to a fluid hierarchy of languages and cultures for the USSR, better served the interests of Stalin's industrializing and modernizing state. His views coincided better with the reigning party formula of convergence-mergence by elevating the non-Russian languages into that hierarchy and presuming their gradual splicing with Russian.

This whole controversy had serious repercussions for the major language reform projects already underway in the field, as masterminded by the structural linguists of the Petersburg and Moscow schools, and their students in the Language Front. By challenging the Marr school for primacy in the forum of theory, they challenged it for primacy in the arena of practice. By failing in one they failed in the other too. The next several chapters examine these projects, along with the scope of Japhetite interference. If the polemics between the Language Front and Japhetidology were bruising, the polemics over language reform were even more painful. The government was sometimes lenient with formalist and structural linguists, but it was much less patient with their projects in the field, which tended to unduly burden and complicate social and political life. Marr's Japhetites, on the other hand, offered much simpler solutions.

Part III
Practical experiments

Chapter 5

Mass mobilizing for Russian literacy: scripts, grammar and style

The first sustained experiments with the Russian language came in the spelling, grammar, and stylistic reforms of the 1920s. Isolated from the masses it was so intent on reaching, the government took a series of measures to fashion a standard language for the new Russian nation and for the broader Soviet public. Like their Italian colleague, Antonio Gramsci, who spent several years in Moscow in the early 1920s, Soviet linguists appreciated scripts and grammars as means to ennoble the speech patterns of the common people in an encoded vernacular, to discipline them within a language of state discourse, to raise them up to a greater historical standard. School grammars played a similar role in nation-building as Taylorist methods in the factories: they helped workers rationalize their labor movements, thought, and speech acts - freeing them for more elevated pursuits. As Gramsci wrote, "written 'normative grammars' tend to embrace the whole territory of a nation and its whole 'linguistic volume' in order to create a national linguistic conformism . . . a more robust and homogeneous skeleton for the national linguistic body, of which every individual is the reflection and interpreter (the Taylor system and self-education)."[1]

Through this process, educators promoted an uneasy dialectic of standardization from above and democratization from below. From above, they depended on formalist and structural linguists and their new spelling and pronunciation rules to help solve the perils of Russian bilingualism. They debated and implemented new scientific grammars and stylistics courses for the schools. They assembled rules and vocabulary lists to promote standard usage. They helped to write textbooks in the compelling language of Bolshevism. But these standardizations were also accompanied by a conscious policy to democratize the schools from below by expanding their social base and by promoting the innovative "complex method" and social dialectology in teaching.[2] Rather than complement each other, the two policies tended to collide.

5.1. The perils of Soviet spelling reform

The Provisional Government left the unfinished business of spelling reform on Lenin's desk. His editorialists promptly began to mock "progressive" bourgeois society for its continued stalling. Linguists sympathetic to the Bolshevik government accused the bourgeoisie of maintaining the difficult old spelling rules to maintain its own cultural hegemony. If the Russian script was a "productive form of speech", it deserved a "maximal rationalization" in the "interests of the proletariat". Polivanov wrote of the superficial letters in the old Russian spelling as playing the very same useless and extravagant "role as the starched collar on the bourgeois intellectual's neck, for any sign which contrasted him to the worker and peasant was of value to him". Obsolete and ornamental letters, he argued, simply do not communicate well.[3]

The new regime took decisive action on the spelling question when, on 23 December 1917, Lunacharskii's Narkompros implemented the earlier Ministry of Education plan by decree, declaring it effective for the government bureaucracy and the schools. Within a year another decree extended the plan to all publications and documents. (Chernyshev 1947: 246-249) By completing the imperial reform project, the regime hoped to unite all Russian speakers under a new spelling standard. But the decrees had the opposite effect. Abroad, many emigre groups simply refused to adhere to them, defending the old letters and rules for decades to come, painting the new spelling as one more example of the "devilish inventions of Bolshevism". Plus, they remarked, it was "unscientific" and "ugly".

One of the most active scholarly emigre groups in the West, the Prague Linguistic Circle, wholeheartedly supported the reform and ridiculed this opposition. As testimony to their progressive ideology, its members argued for the reform so that "millions of children and simple people, who do not have the opportunity to waste years and years on the mastering of a cunning and complicated spelling . . . may with minimal energy come to Russian and world culture. The point is to be able to rationally use our liberating energies".[4] Nor did the 1918 Narkompros decrees resolve the spelling question at home. They failed to sweep the old spelling issues away with the old order. Some radical Bolsheviks condescendingly referred to the decrees as products of the Provisional Government, not Soviet power. The public and scholarly press registered scores of complaints as to how the reform was "incomplete". People still argued that the Russian script and its sounds were terribly mismatched.

In 1919, believing the spelling reform to be insufficient, Narkompros raised the question of Latinizing the Russian and Arabic scripts of the former empire. Educators held that the western Latin alphabet was a "logical" complement to the new government's choice of the metric system and western calendar. For the most idealistic among them, it would finally end Russia's "script separatism" from Europe and serve as a "convergence" (*sblizhenie*) of the Soviet peoples. Leading Russian linguists tabled the proposal, offering their support in principle, but their opposition in fact, given the practical complications of a new Latin alphabet. Narkompros, they argued, had just decreed a new spelling reform and should not burden teachers with any more experimental conversions. Besides, they explained, Latin was no panacea for world unity, because the alphabets of

Europe already suffered from their own internal "discord" (*raznoboi*) given the great sound differences between language systems. Lenin supported Latinization along these equivocal lines, believing it was beneficial in principle, but premature. Lunacharskii even recounted a 1918 conversation with him on the subject. "I do not doubt", Lenin allegedly said, "that the time will come for the Latinization of the Russian script, but to act in haste would be unwise". Better to implement the 1918 spelling reform, which was acceptable to most scholars, and wait until the Soviet state had built its strength and authority for a turn to Latin. "Such was the instruction handed down to us by the leader", concluded Lunacharskii.[5]

Concerned Russians drew from an endless reserve of complaints to describe the continuing plight of their spelling system. One report on the primary schools termed the situation "extraordinarily sad". Others pleaded to throw all of Grot's spelling rules into "the dustbin of history," to free students "from Grot's captivity". Publicists referred to the "struggle against orthographic illiteracy" as the "sorest subject of the contemporary school." People talked of the "collapse of orthography", and of the general "epidemic" of illiteracy resulting from the still unsettled spelling question. One educator referred most figuratively to the new Russian orthography as a Molokh, a "hydra of eight thousand heads", noting that "this pagan god once again demands its victims, just as before". And if the situation was sad in the urban schools, in the rural schools it was "catastrophic". Or as another critic wrote, the "great, powerful Russian language" was "in peril".[6]

Why all of the hyperbole? The crisis was real. Seven years of war and revolution had left their toll. A whole generation of students was now winding its way through the schools, from the earliest grades to the universities, without satisfactory skills in reading and writing. Illiteracy remained high in the 1920s, especially in the villages; half of the population over nine years of age could not read or write. Yet as a result of Bolshevik affirmative action policies, more and more poorly literate and illiterate students, along with their local dialects and resulting spelling mistakes, were becoming a daily part of school discourse. They lacked the proper experience or training with the written language and its new spelling rules.

To make matters worse, the Soviet government began to implement educational reforms during the 1920s that mistakenly assumed a high standard of readiness among teachers and students. Primary among these reforms was a whole new curriculum for the elementary and secondary schools, the "complex method". It put end to the traditional subjects of reading, writing, and spelling; as well as the teaching of "skills" (*navyki*) by way of rote memorization, drills, and homework. In their place, the schools taught students the interconnections between specific subjects, as well as the power of active learning, under the general rubrics of nature, society, and labor.

The social transformations brought on by the revolution, compounded by these new methods, frustrated educators. They warned that the ability of children to draw from the fund of human knowledge, and contribute to it through reading and writing, was at risk. Primary and secondary school students were not mastering the crucial "automatisms, which free children from the necessity of fixing their attention on the process and mechanism of reading, writing and arithmetic, which economize the strengths of children, and save childhood energy for higher creative labor". Instead, Soviet schools were producing children who could not spell, and therefore by the strict standards of the day, were illiterate in general. Teenagers were impoverished when it came to spelling; a commission charged to study the matter in 1929 even concluded that for them, "Russian is a foreign language".[7] Educators must have looked out upon this sea of unwashed humanity and wondered if there was such a thing as the language of Pushkin. The general decline of quality literacy - exacerbated by the new spelling rules, the new complex method, and the new grammar - undermined the authority of Russian. The torturous dictation lessons from prerevolutionary schools came to an end, but this meant that students now wrote "more illiterately" than before, creating anarchy in spelling and a loss of "respect for the written word". The "delicate and dialectical system" of the Russian language was in a shambles.[8]

The plague of mistakes spread into print culture. Publishing houses printed handbooks in the early 1920s to codify the new spelling system for newspapers, the schools and the government bureaucracy. I.V. Ustinov's practical guide to its rules, with an accompanying dictionary, became an important reference source. His "pictures" of the new words were necessary for the reform to assimilate into the public consciousness, to "cultivate sharp-sightedness toward the word-form". (Ustinov 1923: 1-5) Yet there were "hundreds of rules, traditions, systems and practices" governing how to spell, and a total of forty different handbooks published for proofreaders, each with its own rules. The anarchy infiltrated public life beyond newspapers and books; shop signs, billboards and advertisements were littered with wrong spellings. Beginning in 1926, the State Academic Council of Narkompros even asked D.N. Ushakov and A.M. Peshkovskii to compile an orthographic dictionary and code to overcome this "chaos", to establish a "Soviet Grot". Pressure mounted for it year after year.[9]

The momentum for simplification peaked with a wave of mass agitation and debate beginning in the fall of 1929. Frustrated with the burdensome process of learning spelling rules, and emboldened by the rhetoric of the cultural revolution, people from all walks of life - the Arkhangelsk Association of Teachers, the Linguistic Circle of Kazan School No. 15, and the Social Group of the Third Course of the N.I. Bukharin Workers' Faculty, to name a few - began to demand a new spelling system. They repeated the tired slogans that the 1918 reform was "unfinished", a "half-measure", a "pagan god" still worthy of overturning.

During the next few years, they organized "disputations" and sent thousands of letters to the major educational and youth newspapers outlining their project proposals. This ground swell for spelling reform is yet another forgotten chapter in Stalin's cultural revolution between 1929 and 1932. Students and workers were now expected to struggle against religion, to mobilize their energies for better production, and to "learn to understand the language of the machine". To save time and energy, many argued for introducing the principles of NOT (the scientific organization of labor) into spelling lessons. Others wanted to plan language along the lines of Esperanto, "a brilliant example of the rational intervention of people in the creation of an extremely simplified grammar". Dziga Vertov even included some of the new spelling proposals in his classic documentary film, *Enthusiasm: symphony of the Donbass* (1931), together with its images against traditional customs and religion and for the revolution in collective farming and industrial productivity. Enthusiasts hoped that its simpler rules would complement the new rationalities of life and labor.[10]

In answer to these demands from below, state educational administrators in the Main Scientific Directorate of Narkompros established a Committee on Spelling Reform in late 1929. They appointed I.V. Ustinov and G.K. Danilov as its directors, both members of the Subsection of Materialist Linguistics of the Communist Academy and ideologue-linguists representing the radical Language Front program. Ustinov and Danilov quickly seized the ideological high ground and shaped the character and scope of the debate. They compiled and edited spelling proposals from concerned citizen groups in Iaroslavl, Nizhnii-Novgorod, and Voronezh. They bragged that this process of democratic creation, consultation, and criticism was the guiding principle of the new reform, in line with the spirit of the cultural revolution and the Language Front's own ideology. But their enthusiasm and radicalism were soon checked by disagreement and polemic.

Most teachers and workers remained loyal to the sound (phonetic) principle, "write as you speak", and demanded a maximal spelling simplification (*uproshchenie*) in a new set of simple rules. They sent scores of such projects into the offices of Russia's academic institutes. Radical phoneticists planned to match written with oral speech as closely as possible. Teachers tended to support this because they worked at the most difficult language frontier, the classroom, where they needed to conquer spelling rules by teaching people how to write quickly and efficiently. They faced the immense task of bringing millions of workers and peasants, young and old, into literate Soviet society.[11] Marr's Japhetites sought to channel this mass movement behind their cause. Not to be outdone by their Language Front rivals on the official commission, Marr proposed his own extreme phonetic design: collapsing several Russian consonants into existing letters; and, based on his Abkhazian transcription system, exchanging several Russian vowels with new Latin combinations.[12]

Most linguists repudiated radical phoneticism, lobbying instead for various interpretations of the sound-form (morphological) principle to design a spelling system that was both easier for illiterates to learn and for literate persons to use. They argued that the phonetic principle would not simplify but complicate reading with "a whole series of alternating sounds" and countless spellings, based largely the peculiarities of individual pronunciation and the many different regional Russian dialects. This was too high a price to pay for an easier way to teach spelling. After all, people read and write all their lives. Better to make some sacrifices in the schools, they argued, in order to rationalize social use later, guaranteeing "the uniform writing of one and the same word and its parts". Thus the "sound-types of the literary language", based on a close reading of structural phonology, should be applied as a corrective to extreme phoneticism. They were essential to salvage the "integrity of the visual image".[13]

The directors of the reform project, Ustinov and Danilov, steered a delicate course between these various camps; their compromise slogan, "to simplify in accordance with science". They recognized the phonetic principle as an aid in making literacy learning and writing easier; yet they appreciated the morphological principle for its "commanding significance" in providing an economy of literary effect. This "organic", elastic standard was meant to please everyone. When speaking to teachers and workers, Ustinov and Danilov framed it as the sound principle with sound-form correctives; when speaking to other linguists, they framed it as the sound-form principle, which left unimportant spellings to phonetic usage. In speaking to all groups, they avoided these fine yet troublesome distinctions by touting the project as a "rationalization of the Russian spelling"; an example of "social intervention in the life of language"; an attempt to create fully capable and literate technical, administrative, and political cadres. The new spelling freed students from boring and useless spelling lessons for the greater pursuit of knowledge. It ennobled Russian, the language of Bolshevism, with a spelling worthy of its speakers.[14]

The educational and research institutes of Narkompros debated the Ustinov-Danilov reform project, by now codified in a list of new spelling rules, during late 1929 and early 1930. But instead of agreement and approval, they saw the reform project mired by detailed recommendations and designs from the opposing sides, petty disputes about this or that letter and rule. Traditionalists scowled at the project as violating the authority of the Russian language; or questioned the timing of the reform, coming so soon after the 1917 decree. Several leading academicians, guardians of the sacred Russian script, agreed that some kind of reform was needed. But they approved only half of the project's total points, highlighting the inconsistencies and faults within the rest.[15]

D.N. Ushakov, who served as chair of the Committee on Spelling Reform between 1929 and 1931, publicly supported the project for a time, possibly because he was afraid of the political repercussions of opposing it, certainly because one of its central features (replacing the dividing sign with the soft sign) established a Moscow norm of palatalized consonants for pronunciation - his long standing pet project. Yet in the years before and after the reform movement, even in front of the councils of the TsK RKPb, he consistently reaffirmed his stand against radical simplification. Instead he promoted a minimalist "reordering" (*uporiadochenie*) of different ways of writing words so as to establish "uniformity" and "consistency" in spelling. It was to take the form of an authoritative "List and Handbook of Orthographic Rules" (*svoda* and *spravochnik*).[16]

In March of 1930, after a rather nasty debate between the various opposing sides, the Narkompros Directorate approved the basic compromise structure for the project. The new spelling system was to provide for "maximal economy in literacy training and in polygraphical effect" by combining the sound and sound-form principles. Narkompros now planned yet another round of public and scholarly debate, with worker and peasant correspondents in particular, to reconsider and consolidate any subsequent revisions and recommendations into a final draft project. The four hundred different spelling projects which it had considered in preceding months were apparently not enough to appease the hunger of the cultural revolutionaries for democratic debate. So the project dragged on and on, while tens of millions of peasants and workers were waiting to be taught literacy in the next few years. Schools and universities valued the reform project but were bewildered by the delays. In defiance, some even implemented it on their own, according to their own preferences for one point or another. The situation deteriorated; the project lingered without resolution.[17]

Yet all was not lost. Among the enthusiasts for spelling reform was a small group of fanatics who brought some added color to the debates. One of them sent a scrap of paper to the spelling commission proposing to create a new script of numbers rather than conventional letters, such that Moscow would be written as "247031". Another wanted to completely eradicate capital letters, believing that periods were enough to signal the beginnings and ends of sentences. He branded capitals as "aristocratic" signs, letter leftovers from imperial Rome. Yet another lobbied for new, simplified grammatical declinations to eliminate the many complex genetive case endings in Russian. He also proposed doing away with the rules which changed verbal endings by gender; the pronouns *he*, *she*, and *they* were sufficient markers of subjectivity.

Equally interesting, and potentially much more useful, was a proposal to exchange the old order of the alphabet (the "ABCs" or *azbuka*) with the "letter configurator" (*bukvosvod*). Instead of teaching children the traditional series of letters in a one-dimensional row from A to Z, why not represent them by way of a multi-dimensional pentagonal star and several exterior concentric circles? High vowels were placed at the top of the star and circles; low vowels at its bottom points. Consonant pairs faced each other at opposite angles. Children were to learn phonetics and the basic contrastive principles of linguistic science along with the alphabet, now mounted upon the political icon of the Bolshevik cause. The *bukvosvod* offered a perfect emblem of the unity of structural linguistics with communist politics.[18]

Others - many of them Esperantists - revived the earlier proposals for Latinization. They wanted to discard Russia's "Church Slavonic", "half-Asian" alphabet; its characters too hard to learn, and too inconsistent between their written and printed forms. Their slogan: "Down with Biblical Antiquity! Give us Latin!" The streamlined Latin alphabet had a special mystique for them. Having recently overcome the myth of Daedalus with the invention of the airplane, wrote the flamboyant N.V. Iushmanov in 1929, Soviet Russia now needed to overcome the myth of the Tower of Babel by creating a new international Latin alphabet. Lunacharskii believed it would help the Soviet Union keep better pace with the technological West. It would also promote "maximal internationalism" within the USSR by bridging its dozens of languages under one standard.[19]

With Lunacharskii's patronage, and buoyed by the fact that many of the non-Russian peoples of the USSR had already begun Latinization, linguists and educators discussed the issue during 1929 in the Subcommission on the Latinization of the Russian Alphabet, part of the Narkompros academic bureaucracy. Under the direction of N.F. Iakovlev and L.I. Zhirkov, both of whom were amateur Esperantists, the subcommission created a Latin script for the Russian language and disseminated a series of exaggerated arguments to promote it. They blamed the Russian alphabet for its "autocratic oppression", "missionary propaganda", and "national chauvinism". They deemed its "national-bourgeois graphical form" unsuitable for the "socialist content" of Soviet publications. They praised Latin's internationalism, simplicity and rationality. They declared it easier to learn than the Russian script and more economical, promising amazing savings in paper and printing materials, not to speak of time, money and energy. Others applied the same rhetoric and logic in their proposal to adopt the Latin letter *i* in exchange for several analogous Russian letters. A few factory newspapers in Moscow even switched to it, with popular support. Vertov used it in his films.[20]

Yet Latinization of the Russian script faced a powerful and varied opposition. Respected linguists (D.N. Ushakov, M.N. Peterson and G.O. Vinokur) and leading Japhetites (V.B. Aptekar' and N.S. Derzhavin) were unequivocally opposed to it. S.M. Dimanshtein, one of Stalin's official spokespersons at this time, joined them in January of 1930, calling Latin a reactionary "Catholic" script.[21] As a result, Iakovlev's and Zhirkov's measures never moved beyond the debate phase.

5.2. The tenuous "hegemony" of formal grammar

When the Bolshevik regime instituted the new spelling rules in 1918, it also charted new ways of teaching the Russian language and grammar in the schools. Both reform efforts displaced the rote memorization of rules with a new emphasis on freer, intuitive learning. Reformers hoped to exchange the old disciplinary regime with a more creative, humane one. Futurist visionaries spoke of projecting the Russian revolution even into the realm of grammar and syntax. They called for the overthrow of the old speech system along with the old social order. "The words of human speech can be divided into two armies: the old and the red", wrote one of them. What is grammar after all? The regulations of the old army of words." When A.A. Bogdanov designed his curriculum for a proletarian university, he privileged science and social studies courses, but left absolutely no room for language study, such was his aversion to traditional modes of grammar teaching. These visions contrasted sharply with the realities of Soviet life. In most secondary schools, language study comprised four lessons per week, as much time as lessons in the natural sciences and mathematics. Not until the higher grades were language lessons reduced to two per week, the time devoted to social studies.[22] The "red" grammar never materialized; Bogdanov's grammar-less proletarian university remained but a dream. Instead, the formal grammar of Fortunatov's Moscow school became the revolutionary standard of the Bolshevik regime.

The school reforms of the early 1920s opened the final struggle between the proponents of logical grammar, mostly traditionalist teachers, against the formalists, representatives of the new linguistics. The "Moscow doctrine" emerged victorious by 1925 as the "hegemon" in Soviet education. Together with Narkompros, the leading pedagogical associations in the country disseminated formal methods throughout the schools. In publications and lectures, formal grammarians taught and counseled teachers on the basic principles of the new grammar and their relation to spelling and speech rules. In state military schools, only formalists were allowed to direct the Russian language departments.[23] The Central State Publishing house approved the works of Fortunatov's school as its leading teacher's aids and textbooks. Peshkovskii's *Our language* was especially influential. The Prague linguist Kartsevskii called it an "extraordinarily important, expressly revolutionary event in the history of Russian language teaching". To celebrate the union of formalist principles with the mass school, the Soviet government even sponsored the publication of Kartsevskii's own grammar in 1928.[24]

These new formal grammars matched well with the "complex method" of teaching. Both emphasized learning as a self-active process. To the formalists, language was the "greatest means of mutual understanding and rapprochement between people", and should "be at the center of teaching in the schools". They did not teach rote, conventional "skills" (*navyki*), which were the concerns of stylistics; but self-acquired, intuitive "real-life concepts" (*znanie*), the true province of grammar, so most of them believed. They designed grammar lessons to teach students "self-control over language" (*nabliudenie nad iazykom*), how to formulate rules in one's own mind, based on the living sounds of a language and its everyday word forms and word connections. They expected children to learn how to speak and write correctly without knowing the complicated, mechanical rules of spelling, pronunciation and grammar; to learn how to spell by their own acts of cognition and understanding, not by set formulas. The meanings of words did not matter so much as their "formal (grammatical) markers" and how they changed in different syntactical contexts. Like the complex method, formalism emphasized learning as a kind of integrated work activity. As one of the original formalist manifestos declared:

> In order to learn a language as a living spiritual activity, it is necessary to observe it as a function of one's own and others' speech . . . it is necessary to reflect upon these observations and phenomena . . . and it is finally necessary to classify this material and come to one's own conclusions, as one would do in the study of natural phenomena. This process of study and education is *labor activity* in the best sense of the term.[25]

P.O. Afanasiev translated these insights into his popular booklet, *The native language in the labor school*, which defined the broader role of language study within the new curriculums of the 1920s. As he wrote in the tradition of Humboldt, "Language is not simply a translator of thoughts already worked out, but an *organizer* of concepts, a means for the formulation of thoughts themselves, a component part of our thought." The role of grammar, newly defined as the "control over language", was to help students master words and thoughts by knowing the parts of speech and their functional relationships, which are registers of "nature (sounds)" and of "the national life of society". Teachers applauded his stress on active learning and creative self-discovery, on language as "energy" (*energeia or deiatel'nost'*) not a mere "thing" (*ergon or delo*).[26]

Inspired by this project to delve into the minds of students and help shape their conscious mastery over language, several prominent formalists revolutionized the schools by recognizing territorial dialects as useful standards of teaching. The old school grammar presumed that the Russian literary language of the educated caste was the true absolute. They now defined this standard as merely one relative "variation" of the whole literary language. Through official Narkompros directives of 1921, the formalists requested that the language of teaching in grammar and pronunciation lessons be the local dialect spoken by pupils. Only later in their studies was bookish speech to be introduced. This new trend in teaching further legitimized the work of the

Moscow Dialectological Commission. Throughout the 1920s, its formalists continued to revise, expand and perfect their work of producing Russian dialect analyses, maps, and atlases. Without shame or fear of being labeled chauvinists, they published new works for the schools and universities on the "great Russian language" and its wonderful plurality of dialects.[27]

As scholar populists of a kind, linguists also turned to the study of social dialects, identifying the unique characteristics of workers' and peasants' speech, collecting them into dictionaries and textbooks for classroom use. They encouraged teachers to use the slang, ditties, sayings, riddles and songs of popular, everyday speech in their lesson plans. Education was to begin with the lower orbits of language and culture, the simple and accessible, in order to reach the higher orbits, the complex and remote fundamentals of the literary language, with greater ease.[28] This nativizing approach even extended to "criminal jargon" (*vorovskoi zhargon*), which became something of a "plague" in Russian primary and secondary schools during the 1920s. Remarkably durable and widespread, reaching from Odessa in the west to Vladivostok in the east, "criminal jargon" devised new slang expressions for the universal business of fighting, stealing, cheating, and carousing. A revolver became a "little lady chekist" (*chekushka*), a militiaman a "bullfinch" (*snegir'*), a thief a "pigeon"(*golub'*). Students learned these words from the street orphans they met in the movie houses and bazaars; read them in the popular works of writers like Mikhail Zoshchenko; or mimicked them from their very own factory-working parents. They spoke them in the hallways between classes and during their school lessons and official meetings. Not to be defeated by this invasion of the street into the schools, educators encouraged teachers to learn slang so as to convince students of its "aesthetically crude and primitive" character, and of the more expressive and beautiful quality of standard literary Russian.[29]

These novel approaches to Russian language teaching were contentious. Most linguists were resolute about teaching the standard literary language rather than its lesser dialect variations, be they territorial or social. M.N. Peterson wanted to raise the masses to a higher standard by teaching the language of the nineteenth-century classics. With several Moscow colleagues (D.N. Ushakov and G.O. Vinokur) he opposed using newspapers as lesson material in the classroom, citing Gus's studies as proof that they were harmful for students. Contemporary writers, he noted with disdain, were using "dialectisms" and words from "street language" which were not at all appropriate for study in the primary and secondary schools. Ushakov was most adamant about teaching the standard literary language based on the properly articulated speech (orthoepy) of the Moscow dialect. Students, he believed, needed to know how to spell and speak correctly. The "criterion for this task must be the cultured Moscow dialect".[30] He argued mercilessly that schools should use and teach a "general language", an "organ of national culture", to raise students to a higher cultural level.

But teachers did not bend to his demands. They wanted to "mix" the language of literature and the language of the street. They even found themselves becoming improvisers, forced to translate textbooks written in the standard literary Russian into the daily spoken Russian language of their students. Said one teacher, "the books are written in city speech, but I must read them in the everyday speech" of our region. Ushakov's project was unrealistic. The Moscow dialect could not act as the one and only standard to promote "the normalization of the Russian language". It was already in competition with the "general Russian language of educated persons" from other dialect regions of Russia.[31]

The continued use of dialectisms and street language was inevitable given the influx of new students into the schools. Teachers needed to understand the systematic rules and patterns of lower-class speech in order to correct mistakes and maintain vigilance over them. This amounted to a "differential approach" and "comparative method" to match the same strategies which Russian language teachers took to the non-Russian classrooms. Teachers had to know the sub-standard regional and social dialect systems in order to better teach the standard language, and in the process "re-forge" the Russian language for socialism. Most classrooms reached a compromise, applying the "norms of the literary language" by way of a "patient attitude toward the local dialect". It was "impossible to struggle against the local features of speech", but it was also necessary for students to "hear the correct Moscow speech" in order to "guarantee general culture" for millions of Russians.[32]

In a tour-de-force of cultural and class toleration, leading pedagogues even amassed convincing scientific evidence to prove that rural school children and street orphans were no less capable than average city children to learn the high standards of the literary language. Their speech patterns were not cruder or more primitive; they were just different, creative expressions fashioned to meet the needs of a particular environment. Teachers needed simply to meet these students halfway, and teach the higher standards based on native patterns and abilities. As A.R. Luria wrote,

> The dialectical method obliges us to reject a static concept of behavior in which types of behavior are studied independently of the environmental conditions and general context within which they develop . . . child-subjects should never be isolated from their general historical circumstances. Education is always group oriented, and the teacher should focus on the socialized aspects of his pupils as individuals.

Luria, who edited this research, later turned it into his classic and influential studies on the social and cultural foundations of cognitive development. His evidence and insights, forged out of the traumatic social changes that had engulfed the Soviet Union, eventually transformed into progressive teaching methods in many an American classroom. Here was an approach as applicable to the children of market capitalism as to those of state communism, one that accepted students on their own terms, without prejudice. But we should take care to note that although wrapped in a cultural pluralism this work was built on the assumption and concluded with the understanding - both rather elitist - that the written word, literacy, was an efficient standardizing tool to turn all those simple rural children into more abstract and complex urban thinkers.[33]

The new formal grammars and dialect studies helped to establish the hegemony of formalism in the USSR throughout the 1920s. But despite these impressive achievements, all was not well in the house of Fortunatov. Formalists were badly divided into "ultra" and moderate factions, each of which proposed and counter-proposed its own definitions of the different parts of speech. Some formalists demanded that teachers follow a strict regimen: always teaching morphology first and only then moving on to syntax. Others were more lenient, seeing formal grammar as an aid for teachers rather than an obligatory plan of action. In another long-simmering battle, N.N. Durnovo and L.V. Shcherba proposed to teach "content" and meanings along with the "forms" of language. This was heresy to the ears of many formalists, who believed that students should define meanings on their own, or at least not during grammar lessons.[34]

These disputes worked an unhealthy effect on the schools. Teachers did not always fully understand or approve all of the points in the formalist program. So "misunderstandings" began with the very first debates shortly after 1917. Some teachers believed that the Bolsheviks had actually created formal grammar as part of a grand conspiracy to revolutionize the schools, or that they were using it for obfuscated ideological reasons to torture teachers and students. Linguists, others said, were weighing the schools down with too much terminology and too many grammatical complexities. Young teachers appreciated formalism but rarely mastered it; older teachers tended to rely on the equally old logical grammar textbooks. Many simply pretended to use the new grammar while relying on the old; only its methods of rote learning and test dictating provided the discipline to teach the new spelling rules with any efficiency.[35]

Pressure mounted in the schools as early as 1925 to return to the teaching of skills and rules, to transform the ideal of "formative education" into the reality of "practical education". This was an urgent necessity since more and more students were entering the classrooms who were not Russian by birth, or who had not mastered the Moscow literary standard in place before the revolution. Teachers had also become burdened by lack of time and materials. D.N. Ushakov even admitted before the State Academic Council that the radical formalist program from the early 1920s had actually damaged the subsequent literacy campaigns since it was poorly attuned to the actual needs of teachers and students.[36]

Linguists and educators responded by changing the curriculums. The 1927 "Narkompros language program" reorganized its lessons according to the traditional distinctions between grammar (the teaching of concepts) and stylistics (the teaching of skills). By no coincidence, Narkompros also published its first obligatory curriculums for the secondary schools in 1927, which abolished the complex method as the central standard and revived traditional divisions between subjects. Reading, writing and spelling lessons were back. The 1928 Conference of Secondary-School Russian Language and Literature Teachers reaffirmed its superficial support for formal methods but "underlined the great importance of the ability to translate this knowledge into skills". Under the pressure of students, teachers, and Narkompros administrators, the formal grammarians also agreed to include lessons on semantics, the "social functions" of language, and "words and their meanings" into their model lesson plans.[37]

5.3. The cultural revolution in language teaching

None of these concessions saved the formalists from the dragnet of the cultural revolution. Between 1928 and 1932, they came under suspicion for their apolitical, idealistic treatments of language, and for burdening the busy lives of adult learners with cumbersome grammar lessons and terms. Critics argued that the "formal analysis of words" was too difficult a pedagogy for vocational and adult students who only wanted practical knowledge and basic meanings. The Japhetites now assumed their cause. Marr referred to the formalist school grammars of the day as "paper canons" unworthy of implementation. His surrogates on the grammar front slandered mainstream linguists for their sympathetic treatments of bourgeois linguists (Humboldt and Saussure); and for their attachments to Plekhanov's theory of hieroglyphics, Voloshinov's theory of neutral signs, and Peshkovskii's "abstract-formalistic" positions. The formalists, in essence, had compressed the living Russian language into the cramped spaces of phonetics and morphology. They had created a tangled web of terms and rules that interfered with the simple instructions and signals of party politics and industrial power.

Marr's Japhetites stood ready to rescue language back along the liberating paths of history. They now redefined the sentence as an "organizational unit of communication, reflecting objective reality through class consciousness". With Lenin's reflection thesis as backing, they revolutionized grammar studies by establishing a priority for the study of the whole word and its meanings (sentence semantics) over the particular sound or word form (phonetics and morphology). E.N. Petrova's slogan, "down with grammar", was every pupil's dream. She proposed to study the social and historical origins of words, or "language as a manifestation of class ideology". Teachers were expected to use industrial metaphors in their lessons, replacing sentimental bourgeois phrases in their schoolbooks with militant slogans from the pages of the ongoing proletarian revolution. The latter, like "love is stronger than death and the fear of death", usually taught tricky grammatical concepts and case endings. The former, like "the rich peasant [*kulak*] clutches bread in his fist [*kulak*]", tended instead to be simple statements of communist ideology.[38]

Danilov and the Language Frontists, who wielded considerable authority in the higher schools and educational publishing, were not afraid to take on the Japhetite offensive, which they accused of trying to "saturate curriculums with an 'historicism' down to Cro-Magnom man", and of repudiating all linguistic forms with their "harebrained", class meanings. They began their own full-scale "purge" of the Russian language, what they considered to be "one of the most conservative superstructures" in Soviet society, so as to clear away all the "vestiges" of the old feudal and bourgeois orders: remnants like "go to the devil" (*nafik*), "riding breeches" (*galif*), "Ford cars" (*fordiki*); sexist phrases like "marry a man" (*vytti za muzh*). In their place, the Frontists proposed a more rationalized vocabulary to match with twentieth-century technology and the revolutionary language of the Russian worker.[39]

In these projects, according to their own citations, the Language Frontists drew from the best methodological and theoretical sources in bourgeois and structural linguists (Humboldt, Bogdanov, Shpet, Vinokur and Gus). Danilov justified their work based on Humboldt's notion that "language is not only something that is mobile, it is at the same time something settled. Language is not only something expressed, but it is also something stated." (Danilov 1931a: 5) Translated into Marxian terms, this meant that his project to create a workers' dictionary, although "reflecting the development of the social-production collective" by way of words, would also serve as a "regulator of this development". To develop clear and concise dictionaries was to "establish correct relations between the different members of the production collective". Time and again Danilov expressed his Humboldtian and Bogdanovite faith in the power of language to move people to action, for "the organization of language as a means of production is at the same time an organization of production itself". Language is not only a reflection of "social-productive collectives", but also their "regulator".[40]

From their posts in workers' faculties and party schools all over the country, Danilov and his Language Front collaborators had already invented the "mass" Russian language readers of the 1920s, in which they wrote articles on the need for clear and concise speech in socialist society, training young communists in the agitational skills of Demosthenes, Cicero, Danton, Robespierre, and the premier Bolshevik orators; as well as in the intricate linguistic rules of pronunciation. Using Shafir's and Gus's studies of newspaper language as evidence, they advised workers to apply active verb forms in their writings.

Danilov counseled workers and students to organize "language culture" clubs devoted to poetry readings, speeches and the literary classics.[41] I.V. Ustinov, a Language Frontist and Danilov's partner in the spelling reform project, had equally broad access to the masses. His textbooks were designed to make language learning easier and more exciting for the "tens of thousands" of new students occupied with political and economic studies. The revolution had provoked drastic changes in literary culture, he noted; some were beneficial, but most were not. Thus now more than ever the Soviet people needed to use correct speech patterns, based on the insights of traditional and structural linguistics, in order to create and communicate pure and precise thoughts.[42]

In 1932, Danilov and the Language Front even proposed an ambitious Marxist-Leninist program for grammar renewal, one that offered to salvage the best theories and methods of formalism. Their "grammar brigade" wrote the Russian language program for the country's Factory Apprenticeship Schools. Like proper communists, the brigadists opposed the notion of grammar "as a descriptive discipline, a codification of internal language facts". Rather, they taught it "in connection with real language as a changing, developing class phenomenon", as "objective consciousness". Yet like smart structural linguists, they were also dedicated to teaching the phonemic relationships between sounds. They did not jettison the formalist accent on concepts and intuition, but allowed students to learn the "dynamics of language development" by self-discovery and the self-creation of new words and phrases. They promised to teach concepts in union with skills. Attracted as ever to the voluntarist notions of Humboldt and Bogdanov, the Frontists believed that their new grammars would compel workers to change the world through language. "Human consciousness not only reflects objective activity", wrote their leader K. Alaverdov, "but even creates it."[43]

Between 1930 and 1933, the Japhetites battled the Frontists for the authority to dictate new curriculums in the schools. With several other linguists, the ever-opportunistic N.F. Iakovlev tried to bridge the gap between them by recasting his old ideas into new ideological form, a materialist grammar based on Marr's theories. He campaigned to turn the formalist hierarchy, which privileged phonetics and morphology over syntax, back onto its feet, just as Marr has turned the "proto-language" pyramid back onto its base. We must begin language study in the schools with the utterance, the "whole sentence" and "whole word", he wrote, only then moving on to study the word part and sound. Yet Iakovlev, as was his custom, did not altogether betray his formalist and structural learning. His concept of the "word-sentence" contained the phoneme as an integral part of the word, just as the word was an integral part of the sentence - a matter of their dialectical (structural) relations. He also wanted students, as language practitioners, to create knowledge about grammar in their own minds, according to their own formally inspired categories of reasoning.[44]

In the end, these pedantic debates swayed no one. The Japhetites won the field. Linguists had already been bickering for decades about this or that new literary standard. But they had little to show for their efforts: neither effective standards to resolve the spelling crisis, nor agreeable principles to resolve the grammar controversies. Policy makers could only take bitter comfort in knowing that students were learning how to spell in Russian, in fits and starts, based on their own regional dialects. Or that teachers were patching together grammar lessons from the half-dozen or so trends that had been thrown at them over the last decade. In these terms, democratization and confusion ruled in the schools, not standardization and order. The masses had been mobilized for language reform, but more on their own terms, less on the state's.

For all of their faults in learning proper spelling and grammar, working Russians were not held back from the promise of upward mobility. But the Russian language, their emblem of national unity and pride, seemed all the poorer. Mainstream linguists (including the Language Frontists), loaded down with all the baggage of formal categories and esoteric terms, were easy to blame for these troubles. The Japhetites, on the other hand, offered simple, ideologically correct alternatives. Their stress on meanings was something the average Soviet administrator could easily understand. As a result, for the next two decades, E.N. Petrova's class semantics often headlined the country's grammar curriculums. Students might continue to write and read poorly. After all, what students did not? But at least they would receive the signal meanings and commands of Soviet power.

Connection between Latin alphabet for Russian + ~~Akkan~~ for langs of East — continuing parallel?

Chapter 6

"A revolution for the east": Latin alphabets and their polemics

Beyond Russia, in the lands of the Soviet east, language reform was governed by the same play of vernacular culture, the same tension between democratization and standardization, but with far more tragic consequences.[1] National representatives set out to refashion their literary communities, to strive for what E.D. Polivanov called the "genuine democratization of literary culture". But they also disagreed about the detail of implementation, about the course of political control. Established traditions, linguistic complexities, and the interference of the central government and its Japhetic cohorts threatened the viability of language reforms at every turn. Simple letters and grammatical forms became highly disputed markers of group allegiances and national identities. At stake was whose dialect, language or culture would dominate a region or republic. Politicians, linguists, and local activists became ever more frustrated by these disputes through the late 1920s and 1930s. They had not even begun to implement new alphabets and literary languages, as the foundations for new print cultures, before these disagreements presented them with their first defeats.

Yet politicians in Moscow were never unduly anxious about these conflicts, or about their own inconsistencies towards them. At different times, but for the same strategic political advantage, the RKPb tolerated the Arabic script, then attacked it; or promoted the separation of literary languages through new Latin scripts, then entertained a limited pan-Turkism by way of unified Latin alphabets. Language reform offered Moscow a rare opportunity to play the formal patron of nativization policy and national development, yet also manipulate these processes for its own advantages. National leaders raised their own agenda, using the unification of Latin alphabets as a cultural opportunity to recoup some of their political losses in the civil war. Alphabets became a ground for national politics by other means. This convergence of interests made language reform possible, yet inevitably doomed it to failure.

6.1. The sources of alphabet politics: Kazan, Baku and Moscow

The Russian script, so delicately modified and nurtured by late imperial linguists for the peoples of the Muslim Caucasus, Volga-Urals, Central Asia, and Far East, experienced some successes and some setbacks after the collapse of the Russian empire. These peoples, especially those having close contacts with their Russian neighbors, either maintained or revised their Russian alphabets, preferring them to other script options - the Arabic and Latin - then under discussion.[2] But the major educational conferences for the Turkic-speaking peoples between 1922 and 1926 resolved to jettison the Russian script from their emerging literary cultures. A. Baitursunov, leader of the Kazakh national movement, referred to Russian and European scripts as chaotic and obscure hieroglyphics to the Turkic mind; instead he created a more popular, phonetic neo-Arabic script for Kazakh speakers. Galimdzhan Ibragimov and Galimdzhan Sharaf fashioned their own neo-Arabic script from Kazan, the most advanced center of Turko-Tatar publishing and literature. Native linguists did the same for Uzbek, Kirgiz, Karakalpak, Uigur, Karachai-Balkar; the Dagestani languages; and the two Circassian sub-languages, Kabardin-Cherkess and Adygei.

Between 1917 and 1928, these neo-Arabic scripts served as the foundations for renascent literary cultures in the Caucasus and Central Asia. They were the natural products of the reformist Jadid program that mixed the dual initiatives of Turkic localism and federalism. They combined the phonetic principle, a powerful standard of mass literacy, popular democracy, and national independence; with the Arabic script, a unifying standard with supranational Islamic values. Even Polivanov, a dedicated patron of Latinization of scripts, praised the achievements of the neo-Arabic.[3]

Rival reformers simultaneously created Latin alphabets for their peoples with similar democratic and internationalist ambitions in mind. They hoped that Latin scripts would be efficient mediums for mass literacy by providing better script representations for native sounds; and that they would mean easier access to European and American print technologies and publications. They shared these hopes with reformist elites throughout Asia and the Middle East (Japan, China, Afghanistan, Persia and Turkey), as well as with leading international linguists and intellectuals. In one of the most celebrated cases, Kemal Ataturk's Turkish Republic began the conversion to Latin in 1928, years after his brethren in the USSR yet based on their model. (*L'adoption universelle* 1934)

The Iakuts, whose language was previously written in a modified Russian script, were the first of the non-Russian peoples to convert to Latin. Their choice was a conscious act of national liberation. The Iakut intellectual S.A. Novgorodov invented the new script in 1917. Baudouin de Courtenay and E.D. Polivanov, his teachers at the Faculty of Oriental Languages at Petrograd University, inspired him to choose the Latin based International Phonetic Alphabet as its model rather than the Russian Linguistic Alphabet, then in use by Russian orientalist scholars. With Polivanov's help, Novgorodov compiled a reading primer by December of 1917. Displaying his respect for national cultures, Polivanov did not unduly interfere in the project but supported it as a service to Iakut national identity. He knew that Novgorodov did not properly apply linguistic science in modifying the International Phonetic Alphabet to the specific sound structure of Iakut. Novgorodov had created less a streamlined alphabet, more a bulky transcription system, representing an extreme number of native sounds. But his choice was deliberate, a new alphabet designed for mass use, according to the radical phonetic principle, "write as you hear". It contained no capital letters or punctuation marks and used dipthongs and extra letter-signs to represent the special sounds of the Iakut language. (Polivanov 1928a: 316-320; Novgorodov 1977: 8-9)

Several nationalities of the North Caucasus followed Iakutia's initiative and began to convert their existing Arabic and Russian scripts to Latin, often with N.F. Iakovlev's aid, during the civil war and the early reconstruction years. The Ossetians began to convert in 1918-1919, the Karachai-Balkar in 1921, and the Kabardin and Ingush in 1922-1923. Educational congresses approved these alphabets and made preparations for Latin scripts for Chechen and Adygei. Some scholars have argued that Iakovlev was nothing more than a "Bolshevik 'orientalist'", "sent from Moscow" to help create these "completely dissimilar alphabets" in fulfillment of the party's "divide and conquer" policy.[4] On the contrary, the sources show that Iakovlev worked closely with leading native linguists and educators to describe and codify their alphabets according to the latest structural insights. The consummate rationalist, he once argued that the accents and diacritical marks which linguists placed above and around Russian letters, so as to adapt them to the sounds of other non-Russian languages, were like annoying flies buzzing about. Better to integrate sounds and signs into streamlined Latin alphabets, he believed; they were much more hygienic.[5]

Some national communists of the North Caucasus greeted these initiatives with optimism. They proclaimed that the "light of the Latin alphabet" would help to civilize the "wild" peoples of the region. They called it an alphabet of "liberation" and took pride in what they hoped would become an all-union movement. Not everyone shared this enthusiasm. The russified leftist intelligentsia supported the Russian language and its script, while the Muslim clerics in control of the religious schools defended the Arabic. Chechen bandits met the Latin scripts "literally with bayonets raised", using them for target practice. In Cherkessia, one of the more enterprising landowners covered himself in a white sheet and pranced around the schoolhouse at night over the course of two weeks, scaring off some eighty children from attending Latin lessons. Such was the fear of what some Arabists called the "satanic" script.[6]

Thanks to its homogeneous ethnic territory, developed literary culture and emerging elite national consciousness, Azerbaijan enjoyed the most resilient movement for a Latin script. From Baku, during the short reign of the independent government in 1919 (the Azerbaijani Democratic Republic), publicists equated Latin with the new military technology and "civilized" culture of Europe, calling it a "nationalization of our language".[7] Immediately after the Red Army's conquest of Azerbaijan in April of 1920, national communists shaped this momentum into state policy. They reviewed the merits of Kazan's neo-Arabic script, but opted instead for Latin, a better means to promote mass literacy and print culture. By early 1922, the Latinists were already publishing the first issues of their newspaper, *The new path*, with parallel columns in the Arabic and big print Latin scripts. S.M. Kirov, then secretary of the TsK AKPb, backed them with propaganda and administrative support.[8] The debates also moved to an all-Russian forum, the official journal *Life of the nationalities*, when neo-Arabists warned that Latinization would fragment the peoples of the East, given the patterns of ethnic and literary development already in place. The Azerbaijani spokespersons took the lead for Latin, which they hailed for its populism and internationalism.[9]

During these years, amid the civil war and its legacies, the authorities in Moscow were content to leave the matter of alphabet reform to the nationalities themselves. This relative detachment stemmed from their drive to ally with the "national progressive intelligentsia" against the "reactionary clerics" of the established Muslim hierarchy. The Bolsheviks could ill afford to alienate their neo-Arabist allies. So they proceeded cautiously, quietly sponsoring public debate between the neo-Arabists and Latinists. Leading Russian Bolsheviks avoided the subject for fear of inciting opposition among devout Muslims.[10] The RKPb did not formally intervene until April of 1922, when the Baku Commissariat and the TsK AKPb sanctioned the existing Azerbaijani initiatives and established their control over them. In September, combining his responsibilities as Commissar of the Nationalities and chief of the Agitation-Propaganda Department of the TsK, Iosef Stalin delivered a major report before the TsK, approving the Latinist initiatives of Azerbaijani national communists and allocating better funding and support. At the same time, A. Mikoian and the party's Regional Committee began to officially promote Latinization and native language teaching in the North Caucasus. Lenin's opinion on these initiatives was passed down to posterity through hearsay. In a 1922 conversation with the leading Azerbaijani Latinist, S.A. Agamalyogly, he predicted that Latinization would become "a great revolution for the East".[11]

Why did Stalin finally agree to serve as a patron of the movement? What might Lenin's rather cryptic words really have meant? The work of the "Commission for Reform of the Arabic Script," established within the Narkomnats in January of 1923, offers us some tentative answers. The Soviet government, which gave the commission the broad sanction to promote an all-union decision in favor of Latin, saw the new alphabet as a chance to combine local cultural interests with central political needs. In the first place, it was not a Bolshevik creation, and therefore avoided any hint of association with Tsarist russification policies or great-Russian chauvinism. Before 1922, the Russian communist party had not dictated its character or scope. The movements in Iakutia, the Northern Caucasus, and Azerbaijan were products of native interests and designs. By supporting them, the party appeared to promote nativization policy, giving peoples new or revised alphabets designed for mass literacy and education.

Yet Latinization also offered Moscow the perfect opportunity to begin to undermine the power of the Muslim clerical establishment, as symbolized through the strange and mystical letters of the Arabic script. Documents from these years consistently spoke of the need to suppress the influence of Muslim clerical educators, and as a consequence the Arabic alphabet and language of the Qu'ran. By forcing the Latin alphabet as the new medium of script literacy, the party would mount an impassable barrier between traditional Islamic print culture and the masses of new "Soviet" literates. Since the vast majorities of the Turkic and indigenous populations of the east were still illiterate, control over alphabet politics meant control over them.[12]

For the moment, these strategic formulas were premature. The members of the 1923 commission could not agree on the issues. Some favored a common, simplified Arabic base. Others proposed a Russian model so that "all peoples of the east will move to a general, European culture through the medium of the Russian language". Yet others argued for new Latin scripts given their successes in the North Caucasus and Azerbaijan. The mediator, N.F. Tiuriakulov, favored reform of the Arabic scripts in the short term and the introduction of Latin scripts in the long. He successfully argued that the government should not ignore the advantages and popularity of the various new Arabic scripts, nor introduce Latin scripts by "decree". Beset by these divisions, the Commission rendered no decisions. One of its final reports of April 1923 concluded that all hope for resolution in the near future, by party decree or by a general conference of experts, was "downright impossible". The political conditions did not yet exist. Traditional Arabist clerics and neo-Arabist Jadid reformists were still too entrenched in local cultural establishments to force a decision. The commission recommended delay the calling of a Turkological Conference to deal with Latinization.[13]

The TsK RKPb continued to patronize the Latin script in Azerbaijan and the North Caucasus, but hesitated from pursuing full scale Latinization beyond. Azerbaijani national communists were all too willing to fulfill that leadership role. They proposed a novel kind of pan-Turkism based on the model of their New Turkic Alphabet (NTA). From the beginning of their work in 1921, the vanguard Azerbaijani Latinists, many of who were Jadidist reformers, presumed to lead the rest of the Turkic-speaking world to their cause. They sent teachers and activists into the North Caucasus and Central Asia to organize friendship societies for the new script and provided them with printed materials and funding. They promoted Latinization as an "important stage in the creation of a new Turko-Tatar culture".[14] S.A. Agamalyogly, Dzhelal Korkmasov, Umar Aliev and Bekir Chobanzade were the first champions for this cause.

Chobanzade proposed the calling of a Turkological Congress (*kurultai*) in March of 1924 to decide on a "unified" alphabet, spelling system, literary language, and terminology for the "different dialects of Azerbaijani, Crimean Tatar, and Turkmen". The Azerbaijani Committee for the New Turkic Alphabet (AzKNTA) campaigned for such a congress between 1920 and 1925. It even called for an all-Islamic Congress to decide the question for the Turks, Persians and Arabs of Asia.[15]

At first, the Volga-Urals and Central Asia were not moved by the issue. Articles and debates on the script question filled the newspapers. Latinists were active in these regions through friendship societies and committees. But their propaganda was unsuccessful. The Second Congress of Uzbek Educational Workers in 1922 applauded the possibilities of Latin, but sanctioned no further action. The dynamic of power shifted only in 1924. Central Asians became more and more interested in the conversion to Latin and sought out Azerbaijani advice. The Central Asian Bureau and Regional Committee of the RKPb began a coordinated offensive, detailing two hundred Turkic communists to learn and propagandize Latin. They were starting from scratch; the Uzbek and Kazakh publishing establishments had no Latin script print materials at all.[16]

Resolute party support for all-union Latinization came just before the Baku Turkological Congress of March 1926, advertised ostensibly as the first such scholarly assembly to examine the ethnic and linguistic cultures of the Turkic-speaking peoples of Asia. In the weeks before the Congress, on the advice of S.M. Dimanshtein and with the approval of Stalin, the Orgbiuro and Politburo of the TsK RKPb designed the shape and character of the event. Stage-managed to enforce Latinization throughout the USSR, the Baku Congress offered Moscow an opportunity to implement its strategic formulas for nativization and anticlericalism. But Moscow recognized even more pressing incentives. Latinization amounted to an indirect but powerful attack on the neo-Arabist national communists among the Volga Tatars, whom the Bolsheviks feared as self-proclaimed "hegemons" of the east. The RKPb exploited Latinization as yet another humiliation for them, another means to "struggle against the counter-revolutionary, nationalistic", pro-Arabic Sultangalievists. It used Latinization as a lever to impose Russian-backed Sovietization and the "esperantization" of culture that the Tatars, both Volga and Crimean, found so distasteful.[17]

At the preparatory meetings for the congress, the TsK RKPb charged its representatives to support Latinization, but to avoid at all costs portraying it as a policy decreed from Moscow. They were not to "force this process" or "take a categorical decision", but rather stress the policy as an achievement of the Azerbaijani Soviet experience. The TsK in Moscow pre-approved the Congress resolution in favor of a Latin script, stressing its technological advantages, the spontaneity of the Azerbaijani initiative, and the need for republican self-determination on the issue. It was dedicated to avoiding all "arguments and conflicts that might please the many enemies of Soviet power and communism". So it dealt with Latinization "carefully and tactfully". Moscow was so anxious about the potential public opposition of the neo-Arabists that it took detailed measures to ensure a favorable vote at the Congress. Stalin received personal reports on the likely count. The TsK's representatives expressly ordered local party and state organs to choose pro-Latin delegates to the Congress. They, in turn, compiled detailed lists of all persons for and against Latin.[18] The alphabet was becoming a visible public sign of loyalty to the regime.

Debate at the party meetings that prepared the congress centered on several questions. Participants engaged in lively disagreements over strategy. Some criticized the party's detachment and inconsistent support for Latin. Others rallied without apparent fear that communists should have the freedom of opinion to speak out for the neo-Arabic script. Kazan's Ibragimov noted that he was not against Latin "in principle", and that his only desire was to save the five hundred years of Tatar literature, its established print establishment, and the advantages of the reformed Arabic. The communist publicist, M.P. Pavlovich-Vel'tman, of recent fame as one of the leading propagandists at the Baku Congress of the Peoples of the East (1920), micromanaged the Baku Congress to ensure a victory for Latin and save the Russian and Azerbaijani communist parties from any embarrassment.

The evidence of this political interference is often stunning. In one light moment, a pro-Moscow national communist even remarked, "we all know this congress is not really a Turkological affair, we are not here to hear the reports of Russian professors, but to clear the air on the alphabet question (laughter)". For a few moments, the free debate of the closed, preparatory meeting even reappeared at the public sessions of the Baku Congress. Ibragimov and Sharaf made the most scholarly and well-argued cases for the new Arabic scripts. Baitursunov reasoned that they were already in use in books and newspapers. Yet a crescendo of arguments from the party sponsored Latinists sent the neo-Arabists to defeat. True to Bolshevik plans, the congress recommended adoption of the Latin alphabet for the peoples of the Soviet east.[19] The party platform triumphed.

But this choreographed victory was only the beginning of a new struggle. In the coming months, the debates turned into polemics. Latinists denounced the Arabists and neo-Arabists in sweeping, highly charged terms. They ridiculed the "half-baked sheikhs, miuridites, and mullahs" of Dagestan and the North Caucasus. They attacked Ibragimov and Baitursunov for their bourgeois nationalism and "patriotic and chauvinistic attitudes" towards national culture. The pro-Latin Bashkirs accused their rivals, the neo-Arabist Tatars, of attempting to impose their own vile "hegemony" on the Soviet east. In Azerbaijan, a crowd of over three thousand workers demonstrating in favor of Latin subjected the old Arabic alphabet to a "public burning". Others buried it in mock graves, and sent hundreds of books written in the Arabic script to the bottom of the Caspian Sea. Speaking out against Islam and the obstacles it posed to modernization, Agamalyogly likened the Arabic alphabet to "all those narrow, curving streets and small mud houses, together with those cumbersome mausoleums, minarets and medresses, symbols of the defenders of backwardness".[20] Latinists time and again referred to the educational and technical advantages of their script in fitting Turkic sounds to proper phonetic signs, arguing that it was a Taylorist or NOTist medium to economize time and energy, equal in efficiency to the telephone and radio.[21]

In response, the neo-Arabists waged a serious counterchallenge from Kazan during 1926 and 1927 for a common neo-Arabic, Turkic script. Under Ibragimov's influence, the Academic Center of the Tatar Narkompros led a successful defensive throughout the Volga-Urals region against the pro-Latin decision of the Baku Congress. The treasurer of the Tatar ASSR budget refused all requests from the Latinists for funding. Raising their defiance even more, the neo-Arabists roundly attacked the Latinists at the 1927 Congress of Tatar Soviets, publishing a fifty-page summary at the back of the Russian text in the newly reformed Arabic script. By then, wrote one critic, "almost all executive officials of the Tatar republic from the party, soviets, and intellectual groups - and all the press workers without exception - were against Latin". The Latinists labeled this nothing less than sabotage, the continuation of the civil war and Sultangaliev's politics by means of language reform.[22]

With the close cooperation of Sharaf and Baitursunov, Ibragimov even created a reformed, united Arabic script for all of the Turkic speaking peoples of the Volga-Urals and Central Asia. This was a powerful lever in convincing the Turkic intelligentsia that the neo-Arabists were the true pan-Turks. "We Tatars are accused of being too revolutionary", said one neo-Arabist in response to the Latinists, but "we are not futurists, we understand revolution as substance rather than as script. Our position is the most revolutionary . . . while you, occupied with formulas, are without ideas."[23] This new movement toward neo-Arabic, pan-Turkic unity posed a distinct and real threat to Moscow, and set the stage for the next round of political intrigues.

In its preparatory conditions delimiting the activities of the Baku Congress, Stalin and the TsK RKPb demanded that no permanent institution, no "Eastern center" or "special turkological organ", should result from the event. They charged the secret police (GPU) to fulfill this condition. The message was unequivocal. The TsK wanted the educational commissariats of each republic to be responsible for Latinization and language reform work in order to ensure the "control of the party leadership". Nativist separation of languages was the standard of the day. At the Baku congress and its preparatory meetings, party spokesmen sympathized with the so-called "popular democrats", shouting down every hint of "pan-Turkism". They voiced the correct class mentality, favoring the adaptation of the written language to the verbal speech of the "peasant *Hinterland*", to the "spoken language of the so-called 'simple people'".[24]

In spite of Moscow's clear cut warnings, the Azerbaijani delegation to the Baku Congress lobbied seriously, just before and during the event, to establish a central coordinating body for Latinization work. Either Azerbaijan acted willfully, or the TsK RKPb changed its position sometime during the congress, for on the very day after it closed, the AzKNTA held its own conference with representatives of the other Turkic republics. Together they planned the organization of a "leading center" to direct the struggle against all remnants of Arabism and neo-Arabism, and to coordinate the linguistic work of all-union Latinization. The conference asked Chobanzade to organize a scientific council and to create a New Turkic Alphabet, on the basis of the Azerbaijani Latin model, to match with the phonetic systems of the different Turko-Tatar sub-languages. Within a year, the AzKNTA became the All-Union Committee of the New Turkic Alphabet (VTsKNTA), which over the course of the next eight years met in executive session to design new print cultures for the Soviet East. The Azerbaijanis rose to leadership over it after 1926 and began to implement their project to unite all the Turkic peoples of the Caucasus and Central Asia under their script standard.[25]

Why did the party compromise on the issue of an all-union Turkological organization under Azerbaijani leadership? The circumstantial evidence shows that the TsK RKPb understood a unified Latin as the lesser of two evils. The choice before it was simple: either work with Kazan's pan-Turkic and pan-Islamic movement based on the new Arabic script, or with Baku's pan-Turkic and anti-Islamic movement based on the Latin. Russian communists naturally targeted the former, given their struggle against the old Islamic elites and the Tatar "hegemons", once represented by Sultangaliev, now by the neo-Arabic Ibragimov. The Azerbaijani variant of pan-Turkism, reduced to a "purely cultural doctrine" after the Bolshevik reconquest, did not pose such a great threat. Plus, Stalin's loyal allies in the Caucasus, Sergo Ordzhonikidze and S.M. Kirov, guaranteed strict supervision over the Azerbaijani national communists in charge.[26]

Besides these very practical motivations, Latinization also had significant ideological value. It corresponded to one of Stalin's guiding formulas - "national in form, socialist in content" - and to his vision of a future, artificially created international language. The Latin script was flexible enough to adapt to the particulars of each national language, but stable and international enough to provide a unified standard of socialist internationalism between them. "Our aim", proclaimed one Latinist, "is toward a maximal adaptation of the alphabet to the given language as well as toward unification of all the alphabets of the peoples of the USSR". The agitational-propaganda activists of the TsK RKPb openly promoted this slogan.[27]

6.2. Turkic language battles of the 1920s

National leaders were able to operate rather freely within these flexible standards. The majority of educated Turkic and North Caucasus leaders recognized the need for compromise: separate languages for native use, a general language for inter-nationality use. At the Baku congress and the VTsKNTA plenums that followed (1928 to 1932), they proposed Turko-Tatar assimilation through one unitary language, but with different dialect standards within it, a "convergence" of languages rather than total "unification". In fact, they resolved to create a three-tiered "cultural-literary federation". Primary schools were to teach the native language, "oriented to local republican dialects"; secondary schools to teach the more unified, regional Turkic language; higher schools were to teach the Russian and European languages. In form, this hierarchy corresponded well with Bolshevik ideological formulas, and their preferences for leading students from local, through regional, to international language usage.[28]

Yet flexibility also meant room for disagreement. The voices of moderation were not always the first or the loudest to be heard. On the one hand, assimilationists forcefully argued for the full unity of Latin scripts between related language groups, ostensibly in service to the party's call for internationalism, but also in order to reunite language groups fragmented by the Soviet demarcation of nations. With several like-minded colleagues at the Baku Congress, Chobanzade proposed maximal unification of the Turko-Tatar languages. Agamalyogly even boasted that the NTA meant a "unification" (*obiedinenie*) of the "Turko-Tatar tribes". On the other hand, separatists promoted Latin scripts fitted to specific national sound systems, in service to the party's call for new "mass" national languages, and also in fulfillment of the inherent nationalism among the Muslim Caucasian and Turkic peoples. They protested against any attempts, particularly Chobanzade's, to create an "aristocratic supra-national" language which no one would really understand.[29] These fundamental disagreements about Turkic national identity translated into the microlinguistic disputes of the VTsKNTA plenums.

The Baku Congress and VTsKNTA scientific council did achieve a measure of agreement about the general linguistic principles necessary to create a unified alphabet for the Turkic nationalities. They defied the historical spelling and its Arabic and Persian rules. They recommended unitary general signs for the shared general sounds (phonemes) of the Turkic tongues. They agreed to apply the sound (phonetic) and sound-form (morphological) principles in tandem. Spelling was to be as closely and economically matched with sounds as possible, but deviations were allowed to keep words of related meanings spelled the same, even though they sounded differently, as a way to maintain unitary spelling and grammar systems. But given the lack of a decisive stand for one or the other principle, and the lack of simple, consensual definitions for both, there was wide room for interpretation and disagreement in their application. Native peoples also had the "full freedom" to choose their own signs for their own particular sounds. B. Chobanzade and N. Tiuriakulov advanced variations of the sound and sound-form principles to match with their own supra-national or national visions. Others proposed even more divergences from the unified alphabet. By 1927, the bickering Latinists had created over fifty different script projects. They may have accepted Latinization, but almost always on idiosyncratic terms. Chaos began to reign rather than coordination, what became known as the 'discord' (*raznoboi*), not because of the principles themselves, but because of the divisions underlying them between peoples and languages.[30]

To make matters worse, the scientific council of the VTsKNTA, directed largely by the Europeans E.D. Polivanov and N.F. Iakovlev, suffered criticisms from neo-Arabists and Latinists alike, both of whom resented outside advice, no matter how well intentioned. Polivanov and Iakovlev formed a solid target for all those national communist leaders who had their own language reform strategies and tactics in mind. The criticisms began with Sharaf's attacks on the "Russian professors from Moscow and Leningrad" during the Baku Turkological Congress. They continued at the VTsKNA plenums, where local leaders resented the consultations of Polivanov and Iakovlev as interference at best, a new kind of russification policy at worst. Believing they had the best interests of the non-Russian peoples in mind when they advised and argued with them, Polivanov's and Iakovlev's good intentions often showed through as patronizing benevolence. Sometimes they were just plain arrogant.[31]

Several specific linguistic issues complicated the negotiations. Most linguists were of one mind that the capital letters of the International Phonetic Alphabet should be the guiding standard for the new scripts. Although he vacillated on the issue for a time, Polivanov eventually agreed on capitals in order to avoid confusion when the Turkic peoples began to learn Russian. Iakovlev wavered too, but eventually crafted a semiotic theory of graphic shapes to define capitals as phonemes of a kind that usefully distinguished meanings between words. Others supported capitals based on psycho-physiological research that showed their advantage in helping people to read.

Yet the Central Asian representatives, ranging from the moderate Turkmens and Uzbeks to the radical Kazakhs and Kirgiz, opposed capitals as extra and unnecessary burdens on their literacy movements. For the Kirgiz representative who delivered an angry speech at the Third Plenum of the VTsKNTA in December of 1928, capitals were difficult ornamental signs, on a par with Arabic letters, which complicated the energies and the costs of literacy learning. But the plenum simply overrode the Central Asians in favor of international capitals. National leaders seemed to be most angry and frustrated that Polivanov and Iakovlev either changed their positions on the issue or abstained. A representative from Turkmenistan ridiculed their indecision. "Thanks to this, you professors have lost your authority; this means that you have no definite positions, even I have turned against you."[32]

The issue of vowel harmony also surfaced time and again at the plenums and set the participants against each other. As a unique characteristic of the Turkic sound system, it dictated the need for a rather large vowel system in order to provide matching sets of vowels within and between words. But for those Turkic sub-languages with numerous foreign borrowings from the Arabic, Persian or European languages, vowel harmony was no longer a dominant characteristic of the language. So leaders of the Turkic nationalities with more developed literary languages (and many foreign borrowings) tended to oppose its codification; leaders of the least developed (and fewer borrowings) tended to favor its use in their script systems. At the Baku congress, these two forces made ready for years of disagreement and dispute. Agamalyogly and Chobanzade rallied against certain uses of vowel harmony as a brake on unification; Ramiz claimed it as Uzbekistan's right to national identity and self-determination. Polivanov and Iakovlev supported the use of the principle, especially for the Kazakh, Bashkir, Kirgiz and Turkmen peoples. They believed that alphabets should not be made harder to learn for some peoples simply to promote pan-Turkic unification.[33] This agitated the unifiers, especially since the two of them qualified their stand by opposing application of the rule of vowel harmony for the Uzbek script.

All of these problems created discord upon "discord" within the Latinization movement. The "Russian" linguists quite often sent mixed signals to national representatives. Polivanov, Iakovlev and Zhirkov once called for a powerful, centralized Scientific Council for the VTsKNTA, or in Polivanov's words, a "war-revolutionary committee" for the "graphic revolution in the east".[34] Their point was clear: complete and quick unification of alphabets would avoid what Polivanov said was fast becoming an "imminent 'Babel'" of languages and scripts.[35] Yet they also often wavered from such headstrong positions, conceding that each language or dialect should also have its own number and kind of letter signs to match with its unique sound system. They harbored no illusions of full unification of alphabets, because any Latin base needed to be revised according to the distinct sound systems of the different languages, especially if the focus was on mass rather than elite literacy. Their eventual hope was to salvage a minimum of unity by keeping the differences slight. Iakovlev referred to his script formulas not as "magical" in any way, but merely as a "technical means" for the "intuitive creativity of each and every people".[36]

Agamalyogly, having little patience for such nuanced approaches, exploded more than once, not only with these professors and their "project mania", but also with other national representatives. To him, they all seemed to be promoting more and more talking and disputing rather than practical decision-making. "Accept our alphabet", he once shouted to them all, "and if you don't, then God take you, go and create your own separate cultures". He and the other

Azerbaijanis on the VTsKNA often demanded unification on their terms alone, favoring centralization of power and of finances in their own hands. They even fought to prevent specific linguistic questions from receiving too much of a hearing in general debate. Representatives of the smaller and more dispersed peoples of the Northern Caucasus and Central Asia opposed such heavy-handed influence peddling, advocating decentralization of power and activity instead.[37]

Ironically, after linguists and cultural leaders finally compiled and approved a unified New Turkic Alphabet in 1928, Iakutia and Azerbaijan became obstacles to its implementation, refusing to dismantle their existing scripts for the sake of full unification according to the new standards. Polivanov joked that Latinists now faced a two front war against those outside the movement who were opposed to Latinization in general, and those inside who had already established their own alphabets. The VTsKNTA put special pressure on Azerbaijan to convert, without success. Its cultural leaders agreed in principle, but they simply did not have the energy, resources and inspiration to retool their existing Latinized print culture. In a rather pathetic turn of events, the first great leader of the Latinization movement, Azerbaijan, was rendered a pariah state if it did not convert to the new alphabet; or an altogether incapacitated novice if it did.[38]

Between 1927 and 1933, a stunning variety of new Soviet national groups, Turkic and non-Turkic alike, joined the momentum for Latinization. Among them were the Nogai, Volga Tatars, Kazakhs, Karakalpaks, Uigurs, Tajiks, Kurds, Abkhaz, Dagestani peoples, Mountain and Central Asian Jews, Talysh, Oirots, Buriat Mongols, Chinese Dungans and a dozen or so other Volga and Siberian peoples. To highlight the new "all-union" character of the movement, the Soviet government re-christened the VTsKNTA as the "Committee for the New Alphabet". Party propaganda now boasted that Latinization was reaching into the distant cultures of the Soviet Union in the same way that collectivization and industrialization were transforming their primitive economies.

For the Turkic-speaking peoples, the base alphabet remained largely the same. But extending Latinization beyond them turned relative order into chaos. The differences between the sound systems of these "new" languages meant changes in the base New Alphabet (NA) itself as well a whole series of extra letters to represent their new sounds. All hopes for unification of alphabets unraveled. National leaders proudly chose different letter-signs to represent the special native sounds of their languages. But this meant "sounds of one and the same phonetic type were designated in different languages by altogether different letters". When European linguists on the scientific council attempted to dictate standardization, they opened themselves to charges of chauvinism. In one colorful episode, Iakovlev took upon himself to replace a diacritical mark (the triangle) for another (the tail) in the Cherkess alphabet. Cherkessians roundly attacked his arrogant disregard for their preference for triangles. Said one angry local, tails were better suited for devils, not for letters.[39]

As a result of statewide Latinization, the NA grew to a maximum of one hundred and five characters: a base of thirty three, with seventy two extra letter signs representing special sounds in the new languages. Iakovlev hoped to reduce the total number of letters to a maximum of eighty-three. But this was a Herculean task, never achieved. In recognition of this discord, state policy shifted from unification of all alphabets to unification of distinct language groups. Each was to have its own unified alphabet and acronym: the New Turkic Alphabet (NTA), the New Mongolian Alphabet (NMA), the New Western Finnish Alphabet (NZFA), the New Northern Alphabet (NSA), and the New Mountain Alphabet (NGA). Unification had been the ideal on the all-union scale. It became the ideal on the regional scale. But everywhere fragmentation was the reality.

The biggest disappointment was the New Mountain Alphabet. North Caucasus leaders, in cooperation with Iakovlev, had created their alphabets rather spontaneously, without much coordination. They had little choice, for though they may have shared a common territory, their languages were quite different. Some of their rich consonantal systems meant bulky and unwieldy alphabets. Abkhaz had fifty-one letters, Abazin and Adygei fifty, and Kabardin forty-six. North Caucasus leaders campaigned for unification of their Latin alphabets as a means to overcome this discord, as well as the very political divisions imposed by the Bolsheviks just after the civil war. They clearly hoped to use language reform to regain some of the unity that they had lost during the years of demarcation. Their maximal ideal was the New Mountain Alphabet. But they had to settle for alphabet unification only of those languages closely related to each other. New Soviet style acronyms were now created for them: the New Adygeiskii Alphabet (NAA) for Circassian (Adygei, Kabardin, Cherkess); the New Veinakhskii Alphabet (NVA) for Chechen and Ingush; the New Dagestan Alphabet (NDA) for the various Dagestani languages.[40] In the end, even the regional New Mountain Alphabet was but a fiction.

6.3. The fragility of new print cultures

These initiatives in Latinization, burdened though they were by disagreement and divisions, translated into some remarkable successes. The VTsKNA and its local committees were quite competent in propagandizing and agitating for the new alphabet. They were also successful in promoting adult literacy and universal elementary education during the 1930s. Most reports confirmed that Latin was much more effective than the Arabic script in teaching people to read and write.[41] The government had elevated the democratization of literary cultures, and therefore literacy learning, as the new state priorities. Alphabet reform served this project well. But these were meager beginnings. Without the proper resources and real authority, the linguists of the VTsKNA were never able to successfully retool beyond simple Latinization into the more complex realms of creating new grammars, language teaching methods, and terminologies for the non-Russian nationalities. They tried but could not keep pace with demand. Expected to complete decades of work in the span of a few years, they only managed to incur the wrath of their critics for mismanagement and delay. Under the revolutionary banner of the Latin script, "language construction" became an empty proposition.

The creation of terminologies offers a useful case in point. The Baku Congress established several working standards. Nations were to choose Turkic terms before non-Turkic ones. The large numbers of Arabic and Persian terms were to remain in the lexicons, but be revised according to the rules of Turkic phonetics and grammar. Future borrowing of Arabic and Persian terms was to be prohibited in favor of adopting international (European and Russian) terms, always adapted to the rules of native phonetics and grammar. These decisions reflected the rather liberal standard of the 1920s: flexible nativization with a minimal degree of international assimilation. Party ideologues called upon native linguists to create terminologies based on the native stock of the "peasant hinterland", in the "interests of the psycho-physiological economy of the speaker". Yet they also encouraged the adoption of loan words according to their international and Russian forms, as long as they were unknown to the population at large.[42]

This work was successful in some regional cases. In 1922, Azerbaijan linguists began to create an inventory of new scientific and political terms from popular dialects, from the regional Turkic stock, and from the European and Russian languages. Their nationalist program was to "liberate Turkic books from the Arabic-Farsi terms of alien peoples" which were inexact and hard to pronounce. Under Chobanzade's influence, they also aimed for the creation of a united, regional "Turkic scientific-literary language" for the Caucasus and Central Asia. In the Kazakh Autonomous Republic and Turkestan Soviet Republic, linguists followed the same timeline and logic. Under Baitursunov's and Polivanov's slogan of "democratization", they first created scientific and political terms from the native Kazakh, Uzbek, Kirgiz, Turkmen, and Tajik stocks, and only later moved toward assimilation of Turkic or European terms, always adapted to native phonetics and grammar.[43]

By 1932, the Azerbaijanis boasted terminological standards in the fields of Anatomy, General Medicine, Human Physiology, Natural Biology, War Administration, Theoretical Mechanics, Electronics, Mathematics, and Psychology. They were privileged with established spelling rules and published dictionaries too. But they still suffered from "extraordinary discord" given that these were created "by bureaucratic decree, without broad scholarly and especially social control". Among the general Turkic reading public, the standards lacked certainty and authority. Journalists and editors made their own rules in newspapers and books, with the result that most publications were plagued by confusing, incoherent, contradictory and "chaotic" spellings and meanings, imperiling respect for national culture.[44]

Uzbek spelling and terminological standards were in worse shape. When the Uzbeks chose a Latin script between 1926 and 1929, their idealistic and nationalistic young linguists implemented a nine vowel system, characteristic of the "purer", vowel harmonic dialects of northern Uzbekistan. In opposition, Russian Turkologists promoted the six-vowel system of the Iranicized central urban dialect of Tashkent, the existing center of print culture and administrative life. Polivanov believed this a natural choice for a base dialect. In his characteristic tone, he belittled the Uzbek vowel harmonists as infantile parochialists and extremists. Trouble arose when, under the pressure of collectivization and industrialization, the Uzbeks assimilated European and Russian words into their poorly developed terminology. This meant mutating the spelling of foreign words to fit into the larger vowel system, at which point the loan words no longer resembled their original roots. Terms became comically long and bulky, immensely difficult to spell correctly. The combination of the larger vowel system with the use of European and Russian words created such a "spelling anarchy" that the 1934 Congress on Uzbek Orthography replaced the nine vowels with six. The Russians won the day.[45]

Even where native terminologies were in place, the whole system of production and distribution militated against their successful implementation. Chronic shortages of human and material resources plagued every national region of the RSFSR and USSR. Natives could not effectively learn the standards of their own native languages fast enough, let alone their new terminologies. The government gave special patronage to the pedagogical colleges and institutes to better prepare qualified literacy teachers. By 1929, every national region was training schoolteachers in the native language. But in higher education, only pedagogical institutes taught their students in the native language with some success, and even they experienced severe troubles. Of the forty-five pedagogical colleges in the whole RSFSR in 1929, only thirteen conducted humanities and science lessons in the native language. The remaining thirty-two, lacking the necessary teachers and textbooks, conducted these lessons solely in Russian, although the native language remained a required subject in most of them. All other institutions of higher professional education trained students in Russian. This meant that most national cadres were unable to work in close contact with fellow natives unless they could first communicate to each other in Russian language degree programs. The same pattern was repeated in most of the Caucasus and Central Asia.[46]

The emerging print cultures of the Muslim peoples were everywhere under strain. From Azerbaijan to Tajikistan, they lacked the paper and typographical equipment to publish newspapers and books in the new Latin script. Their requests to the Committee for the New Alphabet were routed to the Central Publishing House, re-routed to the State Publishing House, and rerouted from there once again. Still required to print the news, editors published jumbled newspapers, half Arabic and half Latin.[47] Typewriters were for the most part unavailable given poor funding from Moscow and mismanagement at the two factories in the country that produced them. Between 1933 and 1935, six thousand typewriters were reportedly produced in the Latin script for the whole Soviet Union: including several hundred each for the larger republics (Azerbaijan, Uzbekistan, Tatarstan and Kazakhstan), eighty five for Dagestan, thirty for Bashkiria, ten for Iakutiia, three for Abkhazia. The all-union state security police (OGPU), whose business was expanding dramatically with the purges, received a windfall of ten. Even these sad measures of resource distribution were inflated. A 1937 report found massive waste and corruption in the whole VTsKNA system of typewriter production and distribution.[48]

These were not the only troubles with typewriters. The Latin script machines did not even have a standard keyboard with unified signs, styles, and placements; they were so poorly designed that typists could not properly learn how to use them. Given their shortages and the resulting increase in demand, the prices of these inefficient typewriters skyrocketed, up to five times the cost of their Russian equivalents. To correct this imbalance, the RSFSR government subsidized lower prices for the Latin machines. But clever entrepreneurs began to buy them cheap, strip and convert them to the Russian script, selling them for a handy profit. The government prohibited this scam practice in decree after decree, but never stopped it. As a result, many offices in the national regions and republics simply used Russian script typewriters for all of their documents, Russian and native, years before Russian-based scripts were forced upon them. The rare Latin-script machine often went unused, except in one case when it served nicely as a doorstop. National elites preferred to use the Russian language in their official business, sensing that Latin, a script without history or tradition, lacked promise for career advancement.[49]

In light of these developments, Latinization and language reform were incomplete and chaotic throughout the Soviet east. In places like Bashkiria and Kirgizia, the Latin alphabet was in use in the schools and press, but altogether absent or poorly integrated into official documents and book publications. People consequently suffered from a "recidivism of illiteracy". School inspectors openly admitted that the boasts of seventy or even ninety-percent literacy in these regions were outright lies. In the North Caucasus, the regional publishing house was plagued by confused spelling, grammar, and literary standards. Most beginning readers could not understand the artificial style of its publications. School textbooks and political brochures were either incomprehensible or boring. The absence of material for pleasure reading, fiction or non-fiction, created an apathetic reading public. In Azerbaijan and Central Asia, the literacy campaigns faltered after a few years of quantitative success without interesting and well-written books and newspapers for beginning readers.[50] People learned the basics of reading and writing, but remained poorly literate without the more refined skills and the foundations of a mature print culture to support them.

6.4. The cultural revolution and the Marr offensive

During the years of collectivization, industrialization, and the Stalinist cultural revolution (1928-1932), Moscow imposed new standards of conduct on the Latinization movement. Its headquarters moved from the periphery (Baku) to the center (Moscow). Speakers at the Second Plenum of the VTsKNTA called for the "liquidation of the old forms of alphabets", and for quicker tempos of Latinization to match the new pace of life. Umar Aliev boasted that the New Alphabet in print served the same purposes as Western style tractors on the new collective farms; both were proof that the Soviet Union had finally entered the machine age.[51] This new climate left no room for the old Arabic script. Latinists began to publicly demean veteran national communists for still using it by force of habit in their personal work, a wide-ranging practice by most accounts. The Latin alphabet became a means of psychological warfare. People literate in the Arabic, which read from right to left, were now forced to assimilate a whole new script which read from left to right. They had to become illiterate in order to become literate all over again. Those who refused were marked as disloyal Arabists.[52] Latin had become more than an alphabet. It had also become a material symbol, joining both word and image in a display of Soviet power over clerical Islam and traditional Muslim culture.

In an interesting turn of events, Lev Vygotskii and A.R. Luria conducted experiments in rural Uzbekistan during the early 1930s proving these points conclusively and verifying some of Marr's points about "sound signalization". Their research showed that illiterate Muslim villagers tended to think in concrete, practical terms. But the semiliterate and literate activists among them, by now educated in the new "Soviet" alphabets, were already able to think more abstractly - that is, smartly. Their research in human "development" reinforced the basic assumptions of the day about social and cultural "development" in general. Basic literacy, the mediation of concrete signs in the human consciousness, was a fundamental tool or lever of political indoctrination (and human progress). Government censors never allowed this work to be published. Perhaps because of the inherent chauvinism in their experiments, seemingly disrespectful of the Uzbek nation; or because of the stunning conclusions, which unduly highlighted the manipulative dimensions of the "cultural revolution" in the "backward" east. (Joravsky 1989: 364-367; and Kozulin 1986: xl)

With the eager assistance of the Japhetites, the latest power brokers on the language front, Moscow now began to attack the "silent sappers" within the nativization movement, any person caught inside the two front war against the deviations of "great power chauvinism" and "local nationalism". According to the first, pan-Turkists like the "venerable professor" Chobanzade had tried to impose a "general Turkic language" on the autonomous republics of the east. But according to the second, more threatening deviation, national democrats like Baitursunov had erected a "great wall between cultures" with their "nationally pure," "artificial" scripts and terms.[53] With their accent clearly on the needs of the center, the Japhetites degraded the Baku Turkological Congress of 1926. It had exaggerated the importance of national (native) over international (Russian) forms in language. They also attacked the local intelligentsia, which had directed nativization in the early 1920s, for creating "puristic" local languages, to the detriment of international communication within the USSR. A leading Japhetite demanded a campaign to "purge" all scripts and terminologies of their local values in exchange for Russian ones.[54]

Purgists from the RKPb and Marr school now targeted the saboteurs and their allies on the VTsKNA, in national scientific research institutes, and in other orientological associations. They blamed the "bourgeois nationalist" Kamchinbek, a leading member of the Presidium of the VTsKNA, for his tolerance toward Arabism and Turkic nationalism. By 1934, they also accused young nationals who were "fellow travelers" from the early 1920s - people like Batu and Ramiz, representatives of the Narkompros of the Uzbek SSSR - for valuing their own national cultures far too much. Co-opted into their own administrative and regional attachments, they had betrayed the Stalinist party line. This was only the beginning of the purges that decimated the national communist intelligentsia over the next decade. At the service of these national democrats, said the Japhetites, were none other than the formalist and structural linguists (Polivanov, Iakovlev, Bubrikh, and Peterson), panderers of Indo-European idealism and formalism. By helping to create new linguistic "forms" for the national languages of the Soviet east, they had promoted fragmented and stagnant literary cultures too, frozen in place and time.[55]

A dramatic shift was now perceptible in the state's priorities toward Latin. By early 1929, S.M. Dimanshtein attacked the tendency of Latinization to "detach" (*otrezit'*) the national regions away from Russia. Propagandists publicly downplayed the importance of alphabet reform. "Language and alphabet are not goals in and of themselves", wrote one of them, but must serve Soviet power. This was an unequivocal signal that the government would protect the modified Russian scripts of the Mordvinians, Mari, Chuvash, and Udmurts from the VTsKNA campaigns. They had never successfully converted to Latin in the first place, and regardless of propaganda to the contrary, had effective Russian scripts at work within their emerging national literary cultures.[56]

The Japhetites focused most of their attention on a broad campaign against Latinization. Marr openly derided it as the "politics of division" (*razbivanie*), which gave "a special script to every gorge and rivulet" in the Soviet Union. You may all accuse me of "Arabism", he once said, but life was better "under the Arabic because people over a large territory" used "one and the same literature and script. But now all of this has been shattered." He and his Japhetites campaigned instead for the "Analytical Abkhazian Alphabet" (AAA), in their terms a superior alternative to the New Latin. The AAA was not really an alphabet but a phonetic transcription system which mixed Latin, Greek and Russian letters. Marr originally designed it as a means to accurately record his multilingual literary texts and his theories of crossbreeding and stadialism. But in 1924 and 1925, during several trips to the North Caucasus, he also worked directly with Abkhazian educational leaders to design a practical spelling system for them based on the AAA, which they soon tried to implement in the schools and publishing.[57]

The AAA did not last for long. By 1928, Abkhazian teachers rejected it due to the sheer number and lack of distinctions between its seventy-eight letter-signs. They were nearly impossible to memorize and adapt to educational and printing needs. Teachers could not learn them well or fast enough to teach in the classroom. Newspaper articles in the new script "stirred up mass reactions from the provinces as to its practical difficulties". Teachers and secretaries loudly complained that it was even harder to learn than the old modified Russian script from the imperial era.[58]

Linguists were not afraid to denounce the impractical AAA. They compared its graphic complexities, the "insufficient discrimination of its characters (marks above and below)", to the ornamentalism of the Arabic script. One linguist gave it the dubious honor of a place in his pantheon of failed attempts at international alphabets. Even Iakovlev betrayed Marr for a time, mocking the AAA as an eccentric museum piece. Others likened the AAA, with all its "combinations of circles and lines", to the archaic "homestead" (*khutor*) style of farming. Under Danilov's leadership, the Language Frontists and Latinists, who had already been cooperating for several years, used the AAA debacle to attack Japhetidology in general. They ridiculed it as a script of "with bobtails all around", taunting the Japhetic Institute, so preoccupied with dead or insignificantly small languages, for its "full disengagement from practical work". In consultation with Abkhaz linguists, they now created a whole new alphabet for the region based on the Latin NA.[59]

Eager to defend their besieged master, Marr's Japhetites began to use the AAA as a weapon to beat their linguistic opponents - traditionalists, structural linguists and the Language Frontists alike - whom they continued to brand as "counterrevolutionary, reactionary forces". They praised Marr's alphabet and his contributions to the reigning party formula of "convergence-mergence", the process by which the many national languages of the USSR were fusing with the one, dominant "progressive" language, Russian. Marr's followers now used the AAA campaign to fully discredit Latinization. They accused the Latinists of promoting fragmentation between writing systems and merely pretending to unification, arguing that Latin served the individual needs of "penmanship" (*chistopisanie*) rather than the broader technological demands of print culture (typography and poligraphy). They derided the "eclectic" professors Polivanov and Iakovlev, "who today say one thing and tomorrow another". They marked the AAA as the complement to the Marxian "new theory of language" and the true vehicle for unification, based on its phonetic qualities and its amalgamation of writing systems.[60]

These controversies poisoned the Latinization movement between 1928 and 1932. The Japhetite attacks had their intended effect. Latinists from the peripheries, who tended to take the word of Moscow as law, confused the arguments and the ideological labels. In the end, they did not know whom to believe, the Language Frontists or the Japhetites.[61] But the ideological guardians of the RKPb knew. In 1932 they disbanded the Language Front and chose Japhetidology as the premier theoretical school in linguistics. Danilov was removed from the scientific council of the VTsKNA; Iakovlev subsumed to a lesser role, as well as to scathing critiques for his own "formalism" and "Saussurianism".

The Japhetites, who were neither devoted to Latinization nor schooled in the intricacies of traditional and structural linguistics, now shared control over the intricate work of language reform.[62] They allowed some Language Frontists and structural linguists to maintain their positions, though not without harassment. In a remarkable turn of events, the Marr school even co-opted certain structural principles (phonemes) into its own ideological orbit.[63] But with an important caveat. Latin forms were not ends in themselves, but means to serve the state's greater ideological ends. Alphabetical literacy counted less now than political literacy. Forms were giving way to content.

The sad results of the Japhetite victory soon became clear. Between 1933 and 1937, Narkompros and TsK RKPb investigations found rampant inefficiency and disorganization throughout the VTsKNA system. It was notorious for ignoring local pleas for assistance. It had such poor ties with the Azerbaijani, Kazakh, Kirgiz, Tatar, Kabardin-Balkar, and Iakut committees that it did not even know who staffed them. Iakovlev once admitted that some sectors of the VTsKNA existed only on paper. As a result, year after year their budgets went unspent. The academic cadres of the national scientific research institutes, which were supposed to help conduct the language reform campaigns, were hopelessly understaffed. Many had only one specialist, usually unqualified, involved in linguistic research.[64]

As their linguistic projects fell into more and more disarray, people all over the country had better reason to appreciate the integrating value of Russian. The multiplicity of languages and cultures in the Soviet Union, once heralded as enriching the Soviet experience, was turning out to be less of a blessing, more of a curse, especially for the non-Russian peoples themselves. With the help of the Marr school, Moscow had placed the distant republics on notice that loyalty and service to it and the Russian language mattered most of all.

Part IV
Statist solutions

Chapter 7

The official campaign for Russian language culture

The "great transformation" after 1928 highlighted rather than resolved the challenges posed by the democratization of national cultures. Nativization of Russian cadres was a remarkable success. A whole new generation of 'promoted ones' (*vydvizhentsy*) from the lower and middle classes entered higher education and acquired administrative power in the wake of the purges. The greatest beneficiaries were young Slavic men of peasant or worker origins. But these achievements were more about quantity than quality. The new jobholders were unprepared, both culturally and linguistically, for their new status. Most of them had poorly mastered Russian. Yet they came to manage the millions of peasant-workers who migrated to the cities after 1928. Together these promoted ones and new city dwellers created a strange hybrid of city life, an "urban peasant subculture", by which they retained their previous rural communal contacts, their undisciplined work habits, and even the cultural dialects and identities of their home villages. They were torn between their own village values and the need to become something urban, something more "respectable", something more Russian.[1]

The nativization campaigns among the non-Russians also enjoyed impressive successes, with variations. They too had their newly promoted cadres in education and administration.[2] But for all of its success, the government still faced a whole series of glaring "contradictions and limitations". The numbers of new jobholders, often simply achievements on paper, masked deeper and more abiding failures. Stalin's economic priorities dictated that the non-Russian promoted ones be placed at the lowest echelons of industry and the bureaucracy; or that where they held higher posts, be supervised by more efficient and reliable "Europeans". Even when natives were successful in achieving some upward mobility, their poor literacy, sometimes in their own native language but most often in Russian, placed severe limits on their career advancement.[3]

The country now faced a choice. Either continue with the course of radical experimentation so characteristic of the NEP period and the early Stalinist cultural revolution, or establish a new regime of "cultural orthodoxies". Soviet leaders chose the latter. In the workplace, they promoted specialist and wage hierarchies at the expense of class egalitarianism or nativization. They brought order and discipline to the schools, professions and sciences by ending experimental methods and leftist "harebrained scheming". In exchange they imposed a unitary, conservative order.[4] These trends were not simply imposed from above. The new cadres of jobholders wanted little more than to settle down into their newly found posts and status. They yearned for cultural norms and security, what Vera Dunham has called *kul'turnost'*, a middle class "program for proper conduct in public", modeled in behavior and dress. Their ardent desires were for material possessions - symbolized by the pink lampshade, lace curtain or rubber plant - and tasteful forms of entertainment and music. In film and literature, they saw their strivings reflected in public celebrations of family values, folk culture and the capital city, Moscow. They expressed their centrist values in language as well, desiring to speak and write correctly, both according to the high literary standards of Russian and the party's correct ideological idiom.[5]

These cultural conservatisms spread throughout the multiethnic USSR. Russian middle class values eventually translated into Russian national values. The government subjected the non-Russian languages to several waves of russification, at different times in the 1930s and with varying effects, which stamped Russian terms and spelling systems onto their literary cultures. This policy represented a blatant violation of the political compact between the center and the peripheries from the 1920s. Where the state had already been successful in sovietizing by proletarian content, it now attempted to russify by national form. In little more than a decade since the establishment of the USSR, its leaders fancied that they were living the very formula of convergence-mergence announced in party ideology. Boasting a supreme confidence, they believed that they were making the ABCD hierarchy and Marr's crossbreeding and stadialism come true. For there was no better proof to them that the historical dialectic of convergence-mergence was happening than when non-Russians combined native and Russian sounds, letters, and terms in their spoken and written speech.

Yet the common theme here was that the Soviet Union was still a country only becoming literate. If there is an emblem for the decade of the 1930s, one becoming ever more acceptable to Soviet historians, it is that rising Stalinist elites were 'semiliterate' or 'half-literate' (*malogramotnyi*), with all of the values and behaviors attendant to such a state of mind. They were still unformed, raw recruits, anxious to establish a place for themselves in the apparatuses of power, vulnerable to the conformist, sloganeering orthodoxies of the day.[6]

7.1. Mastering the 'great Russian literary language'

By 1932, the party signaled that the cultural revolution in linguistics was over. It targeted "naked technics (formalism)"; the concept of language as internal, "neutral ideological sign (Voloshinov)"; and the "fascist theory" of Indo-Europeanism. Lenin's reflection thesis, reinforced by Marx's authority from *The German ideology*, taught the country greater truths. Language was indeed "objective reality", real "practical consciousness". The latter schools of thought were effectively banished; Lenin's reflection thesis became the official party dogma. Or in Iakovlev's words, "Saussure's false theory of signs" was to Marxist-Leninist reflection theory "as the heavens were to the earth". Party leaders simultaneously berated all those "language politicians" who were peddling utopian ideas about language reform (be they Language Frontists, Japhetites or Esperantists), caring little for their esoteric linguistic debates over spelling and grammar. They had even less patience for their disruptions in the schools. Abandoning the earlier debates and experiments, they now demanded conservative standards to bring the classroom up to Russian rather than Russian down to it.[7]

The 1929 spelling project, which I discussed in chapter five, promised its benefits only in the distant future, mostly to generations still illiterate. For the present, it guaranteed only the same kinds of dislocations which people had already experienced in the 1920s, with most damage to the recently literate generation just coming into or consolidating power. It would have had to learn spelling all over again. Party cadres dreaded their own spelling lessons, not to speak of the promise of more. The "thousanders", urban cadres who descended on the countryside to promote collectivization, had to complete four or five years of education in six months. They were seasoned and tough activists. Of physics, mathematics and Russian language lessons, they disliked the latter most of all, and spelling lessons even more.[8] They were one of many influential interest groups that did not need further educational turmoil on the spelling front.

Throughout the 1930s, linguistic commissions at the highest state levels continued to experiment with spelling codes, handbooks and dictionaries in order to achieve a proper "reordering" of the orthography. But even these minimalist projects stalled time and again in committee debates, sometimes thanks to continuing arguments between the Language Frontists and Japhetites. Linguists bickered, as always, about specific sounds and spelling principles. Their handbooks, filled with contradictions, still promoted more confusion than clarity among typographers, publishers, journalists and students.[9] As chair of the Narkompros Governmental Commission on Reordering the Orthography in 1936, A.S. Bubnov angrily reacted to the delays. "The young generation is today without tradition", he said, "'without fear or fault'". He called on the state to clear away "all of the deposits, the dirt of the ages", and finally establish new spelling standards for better literacy.[10] Discipline was the new slogan of the day. But Bubnov was not long to serve in his post, for he was soon counted as a victim of the purges. These were not the times for decisiveness on such delicate issues. So the Narkompros decrees of 1917 and 1918 and the disputes about them lingered in dispute.

On the grammar front, the formalists were able to recover some of their losses from the Japhetite barrages. True, they remained open to charges of "left deviation" and ideological disloyalty. Yet the government recognized the utility of formal grammars in the schools. Given the poor quality of Russian language studies in the eighth grade for the 1932 school year, Narkompros reduced the portion of classes dealing with historical issues and Japhetidology and devoted more time to the "concepts and skills of correct reading, writing, and speaking". By the late 1930s and 1940s, Narkompros also began to approve more and more school textbooks by formalist grammarians. Simultaneously, the Council of People's Commissars approved new language teaching curriculums for university education that emphasized the linguistic principles of Potebnia, Fortunatov, Shakhmatov, Ushakov, Peshkovskii, and Afanasiev.[11] Marx, Lenin, Stalin, and Marr were still obligatory readings, but the emphasis was now on the disciplinary value of these other classics.

The Seventeenth Party Conference of 1932 set the tone for this new conservatism, committing the government to the fight for cultured speech, to the struggle against "street language" (*blatnaia muzyka*), "hooliganism in language", "lisping language" (*siusiukanie*) and "narrow-mindedness" (*deliachestvo*) in speech. It called for a Bolshevik-Leninist vocabulary, one which was "scientifically correct" and which "objectively reflected real reality". Menshevik terms like "alienation" (*otchuzhdenie*) were out; Leninist phrases like "expropriation of the land" (*ekspropriatsiia zemel'*) in. This did not mean the creation of a dialogic communist language for all of Soviet society, in the manner of the Language Front's proposals. The elite language of the party remained explicitly inviolable and separate from the everyday language of society. The vanguard party spoke to the masses in one voice so as to raise them up to the proper class consciousness in the correct ideological idiom. It very nearly amounted to the creation of a "totalitarian" language, with immense power to impose new ways of "one-dimensional" thinking on people's minds.[12]

The party idiom, disseminated among the masses of workers and peasants, enjoyed its own unique style. Through noun phrases and passive verbal constructions, it reflected a syntax of political obedience. In typical ideological statements, the absence of active verbs hinted at a preexisting, even "magical" reality, always immutable and true. Through the polarity of words or phrases and the formulaic repetition of stereotypes - "Soviet internationalism" versus "capitalist imperialism" - the party idiom expressed its own "axiological" contrasts between good and evil. Through "the uncritical use of authoritative quotations" and a ritualistic, solemn style, it commanded respect and loyalty.[13]

The press remained the party's "decisive weapon" by which to enforce its truths, far stronger than any bureaucracy in its direct links to the people. In a stroke of Pavlovian genius, with a little help from Marr's new theory, the party used its central media organs, *Pravda* and *Bolshevik*, to send waves of messages, what it called command "signals", to party members and the public who lived below the rarified heights of Moscow. Signal articles, repeated time and again in the central and local press organs and radio, ensured the proper translation of party messages, by substantive content and language form. As Suzanne Rosenburg wrote of her years in journalism, "you arrived in the morning and carefully perused every line of the *Pravda* editorial. In it were the cues for your topics and how they should be presented to the reader. Whatever you contributed, regardless of your beat, had to be an enlargement and illustration of the Party stand."[14]

The government began to vigorously promote its political idiom in the form of a new proletarian literary genre and class dialectology. Maxim Gorkii's new journal, *Literary studies*, offered a common proletarian standard, "socialist realism", to all the young writers not yet attuned to the standard Russian literary language. Given his abiding fear of a possible corruption or "dialectization" of the Russian language among the rabble of workers and peasants, Gorkii displayed his own middle brow fiction, in a socialist realist style, as a model for young writers to imitate. As he wrote,

> In the realm of verbal creation, linguistic and lexicological ignorance always appears as the sign of a low cultural level and is always accompanied by a lack of ideological formation. It is finally time to recognize this . . . . Literature must be purged of its linguistic weaknesses; we must struggle for simplicity and lucidity, for those skillful and honest techniques without which there can be no ideological clarity.[15]

Several linguists, L.P. Iakubinskii and V.N. Voloshinov, by now co-opted into the Marr school, contributed a series of articles to Gorkii's journal. The Bolshevik revolution, they argued, had undermined some traditional forms of the Russian literary language, namely through the vernacular elements of class and social dialects. They discussed how the new generation of Soviet writers might fulfill their roles as linguistic modernizers by maintaining the stability of traditional forms for correct usage, yet also by drawing from the new proletarian and collective farm lexicon and style. The point, as Iakubinskii put it in a most revealing statement, was not to create automatons who simply parroted party formulas and Leninist phrases, but competent readers and writers who precisely understood words and their "concrete" meanings. From the Japhetite ILIaZV, V.M. Zhirmunskii studied the Russian and non-Russian dialects of the USSR in their class, social, and national contexts. He similarly argued that the national language was a stable, overarching standard, while class and social dialects served special social functions within its realm, if always dialectically "interconnected" and mutually enriching. The ballast of national linguistic form was not a burden to be despised, but a heritage to be adapted to the new purposes of communist ideological content.[16]

Throughout the 1930s, as such attention to the class aspects of language grew, the study of regional Russian dialect variations waned. The Japhetites closed down the Moscow Dialectological Commission in 1932, subsuming its activities within the renamed "Institute of Language and Thought" (formerly the Japhetic Institute). Dialecticians, once concerned with territorial and linguistic distinctions, now focused on peasant dialects by their class categories and sociopolitical vocabularies. Jettisoning decades of detailed work by Moscow's dialectologists, government administrators became almost blind to the regional dialect variations of Russian. Unlike the class dialects of urban workers and collective farmers, they were a mark of Russia's backwardness. As such, educational administrators trained teachers to detect the speech habits of different strata of the rural population with the aim of suppressing them for more ideologically correct forms.[17]

In defining these new approaches to word study and usage, the government did not pretend to impose a new communist language upon the USSR for all functions and for all time. It simply wanted to standardize ideological discourse, to discipline political thinking, and to calibrate public behavior. It strove to create a minimal working vocabulary as part of its political "catechism", not to refashion the Russian language as a whole. No matter how heavy and formulaic, it was quite effective as a standard and as a shaper of ideas and attitudes, especially among those very party activists who disseminated it. They after all, tended to believe in the very slogans they enunciated.[18] But the government was never completely able to control how these standards were received among the people, or how they combined with the stubbornly resilient regional dialects. After all, Humboldt had already taught several generations of educated Russians that language was, by its very nature, always something stated and something expressed; something stable, yet also something mobile. The new party standards did not mean that people immediately lost their sense of play and metaphor, their ability to shape the singular forms of language into new, shaded, plural meanings. Russian speakers always maintained their power of protest through the ironic use of political idioms, the slang speech of the labor camps, and the parodic style of jokes and anecdotes. Thus even the "official language" and "linguistic imperialism" of the Soviet regime, as Katerina Clark has noted, could not escape the "latent ambiguities" and "cross-fertilization" of individual minds.[19]

These centralist strategies were also a function of the government's continuing struggles with "backwardness" and illiteracy. The country had undergone a rapid democratization process and literacy campaign through the 1920s, which had brought newer and greater numbers of Russians into the schools and had taught them how to read and write. But the process was irregular in its successes. The "Down with Illiteracy Society" enjoyed only spotty progress in the 1920s. It was created with great publicity, but in practice could only boast of "paper achievements". This was a result, in part, of political tactics. Even when supplied with funds and materials, the society focused on adult illiteracy, in the interests of building a pro-Bolshevik political consensus, at the neglect of teenagers and children. (Kenez 1985: 154-166) This tactic changed with the militancy of collectivization and industrialization in the 1930s. As the government conquered the economies of the peasant villages in these years, it also established programs for compulsory education and universal literacy. The number of rural students rose from eight million in 1928 to fourteen million in 1933. The growth of literacy enjoyed similarly remarkable success. But advances in the numbers of literates did not automatically mean the creation of a literate culture. Most people read and wrote poorly, thanks in part to the poverty of educational resources. Rural schools suffered from dilapidated physical plants, shortages of textbooks, paper and pencils, as well as poorly paid and poorly trained teachers. The literacy reading rooms, libraries, clubs, and cultural houses of the USSR were inadequately staffed and equipped.[20]

In sum, the literacy campaigns did not give many Russians a full "mastery over the standard Russian language". Most workers and peasants remained only 'semiliterate' (*malogramotnyi*), poorly tutored in correct speech, spelling, grammar, syntax, and style. Or in the pithy words of a TsK RKPb statement, the USSR had failed to experience the Hegelian leap from quantity to quality.[21] Equally troubling were reports that droves of Russian secondary and university students were failing their Russian language courses. In north central Russia, most "failing" students were not able to successfully complete their secondary education because of poor grades on their written Russian examinations. Government leaders of the area recognized that the crisis spread into all corners of their districts, although it was "especially bad" in some schools, where the failure rate in written Russian reached up to seventeen percent of the student body. In the higher schools, spelling illiteracy remained a special problem.[22]

During the middle and late 1930s, linguists and educators took recourse against these failings by increasing the hours of Russian language instruction, fortifying grammar teaching from the primary to the higher schools, and attempting to instill in students a respect and love for the Russian language. "Literacy must become a matter of honor for every student", commented G.A. Mel'nichenko, a language teacher and patron of formal methods at the Iaroslavl Pedagogical Institute. Party media watchdogs also targeted imprecise, boring and downright "bad" language and "semiliteracy".[23]

The Secretariat and Orgbiuro of the TsK RKPb, under the authority of V.M. Molotov and A.A. Zhdanov in particular, took a special interest in these problems. They promoted the "cultivation" of correct Russian speech along with Gorkii's new genre of proletarian "socialist realism". The Orgbiuro reprimanded the Moscow Finance-Economics Institute in 1934 for enrolling Russian students who were not sufficiently literate in their own language, demanding that similar higher schools impose stricter standards. It took care to provide beginning readers with their own simplified, weekly special-format pages in their favorite newspapers.[24] Thanks to Molotov's personal intervention and the patronage of the TsK in 1935, D.N. Ushakov was able to complete Lenin's beloved language project from civil war days, the *Dictionary of the Russian language*. Uniting words from the classical writers of the nineteenth century and the best Soviet writers and orators of the twentieth, the dictionary was proof positive of the USSR's fortifying speech community. At the same time, G.O. Vinokur went to work planning courses on the history of the Russian literary language for the higher schools, as well as a "normative grammar of the Russian literary language" to supplement ongoing work on the dictionary and spelling projects.[25]

The government did not act alone in reestablishing these standards. A popular conservatism from below helped to reinforce them. It developed from the scope and character of the literacy campaigns in the 1920s and 1930s, which left a lasting impression in people's lives. Workers and peasants who were becoming literate disapproved of slang and colloquial language in print. They admired the simple, standard speech of high culture, just as they demanded literature with a "readable and clear message" and realistic and meaningful portrayals of their lives. People who rose to urban employment and literacy so quickly became proud guardians of the Russian language. They also became respectful admirers of the linguists who helped to create their alphabets, grammars and lexicons.[26]

Most crucial was the advent of mass radio in the 1930s, which allowed Russians to listen to themselves for the first time, to highlight the differences in their regional dialects, and to come to appreciate the need for new, inviolable standards. Thanks to the "language creativity" of the masses, wrote the linguist S.I. Bernshtein, our cities are now filled with the dialects of "Vologda and Smolensk, Pskov and the Don, Siberia and the Volga". His insights had clear political implications, which he was not afraid to voice in public. The united worker-peasant state was something of a myth. "In terms of language", he wrote, "the proletariat is not homogenous." Linguists realized the difficult truth that the speech rules and standards from before the revolution were no longer valid. But they could not agree how to institute new norms. A mood of pessimism filled their reports given the enormity of the problem. They needed to rewrite the rules for dialect configurations that had not yet been studied and codifed. They had to train teachers who were almost totally ignorant of such standards and who spoke in dialectisms themselves.[27]

D.N. Ushakov, the unbending conservative, was perhaps the most successful linguist to establish new speech standards. Between 1932 and 1941, he served on the All-Union Radio Committee as a consultant to announcers, giving reports and seminars to correct their pronunciation errors on the air.[28] Radio renewed his hopes from decades before to establish the Moscow dialect as an all-union standard. Radio gave him and Russians the "opportunity for real interaction between the speakers of the center and the listeners of the peripheries". Although he concurred with most educated Russians that "there is no single Russian language in the expanse of its expanding territories", he still yet found general agreement among radio listeners that his Moscow norms were the proper standards. Ushakov publicized them on radio programs, in booklets, and in dictionaries; they even became "obligatory for all announcers in all republics and regions of the USSR". But the imposition of these norms brought more disputes than agreement from everyday listeners. Their letters to the committee and Ushakov from 1938 are filled with questions and criticisms regarding what, to them at least, were confusing and contradictory standards of speech. As one report summarized, listeners "react to every little mistake" of pronunciation; they "do not want to hear even one incorrect stress, even one mistaken word, from the mouth of the announcer". They want "pure, precise, lucid" speech.[29]

As such attention to the "great Russian literary language" increased, so too did praise and honor for the great linguists and grammarians from the past: Potebnia, Fortunatov, Shakhmatov, Baudouin, and Peshkovskii. Their portraits now graced the academic journals. In 1937 the country celebrated the centennial of the death of Alexander Pushkin, the "creator of the Russian literary language". The government republished his works in mass editions, converted his stories into plays, operas and musical extravaganzas for popular consumption; and promoted ritualistic worship of Pushkin through libraries, shrines, pilgrimages, and state prizes.[30] By 1938, earlier critiques of "bad" language and semiliteracy were curtailed, replaced by panegyrics to the Russian language of Lenin, Stalin and Bolshevism as the "most accessible, clear, living" language, the "best literary language", the "language of the party" which the "masses love and value".[31] New standards of loyalty and minimal standards in correct speech had been defined; pluralism in either ideology or word choice was put at risk. Stock in the Russian language was on the rise.

7.2. Political literacy for the languages of the east

In the lands beyond Russia, Stalin's revolution in industry and agriculture forced a new regime in language reform. The goods and services of modernization demanded a closer, layered fusion of the native and Russian tongues. Soviet society now needed a single working vocabulary for science, technology and ideology. "By the term 'literacy'", wrote S.M. Dimanshtein, a director of the official campaign, "we now mean not simply alphabetical literacy. This is not enough anymore. Today we demand political and technical literacy in the broadest sense of the term."[32] For the national republics and regions, the government shifted its ideological attention from the simple ABCs to the ABCs of communism. Language development became subject to the dictates of an authoritarian dictatorship presiding over a massive and unprecedented economic transformation. Power and production became more important than the people.

The first distinct attempts to coordinate russification of the eastern languages came in 1932. With the sanction of Narkompros, the Language Front and the Scientific Research Institute for Linguistics (NIIaz) set out to displace the VTsKNA and take central control over language reforms throughout the country.[33] They focused their attention on non-Russian terminologies, which were so poorly developed that translators were unable to convey the crucial distinctions of Marxist-Leninist theory from Russian into the native tongues. The party's most important political brochures were rampant with distorted political meanings. In mild cases, the Russian word "proletariat" (*proletariat*) was translated into Tatar as "people" or "nation". In more serious cases, such lapses entered the realm of counterrevolution and sabotage. A Bashkir translator once defined the communist party's role not as the "resolute rudder" of the working class but as its "tail". Azerbaijani translators filled Stalin's *Problems of Leninism* with amazing political distortions, turning "colossal" (*kolossal'nyi*) into "terrible" and "soviet power" (*sovetskaia vlast'*) into "soviet dictatorship". Moscow was saying one thing, the peripheries another. Such commentaries reaffirmed the need for a decisive terminological reform.[34]

G.K. Danilov and the Language Front came to the rescue. Their terminological brigades combined the structural principles of their teachers with a public campaign to russify the languages of the east. They focused their efforts on terminologies because, as plastic and artificial systems, they were the "most socially expressive aspects of language". Terms, they argued, were also the most structured elements of the lexicon, for they always derived their precise meanings from their position in the broader terminological system, in direct point of contrast with other terms. In this work, Danilov's brigades openly promoted the "interests of the governing class" and "hegemon of the revolution", the Russian proletariat. If the Russian industrial and collective farm worker were now the frontline soldiers in the class struggle, then Russian as the "language of the proletariat" should become the standard around which all languages revolved. This meant that the non-Russian nationalities should always borrow "national" terms (dealing with Marxism-Leninism and the Soviet state) wholly and directly from Russian; and "international" terms for science, technology and general politics from the languages of the developed capitalist countries, but always through the grammatical forms of Russian.[35]

The Soviet government may have disbanded the Language Front, but it also deftly salvaged some of its terminological principles. In his manifesto for the russification campaign, Dimanshtein stressed that the non-Russian peoples of the USSR were now to extensively borrow any and all terms that met "the demands of Soviet reality". Words with a special "piquancy" from the Marxist-Leninist vocabulary and from international terminologies - *bolshevik, sovet, proletariat, klass, dialektika, sotsializm, materializm, filosofiia, induktsiia, kondensator, radiofikatsiia* - were to be adopted whole, according to Russian spelling and pronunciation. Form had to follow content. The spelling and pronunciation of some words and terms were simply too important to be left to native, non-Russian forms. Dimanshtein thus announced the unity of socialist content with national linguistic form. To fight "vulgarisation" he also demanded more precise translations and distinct meanings of certain class based Russian terms. The non-Russians had to better understand the differences between "price" (*tsena*) and "value" (*stoimost'*), "state" (*gosudarstvo*) and "people" (*narod*), "dictatorship" (*diktatura*) and "power" (*vlast'*), "agrarian" (*agrarnyi*) and "peasant" (*krest'ianskii*). After all, the party nomenclature was all about words, which in turn were all about objects and actions in the real world. Ensuring the precision of meanings between "name" and "object" was worth the trouble, a guarantee for proper conduct and behavior.[36]

In the wake of these broad policy statements, the Commission for Technical Terminology of the All-Union Academy of Sciences started work almost immediately to establish a scientific-technical terminology for the whole USSR.[37] But the government's primary interest was in standardizing words of the official political idiom. In the years just after Dimanshtein's pronouncements (1933 to 1937), the Orgbiuro TsK RKPb centered its concerns around correct, coherent translations of the classics of Marxism-Leninism from Russian into the native non-Russian languages. It patronized courses for translators at the Orientological Institute in Leningrad, at the Nationalities Institute in Moscow, and in the capitals of most major republics (especially for the Tatars, Bashkir, Chuvash, Kazakh, Kirgiz, Uzbek, Tajik, Turkmen and Buriat-Mongols). It took attentive care to publish the classics of Marx, Engels, Lenin and Stalin in native-language, multiple-volume sets for all of the small and large nationalities of the RSFSR and USSR.[38] Moscow bureaucrats now redoubled their efforts to apply Russian as the official state language. In one case, the USSR Commissariat of Communications decreed a set of minimal norms necessary for national communication workers to master Russian. Central Asians complained that this was a crude example of "great power chauvinism", a case of how Moscow "underestimated the importance and urgency" of nativization policy, trying to impose one dictate upon all the varied peoples of the country. Yet no redress was forthcoming. The minimal norms stood fast.[39]

The government put the Language Front's principles to its own uses. But in their haste to revolutionize language, the Frontists had mistakenly repudiated the ABCD hierarchy and Marr's model of language crossbreeding and stadialism, what Dimanshtein called the "differential approach", based on the "concrete conditions" of each "given national culture", or in short the "law of language interaction". The government was not out to russify whole languages, only certain of their parts. Its aim, to create a network of communicative power, an economy of linguistic scale, centered on the Russian language. The new standards and borrowings were not meant to threaten the basic lexical funds and grammar systems of the native tongues. Local languages would not suddenly and totally lose their significance to an all-powerful Russian language. Besides "piquant" terms, all other borrowings were in fact still to be fitted to national linguistic forms (native phonetics, grammar and syntax). These proposals were no less russifying than the Language Front's. They were simply more tolerant, more flexible, more dialectical. Based on the ABCD hierarchy and the pyramid of convergence-mergence, they recognized both the status and plasticity of the non-Russian languages, including the Slavic languages, Ukrainian and Belorussian. But they also placed them at the lower end of the historical scale. Within most native print cultures, for example, native terms and styles were most common in children's texts or in elementary school usage. Russian terms and styles dominated adult political and technical publications, as well as in the secondary and higher schools. By way of a curious "division of labor", in George Liber's apt terms, the native tongue was left to the home, street, and personal communication. Russian was centered in the serious world of public discourse.[40]

7.3. Iosef Stalin's utopian moment

The pyramid of convergence-mergence may have begun with the non-Russian languages, fusing them with Russian, but it did not end there. As Marr had once proclaimed, "the problem of terminology is the problem of the language of the future". Stalin too had argued that languages developed from "differentiation to assimilation", in conjunction with the forces of production, a process which would lead to a single world language. By 1935 he even proposed that a "fusion" language - a mixture of English, French, Russian, and perhaps even Esperanto - was quite possible in the future, as opposed to any one "victor" national language. "In the period of the victory of socialism on a world scale", he wrote, "the national languages without exception will merge into one general language".[41] Enthused in part by this theory on the "inevitable fusing of languages", in part by his own longing for an "administrative utopia" of managers and engineers, Stalin's regime now promoted the creation of an international scientific-technical terminological code. It was based on the Latin alphabet and the Esperanto language, two linguistic projects that he had patronized since the beginning of his revolutionary career. Perhaps remembering those lonely days of imprisonment and exile when he learned Esperanto, Stalin still entertained its utopian possibilities.[42]

The Esperantists now received a new lease on life through the Technical Code Commission of the All-Union Committee for Standardization, under the direction of their longtime leader and former Language Frontist, Ernst Drezen. All of his writings on office management, Taylorism, and Esperanto now converged in the service of a vital national interest, the Second Five-Year Plan (1933-1937). Besides Stalin, his patron was the leading Taylorist theoretician in Soviet Russia, A.K. Gastev, who with a host of technicians and engineers mounted a "struggle for the standardization" of techniques and instrumentation in the field of production. Drezen raised his own banner for the classification and standardization of an international scientific-technical terminological code, "the basic means for the organization of labor, knowledge, and thought". The lack of coordinated and clear language was promoting waste and confusion in the Soviet economy.

The technical schools and colleges suffered from tens of thousands of unstable "specialized terms", either difficult foreign terms or multiple Russian terms for the same scientific-technical meaning. Compound words needed to be "economized" in order to save print space and mental energy. "Gasoline-dispensing pump" (*benzino-podaiushchaia kolonka*), for example, might become "gas pump" (*benzokolonka*). Otherwise, lacking simple and standard terms, mechanics and technicians would continue to misunderstand their own repair instructions and orders. Drezen settled for nothing less than the full unification of terms and symbols within the theoretical, technical, and applied disciplines. He even aimed for the "fixation of terms for each mechanical component of each elemental process". His goal, "to repudiate every figurative and allegorical style" in order to avoid the "imprecision and multiple meanings of different expressions".[43]

The pace toward Drezen's code quickened at the Stockholm Conference of the International Standardizing Association in September of 1934, where he delivered a "critical historical survey" of proposals for "international terminological unification". The major technical and electrical engineering reviews of Europe and America approved his report, mandating him the task of preparing a final project, under the official sponsorship of the Soviet government. The national standardizing associations of nineteen developed industrial countries "unanimously accepted" it within a year.[44]

In order to achieve "precision in meaning" and facility in practical application, Drezen based his code on the simplified, phonetic signs of the Latin alphabet. It was already in use in the European west and the Soviet east, and he hoped that the Soviet government would soon Latinize the Russian alphabet system as well. This hope was not too far-fetched. Most commentators of the day considered alphabets to be neutral mediums, nothing more than formal representations of languages, a notion that became widely publicized during the debates over language reform in the 1920s and 1930s. According to this logic, Russian in a Latin script would have been as dominant a force over the non-Russian languages as Russian in its own traditional script. Some government leaders may have agreed. In 1935 and early 1936, they revived their support for the Latinization movement, promising it even more resources and financial credits. The TsIK SSSR ordered the VTsKNA to redouble its efforts to organize local conferences for the improvement of orthographies, terminologies, and literary languages based on the Latin script. Specialists were slated to receive better salaries and support. The VTsKNA was reorganized and new funding given to scientific, publishing and organizational work. Linguists and cultural leaders remained at work perfecting Latin orthographies into early 1936. Drezen even headed the Ugro-Finnic section of the VTsKNA.[45]

In order to promote the "greatest internationalism in form and content", Drezen based most of the code's root words, affixes, prepositions, conjunctions, and grammatical rules on Esperanto, what he called his "conditional standard". During this work, he stayed in close contact with the leading German standards engineer and Esperantist, Eugene Wüster, as well as with the president of the Universal Esperanto Association, Louis Bastien. The code's phonetic simplicity, all-European character, and non-European agglutinative structure were a "most rational solution" to the world language problem. For Drezen, victory for the code meant a partial victory for Esperanto. "*Ciuj de vojoj*", he wrote, "*kondukas al Romo.*" His hopes for the code and for Esperanto were so serious that in March of 1936 he approached Bastien about the possibility of a new, world Esperanto alliance to include the Soviet Union.[46]

7.4. Russifying the eastern scripts and schools

All of Drezen's work came to naught. His code failed in the spring of 1936 as the governments of the industrialized West, one by one, refused to implement it. The Soviet Union, sponsor of the code, could not proceed alone with a new international standard, so it capitulated. Stalin's leap into "mergence" on an international scale had failed. So he retreated into his "zonal" defense. The advent of new russified terms, coupled with the failure of Drezen's code, meant that the Latin script became an archaic relic, and Russian the standard of a new regimented life. In May of 1936, the Orgbiuro TsK RKPb made a comprehensive accounting of the successes and failures of the Latin scripts in use by the nationalities of the RSFSR (the small peoples "living scattered among the Russian population"). It then approved the first conversion of a Latin alphabet, the Kabardin NA, to a new modified Russian script. Kabardia had been one of the first territories to turn to Latin, thanks to N.F. Iakovlev's formulas for the creation of scripts. But the Kabardin-Balkar Regional Committee and Northern Caucasus Regional Committee of the RKPb now complained that literacy and education were under strain in the area given the "extreme complexity" of the Latin script and public clamoring for Russian.

At the same time, the TsK Orgbiuro approved the formation of the Central Scientific Research Institute of Languages and Alphabets (TsNIIIaP) to direct the coming tasks of "language construction" (*iazykovoe stroitel'stvo*), a new code phrase for conducting the broader russification campaign that followed. In February of 1937, the Seventh Plenum of the VTsKNA formally approved the conversions of the North Caucasian (Kabardin, Adygei, Cherkess, Abkhaz, Abazin) and the Northern Siberian (Saamy, Nentsy, Man'si, Khanty, Nanai, Nivkhi) scripts from Latin to Cyrillic. By the end of the year, the rest of the national regions and republics of the RSFSR had converted too.[47]

The government logic behind these conversions was simple. The Latin script had become fragmented and divisive, an "obstacle to the mastery of the Russian language". Most of all, Latin was poorly suited to the sound, spelling and print needs of the Soviet peoples, especially since more and more non-Russians were now learning the Russian language and its word borrowings.[48] They first learned their own languages, written in Latin scripts, in the primary schools. Only later did they turn to learning Russian in Cyrillic letters. The resulting script discrepancies made for confusion and inefficiency in learning. For native cultural and political leaders who had survived the purges and who increasingly depended on Moscow for patronage and power, one standard Russian-based script for both varieties of language learning made sound sense.

Between 1939 and 1940, the Soviet government decreed Russian-based scripts for the remaining nationalities of the USSR, with the exception of the Georgians and Armenians. Several leading Japhetites on the TsNIIIaP, B. Grande and N.K. Dmitriev, reviewed the new script projects according to two precise measurements, drawn from Marr's theory of crossbreeding and stadialism. Firstly, to promote the unity of national literary cultures under a Russian standard, the new letters of the non-Russian languages were required to represent the same function or "significance" as Russian letters. The spelling of international terms was to match as closely as possible with Russian spelling forms rather than create any "artificial divergences". This meant that such languages received altogether new Russian sounds for their phonetic systems, to match with the new Russian letters necessary for the integral spelling of "international" terms. Secondly, once the script projects met this standard, each region or republic was left to create a Russian alphabet system to best serve the needs of mass literacy. Teachers met to discuss the viability of various signs and rules for the mass schools, arguing for this or that letter based on the needs of their students.[49]

The TsNIIIaP took no care whatsoever to unify the different national projects between themselves. In spite of the obvious lessons of the Latinization campaigns, and the many available studies on specific linguistic questions, it did not even coordinate phoneme representations between the cohesive Turkic sub-languages. Its directors allowed a whole new set of discrepancies to fragment literary cultures: the use of one Russian letter for several different Turkic phonemes; or the use of several Russian letters for one and the same Turkic phoneme; or the representation of the same phoneme in different sub-languages by different letters. Representatives of the Turkic-speaking republics protested, demanding an end to these needless discrepancies. In November of 1940, the School Division of the TsK VKPb even met with them to discuss "unification of the new alphabets". But "unification" in 1940 did not mean the same as "unification" in 1926. Instead of debating, the assembled guests heard a short and simple lecture from Moscow about the primacy of the vertical unification of the non-Russian scripts under a Russian standard, not the horizontal unification between the scripts of the Turkic peoples.[50] The party had made its decision; the case was closed. Russian scripts, visible on every public sign and every printed page, would help all of the Soviet peoples speak and think like good, proletarian Russians.

New terms and scripts were hardly enough to fuse the native and Russian languages into the pyramid of convergence-mergence. The non-Russians also had to master Russian itself in order to become fully Soviet. Yet their record on this score was atrocious. Complaints about their poor teaching and mastery of the Russian language reverberated into the 1930s. At an educational conference of the party's Central Asian Bureau in 1934, national representatives criticized how some children attending pedagogical and other training colleges were barely literate in the native and Russian languages. Some were as young as nine years old and still "wet their beds", enrolled simply to meet nativization quotas. State and party leaders complained time and again that their students could not advance to vocational, professional and university education because they were not sufficiently literate in Russian. Between 1935 and 1937, the success rate of non-Russian students in the Russian language remained unsatisfactory across the USSR. Many schools were getting worse every year. Russian language teaching was in peril. The RSFSR Narkompros warned that the vast majority of primary and secondary schools in Dagestan and Chechnia did not teach Russian. In the Volga-Urals, Northern Caucasus, and Central Asia, it was often a subject in name only.[51]

In Azerbaijan, Russian language teaching was deficient all the way from the second grade to graduate school. Of 3,104 native-language schools, a total of 1,212 did not teach Russian at all; those that did taught it very poorly, especially the rural schools. The higher pedagogical colleges and institutes were mostly to blame; they prepared very few qualified Russian language teachers, most of them still teenagers with just a few weeks of special training. One analyst summarized this sad state of affairs by noting that Russian had always taken a "secondary" place in most schools. The worst teachers were assigned the Russian language courses. They taught them in the afternoon, when all the students were tired, and when many had already left for home or work. And they promoted children to the next grade regardless of their proficiency. The situation in Uzbekistan was equally bad. Of 2,508 primary schools, a total of 1,679 had no Russian language teachers at all.[52]

These complaints and recommendations contributed to the 13 March 1938 decree of the TsK RKPb, "On the Obligatory Study of the Russian Language in National Republic and Regional Schools". It established a set of formal, universal standards for the whole USSR: students were required to enter secondary school with basic reading, speaking and writing skills in Russian sufficient to carry a conversation and conduct work in an office setting. It charged the RSFSR Narkompros to begin work on fortified curriculums and texts, and to fulfill the plan of sending a wave of "thousanders" into the union republics to teach Russian, reminiscent of the party cadres sent to collectivize the villages years before. Azerbaijani and Uzbek party leaders promised to train their own Russian language "thousanders", backed by new teacher colleges, bilingual dictionaries, and government inspectors. They vowed to establish remedial Russian classes for their own staffs, and to increase the hours of Russian language teaching in the schools.[53]

Moscow took these directives and promises with utmost seriousness, fashioning a regulatory hierarchy to chart their implementation. Local educators reported to regional party leaders, who in turn reported to the School Division of the TsK RKPb, or directly to A.A. Zhdanov, the Orgbiuro Secretary responsible for the official campaign. Not trusting the reports within its own party structure, the TsK sometimes sent plenipotentiary inspectors into the peripheries to investigate results. During one such episode, the Uzbek Narkompros proudly reported that over 2,000 people had already finished four-month courses in Russian language teaching. But the TsK inspector soon turned the meeting into an inquisition, and discovered that these new teachers were still poorly prepared, both in Russian and in Uzbek. The local authorities grudgingly admitted that the increased hours of Russian language teaching in the schools were a farce.[54]

Results were so disappointing at first because of the coercive nature of the campaign. National educators became overloaded by the new, monolithic Russian language programs. They were required to implement them in the schools without question or qualification. They complied, no doubt fearing for their lives. But after several months of impractical and unsuccessful work, educators met to discuss their shared problems and joined together in a campaign for "differential" Russian language teaching programs, based upon the "local conditions". A sympathetic TsK RKPb School Division approved their requests. In promoting the teaching of Russian in the non-Russian territories of the USSR, the government still had to depend on the differential approach and comparative method. Russian language teaching had to be founded upon the specific linguistic conditions of each native language. Non-Russian students still had to know their own native languages well enough, and to apply the comparative study of native phonetics and grammar, to successfully learn Russian. Thus the legal terms of the 1938 decree recognized the importance of native language learning, obliging all teachers to learn the native languages and dialects of their students before ever attempting to teach them Russian.[55]

Still, these were small concessions. The government sent a more unequivocal message that the native languages were to remain weak and submissive. The network of national scientific research institutes in the RSFSR and USSR fell into complete disrepair. Moscow's own Scientific Research Institute for the Non-Russian Schools was closed "for unclear reasons" in 1938, at which point aid "from the center" stopped cold. The TsNIIIaP received less and less funding and attention during its brief existence between 1936 and 1944, when its administrative structure was transferred wholesale into the Marrist Institute of Language and Thought and its activities withered, leaving the nationalities of the USSR without any administrative patrons.[56] The 1938 decree highlighted once and for all the power of Russian as the formal language of the supra-state over its territorial units. The grandfatherly L.V. Shcherba, Baudouin's close friend and colleague from before the revolution, now celebrated Russian as the true symbol of civic concord. "It is ours [*nasha*] and this is so much more than mine [*rodnoi*]". (Shcherba 1939: 19-26) The new Soviet person, even though often born without the Russian language, would eventually come to possess it, and the noble internationalist and humanist ideals expressed within it, through the good graces of Soviet power.

Chapter 8

Stalin's linguistic theories as cultural conquest

> *Comrade Stalin, you are a great scholar,*
> *In linguistics, you've mastered it all.*
> *Me, I'm just a poor Soviet convict,*
> *My comrade, the gray Siberian wolf.*
> *Russian folk song (circa 1950)*

By 1938 - through such institutions as the Narkompros, Orgbiuro and Secretariat - the Soviet government had finally crafted a series of conservative approaches to the teaching of the Russian language and a set of russification initiatives for the non-Russian languages of the east. Almost all of the maximalist language reforms from earlier years had failed. They were little match for the new priorities of industrialization, collectivization, and state consolidation. Minor spelling improvements and modified formal grammars took the place of the radical reforms of the 1920s. Latin letters yielded to Russian. Language nativization lost what earlier priorities it enjoyed in funding and administrative support. Drezen's proposal for an Esperantic terminological code gave way to strictly Russian terminologies. Only the Language Front's principles of terminological standardization, which elevated the prestige status of the Russian language, survived the 1930s.

During and after World War II, Soviet class values fused decisively with a patriotic Russian nationalism. Propagandists reinstated ancient heroes, Alexander Nevskii and Dmitri Donskoi, even reviving the Orthodox religious pageantry of old. They tried once again to promote a purer Russian language in the hearts and minds of the Soviet people. These new policies circumscribed the scope of linguistics and national literary development but did not completely eradicate them. Between 1948 and 1950, the fortunes of formalist and structural linguists rose or fell as their different patrons in the Politburo struggled over the relevance of Marr's Japhetidology. National cultures even enjoyed something of a limited revival. Moscow allowed selected non-Russian national heroes and symbols their own orbits around the central theme of Soviet Russian patriotism.[1] But what was the place of Marr's theories in this new order? Would his heroic status survive? Iosef Stalin delivered the final word on these questions in his famous booklet on linguistics. The shape and trajectory of Marr's stadial pyramid remained, but now Stalin made it altogether his own.

8.1. The resilience of structural linguistics

Most scholars argue that the Marr school was an absolute power within linguistics and language reform in the 1930s and 1940s, noting with good reason that it enjoyed the "sanctions of a dictatorial government".[2] But we can also muster convincing evidence that the Japhetites did not enjoy a total victory after 1932. The party forced a compromise. Marr's theories of language development exercised only a partial hegemony. His students retained control over its ideologization and popularization, including primary institutional power. But structural linguists, in league with traditional comparativists and formalists, maintained important dominions over linguistic studies and language reform projects. These developments square with other findings about an undercurrent of professional conservatism during the 1930s. Like many academics and scientists, linguists were assured of job security from the state so long as they maintained a "dedicated apolitical professionalism" and loyal service to the party and its ideals. (Fitzpatrick 1992: 244)

The Japhetites and their rivals remained locked in a balance of forces on most directorates and committees. Language Frontists, along with more traditional members of the Petersburg and Moscow schools, found sanctuary in several institutions: the Communist University of the Workers of the East, the Moscow State Institute of Foreign Languages, the Moscow Pedagogical Institute of Foreign Languages, the Moscow City Pedagogical Institute, and the Moscow Institute of History, Philosophy, and Literature. The government depended on their expertise to teach needed courses on the History of Ancient Slavic, the History of Contemporary Russian, and Russian Dialectology.[3] Japhetite theories were engaged in a healthy competition with formalist and structural linguistics as well. The study of language history and semantics dominated the all-union curriculum for university linguistics throughout the 1930s and 1940s. The government obliged students to learn about language as "practical conscious activity"; and to read Marx, Engels, Lenin, Stalin, and Marr, in descending order of importance.

But students also learned about structural phonology and formal grammar, through readings of Humboldt, Potebnia, Baudouin, Shakhmatov, Ushakov, Peshkovskii and their colleagues. In her translations of the "Linguists of the West Series" (Saussure, Sapir, Vendryes and Meillet), widely available in the late 1930s, R.O. Shor and her collaborators also stressed the value of the bourgeois heritage in linguistics from abroad. Part of the very reason for publishing a critical edition of Saussure's *Course in general linguistics* was to make better ideological sense of its adherents in the USSR, whom the editors considered a dominant trend, however faulted in some of their structural and sociological methods.[4]

In government meetings of the early 1940s, several linguists were even bold enough to criticize the scholarly work of the Marr school. One of them targeted a Japhetite school textbook as vulgar "phraseology", weighed down by the "scientific linguistic baggage" of Marr and Aptekar'. Another labeled the author as a "dilettante" who represented the "most primitive and crude doctrine" of Japhetidology, who filled the text with an "empty flow of words". Narkompros rejected the book. In May of 1941, scholars assembled for a theoretical conference on the topic of Lenin's philosophical works, which included papers on their significance for linguistic science. Vinokur used this opportunity to speak out against Japhetidology, that "vulgar-materialistic deviation" in philosophy and linguistics, arguing rather for the crucial distinction "between the objective and subjective moment in language, without ignoring the latter, as the vulgarizers do".[5] His words proved that linguists could sometimes express, however rarely, the philosophical idealism that informed their principles.

The fates of structural linguists during these years were mixed. Bubrikh kept his chair over Finno-Ugric studies at Leningrad State University until his death in 1949, yet the Japhetites constantly harassed him and his work. The party forgave the young Language Frontist, Lomtev, for his belligerence. He spent most of the 1930s directing linguistic work in Belorussia and eventually became a specialist on Russian syntax, and a successful publicist of structural principles. The party reprimanded M.S. Gus for his "theoretical mistakes in journalism" in 1931; he held minor posts in Moscow theaters in the 1930s and became a successful publicist and critic at several journals and newspapers by the 1940s.

Those who openly defied Marr (who died of old age in 1934) or who violated the party line, as in the case of Danilov and Polivanov, suffered accordingly. The party persecuted them not so much for their beliefs or methods as for the ways in which they expressed or politicized them. Danilov disappeared from active public life. Polivanov was arrested in March 1937 and executed on 25 January 1938, ostensibly for espionage during his field trips to the Far East and Japan. Others shared a similar fate. The Moscow formalist, N.N. Durnovo was accused of participating in a White emigre clique because of his working partnership with Prince N.S. Trubetskoi through the 1920s in the Prague Linguistic Circle. He died in the camps. An estimated five thousand Esperantists, including Ernst Drezen and his collaborators, also perished in the Gulag after 1937, accused of conspiratorial ties with other Esperantists abroad. Shpet lapsed into obscurity and harassment, translating Byron, Shakespeare, and Dickens for the State Publishing House. In 1936, not the best year for dialectical idealism, he finished a translation of Hegel's *Philosophy of spirit*, accompanied by several popular essays.[6] He eventually died in the camps as well. Nor were the Japhetites immune; Aptekar' and Bykovskii perished in the purges of the late 1930s.

Most linguists were ready and willing to attend to government policies, most notably in their service to Russian as the official, prestige language of state communication. They continued to apply specific formalist and structural insights to their work into the early 1950s, albeit within party ideological limits. Only the philosophical foundations of structural theories - as in the case of Hegelian idealism, Shpetian aesthetics and Western structuralism - remained publicly disreputable. (Zvegintsev 1956)

8.2. The Japhetite offensive and the fall of Marr

Between 1945 and 1948, the Russian language became the object of popular veneration, a sacred relic of the war against fascism and a living symbol of the might and right of the victorious Russian people. As in 1880 and 1937, Pushkin once again became the central figure in official celebrations of the national literary language and culture. The party subsidized the publication of 45 million copies of his works in 1949 alone, part of its attempt to bring the masses up to high brow culture and the great Russian literary language.[7] The TsK RKPb promoted Russian language classes as the preferred foundation for "the cultivation of Soviet patriotism and national pride, love of the motherland, and loyalty to the ideas of communism" - a campaign which reached into nearly every facet of public life. It charged language teachers to inspire students with the "unique significance of the Russian language, its richness, sonority, beauty and expressivity, and in this way instill love for this 'great and powerful' language".[8] The government's message was clear. Only by mastering the intricacies of their native tongue could students begin to imagine themselves as Russians.

Formalist and structural linguists now enjoyed a remarkable public revival. These years saw the publication of V.V. Vinogradov's *The Russian Language*, A.N. Reformatskii's *Introduction to Linguistics*, G.O. Vinokur's *The Russian Language*, and A.S. Chikobava's *General Linguistics*. They saw Ushakov, Peterson, Reformatskii, and Kuznetsov rise to new leadership posts in academia. Working from Werner Hahn's revisionist interpretation of the postwar era, we can account for the revival of mainstream linguistics given A.A. Zhdanov's promotion of objective and creative standards in scholarship between 1945 and 1948. At this time, the TsK Propaganda and Agitation Department promoted relatively free discussion in the major party and academic periodicals. (Hahn 1982) Zhdanov, a longtime patron of "language culture" in the TsK RKPb, promoted the revival in linguistics as well.

The logic of the revival was sometimes quite compelling. R.I. Avanesov, working in the tradition of Fortunatov's dialectology, reasoned that the Russian national language was a living, complex organism, and regional dialects a kind of pathology within it. Just as a medical doctor needed a detailed sense of the human anatomy and physiology in order to identify the symptoms of disease and diagnose a cure, so too did the dialectologist need to recognize the specific sound, word and word-combination systems within regional dialects to maintain the health and integrity of the national linguistic body. Dialect pathology was especially useful for teachers in the cities, who needed to detect the diseased speech patterns of their students to better correct them. (Avanesov 1949: 3-33)

Threatened by the resurgence of their rivals, and remembering their first victory over the Language Front some sixteen years before, the Japhetites were now moved to militant action. They were assisted by political developments within the Politburo itself, especially after Zhdanov's fall from favor, when G.M. Malenkov and L.P. Beria began to promote a more dogmatic line in academia during the "triumph of reaction" and the anticosmopolitan campaigns between 1948 and 1950. First and foremost among the new winners was the eccentric geneticist, T. Lysenko, who rose to prominence in August of 1948 declaring that the environmental manipulation of plant genetics, based on his proletarian theories, would ensure a revolution in Soviet agriculture. Within a month after his successes, the Japhetites attempted to reintroduce a similar polemic into linguistics in order to undercut the resurgent Indo-European and structural schools, and to further safeguard and advance their own careers. Under Malenkov and Beria, party ideological guardians sympathized with Japhetidology, believing that the "structuralists and Saussurianists" were "combining the positions of prerevolutionary Russian linguistics with the ideas of reactionary foreign linguists" in a conspiracy to dominate the field. In targeting these scholars for attack, the leading Japhetites of the day - I.I. Meshchaninov, F.P. Filin, G.P. Serdiuchenko and S.D. Katsnelson among them - now established the infamous "Arakcheev regime" in linguistics.[9]

Marr's students once more defiled the Indo-European school, the historical-comparative method and structural phonology. Again they forced their enemies to "repent" and "disavow" their views under the threat of "administrative repression". The reputations of leading scholars littered their battlefield. V.V. Vinogradov lost his chair at the Philological Department of Moscow State University; with several colleagues he recanted his work. In support of its Marrist Institute of Language and Thought, the directors of the Academy of Sciences consigned the premier linguists of the USSR (Vinogradov, Chikobava, Peterson, Reformatskii, Zhirmunskii and Bubrikh) to slander and abuse. Not even the Prague Linguistic Circle was immune from the onslaught, which swept into Czechoslovakia with the communist seizure of power. R.O. Jakobson was dubbed "the genuine evil spirit of our linguistics" and the "chief pillar of structuralism".[10]

The Japhetites flooded periodicals and public lectures with broadsides reviewing the notions of gesture speech; language as a second signal system and as a tool of production; the superiority of semantics over phonetics.[11] In the spirit of Marr and Lysenko, they reminded the Soviet public that the real world could be known and mastered by its natural, or even imagined, laws. They championed the willful conquest of nature by reaffirming that to name something was to know it, to control it, to transform it to one's own purposes.

But the Japhetite offensive was brief. Its end was foreshadowed as early as December of 1949, when the Ministry of Education (RSFSR) sent out decrees to all regional and local school districts, calling on teachers to extend the number of hours for Russian language teaching in the secondary schools; to "attentively examine the quality of knowledge and skills of students in Russian"; and to take special care in the teaching of grammar.[12] Scores of internal school, government and party reports between 1941 and 1950 once again revealed that the Russian language was in peril. Russian children were not becoming fully literate in their own language. The schools were creating literate students in the primary grades, but the process broke down through the secondary years. By 1948, the success rate of students on written Russian examinations was disastrously low in the Iaroslavl region, mostly due to spelling and grammar mistakes. The problem crept up into the higher schools. Even the teacher colleges graduated people who were "semiliterate" and who had not "mastered" a basic knowledge of Russian.[13]

The Council of Ministers of the USSR was so frustrated with the "drift" and "chaos" on the spelling issue that it appealed directly to TsK Secretary Beria to publish a definitive set of spelling rules which had recently been compiled. A campaign for a "united orthographic regime" in the schools followed during the winter and spring of 1949, whereby administrators and teachers in all schools and all classes were told to carefully inspect student spelling notebooks and organize learning circles.[14]

Russian language teaching in the non-Russian schools was in even worse straits. The 1938 state decree remained a standard unfulfilled. The Ministry of Education reported severe problems in Russian teaching and textbook publishing in the national schools between 1948 and 1950. Students were failing to move from native language instruction in the first years of primary school to Russian language instruction in secondary and higher schools. The situation was desperate in the North Caucasus and Buriatia, which completely lacked the resources and standards necessary for such a conversion. Udmurt children were unable to speak communicable Russian because they spoke their native tongue at home, while Russian language teaching methods were "primitive", their own teachers illiterate in Russian. Oirat, Khakass, Cherkess and Adygei representatives complained that their schools had no Russian language textbooks designed for their needs. Uzbek, Tatar and Mari schools admitted that they were incapable of producing cadres of educated students to move on to higher education given failing rates in Russian.[15]

The Japhetite offensive coexisted for a time with these developments in Russian language teaching. Party ideologists promised to revive the status of Russian in Soviet society in partnership with the Japhetites, granting them free access to propagate their theories in the schools and colleges. But this is precisely where the offensive began to unravel. The Japhetites went about their way, exaggerating the importance of semantics and lexical studies, devaluing the role of spelling and grammar lessons, eagerly attacking Reformatskii's "Humboldtianism" or Chikobava's "Saussurianism". They left thousands of dumbfounded teachers and students in their wake. The Ministry of Education and Academy of Pedagogical Studies even capitulated to the Marr school's ideological demands by reducing the time allotted to pronunciation, spelling, and grammar lessons in the primary school curriculums. In their place they imposed E.N. Petrova's special "clustering" method, which taught such useless information as the etymology of the word *iarovizatsiia* (from the ancient god name, *Iarilo*). Teachers protested that it was wasting precious time in their language classes.[16]

The days of the Japhetites were numbered given these crises and contradictions in Russian language teaching. Simply put, they no longer served the practical needs of state. Since most internal reports between 1949 and the early 1950s blamed the hegemony of the Japhetites for the high failure rates in Russian, the government saw the perfect opportunity to displace them from power in academia and thereby reinforce its commitment to the Russian national language. The tide finally turned when a series of internal TsK RKPb reports criticized Japhetidology for a lack of "Bolshevik principles" and for its arrogant "intolerance" of other trends in linguistics. The TsK highlighted its dangerous effects on Russian language teaching, and its lack of responsible work with the national languages of the union.

Analysts from the Agitation and Propaganda Department, who admitted to having patronized the Japhetite campaign from the beginning, now turned to TsK Secretary M.A. Suslov for action. They urged him to write an authoritative press article to bring order to the field of linguistics and to critique the deficiencies of the Marr school and all those who saw his theories as "infallible".[17] Suslov had recently become TsK secretary in charge of agitation and propaganda, editor of *Pravda*, and the architect of yet another phase of Politburo intrigues and cultural orthodoxies that began in 1950. Under his watch, the party retreated from Japhetidology and promoted mainstream trends in linguistics. But the ever-modest Suslov did not lend his name to this reversal of fortunes. The campaign demanded a more experienced guide.

8.3. Iosef Stalin, coryphaeus of linguistics

The anti-Marr campaign began in earnest when the Georgian linguist and longtime critic of Japhetidology, A.S. Chikobava, was called to Stalin's dacha outside of Moscow on 10 April 1950. The two met and discussed the general situation in linguistics, including Chikobava's recent survey text, which Stalin had read with interest. He thereupon asked Chikobava to write a review article for *Pravda*; they met several more times in coming weeks to discuss it. The piece, which berated the Marr school and argued for the legitimacy of Indo-Europeanism, historical-comparativism and formal methods, was published on 9 May 1950. But this was only the beginning of the linguistics debate in which both he and several other leading linguists were already engaged, including V.V. Vinogradov and D.N. Ushakov.[18] Stalin soon intervened with three leading *Pravda* articles of his own (20 June, 4 July, and 2 August).

For years now, these articles, later reprinted in millions of booklet copies as *Marxism and the problems of linguistics*, have understandably bewildered historians as to their practical significance.[19] But when we place the articles in the broader historical context of linguistic science and language reform, they begin to make better sense. Stalin was no stranger to language issues, as we have already seen with regard to the Latin alphabet and Esperanto. His pronouncements marked Soviet Russia's final conquest of its early national frontiers. In an instant, Stalin elevated his own cult of personality and the status of the Russian language, once and for all, as the paramount state principles of the USSR.

In *Marxism and the problems of linguistics*, written in the form of a classical Greek dialogue with several ordinary Soviet citizens, Stalin joined Potebnia, Baudouin, Fortunatov, and Shakmatov as a "coryphaeus" of science. He now defined historical-comparative linguistics as the premier school in the discipline, if still in his shadow. In repudiating Marr's crude materialist formulas, point by detailed point, he took modern linguistic insights for his own. With Polivanov and the Language Front, he agreed that the bourgeois "heritage" was valuable. Japhetite "proletarian" grammars were the workings of "troglodytes", he wrote, who would have destroyed functional bourgeois railroads to make way for dysfunctional proletarian ones. Stalin redefined language in Humboldt's terms as a means of communication rather than in Marr's as a means of production. "Sound language or the language of words was always the sole language of human society able to serve as a genuine means of human communication." It was "one of those forces which enabled people to be differentiated from the animal world, to join together in societies, to develop their thinking".

In the tradition of Humboldt, Stalin agreed that grammar "gives language a harmonious, intelligent character" because of its abstractive power. He effectively superimposed the authority of Russian grammar upon the authority of the Bolshevik nomenclature. Form now better served content. And in a most stunning defeat for Marr's ideas about gesture language and the second signal system, Stalin wrote that "sign language cannot be equated with sound language, just as it is impossible to equate the primitive wooden plow with the modern caterpillar tractor with a five-frame plow and a row tractor drill".[20] Sound makes us human, he mused, just as machines make us modern.

Historical-comparative methods were, in Stalin's words, "an impetus to work, to studying languages". In contrast, Marr's four-element analysis was black magic, like "lying on top of the oven and reading teacups". At Stalin's side, Polivanov's old students and veterans from the Language Front movement now promoted the study of sound and word changes through time based on the strict, precise methods of traditional linguistics. Their revival and celebration of the historical-comparative method may seem irrelevant and inappropriate at such a late date in the history of linguistics. Yet on the Soviet scene it retained legitimacy and vitality as the traditional rival force to Marr's methods. It was also the best initial means to revive structural methods in linguistic work, which were becoming ever more valuable in the Soviet project to develop cybernetics and computer science to compete with the USA in the cold war.[21]

In its central argument, the essay transformed Marr's notions of class language development into Stalin's notion of a "non-class, national language, the common knowledge of which constitutes an indispensable condition for the nation's formation". Marr's ideas had become obsolete after the Soviet victory in World War II and Stalin's new dedication to Russian nationalism. The government could no longer tolerate their practical devaluation and neglect of the Russian language, and their superficial patronage of the non-Russian languages of the periphery. Stalin therefore established the theoretical and ideological primacy of modern standard Russian for all peoples of the USSR. He jettisoned Marr's views of language crossbreeding and stadialism, processes that were to lead to a brand new international language, in favor of his latest (and final) theory of one language (Russian) being ultimately victorious. This winning Russian now became the capstone of a common state identity for the whole USSR. Stalin recapitulated from the linguists of the 1920s that, for all of the changes in vocabulary and grammar teaching brought about by the Bolshevik revolution, "the structure and grammar of Pushkin's language" and "its basic lexical fund" had remained the same. With them, he recognized that jargons and dialects work as the sub-languages of social groups, but always within the greater sphere of the national language. In waves of reports and books that accompanied these words, linguists scolded the Japhetites for devaluing the "lexical and grammatical richness of the great Russian language".[22]

Perhaps most significantly, in terms of practical effects *Marxism and the problems of linguistics* promoted a massive "restructuring" (*perestroika*) of Russian language teaching in the schools. We must remember that practical issues motivated Stalin's intervention in the first place. His essay was not about "totalitarian logic" or linguistic absolutism. (Gray 1993: 16) It was more about the Soviet government trying to keep its disorderly house in some kind of order. To what must have been the utter despair of millions of children, Stalin's words revived morphology, grammar, and orthography lessons in the schools, as well as the teaching of concepts and skills. His message was simple: that teachers inculcate a "love and a political conscious attitude for Russian". He wanted them to "teach students how to read intelligently, properly, easily and expressively; to write literately; to expound their thoughts in speech and in print both freely and correctly".[23]

From these instructions, educators in the Academy of Sciences, Ministries of Education, and Academy of Pedagogical Studies now remade language teaching in the schools, all the way from the first grade up to postgraduate education. They wrote new curriculums, teaching and grading standards, textbooks, and teaching methodologies. Grammatical "analysis" (*razbor*) and the integrated teaching of concepts and skills became the catchwords of the day. Regional committees of the RKPb scrambled to take charge over the campaign. They directed seminars, conducted inspections, and monitored the new curriculums. Party cells organized "Russian language corners" in the schools, filled with the latest textbooks and learning aids for student use. At summer camp, young communists in the Pioneer organization gave up canoeing and hiking to conduct group discussions and lessons on noun suffixes and the comma.[24]

Everyone from members of the Council of Ministers of the RSFSR, to lowly primary school teachers, were soon reporting that these policies were raising grades, that students were applying orthographic and grammatical rules with more confidence. They praised Stalin's essay for defining morphology as the most important part of grammar, grammar as the most important part of Russian, and Russian as one of most important languages of the world. One teacher even reported that Stalin's linguistic principles had helped her renew the teaching of the substantive noun.[25]

The government also publicized Stalin's essay as the new standard by which to renew the teaching of Russian in the native non-Russian schools. It organized yet another "thousanders" movement, calling up teachers from the Russian-speaking regions of the RSFSR to fan out into the non-Russian areas of the USSR spreading the Russian "word". In 1951, apparently at the request of native leaders, who were merely responding to the new conditions of Soviet life, state educational ministries moved the teaching of Russian as a subject back to the second half of the first grade for Tatar, Mari, Bashkir and Chuvash schools. Primary school teachers apparently needed this extra time to prepare students for advancement into Russian language higher schools. In Central Asia, educators similarly raised the number of hours of Russian language instruction in the primary grades - from ten to seventeen hours per week.[26]

Amid all of these developments, party and state administrators once again realized that dictates from the center could not be implemented effectively without consideration of local needs. The government was not a monolith; the administration and society below not always meekly compliant. A.V. Mirtov, a noted dialectician, called upon the Ministry of Education and the Academy of Sciences to establish dialect laboratories in all of the pedagogical institutes of the

RSFSR. Only by recognizing and correcting dialect patterns in their students, he argued, could teachers help raise them up from lowly provincial to higher all-Russian culture. The government accepted his arguments, demanding that school administrators and teachers take special care to account for the dialect variations and individual needs of Russian students. It expressly prohibited the imposition of a "single obligatory state program" in Russian language teaching. And it promoted new studies and textbooks on the regional dialect variations of Russian, primarily for use by teachers.[27]

The greater prestige of Russian only heightened the need to teach the non-Russian languages more attentively as well. Native languages were not disappearing but coming into fuller relief. Stalin acknowledged so much in the debates when he sided against any attempts "to liquidate an existing language and build a new national language ('sudden language revolution')"; or when he verified the long-term stability of speech communities. Part of the very reason for Stalin's essay was to legitimize the study of the non-Russian languages in all manner of their linguistic levels and dialectical bonds. The Ministry of Education (RSFSR) and the Academy of Pedagogical Studies had already united forces between 1946 and 1948 to revive the Scientific Research Institute for the Non-Russian Schools, dedicated to providing better language teaching methods, textbook publishing, and alphabet reform.[28] Native leaders even began to lobby for reforms of those Russian alphabets imposed so hastily in the late 1930s, and for a reunification of the intra-Turkic sign systems, calling for a new "scientific linguistic center" to coordinate language reform work. They pressed for the teaching of the native languages in the higher grades in order to save national culture.[29] Stalin's essay legitimized these initiatives.

The "comparative method" became the accepted standard of Russian language teaching throughout the USSR. It was the slogan of several teachers' conferences in the summer of 1948. Linguists now spoke of the "Russian language community in the RSFSR and USSR that exists, and still yet needs to be created"; and highlighted the importance of native and Russian language teaching by way of comparative "paradigms" since Russian otherwise remained a "purely amorphous language". The Academy of Pedagogical Sciences also began to direct research studies and publications based on the comparative approach to the native and Russian languages in their "dialectical" relationships.[30] Azerbaijani, Tatar, Mari and Uzbek educational leaders likewise campaigned for it, realizing that Russian language teachers needed to be attuned the "specific characteristics" of the native languages in order to teach Russian well. Weak native language teaching, they argued, translated into weak Russian language teaching. To fortify one language meant to fortify the other.[31]

The underlying theme in all of this was one of Soviet-Russian patriotic nationalism. But beneath the pomp and circumstance were troubling realities. In each of its dimensions, the linguistic campaign of 1950 revealed just how vulnerable and unsteady the Soviet state was in the most basic of cultural terms. It could not even successfully teach the official state language to its own nation, let alone the non-Russian peripheries of the union. And when it did impose new curriculums upon them, it could only do so by respecting, to some degree, their very own languages and cultures. On every linguistic front, then, Stalin's essay yielded to form: to formal historical-comparativism, to Russian grammatical forms, and to the non-Russian linguistic forms as well. The echoes we may be hearing here call us back, ultimately, to Shpet's work: to the tenacity of "social facts", to the "collective" meanings embodied in them, and to the speech communities which encircle themselves as nations. Thus, although cloaked in the superficies of the "great Stalin" and the "great Russian people", the campaign was in reality a capitulation. For both the Russian and non-Russian peoples alike, it was an attempt to discipline the undisciplined, to fashion a common institutional and authoritative bond between such apparently indolent and disparate peoples. It recognized that alphabetical was as important as political literacy, that grammatical form mattered perhaps just as much as Marxist content.

In the life of the average Soviet person, Stalin's booklet on linguistics had momentous overtones. Those who held party or government posts, and those who someday hoped to hold them, bought the booklet and pondered its linguistic insights and commands. Children of every Soviet nationality learned about it in the schools. People immortalized it in fiction, in folk song, and in the thousands of telegrams and letters they sent to the TsK, praising the "coryphaeus" of linguistic science and his contributions to the "spiritual freedom of mankind".[32] It all added up to a rather bizarre yet comprehensible episode in the history of the USSR. Iosef Stalin, the alpha and omega of the Soviet state, taught his countrymen that the native language and Russian were the alpha and omega of Soviet citizenship. People should master both, just as he acquired Georgian in his youth and learned Russian in adulthood. In a parable from his own life, he taught them that the national frontier was something they could only conquer in themselves, by maintaining the language of the home, but especially by learning the language of the state.

This was not the first time, nor the last, that Stalin played the role of philosopher king and great editor of public discourse. Just a few years before, he actually rewrote parts of Lysenko's notorious speech on Marxist genetics (1948), correcting his writing style and toning down his class polemics, highlighting the objectivity of the natural sciences. And within a few years, he would write his last great treatise, *Economic problems of socialism in the USSR* (1952), reaffirming the tenacity of the economic laws governing social change, validating the "objective character of scientific laws".[33] None of these messages, including his essay on linguistics, were inconsistent with what Marr had been saying all along, usually in conjunction with Lenin's reflection thesis. Words were mirror images of the real world. Language reflected objective reality. To name was to know. In these late essays, Stalin humbly recognized the objective laws of nature (in genetics, language, and economics), but pronounced them in a most subjective way, through his own will and authority. He revived the grand old theories of sound and grammar "representations", but only by way of his own peculiar "alchemy of representation".[34] In a strange way, Stalin's linguistic principles of 1950 represent a phenomenology of language for the many; he did, after all, recognize what Shpet would have called the "ontological" or actual conditions of our lives. But all of this was advanced through the phenomenon of one man. Objectivity was not self-evident, but a function of his own will. Language made it so.

Conclusion

> *Vulgar tongues are written down when*
> *the people regain their importance.*
> *Antonio Gramsci*[1]

Under the best of circumstances, the Soviet government reaffirmed this principle of local linguistic autonomy. Through a policy of nativization from above, and a process of national literary creation from below, it provided the Russian and non-Russian peoples of the USSR with new or improved language forms to promote literacy. Most national languages achieved the impressive gains of new alphabets, grammars and various degrees of literary development. In these terms, language reformers were quite successful in diagramming and codifying the national languages. Yet many of these reforms were benign in practice. The gains matched with the unrequited losses of truly viable print cultures and language status. They did not even approach the self-determination and equality of rights necessary for autonomous cultural development and mature, reciprocal relations between peoples. Even well informed language reforms were empty propositions without adequate social supports. The linguistic building blocks of literacy, along with new quantities of literates, were nothing without the qualities of print and literary cultures to empower them. Readers without newspapers and publishing networks, readable and interesting books, and official documentation in their native languages were not truly readers at all. In these terms language reform was a grand failure, most certainly for the non-Russian languages.

The non-Russian languages enjoyed the right to autonomy but not the right to equality. The government allowed them to develop in various ways, but never so much as to become coequal with the status and prestige of Russian. In part because of central state designs, in part because of local national contexts, the Soviet experience subjected the non-Russian peoples to pressures that either devastated the development of some languages, or doomed others to stagnation, or prevented yet others from reaching their full potential. The effects of language reform were as varied as the languages involved. But in the aftermath of industrialization, collectivization and world war, the development of each of the non-Russian languages was sacrificed for the benefit of Russian. Soviet leaders strengthened its prestige functions. They refashioned the literary language of newspapers and books. They established new parameters of literacy - Russian terms and letter-signs - so as to speak to and hear, in one voice, the peripheries of their unwieldy state of nations.

From the Bolshevik Revolution of 1917 to Stalin's death in 1953, the history of early Soviet national policies consistently reveals this mixed pattern of development and dominance. At various times and with various effects, this pattern took shape in the ABCD hierarchy and its comparative method, in Marr's theories of crossbreeding and stadialism, and in Stalin's historical formula of convergence and mergence. The Soviet regime, a discriminating consumer of linguistic and ethnographic knowledge, institutionalized the principles of either the structural or Marr schools, to different degrees and at different times, in the service of its modernizing agenda. The formal language classifications of the structural school helped the government lock the nationalities of the complex, multiethnic USSR into a manageable hierarchical space. The historical paleontology of Marr's theories helped bind them into a submissive historical time. The struggles between these two schools illuminate the power of academic elites to shape state agendas through new knowledge, as well as their vulnerability and weaknesses before the awesome power of the state. The struggles also reveal that party leaders were never blinded by their own ideology, nor by the Marr school's exploitation of it. They consistently used the achievements of both the structural and Marr schools, depending on their practical applications and results.

Practicality remained the rule throughout the 1950s, long after Stalin's death, as the government began to promote structural linguistics for the nuclear age, specifically for use in machine translation and cybernetics technology. Structural methods now developed in force. Beginning with his dissertation work on phonological theory (1951) and continuing with his classic studies of the 1960s, S.K. Shaumian became the most radical voice for a new structural linguistics independent of psychological, or semantic, or sociological associations. At the Seminar on Mathematical Linguistics at Moscow State University (1956), old and new generations of structural linguists laid out a future program for the purely "formal description of linguistic facts".[2] The decisive turn came at the All-Union Conference on Machine Translation in Moscow (1958), which opened the fullest and freest discussions of structural methods to date, and which outlined the basic circle of questions to be explored: on logical semantics, sign and code systems, phonology, morphology, syntax, and transformational grammar. Even Roman Jakobson was invited back to the country. "The topic of the conference is very urgent", wrote V. Toporov, but it "could hardly be called timely; it could just as well have taken place thirty years ago." Much had transpired in the intervening years on the linguistics front, but the linguists themselves retained their professional memories. The contributions of earlier formalist and structural thinkers had not been made in vain.[3]

Stalin's essay imposed a new order on Soviet linguistics, but gave it little peace. New debates raged on about old themes. Former Marrists, seeking a newly found respectability and legitimacy, criticized abstract structural methods for lacking the "human" element. The veteran structural linguist, P.S. Kuznetsov, made a reasoned plea to study "language not as pure structure but in its broader (social-historical) dimension". Following Kuznetsov's lead, his colleagues V.V. Ivanov and I.I. Revzin criticized the new structuralist purism, calling on the authority of the Petersburg, Moscow and Prague schools as support, and arguing that language was a system of social signs and meanings, always operating in particular places and times.[4] In one of the most interesting developments, the leading members of the Moscow-Tartu school of semiotics (Yuri Lotman and Boris Uspenskii, among others) raised Mikhail Bakhtin to unprecedented personal and professional celebrity. He became the new "coryphaeus of modern semiotic thought". (Titunik 1976: 327) In a sense, Bakhtin became the new Marr, his name synonymous with a rebellion against formalism and structuralism in linguistics, especially in the context of Shaumian's rising fame. Under his banner, linguists and literary critics were charged to reveal all that was social and historical, all that was equivocal and relative, in the written text. From Bakhtin they learned the value of flexible sense over fixed meaning. Or as he wrote, "each word tastes of the context and contexts in which it has lived its socially charged life; all words and forms are populated by intentions". (Bakhtin 1981: 293)

Scholars are right to say that Bakhtin raised a quiet but powerful call not only against purism and abstraction, but also against the "official discourse" and "monologism" of state authority; that he celebrated the carnivalesque; that he ultimately proposed the need for a democratic speech community for Russia.[5] But their claims may be somewhat overdone. After all, Bakhtin's rich notions of plural discourse matched well with the intricacies of the ABCD hierarchy already in place in the country. His literary principle of dialogue reflected the political reality of discourse already at work within the Soviet system. Bakhtin was less the rebel protesting the "monologic" voice of the one-party state, more a reflection of the very "dialogic" tensions inherent in it. For "languages do not exclude each other, but rather intersect each other in many different ways". (Bakhtin 1981: 291)

In the end, the regime always offered a mixed repertoire of linguistic choices, and therefore social identities, to the non-Russians of the USSR. They could always learn the ritual language of state discourse, Russian; but they would always speak the familiar majority language of their native homeland. Even the communist party's ideological boasts that the Soviet nationalities were experiencing a process of "convergence" contain an element of truth. Non-Russian children learned both their native languages and Russian, an "obligatory" subject for every student, in school classrooms throughout the distant expanses of the USSR. New generations of non-Russians became bilingual, mixing and matching their native and adopted Russian tongues at will, depending on the moment and the desired meaning. Dimanshtein was both ideologically and objectively correct when he said that such learning amounted to a "convergence" between "Russian proletarian culture and national cultures developing along revolutionary paths".[6] His words reflected the party's compromises with reality as much as its ideological pretenses. It took two forces, after all, to converge. The ABCD hierarchy, which ranked and privileged languages by status and function, continued to shape everyday lives and labors. The native peoples responded to its dictates at their own paces and in their own interests. Non-Russian school children continued to fail their Russian language classes, whether by circumstance or by choice. In sum, what stands out in the Soviet experience is the resilience of native dialects and languages as objective forces through history, more often impermeable to the subjective will of political authorities than not.[7]

The daily business of state demanded that Russian become the linguistic ground for a newly created Russian nation, that it remain the language of social mobility and state communication for the whole USSR. Census statistics show that concentrated elites in the major republics regularly claimed Russian as a second language. It dominated the higher schools and those privileged to attend them. Its publications received priority attention and funding. But Russian never became the language of nations. Nor did nativization ever become altogether incompatible with the demands of the Soviet government. The native languages, despite the best efforts of the center, prevailed as cultural sanctuaries in family and daily life. Statistics show that the vast majority of non-Russians retained their mastery. They enjoyed dictionaries, school textbooks, newspapers, and national literary works in the native languages. This balancing of russification and nativization policies became institutionalized after 1953 in what scholars term a system of "differentiated bilingual education", "limited language rationalization", and "unassimilated bilingualism".[8] These were rather polite and learned ways of saying that the ABCD hierarchy remained in place, with the Russian language at the center and the many non-Russian languages still functioning at the peripheries of officialdom.

These very terms are, ultimately, too cold and indifferent to match with the human inequalities that they represent. For these varieties of "bilingualism" were expressions of deeply rooted social and ethnic divisions within the country. As one russified Azerbaijani language teacher noted in 1994, "the city of Baku was surrounded by a great wall. Beyond it we could no longer speak in Russian. We became like strangers in our own land."[9] Events at the end of the Soviet regime only highlighted the conflicted nature of language maintenance and use in the USSR. When M.S. Gorbachev's *glasnost'* policies opened the way to greater autonomy and more equality for the non-Russian borderlands, popular front movements took vengeance on the prestige status of Russian (and its local elites). They promoted local legislation to raise the native languages as the official mediums of state discourse, setting goals for their preferential social, educational, and political use. These were powerful statements about the resilience of the native languages, about the unevenness of their development, and about popular resentment at the dominance of Russian and its russified speakers.[10] At this moment of political and social crisis, filled with danger and promise, people once again took refuge and hope in their native languages.

The national language laws of the late Gorbachev years were telling examples of the legacies of seventy years of Soviet rule, proof at once of the constraints and opportunities of the ABCD hierarchy. As new policy making, the laws did little more than set the balance of the hierarchy straight again, in the spirit of Lenin's "egalitarian" national policy. There was very little that was revolutionary about them. True, the old party ideological formulas about the "convergence" and "mergence" of nations were discredited. Instead, communist party ideologues and educators revived such slogans as "reciprocal bilingualism" and "Soviet language union" from the distant past. N.S. Trubetskoi's works, once banned as vile, "bourgeois-reactionary" linguistics, were now published, provoking much interest and debate. In a new "Eurasian" imperative in language and national policy, Gorbachev's government promoted a multicultural and tolerant "system of interrelated instruction of the native and Russian languages".[11] Yet these new formulas still retained the priority of Russian as the "first among equals", the leading language of the USSR. Indeed, each of the new language laws was framed within the continuing relevance of Russian as the official language of state discourse. The laws were products of the cumulative effect of many decades of russification. They were historical markers of just how far the non-Russian nationalities still had to go in order to achieve the new linguistic standards of independent national cultures.

During my own trips in the Caucasus and Central Asia in 1992, just after the collapse of the Soviet Union and the sudden appearance of the "newly independent states", I sometimes felt as though I was observing the 1920s, at least as I understood them. Azerbaijan and Uzbekistan, along with their neighboring Turkic states, had already begun to implement a conversion to their former Latin alphabets. They were mostly visible on street signs, or in children's ABC books, or in the odd Latin script newspaper. In the cities, especially among professional and business circles, the Russian language and its script dominated spoken and written speech. But everywhere else - in the side streets of Baku, filled with refugees escaping the war with Armenia, or in quiet mountain hamlets, seemingly untouched by the twentieth century - the native language was spoken as it generally had been before.

Soviet leaders may have wielded a singular kind of power, but they were always forced to inhabit plural worlds. From the beginning of their rule over the broad and varied expanses of the USSR, they recognized the limits of that power and the demands of colonial rule in the twentieth century. They could not escape nativization. They could not but help to frame the development of the non-

Russian languages as the single best mediums for the dissemination of Russian. The multiethnic Soviet state required some measure of dependence upon the ruled in order to ensure effective dominance over them. The cultural and ethnic realities of the former Russian empire locked Soviet rulers into such a hegemonic imperative throughout their regime. These most fundamental realities offer us compelling proof about the central paradox of Soviet power; the gap between the political space which by force it could conquer, and the cultural space which in real terms it could never possess. The opportunities and constraints of language reform may have given Soviet leaders their most enduring insights into national relations. To their ultimate frustration, they learned that language, an essential tool of the dialectical process in history, was also a troublesome and treacherous dimension of the human experience.

Abbreviations and acronyms

AAA	Abkhazskii analiticheskii alfavit
AAN	Arkhiv ANSSSR
ANSSSR	Akademiia nauk soiuza sovetskikh sotsialisticheskikh respublikakh
AO	Avtonomnaia oblast'
ASSR	Avtonomnaia sovetskaia sotsialisticheskaia respublika
Az	Azerbaidzhanskii
GAIaO	Gosudarstvennyi arkhiv iaroslavskogo oblasti
GAIMK	Gosudarstvennaia akademiia istorii material'noi kul'tury
GAKhN	Gosudarstvennaia akademiia khudozhestvennykh nauk
GANI	Gosudarstvennyi arkhiv noveishei istorii Azerbaidzhanskoi respubliki
GAPPOD	Gosudarstvennyi arkhiv politicheskikh partii i obshchestvennykh dvizhenii Azerbaidzhanskoi respubliki
GARF	Gosudarstvennyi arkhiv rossiiskoi federatsii
GBOR	Gosudarstvennaia biblioteka oktiab'rskoi revoliutsii
GIA	Gosudarstvennyi istoricheskii arkhiv Azerbaidzhanskoi respubliki
Glavnauk	Glavnoe upravlenie nauchnymi, muzeinymi i po okhrane prirody uchrezhdeniiami
Glavsotsvos	Glavnoe upravlenie sotsial'nogo vospitaniia i politekhnicheskogo obrazovaniia detei
Gosizdat	Gosudarstvennoe izdatel'stvo
GPU	Gosudarstvennoe politicheskoe upravlenie
GUS	Gosudarstvennyi uchenyi sovet
ILIaZV	Institut literatury i iazyka zapada i vostoka
IzhS	Institut zhivogo slova
Komnats	Komitet natsional'nostei
KTT	Komissiia tekhnicheskoi terminologii
LGU	Leningradskoe gosudarstvennoe universitet
LOIKFUN	Leningradskoe obshchestvo issledovatelei kul'tury finno-ugorskikh narodnostei
MGPI	Moskovskii gorodskoi pedagogicheskii institut
MGU	Moskovskoe gosudarstvennoe universitet
MIIFL	Moskovskii institut istorii, filosofii i literatury

182 Abbreviations and acronyms

MLK	Moskovskii lingvisticheskii kruzhek
MLO	Moskovskoe lingvisticheskoe obshchestvo
MP	Ministerstvo prosveshcheniia
NA	Novyi alfavit
Narkomnats	Narodnyi komissariat po delam natsional'nostei
Narkompros	Narodnyi komissariat po prosveshcheniiu
NEP	Novaia ekonomicheskaia politika
NIIaZ	Nauchno-issledovatel'skii institut iazykoznaniia
NKN	Narodnyi komissariat po delam natsional'nostei
NKP	Narodnyi komissariat po prosveshcheniiu
NKRKI	Narodnyi komissariat raboche-krest'ianskoi inspektsii
NKVD	Narodnyi komissariat vnutrennykh del
NOT	Nauchnaia organizatsiia truda
NTA	Novyi tiurkskii alfavit
Obkom	Oblastnoi komitet
OGPU	Ob'edinennoe gosudarstvennoe politicheskoe upravlenie
Orgbiuro	Organizatsionnoe biuro
Raikom	Raionnyi komitet
RANION	Rossiiskaia assotsiatsiia nauchno-issledovatel'skikh institutov obshchestvennykh nauk
RAPP	Rossiiskaia assotsiatsiia proletarskikh pisatelei
RGAE	Rossiiskii gosudarstvennyi arkhiv ekonomiki
RGALI	Rossiiskii gosudarstvennyi arkhiv literatury i iskusstva
RKK	Rastsenochno-konfliktnaia komissiia
RKPb	Rossiiskaia kommunisticheskaia partiia (bol'shevikov)
RSDRP	Rossiiskaia sotsial-demokraticheskaia rabochaia partiia (bol'shevikov)
RTsKh	Rossiiskii tsentr khraneniia i izucheniia dokumentov noveishei istorii
SAB	Sredne-aziatskoe biuro
SAT	Sennacieco asocio tutmonda
SEU	Sovetrespublikara esperantista unio
SESR	Soiuz esperantistov sovetskikh respublikakh
SM	Sovet ministerov
SNK	Sovet narodnykh komissarov
Sovnarkom	Sovet narodnykh komissarov
Sovnatsmen	Sovet po prosveshcheniiu narodov nerusskogo iazyka
SSSR	Soiuz sovetskikh sotsialisticheskikh respublikakh

Abbreviations and acronyms

TKK	Terminologicheskaia koda komissiia
TsDNIIaO	Tsentr dokumentatsii noveishii istorii iaroslavskogo oblasti
TsGALI	Tsentral'nyi gosudarstvennyi arkhiv literatury i iskusstva
TsGANI	Tsentral'nyi gosudarstvennyi arkhiv noveishii istorii
TsGANKh	Tsentral'nyi gosudarstvennyi arkhiv narodnogo khoziastva
TsGAOR	Tsentral'nyi gosudarstvennyi arkhiv oktiabr'skoi revoliutsii
TsGA RSFSR	Tsentral'nyi gosudarstvennyi arkhiv RSFSR
TsGAUz	Tsentral'nyi gosudarstvennyi arkhiv uzbekistana
TsIK	Tsentral'nyi ispolnitel'nyi komitet
TsK	Tsentral'nyi komitet
TsKSESR	Tsentral'nyi komitet soiuza esperantistov sovetskikh respublikakh
TsNIIaP	Tsentral'nyi nauchno-issledovatel'skii institut iazykov i pis'mennostei
Uchpedgiz	Uchebnoe pedagogicheskoe izdatel'stvo
UEA	Universala esperantista asocio
VKPb	Vsesoiuznaia kommunisticheskaia partiia (bol'shevikov)
VKS	Vsesoiuznyi komitet po standardizatsii
VTsIK	Vsesoiuznoe tsentral'noe ispol'nitel'noe komitet
VTsKNA	Vsesoiuznyi tsentral'nyi komitet novogo alfavita
VTsKNTA	Vsesoiuznyi tsentral'nyi komitet novogo tiurkskogo alfavita

Notes

Introduction

1. A free translation from the poem, "Rodnoi iazyk" (1911), in Briusov (1973, 2: 66). For more on Briusov's failed project to renew Russian culture through poetry and literature, what he had already recognized as the broken, decaying strands of language, see Grossman (1985) and Rice (1973).
2. Weber (1976) argues this claim. Kaiser (1994: 44-45, 67-71), provides evidence for the Russian case; as does Lewis (1972b: 55-57). Hosking (1997) offers a general survey based on these insights. The new Soviet government was most troubled by the situation, comparing its high illiteracy rates to its meager harvests and high mortality rates (represented to the unwashed masses by thin bags of grain and ghastly skulls). See *Vse na bor'bu s temnotoi* (1923).
3. The quote is from a 1927 report by G.G. Mansurov, a director of the National Minorities Council (Sovnatsmen) of the Commissariat of Education (Narkompros), in TsGA RSFSR f.2306 o.69 d.649 l.8.
4. For discussions of these twin perils - ruralization and easternization - during the civil war era, see Lewin (1985); and Carrere d'Encausse (1978). Quoted from S.M. Dimanshtein in a Communist Academy debate on the question of national cultures, AAN f.350 o.2 d.147 l.135. Semen Markovich Dimanshtein (1886-1937), a leading publicist on national issues, joined the Russian Social Democratic Labor Party in 1904. After the Bolshevik Revolution, he held a variety of important posts: assistant director of the People's Commissariat of the Nationalities and a member of its Director's Board; chair of the Central Bureau of the Jewish Section of the TsK VKPb; member of the Turkic Bureau of the TsK VKPb and of the Committee for the Peoples of the North; assistant director of the Agitational and Propaganda Department of the TsK VKPb; and chair of the Commission for the Study of the National Question of the Communist Academy. From biographical data in AAN f.350 o.3 d.207 l.1.
5. Quotes respectively from Ia. Iakovlev (1924: 3-4); *Stenograficheskii otchet pervogo* (1927: 1); a report to the TsK RKPb (1927), in RTsKh f.17 o.112 d.405 l.178; and a circular of the Commissariat of the Nationalities (1918), in AAN f.350 o.2 d.276 l.31.
6. Lunacharskii's comments in *Rodnoi iazyk i literatura v trudovoi shkole* 1 (1928: 67-80). Danilov (1931d: 3).
7. In the Caucasus, the Soviet government rediscovered the indigenous and related Circassian sub-languages of Adygei, Kabardin, Cherkess, Abazin and Abkhaz; the indigenous languages of Chechnia, Ingushetia and Dagestan

(including Avar, Dargin, Lak, and Lezgin); Ossetian and Talysh (Iranian languages); Kalmyk (a Mongolic language); the Turkic languages of Azerbaijani, Karachai-Balkar, Nogai, Kumyk, and Gagauz (a Turkic language spoken in Moldavia and Ukraine). In the Volga-Urals region and Central Asia, they discovered the Turkic sub-languages of Tatar, Bashkir, Kazakh, Kirgiz, Chuvash, Turkmen, Uzbek, Uigur; and Tajik (an Iranian language). To the north and east, they found the Finno-Ugric sub-languages of Mordvinian, Mari, Komi, Izhor, and Veps; Iakut, Khakass, Shor, and Oirot (Turkic languages of Siberia); Buriat-Mongol; Dungan-Chinese; and the conglomerate Paleo-Asiatic languages of the North. I take the term "sub-language" from Allworth (1967). This is not an exhaustive list, but merely one representing those languages discussed here. For more on the many languages of the former USSR, see Comrie (1981).

8. For discussions of these issues, see Pipes (1964), Rakowska-Harmstone (1974), Connor (1984), Simon (1991), Liber (1992), and Suny (1994).
9. See Patenaude (1995: 552-570) for the interesting historical context. Quoted from *Revoliutsiia i pis'mennost'* 3 (1932: 71).
10. Quoted from Samuelian (1981: 83); and Stalin's *Marksizm i natsional'nyi vopros* in (1951, 2: 296). Stalin wrote this work during 1912 and 1913. For evidence of this mentality, see the 1927 report on "national cultures" in AAN f.350 o.2 d.147 ll. 20-23; the 1928 debate in the Turkmen Communist Party, in RTsKh f.62 o.2 d.1631 l.30; and the debate on nation-making in the Central Asian Bureau of the TsK RKPb, in RTsKh f.62 o.1 d.25 l.41.
11. This problematic formula of the nation, as deriving both from a stable set of objective conditions and a shifting range of subjective choices, dominates today's scholarly discourse. The two sides in the debate are best represented by Smith (1986); and Anderson (1991). Also see the discussion in Deutsch (1966: 78-79); and Suny (1994: chapter 1).
12. I discuss this hierarchy, as yet unexplored in the secondary literature, in chapter two. On Lenin, see Haarman (1992: 118-119).
13. My approach best matches with Kaiser's (1994: 101-105). In contrast, Slezkine (1994: 443-445), notes that "the idea of a formal ranking of ethnic groups was absent from NEP nationality policy". Kirkwood (1991: 64) also argues that "hierarchies of importance were worked out for languages and crudely linked to the politico-ethnic divisions of the Soviet Union" only in the late 1950s.
14. Levi-Strauss (1973: 336-338) has even called writing a modern form of slavery. Historians have otherwise identified language as a simple tool of political power to better control subject populations through the corresponding institutions of education, military service, and industrial labor: See Foucault (1973); Fabian (1986); Bourdieu (1991: part II); Bell (1995: 1403-1437).
15. See Grillo (1989: 4); Lelyveld (1993: 192-193). Quoted from Laitin (1992: 5).

16. For discussions of these and other models, see Fierman (1991); Pool (1976: 425); Kreindler (1985: 2); Moskovich (1989: 85-99).
17. See Fitzpatrick (1992: ix) on "hegemony" and "autonomy". Rieber (1991: 344), on "state institutions" and "social movements". Dunham (1990: 13), on the "coercive powers" of terror and paranoia, and the "regenerative powers" of "accomodation and settlement".
18. See Eklof (1986); Thurston (1991: 541-562); Robin (1990: 26); Clark (1981); and Stites (1992). More recently, scholars have discovered the dialectic between power and resistance in language issues. See the articles (by Mark Steinberg, Caryl Emerson, Diane Koenker, James von Geldern, and Michael Gorham) devoted to the theme, "Language and meaning in Russian history", in *The Russian review* 55 (July 1996).
19. For a revealing statement of his linguistic pretensions, see Stalin's remarks comparing the Bashkir and Tatar languages, during the Orgbiuro reports (26 April 1926) in RTsKh f.17 o.113 d.190 l.62.
20. Quoted from Liber (1992: 33-36). Quoted from the 1924 communist party report on national policy in Azerbaijan, in GAPPOD f.1 o.74 d.42 ll.9-24.
21. From the stenographic report of the meeting in Pavlovich's personal files, TsGAOR f.5402 o.1 d.109 l.27.
22. On the relevance of the "structural method" and its contribution to Soviet language reform, see Arutiunova & Klimov (1968: 155). Jakobson called this "the structural bent in the science of language", in Jakobson (1971: 670). Jakobson & Bogatyrev (1922: 457-458) and Vinokur (1923b: 104-106) were some of the first linguists to define these aspects of language study as the proper ground for 'language planning' (*iazykovaia politika*).
23. I am grateful to David Rich and Eileen Consey for sharing these insights with me, from Richards (1993: 21, 112); and Foucault (1982: 777-778).
24. For more on these varieties of language planning, also known as corpus planning, status planning, and prestige planning, see Haarmann (1990: 103-126); and Cooper (1989).
25. I have benefited from the discussions of these issues, in the American context, in Brown (1992); and Larson (1984: 28-29).
26. "The distinctive feature of Soviet structuralism is that it never developed a special theory of structuralism and never indulged in para-theoretical speculations." Segal (1974: 25-26). For a critical history of structuralist ideas in the twentieth century, see Pavel (1989: 1-18).
27. To cite two of the most interesting examples, Emerson (1996: 359) calls Bakhtin "the patron saint of dialogue". Holquist (1990a: xxxii) refers to certain aspects of Bakhtin studies as "sport only for the initiated".
28. Not so strange perhaps if, following the deconstructive tenets of Roland Barthes and Michael Foucault, we count authors not as willful individuals but as social creations, as functions of the larger discourses of power and the

networks of critics and academics who "create" them in the first place. See Barthes (1977: 147); and Foucault (1980: chapter 2). On the controversy about Voloshinov, who some say was a simple prop for Bakhtin's pen, see Titunik (1986: 91). I follow the practice of the professional linguists who knew and worked with Voloshinov during the 1920s and 1930s in accepting his works as his own. For example, V.A. Desnitskii, one of Voloshinov's academic mentors, judged him a "fully mature" thinker, well read in linguistics and philosophy. From 1929 documents in Voloshinov's personnel file, in TsGA RSFSR f.4655 o.2 d.462 ll.1-4.

29. Ivanov (1976: 270). This approach is inspired by two models: Aarsleff (1982: 314) who writes that "the 'heroic' theory of science reveres discovery and invention, and by the same token plays down or ignores the context"; and Susan Gross Solomon's (1980:4-8) "contextualist" approach.

30. "In the combination of distinctive features into phonemes, the freedom of the individual speaker is zero: the code has already established all the possibilities that may be utilized in the given language. Freedom to combine phonemes into words is circumscribed; it is limited to the marginal situation of word coinage. In forming sentences with words the speaker is less constrained. And, finally, in the combination of sentences into utterances, the action of compulsory syntactical rules ceases, and the freedom of any individual speaker to create novel contexts increases substantially." Jakobson (1971: 242-243).

Chapter 1

1. For the historical background, see Kristoff (1967: 238-255); and Cracraft (1986: 524-540).
2. Rogger (1960: 87-88). Quoted from Hroch (1985), and Levitt (1989: ix, 4-5, 151-156).
3. On the first politicized debates within linguistics, see Gasparov (1985: 297-333).
4. Koerner (1982: 1-39). Müller quoted in Leopold (1987: 501-512).
5. For example, see Müller (1865), Müller (1868-1870), and Müller (1891). For background, see Chemodanov (1956); Mallory (1989); and Renfrew (1987).
6. The phrase is Hans Aarsleff's. For background, see Sliusareva (1974: 265-274), Ferrari-Bravo (1983: 122-139), and Bushnell (1992:1-14).
7. Taylor (1975: 5-29, 81-85, 565-571). Hyppolite (1972: 160-162).
8. Quoted from Humboldt (1988: 48-49, 54-59, 60-77, 93, 169-175). This same text was published in the *Journal of the ministry of national education* in 1858 (numbers 97, 98, 99, 100) with a most congratulatory editorial note praising

Humboldt (1767-1835) as the founder of a "whole new science of language" with important implications for history and anthropology (number 97: 1).
9. See Shpet (1927: 13, 35, 79); and Bakhtin (1981: 270).
10. Locke (1898). Quoted from Litvinova (1892: 45-48). Note also Gorodenskii (1898).
11. Quoted from Potebnia (1892: 164-167); see also the section in it on the "language of feeling and the language of thought" (90-93). This work was published in five editions between 1862 and 1923. Quoted from the comments of I. Plotnikov and A. Betukhov in *Rodnoi iazyk v shkole* 1 (1917: 11-18); 1 (1919-1922: 110-116); and from Potebnia (1913a: 190). A.A. Potebnia (1835-1891) was born in the Poltava province of Ukraine, and educated at Kharkov University and at various universities in Western Europe. His doctoral dissertation of 1874, *Iz zapisok po russkoi grammatike*, was universally recognized as a classic work, and he later received several awards for it, including membership in the Academy of Sciences.
12. Potebnia (1913a: 197, 206-209). This essay was originally published in the journal, *Vestnik Evropy*, in September of 1895.
13. Quoted from Holenstein (1976b: 61-62). Jakobson (1971: 543, 713); and (1988: 168), has testified to the influence of Hegel and Humboldt on structural linguistics; as has De Mauro (1978: 283-363). For background, see Gukhman & Iartseva (1964: 15); and Sliusareva (1976: 442).
14. I take these terms from Anderson (1985). Jan Ignacy Baudouin de Courtenay (1845-1929) finished a master of arts degree at Warsaw (1866) and a doctorate at Leipzig (1870) before holding a number of university posts in the Russian Empire (Kazan and Tartu), becoming a Corresponding Member of the Academy of Sciences (1897) and a professor at St. Petersburg University (1900-1918). Filip Fedorovich Fortunatov (1848-1914) was a professor at Moscow University from 1884 and member of the Academy of Sciences from 1898.
15. Quotes from Stankiewicz (1972: 7-8, 68, 50-52, 141-142, 268); and Badouin de Courtenay (1963: 50, 58). For a critical but balanced biography, see Mugdan (1984). On Baudouin and Fortunatov as founders of a structural approach to language, see Jakobson (1971: 711).
16. Baudouin de Courtenay (1908). Brandt's articles proselytizing Esperanto are collected in the Manuscript Division of the Lenin Library in Moscow.
17. Quotes from Jakobson & Pomorska (1983: 10-11); Erlich (1980: 171); Reformatskii (1988: 30-31); and Peterson, (1956: 12-15). For background on Fortunatov's methods as a transitional approach to structural insights, see Zhuravlev (1990: 22-30); and Gasparov (1970: 177-207).
18. Golanov & Durnovo (1924-1925: 749-756). Vysotskii (1961: 30-66). A.A. Shakhmatov (1864-1920) was a graduate of Moscow University in 1887, becoming a member of the Academy of Sciences in 1894 and professor at St. Petersburg in 1910. Editor of *The dictionary of the Russian language* between

1891 and 1916, he wrote pioneering studies on the history of the Russian literary language and Russian syntax. On the itinerant painters, see Valkenier (1977).
19. Quotes from Erlich (1980: 49, 60). For background, see Jakobson (1971: 523, 529-530, 533); Shklovskii (1966: 91-95); and Burliuk (1914: 81-85).
20. Bradley (1991: 131-139); and Ruane & Eklof (1991: 199-211). Alston (1969: 247-248).
21. Sinel (1973: 215, 250). Wildman (1980: 38). Bushnell (1981: 565-566). Eklof (1986: 124-125, 256, 282, 471).
22. Stites (1992: 24-25); Brooks (1985b); McReynolds (1991: 8-9, 45, 283); Neuberger (1993); Brower (1994: 147-167).
23. Grot (1885-1912). For a review of spelling issues, see Comrie & Stone (1978: chapter 8). Shor & Chemodanov (1945: 269-270).
24. Seregny (1990: 141). Eklof (1986: 401-405, 479, 481-482). Quoted from Brower (1990: 159-160).
25. Chernyshev (1970, 2: 22-23, 680-681); and Chernyshev (1947: 174-182).
26. *Rodnoi iazyk v shkole* 3 (1915: 113-122); 2 (1919-1922: 21-24); 7 (1925: 99-104).
27. Peshkovskii (1914). *Rodnoi iazyk v shkole* 3 (1914: 179-181); 3 (1915: 122); 6 (1915: 296-299).
28. *Rodnoi iazyk v shkole* 1 (1914: 19-24); 4-5 (1914: 284-285); 4-5 (1915: 167-177).
29. For a historical review, see *Rodnoi iazyk v shkole* 4 (1923: 62-64).
30. Quoted from Fishman (1977: xvii). Chernyshev (1947: 170, 176, 182-188, 209-219, 242-246).
31. Brower (1990: 153-155, 164-169). Sinel (1973: 219-226, 231); Eklof (1986: 41). Hans (1964: 157).
32. Brower (1990: 180-181). Frank (1994: 74-76).
33. Zhitomirskii (1915: 257). Mirtov (1915). *Rodnoi iazyk v shkole* 2-3 (1916: 106-107); 6 (1916: 264); 2 (1915: 101-103); 4-5 (1915: 190-193).
34. *Rodnoi iazyk v shkole* 6 (1917: 254-269); 6-10 (1918: 181-187); 5 (1927: 293-298); *Russkaia shkola za rubezhom* 5-6 (1924: 112-118).
35. *Rodnoi iazyk v shkole* 8-10 (1917: 357-364). Budde (1917).
36. *Rodnoi iazyk v shkole* 1 (1917: 18-21); 2-3 (1917: 97-103); 6-10 (1918: 181-187). Ushakov (1917). Quoted from Sakulin (1917a: 1-16). Polivanov (1917: 4).
37. Quoted from a circular of the Ministry of National Education (14 June 1913), in GIA f.309 o.1 d.958 1.3; and Kreindler (1979: 5-26). For the historical background regarding the western provinces, see Thaden (1984) and Weeks (1994).
38. Quoted from Bassin (1991: 9-17); and Kristoff (1968: 352, 364, 369-373).
39. Riasanovsky (1964: 207-220) and (1972: 19-23) has consistently argued this point of view.
40. For a review of Uvarov's policies, see Whittaker (1984: 189-191, 207-212).
41. See Jersild (1996: 641); Slezkine (1993: 120-122); Clay (1995: 45); and Brower & Lazzerini (1997).

42. For three penetrating views, see Crisp (1985: 146); Byrnes (1968: 122-130, 188-202); and Dowler (1995: 516-538).
43. Kreindler (1979: 5-26) argues that Soviet nativization policies were an extension of these imperial policies. Jersild (1996: 646) discusses "an Imperial precedent to the Soviet version of federalism". Dowler (1995: 537) discusses the continuity of a "differential language policy" between the empire and union as well.
44. Baudouin quoted in Rothstein (1975: 395). Stankiewicz (1972: 65-66, 127, 215, 217, 241, 269, 304).
45. See "O smeshannom kharaktere vsekh iazykov" (1901) in Baudouin de Courtenay (1963: 371). "O poniatii smesheniia iazykov" (1923) in Shcherba (1974: 60-74). Bogoroditskii (1934). Polivanov (1968: 143-145, 156-164). Lev Vladimirovich Shcherba (1880-1944) graduated from St. Petersburg University in 1903, and taught General Linguistics there beginning in 1916.
46. See Chernyshev (1970, 2: 679, 685, 688). Rothstein (1975: 390-401); and Toman (1991: 47-50).
47. Shklovskii (1966: 95); Kaverin (1976); Otsup (1961: 76-87). Lartsev (1988). Quoted in Polivanov (1974: 12-13). Evgenii Dmitrievich Polivanov (1890-1938) graduated from St. Petersburg University in 1912 and became a leading specialist in the Turkic and East Asian languages during the 1920s. He joined the communist party in 1919 and worked as a translator for the People's Commissariat of Foreign Affairs and the Communist International between 1917 and 1921, with special responsibility for translating the secret treaties of the Tsarist regime, and for overseeing the organization of Chinese communists.
48. *Slavia* 3 (1924-1925: 749-756); *Slavia* 1, 2-3, 4 (1922: 171-184, 457-469, 626-634). Trubetskoi (1975: viii) and Trubetskoi (1969: 310-311). Jakobson & Pomorska (1983: 13-15).
49. Quoted from *Rodnoi iazyk v shkole* 4-5 (1914: 207-209); 6 (1917: 259-261); 8-10 (1917: 357-358, 426-428); 5 (1927: 293-298). Kreindler (1985: 347).
50. Zenkovsky (1960: 33, 49-51). Bennigsen & Quelquejay (1960: 418-465).
51. Quoted from Rorlich (1986: 88-89). Validov (1986: 74-76, 85, 154-157).
52. Lazzerini (1973: 210-211, 224-229). For a list of the different Turkic newspapers at the turn of the century, and their different "dialects" or sub-languages, see *Musul'manskaia pechat' rossii* (1987); and Bennigsen & Quelquejay (1964).
53. *Politicheskaia zhizn' russkikh musul'man* (1987: 34, 78, 91). Allworth (1990: chapter 8). Swietochowski (1991: 55-63).
54. *Programmnye dokumenty* (1985: 25, 51, 73, 79, 87, 90-91). Shorish (1984a: 249); and Davlet (1989: 23).
55. Quoted from the "top secret" report from the Department of Police (Ministry of Internal Affairs) to the Baku Governor (31 December 1900), in GIA f.45 o.1 d.35 l.1, which discusses Gasprinskii's work and influence.

Chapter 2

1. Quoted from the protocol of the Plenum of the TsK AKPb and Caucasus Bureau of the TsK RKPb and Baku Commissariat AKPb (8 November 1920), in GAPPOD f.1 o.1 d.14 1.20.
2. Lunacharskii's comments in "Rechi," *Zapiski instituta zhivogo slova* 1 (1919: 12-22). Maiakovskii (1978, 3: 250-252). For background, see Rabinowitch (1976).
3. Quoted from Vinokur (1971: 136). The full-page layouts on language problems, under the headings, "Rabochaia zhizn'", in *Pravda* 284, 285, 286 (21, 22, 23 November 1923); Trotskii (1923).
4. *Zhurnalist* 1 (1922: 46), a good source of articles dealing with these issues.
5. Selishchev (1925: 207); and the classic work, Selishchev (1928). Uspenskii (1931: 273-281), offers a valid critique of Selishchev's methods. For background, see Brooks (1982: 187-202); and Gorham (1994: 33). Afanasii Matveevich Selishchev (1886-1942), born in impoverished rural surroundings, graduated with a diploma from the Historical-Philological Faculty of Kazan University in 1911, soon becoming a professor at Moscow State University and a specialist in the study of the Slavic languages.
6. Selishchev (1928: 158-161); Shafir (1923); Shpilrein & Reitenberg & Netskii (1928); Larin (1928: 175-184); and the articles in *Krasnaia pechat'*, *Zhurnalist*, *Russkii iazyk v sovetskoi shkole*, and *Pechat' i revoliutsiia* between these same years. Stites (1991: 300-301). For an account of the gap between city and village speech during the Provisional Government, see Figes (1997: 342-344).
7. *Zhurnalist* 14 (1924: 15-16); Lunacharskii quoted in *Rodnoi iazyk i literatura v trudovoi shkole* 1 (1928: 64, 72-74). *Zapiski kommunisticheskogo universiteta imeni Sverdlova* II (1924: 242).
8. Stites (1989: 88-89). Quoted from Tugenkhol'd (1926: 57).
9. For background, see Stites (1992: 41-45); and Russell (1982: 390-412). Shaginian (1991) is a leading example of just this kind of fiction.
10. Quoted from *Zhurnalist* 4 (1923: 5); 3 (1923: 5, 21-26). *Narodnyi uchitel'* 3 (1925: 110-114). For background, Kenez (1985: 224); and Brooks (1989: 20-22).
11. Kenez (1985: 227-233). *Zhurnalist* 1 (1922: 59-60); 2 (1922: 3-8).
12. *Vremia* 3 (1923: 48-49); *Narodnyi uchitel'* 3 (1924: 13-19); *Zhurnalist* 1 (1922: 32-35).
13. Von Hagen (1990: 107, 161). Robin (1991: 253-267). Coe (1993) offers a detailed study of the "correspondence" movement.
14. Rubakin (1924: 10-14). Shafir (1927: 63). Rubakin (1929: 108). Iakov Moiseevich Shafir (born in 1887) was a member of the Odessa War-Revolutionary Committee during the Russian Revolution and a member of the RKPb from 1920. From biographical materials in AAN f.350 o.3 d.324 1.26.
15. Gus (1927: 57-61). Gus (1930: 65-68); Broz & Gus (1928: 91). Mikhail Semenovich Gus (1900-1984), a graduate of the Juridical Faculty of Kiev

University in 1918, and an active participant in the Russian Revolution, joined the RKPb in 1920. A party journalist and member of the NOT League in Ukraine between 1919 and 1926, he later worked as a teacher and administrator at the State Journalism Institute (1927-1930).
16. *Zhurnalist* 4 (1923: 55-56); 1 (1922: 47-48). Karpinskii (1923: 1). Shafir (1926).
17. Gus & Zagorianskii & Kaganovich (1926). Their newspaper sources were *Kommunist* (elite), *Rabochaia gazeta* (mass worker), and *Bednota* (mass peasant).
18. *Zhurnalist* 1 (1925: 12-14); 2 (1925: 5-10); 3 (1925: 13-16); 4 (1925: 11-14); 8-9 (1925: 40-43).
19. Instructions of the "Down with Illiteracy" publishing house (1927), in TsGA RSFSR f.296 o.1 d.72 ll.192-193. *Russkii iazyk v sovetskoi shkole* 1 (1931: 37-39).
20. "Rechi", in *Zapiski instituta zhivogo slova* 1 (1918: 12-22).
21. *Zapiski instituta zhivogo slova* 1 (1918: 13-14, 52-53).
22. From the course syllabi of L.V. Shcherba, V.I. Chernyshev and others, in *Zapiski instituta zhivogo slova* 1 (1918: 29-31, 62, 69, 71, 85). Bernshtein (1927: 41-53). Quoted from Pashkov (1925: 164-169).
23. AAN f.502 0.3 d.96 ll.2-3 contains a list of the writers from whom dictionary entries were collected (including 6,975 words from Viacheslav Ivanov, 5,482 from Demian Bednyi, 5,067 from Mayakovskii, and 3,770 from Lenin). Brooks (1985a: 159); Kenez (1985: 97-104). Maguire (1987).
24. Kruchenykh (1928: 7-12). *Uchenye zapiski instituta iazyka i literatura RANIONa* 1 (1927: 130-133).
25. Documents of the Central Bureau of the Communists of the East (1919-1921), in RTsKh f.583 o.1 d.123 l.12; and of the Council of National Minorities, in TsGA RSFSR f.296 o.2 d.41 l.9. Allworth (1990: 178-179).
26. Debates in TsGAOR f.1318 o.1 d.665 l.11; d.706(1) ll.1-2; and d.706 (2) ll.96,113. Documents in TsGAUz f.17 o.1 d.1062 l.30; f.34 o.1 d.1792 ll.1,15.
27. Reports on the Turkic peoples to the RKPb (1920-1921), in RTsKh f.583 o.1 d.160 ll.5,14; d.179 l.2; d.19 ll.18-19,29; in TsGA RSFSR f.296 o.2 d.37 ll.2-3; and in RTsKh f.61 o.1 d.68 ll.2,26. Telegram from the Kazan Reinforcement Staff to Trotskii (27 June 1919), in RTsKh f.583 o.1 d.145 l.54. Reports on the RSFSR nationalities (1923-1926), in RTsKh f.17 o.60 d.1023 ll.6-12; d.1034 l.24; and in TsGAOR f.3316 o.19 d.355 ll.12-18.
28. For an open discussion of party chauvinism, see Riddell (1993: 104-107, 293). Quotes respectively from the reports of the RKPb on the Communist Party of Turkestan, in RTsKh f.17 o.112 d.374 l.42; and RTsKh f.62 o.1 d.20 l.200; comments in *Izvestiia iugo-vostochnogo biuro TsK RKPb* 6/13 (November 1922: 47); and TsIK RSFSR documents in TsGAOR f.1235 o.119 d.39 ll.73-77.
29. As reported in TsGA RSFSR f.2306 o.1 d.182 ll.87-8. Blank (1994: 23-24, 93, 115). Krasovitskaia (1986).
30. These charges were made respectively from Narkomnats (1918), in TsGA RSFSR f.2306 o.2 d.306 l.5; from Narkompros, in TsGA RSFSR f.296 o.2 d.7 l.5; from

Sovnatsmen (1923), in RTsKh f.17 o.60 d.1017 l.5; and from Turkestan (1919 to 1923), in RTsKh f.122 o.1 d.58 l.108; in TsGA RSFSR f.296 o.2 d.35 l.40; and in TsGAUz f.25 o.1 d.1021 l.395; TsGAUz f.34 o.1 d.1935 l.21.

31. Quoted from Narkompros directives and instructions in TsGA RSFSR f.2306 o.1 d.182 ll.87-8; o.2 d.563 l.12.

32. Pokrovskii's remarks in RTsKh f.17 o.60 d.1017 l.5. Narkompros and Sovnatsmen reports between 1919 and 1923, in TsGA RSFSR f.2306 o.2 d.622 l.220; o.1 d.2197 ll.23-35. The Turkestan TsIK report of 1923 in TsGAUz f.17 o.1 d.1084 l.1.

33. Narkompros RSFSR reports in TsGA RSFSR f.296 o.1 d.60 l.1; TsGAOR f.1235 o.119 d.39 ll.1, 93-102. The 1921 Letter to Stalin, in TsGA RSFSR f.296 o.2 d.34 ll.1-7.

34. The quote is from a member of the Central Bureau of Communists of the East, in RTsKh f.583 o.1 d.179 l.83. For Stalin's support of these measures, see his "Dolkad o sovetskoi avtonomii Terskoi oblasti" (17 November 1920) in Stalin (1951, 4: 399-407). For background, see Nenarokov (1990: 4).

35. See the boasts in Durdenevskii (1927); and Dimanshtein (1936). For the 1921 decrees of the Azerbaijani Revolutionary Committee and its successors, see GANI f.411 o.3 d.2 l.14; f.57 o.1 d.170. The 1921 and 1923 decrees of the Sovnarkom and TsIK of the Turkestan SSR (see TsGAOR f.1235 o.118 d.1 ll.117,131) recognized Uzbek, Kirgiz (Kazakh), Turkmen, and Russian as the equal native languages of the republic.

36. The quotes are from TsIK RSFSR documents in TsGAOR f.1235 o.118 d.1 ll.27,59,176,357; o.119 d.25 l.5. Tsentral'nyi Ispol'nitel'nyi Komitet (1927).

37. Samurskii (1925: 116); and his articles in *Sovetskoe stroitel'stvo* 1 (1928: 128); and *Revolutsiia i gorets* 3 (1931: 62-63). In 1925, at an all-Dagestani conference, the communist party resolved to promote both Azeri Turkic and Russian as the dual "state languages", from TsGAOR f. 5402 o.1 d.94 ll.38-48; and RTsKh f.17 o.113 d.268 l.28.

38. On Ukraine, see Shevelov (1989: chapter five); and Liber (1992: chapter six). On Belorussia, see Vakar (1956: 139-142); Wexler (1974: chapter 10); and Guthier (January 1977: 58-60) and (April 1977: 273-274).

39. On the high costs of nativization, see Vareikis (1926); and such documents as the 1922 report of the Turkestan Narkomnats, in TsGAUz f.17 o.1 d.1079 l.44. The guidelines (dated 13 August 1923) are located in RTsKh f.62 o.2 d.158 ll.12-19. Materials on the Uzbek nativization commissions (1927-1928), in TsGAUz f.837 o.5 d.519 ll.7,44-45,197,200; and (1930-1931), in TsGAUz f.837 o.8 d.458 ll.7,74. Fierman (1991: 178).

40. Quoted from Tsentral'nyi Ispol'nitel'nyi Komitet (1927: 19). Mekhmedzade (no date). Kurbangaliev & Gazizov (1925). Reports from the early 1920s, in TsGAUz f.34 o.1 d.974; TsGAUz f.94 o.5 d.606 ll.18-20. TsK KPUz circular (1927), in TsGAUz f.837 o.3 d.503 l.64.

41. Protocol of the Meeting of the full TsK AKPb and Stalin (8 November 1920), in GAPPOD f.1 o.1 d.14. On autonomization, see "Doklad o sovetskoi avtonomii Terskoi oblasti" (17 November 1920), in Stalin (1951, 4: 399).
42. For background, see Rorlich (1986: 131-145); and Schafer (1995: 452-454).
43. Allworth (1990: 179-209) offers a leading interpretation. On Stalin's role in subduing 'frictions', see the report of the Central Asian Bureau (2 June 1924) in RTsKh f.62 o.2 d.87 1.155; the Protocol of the Orgbiuro meeting (4 June 1924) and the report of the Central Asian Bureau to the Orgbiuro (4 June 1924), both in RTsKh f.17 o.112 d.566 ll.3, 16-28; and the 1924 report of the Communist Party of Turkestan in RTsKh f.62 o.2 d.158 ll.1,46. On policy towards the Uzbeks and Kazakhs, see the heated debates in the stenographic report of the meeting of the Central Asian Bureau (28 April 1924), in RTsKh f.62 o.1 d.25 ll.26-63. On policy towards the Tatars, see the stenographic report of the Central Asian Bureau (13 April 1924), in RTsKh f.62 o.1 d.20 ll.45-46.
44. Remarks from the Central Asian Bureau of the VKPb (1931), in RTsKh f.62 o.2 d.2470 l.113.
45. For examples of this argument, see Iskhaki (1933: 52-54); Caroe (1953b: 154-159); Bennigsen (1967: 250); Rywkin (1990: 92); Pipes (1989: 205).
46. The hierarchy is paraphrased from I. Davydov's "project resolution" (July 1926), in TsGA RSFSR f.296 o.1 d.169. Narkompros accepted it officially and distributed it widely in government forums. For more on debates about state-building and nation-making, see Kaiser (1994: 108-110); and Hirsch (1997: 251-278).
47. See the reports, "Natsional'nye momenty v partiinom i gosudarstvennom stroitel'stve," and "Doklad o natsional'nykh momentakh v partiinom i gosudarstvennom stroitel'stve," in Stalin (1947, 5: 181-194, 236-263). Dimanshtein quoted during the debates (February of 1926) at the Communist Academy, in AAN f.350 o.2 d.21 l.65.
48. Statistics reported in TsGA RSFSR f.2306 o.2 d.306 ll.6-17.
49. Narkompros circular (1924), in TsGA RSFSR f.1575 o.1 d.524 l.66. *Sovetskoe stroitel'stvo* 12 (1927: 97); *Narodnoe prosveshchenie* 11-12 (1927: 229-233); *Voprosy prosveshcheniia na severnom kavkaze* 12 (1926). The Sovnatsmen report (1926), in TsGA RSFSR f.296 o.1 d.212 l.2. Azerbaijani Narkompros correspondence (1923), GANI f.57 o.1 d.260 l.274.
50. Stenogram of the TsK AKPb Presidium (18 January 1926), in GAPPOD f.1 d.74 o.153 l.62. Quoted respectivley from Dimanshtein's comments in the Communist Academy, in AAN f.350 o.2 d.156 l.35; d.267 l.24; I. Davydov's and N. Chekov's comments in *Prosveshchenie natsional'nostei* 1 (1929: 17-29, 87-93). *Spravochnik dlia postupaiushchik* (1926: 5, 14-15, 21).
51. As pithily stated in Enukidze (1926: 50-53).
52. For Stalin's pronouncements on language issues between 1904 and 1929, see Stalin (1946-1951, 2: 330; 3: 138-139; 11: 341-349; and 13: 5). Quoted from Connor (1984: 259, 394-396).

53. Quotes respectively from *Rodnoi iazyk i literatura v trudovoi shkole* 1 (1928: 41, 67-81); Gasilov (1929: 17). Also see a review of Mikoian's speech at the 1925 conference on "The Problems of Culture and Education for the Mountain Peoples of the North Caucasus," in *Voprosy prosveshcheniia na severnom kavkaze* 8 (1927: 41). In the words of the Theses of the Second Plenum of the TsK KP(b) of Turkmenistan (1928), "without the Russian language, the Turkmens are not in a position to master the cultural achievements of humankind . . . ." Quoted from RTsKh f.62 o.2 d.1631 l.62.
54. I have liberally assembled these quotes from a variety of sources: educational reports in TsGA RSFSR f.296 o.1 d.267 ll.6-14; d.268 l.18; d.308 ll.10-13; d.434 ll.117-123. Mirtov (1926: 7). Birger & Chekov (1928: 5-6). Report on cultural work in Turkmenistan (1931), in RTsKh f.62 o.2 d.2590 l.16. The internal police (NKVD) circular (1924), in TsGAOR f.1235 o.119 d.39 ll.73-74. The report on the Bashkir party organization (26 April 1926), in RTsKh f.17 o.113 d.190 l.25. Enukidze quoted from a 1927 debate in the Presidium of the Council of Nationalities of TsIK, in TsGAOR f.3316 o.20 d.153 ll.36-37,47,52.
55. The debate on nativization, in TsGAOR f.3316 o.20 d.431 l.34. Report on the work of the Bashkir party organization (1926), in RTsKh f.17 o.113 d.190. The Sovnatsmen informational report on literacy work in Kazan, Vladikavkaz and Moscow (1925), in TsGA RSFSR f.296 o.1 d.112 l.8. *Voprosy prosveshcheniia na severnom kavkaze* 12 (1926: 52).
56. *Revoliutsiia i gorets* 1 (1928: 40). Debate in the Communist Academy, in AAN f.350 o.2 d.266 l.14. Report from Saratov (1923), in TsGA RSFSR f.296 o.1 d.70 ll.2-4. Comments in Tsentral'nyi Ispol'nitel'nyi Komitet (1927: 47).
57. Narkompros RSFSR Director's Board and inspection reports (1927), in TsGA RSFSR f.2306 o.69 d.847; d.1342 ll.10-11. Quotes from *Voprosy prosveshcheniia na severnom kavkaze* 2 (1926: 133-135); 1 (1927); 3 (1927); 4 (1927); 7 (1927: 52). For background on Russian as the new *koine* of the USSR, and the varied types of language contact and mixing in the early Soviet experience, see Lewis (1972b: 273, 275-293).
58. Atadzhanov (1976: 129-130). The TsIk and SNK circulars of 1925, in TsGAUz f.837 o.5 d.519 ll.204-208. 1927 materials of the Uzbekification Commission (UzTsIK), in TsGAUz f.837 o.5 d.519 l.194. The reports on nativization between 1924 and 1929 in the Uzbek archives are replete with these complaints: TsGAUz f.25 o.1 d.875 ll.8,29; f.94 o.5 d.466 l.5,18; f.837 o.3 d.593 l.32; o.6 d.495 l.7; o.6 d.494 l.75.
59. Dimanshtein quoted in 1928 during debates at the Communist Academy, in AAN f.350 o.2 d.267 l.90. For similar problems with Kirgiz (Kazakh) 'promoted ones', see the documents of the Nationalities Department, in TsGAOR f.1235 o.118 d.1 l.331.
60. On the failure of the courses, see the reports of the Central Asian Bureau of the VKPb (1930), and Central Asian Bureau correspondence (1931) with the internal

police (OGPU) on national antagonisms, in RTsKh f.62 o.2 d.2390 ll.76,162; d.2575 l.48. Quoted from reports on Uzbekification (1927-1931), in TsGAUz f.837 o.5 d.519 l.194; o.8 d.458 ll.90,136,160,200; o.9 d.172 ll.2,15; d.173 l.12. Dimanshtein's report to the Communist Academy (13 April 1927), "The national minorities in the USSR and abroad," in AAN f.350 o.2 d.156 l.33.
61. On the schools, see the Narkompros report on national education (1926) in Ulianovsk, Kursk and Voronezh, in TsGA RSFSR f.2306 o.69 d.720; and the Main Committee for Social Education (Glavsotsvos) circular (1924), in TsGA RSFSR f.1575 o.1 d.524 l.66. A Russian student quoted from the debate comments in Tsentral'nyi Ispol'nitel'nyi Komitet (1927: 25, 41). For confirmation of Russian chauvinism in the 1920s and 1930s, see Payne (1995: 237, 285, 306-307).
62. V.N. Shul'gin's 1928 report, "O natsional'nykh antagonizmakh i bor'be s nimi," presented to the State Academic Council of the Narkompros RSFSR, in TsGA RSFSR f.298 o.1 d.40 l.6. N. Konoplev (1931: 46-52).

Chapter 3

1. Quoted from Shpet (1927a: 16-17, 12-13).
2. Fitzpatrick (1992: 42-47). Vucinich (1984: 80, 111-113). Graham (1993: 174).
3. *Uchenye zapiski instituta iazyka i literatury RANIONa* 1 (1927: 128-133). Documents of the Moscow Linguistic Society in AAN f.696 o.1 d.58 ll.1-5; d.155 ll.1-6, 54-64. Mikhail Nikolaevich Peterson (1885-1962) was a professor at Moscow State University between 1919 and 1937, a specialist in Comparative Linguistics and Sanskrit languages. Dmitri Nikolaevich Ushakov (1873-1942), professor of Linguistics at Moscow State University, was perhaps best known for his work on Russian pronunciation and orthography, as well as his very popular, *Short introduction to the science of language* (1913).
4. Quoted from Peterson (1928: 206-207). For discussions about Saussure, see the reports of the Moscow Linguistic Circle (1923), in TsGALI f.2164 o.1 d.1 l.2; TsGA RSFSR f.2307 o.2 d.431 ll.4-5; and TsGA RSFSR f.2307 o.2 d.431 l.4. For early favorable reviews of Saussure's structural insights, see Vinokur (1923c: 104-113); and Nikiforov (1924: 236).
5. The quote about Kartsevskii is from Jakobson (1971: 518, 713, 531-533). Kartsevskii's remarks in *Rodnoi iazyk i literatura v trudovoi shkole* 1 (1928: 24). Also see the critiques of formalism in Kartsevskii (1927); his articles in *Russkaia shkola za rubezhom* 12 (1924: 47-65), and *Slavia* 4 (1925-1926: 197-198); and his series of book reviews in *Russkaia shkola za rubezhom* between 1923 and 1927.

6. See Peshkovskii's comments in *Rodnoi iazyk i literatura v trudovoi shkole* 2 (1928: 50-57). Quoted from Hjelmslev's personal letter to Peterson (30 September 1929), in AAN f.696 o.1 d.692 l.13; and Hjelmslev (1976: 40, 43, 94, 95, 107, 115-118, 125). Aleksandr Matveevich Peshkovskii (1878-1933) was a 1906 graduate of Moscow University and professor there between 1926 and 1933, a specialist in scientific grammars, intonation studies, and teaching methods.
7. See the moving personal statement in the "Preface" to Shpet (1989: 11-19). Much of the material that follows is drawn from Shpet's own autobiography (along with testimony by P.S. Kogan), contained in his statement before the RKPb purge hearings in July of 1930. TsGA RSFSR f.4655 o.1 d.283, beginning with ll.248-252. Gustav Gustavovich Shpet (1879-1937) was born in Kiev to a family of impoverished Polish textile workers, owing much of his future success to his own self-education. During his late teens, he read Marx and Plekhanov, Kautsky and Lenin, soon becoming a member of the "Workers' Will" (*Rabochaia volia*) movement, for which he was imprisoned for a time while he was a student in the Historical-Philological Faculty at Kiev University. After 1905, graduate work took him to Moscow, France, England, Scotland, and finally to Germany for studies with Husserl.
8. Quoted from the testimony of Kaverin (1978: 277). Quoted from Asmus (1927: 250-251).
9. Quoted from Jakobson (1971: 518, 713, 532-533); TsGA RSFSR f.2307 o.2 d.431 l.4. Erlich (1980: 62). For a fine study of Shpet's thought, especially his "sociological" approach, see Haardt (1993).
10. Shpet put this principle eloquently when he wrote that "language is universal for everyone; each person carries within their self the key to understanding all languages". From Shpet (1927a: 28). See also Investigation I, "Expression and meaning", Investigation III, "On the theory of wholes and parts", and Investigation IV, "The distinction between independent and non-independent meanings", in Husserl (1977); and Edie (1987). Shpet (1914) surveyed Husserl's thought.
11. See respectively Shpet (1927a: 12, 16-19, 38, 46, 51, 68, 178); and Shpet (1927b [1989]: 564-565).
12. Quoted from Shpet's remarks at his purge hearings, in TsGA RSFSR f.4655 o.1 d.283 l.268. Quoted from descriptions of the work of N.N. Volkov, A.F. Losev, V.V. Vinogradov, E.Iu. Shabad, N.F. Iakovlev, and others, in the series, *Biulleten GAKhN* 4-11 (1926-1928).
13. Shpet (1917), later expanded and revised as Shpet (1927b [1989]: 514-515, 560, 573-574; 482, 568).
14. Vinokur's "O vozmozhnosti vseobshchei grammatiki," delivered before the Philosophical Section of GAKhN on 8 March 1927. See *Biulleten GAKhN* 8-9 (1927-1928: 17); reprinted in Vinokur (1988: 71-90).

15. I discuss the party's campaign against him in chapter four. Contemporary Soviet semioticians, though they often speak in Shpet's very own terms, have largely branded him as a "subjective idealist". For example, see Lotman (1976: 15-17). Nemeth (1995: 103) terms Shpet's work "at best a mundane phenomenology of the social". Clark & Holquist (1984: 379) dismiss him as an "eccentric and brilliant phenomenologist". Joravsky (1989) does not even mention his name. On the other hand, for favorable estimations of Shpet's work and influence, see Steiner (1988: 81); Ivanov (1976: 266-269); and Holenstein (1976a).
16. See the comments of Zhirkov and his colleagues (A.M. Peshkovskii, M.N. Peterson, and N.F. Iakovlev), in the protocol of the meeting of the Moscow Linguistic Circle (4 February 1923), during a talk by R.O. Shor about Saussure, in AAN f.696 o.1 d.155 l.87. Vinokur's comments in his report, "O vozmozhnosti vseobshchei grammatiki", in Vinokur (1988: 71-90). On teleology, see Iakubinskii (1974: 323); Vinokur (1923a: 205); Erberg (1928: 163); and Jakobson's 1927 essay, "The concept of the sound law and the teleological criterion", in Jakobson (1962: 1-2).
17. Iakovlev (1923). Karinskii's lectures on "struktura iazyka," in AAN f.468 o.1 d.24 ll.2-17; d.42 ll.17-25.
18. Shor (1926) combined a study of phonetics and phonology with sociology and geography. Beliaev (1928: 128-135) offered a first, tentative step toward a materialist conception of semiotics. Shcherba's "O troiakom aspekte iazykovykh iavlenii" (1931), in Shcherba (1974: 24-39) discussed the physiological, psychological, and sociological aspects of language.
19. Vinokur's autobiographical remarks in TsGALI f.2164 o.1 d.41 ll.3-5. Vinokur (1925: 21-31) contrasted the dual aspects of the "word" as either "scientific term" or as "symbolic image". In the 1920s, he published a series of articles in *LEF, Pechat' i revoliutsiia, Zhurnalist*, and *Russkii iazyk v sovetskoi shkole*, later compiled into Vinokur (1929b). Shor (1927: 66-69). Grigorii Osipovich Vinokur (1896-1947) studied at Moscow University under Ushakov and Peterson, was intimately involved in the Futurist movement of the 1920s, later teaching at the university and becoming a member of the Academy of Sciences in 1933. Rozaliia Osipovna Shor (1894-1939), one of the few women linguists of the interwar years, did graduate work in Comparative Linguistics and Sanskrit at Moscow State University in the 1920s.
20. Gus referred to structural linguistics as the "elucidation of the semasiological and morphological characteristics of language", in a letter to Vinokur of 17 February 1927, in TsGALI f.2164 o.1 d.9 ll.1-2. Broz & Gus (1928: 89, 91-94, 113, 134). Gus (1930: 76, 81).
21. *Iazyk i literatura* 3 (1928: 156-178). *Krasnaia gazeta* (12 April 1930: 2). Lev Petrovich Iakubinskii (1892-1945) was a graduate of St. Petersburg University

(1913), author of two influential tracts, "On the sounds of poetic language" (1916-1919), and "On dialogic speech" (1923), both of which drew from Baudouin de Courtenay's language theories to discuss the relationship of sound to meaning.
22. Polivanov (1931: 267). TsGA f.4655 o.1 d.389 ll.10-11,12,71; d.407 ll.1-2; d.415 ll.6-10,11-26. AAN f.468 o.3 d.21 ll.1,20; d.22; d.28.
23. Vinokur quoted from *Zhurnalist* 5 (1923: 46-50); and 14 (1924: 32-35).
24. Reformatskii (1933a: 42-58). Reformatskii (1933b: 95-101). Reformatskii partly conducted this work on the legibility of the "sign" at the Moscow State Institute of Psychology under B.A. Artemov's direction.
25. Reports to Narkompros (1927), in TsGA RSFSR f.2306 o.69 d.847 ll.53-54. Resolution of the Orgbiuro of the TsK (1936), in RTsKh f.17 o.114 d.601 l.94. Comments at a general meeting of workers' correspondents and newspaper editors of the Iaroslavl region (1936), in TsDNIIaO f.272 o.223 d.228 ll.15,32,43,68.
26. Jakobson (1971: 712). Trubetskoi (1975: 87, 121, 143, 150, 200, 229). Roman Osipovich Jakobson (born in 1896) was a graduate of the Lazarev Institute of Eastern Languages in 1914 and of Moscow State University in 1918. He helped to establish the Moscow, Prague, and New York Linguistic Circles. Nikolai Sergeevich Trubetskoi (1890-1938) graduated from Moscow University in 1913 and taught there between 1915 and 1916. After the Bolshevik Revolution, he eventually settled in Vienna, holding its chair in Slavic linguistics until his death.
27. Trubetskoi quoted from Toman (1995: 193-196, 200-210), which also offers a review of Trubetskoi's theories, emphasizing his cultural relativism rather than Russian exceptionalism. For background, see Liberman (1991: 322); Pomorska (1977: 371-372); and Gamkrelidze & Ivanov & Tolstoi (1987: 492-501).
28. See the essay, "K kharakteristike evraziiskogo iazykovogo soiuza" (1930), in Jakobson (1971: 144-201). See Jakobson's praises of Shpet in the protocols of the Moscow Linguistic Circle, AAN f.696 o.1 d.155 l.7; and in a private letter to Shpet (December 1928) from Prague, in GBOR f.718 o.25 d.67 ll.2-4. Savitskii's 9 August 1930 letter to Jakobson is translated in Toman (1994: 132).
29. Kristoff (1968: 376-387). Liberman (1991: 233, 345). Trubetskoi (1991: 147). *Evraziistvo* (1927); and *Evraziistvo* (1932). For a stunning presentation of the Eurasian thesis in the official journal of Narkomnats, see Arkhincheev (1924: 45-55).
30. See and compare Iakovlev's varied works: (1922: 4-5), (1923:5), and (1928: 123-148).
31. The 1922-1924 reports of the Circle, in TsGALI f.2164 o.1 d.1 ll.2-19; and TsGA RSFSR f.2307 o.2 d.431 ll.4-5. The reports of the Institute, in TsGA

RSFSR f.2307 o.10 d.275 ll.37-39; d.278 ll.161-162; and TsGA RSFSR f.4655 o.1 d.289 ll.54-59. Nikolai Feofanovich Iakovlev (1892-1974) graduated from Moscow University in 1914, a specialist in the North Caucasian languages. His close collaborator, Lev Ivanovich Zhirkov (1885-1963) was a graduate of the Lazarev Institute of Eastern Languages (1911), a specialist in Persian philology. He also studied under Baudouin de Courtenay at St. Petersburg after 1914.

32. RANION reports in TsGA RSFSR f.4655 o.1 d.45 l.13; ll.45-47. Narkompros RSFSR reports (1925-1927), in TsGA RSFSR f.296 o.1 d.118 ll.1-2,12; d.412 ll.37-38; o.2 d.388 l.27; and in TsGAOR f.1318 o.1 d.62(b) l.34; d.64; f.3316 o.19 d.332 l.16.

33. Davydov's reports between 1925 and 1931, in TsGA RSFSR f.296 o.1 d.116 ll.113-114; d.72 ll.85-93; d.470 ll.175-176. Bubrikh (1929: 73-74). Iakovlev's remarks in *Stenograficheskii otchet tret'ego* (1928: 10-11). Dmitrii Vladimirovich Bubrikh (1890-1949) graduated with a Master's Degree from St. Petersburg University in 1920, where he studied under Baudouin de Courtenay. A specialist in the Finno-Ugric languages, he was appointed a professor at Leningrad State University in 1925 and Corresponding Member of the Academy of Sciences in 1946.

34. The 1918-1919 reports of the Orientology Institute, in TsGAUz f.17 o.1 d.1062 l.29; reports in TsGAUz f.34 o.1 d.1191 l.67; d.1190 l.2. *Prosveshchenie* 1 (Tashkent, 1922: 14), and 6 (1921: 15).

35. Mansurov & Epshtein (1927: 6-10). On the method, see the debate of the Presidium, Council of Nationalities, TsIK SSSR (1927), in TsGAOR f.3316 o.20 d.153 l.343; I. Davydov's remarks (1929 and 1931) in TsGA RSFSR f.296 o.1 d.434 l.33; d.470; Mirtov (1926: 7); Luk'ianennko (1926); *Russkii iazyk v sovetskoi shkole* 3 (1930: 179-180); *Natsional'naia kniga* 1 (1930: 38-41); *Prosveshchenie i natsional'nostei* 6 (1930: 96).

36. D.V. Bubrikh, "The Russian Language and its Distinctions from Mordvinian," in TsGA RSFSR f.296 o.1 d.447 ll.1-18. *Russkii iazyk v mordovskoi shkole* (1928). *Kul'tura i pis'mennost' vostoka* 10 (1931: 128-131); and 7-8 (1931: 85, 88).

37. Polivanov (1927: 111-122). Danilov (1931d: 3, 6-7, 161-163). Danilov & Ustinov (1928: 5-20, 31. Georgii Kondratievich Danilov (born in 1896) attended Moscow University in 1914, sympathized with the Socialist Revolutionaries during the civil war, and joined the communist party in 1920 (he was purged in 1922 for "intellectual unreliability" but rejoined in 1925). He was a member of the Institute of Language and Literature (RANION) and of the Linguistics Faculty at the Communist University of the Workers of the East. From biographical materials in TsGA RSFSR f.4655 o.1 d.371 l.45; and o.2 d.485 ll.1-100.

38. Polivanov (1931: 315, 321, 67-72). Nikiforov & Danilov (1928: 15). Danilov's reports, in TsGA RSFSR f.4655 o.1 d.369 l.110; d.394 f.32.
39. Quoted from Taylor (1981: 58-59). *Vremia* 1 (October 1923: 5-6). *Pravda* 23/XI (1923: 5); *Narodnyi uchitel'* 11 (1926: 2); 1 (1926: 158). For the historical context, see Bailes (1978) and Beissinger (1988).
40. Gastev quoted from Brodskii & Sidorov (1924: 263-267). Bogdanov (1914: 59).
41. Quotes from Bogdanov (1922: 6); Bogdanov (1925b: 72-79); Bogdanov (1923: 20-24); and Bogdanov (1980: 2-3, 17-19). For a review of the historical context, see Sochor (1988: 46-47); and of Bogdanov's philosophy, see Jensen (1978: 34-35).
42. Nikiforov & Danilov (1928: 6-15). *Vestnik znaniia* (1926-1928) was filled with such articles. Rybnikova (1931: 84). Barkhin (1933: 118-119). Iakovlev and Polivanov's comments in *Stenograficheskii otchet pervogo* (1927: 146); *Stenograficheskii otchet tret'ego* (1928: 10).
43. Kruchenykh (1923b: 3-6). The essay, "The general phonetic principle of any poetic technique," in Polivanov (1974: 350-367). Gofman (1936). Drezen (1926-1927). On the Bolshevik revolution and "word-creation" (*slovotvorchestvo*), see Gorlov (1924: 21-48); and Mally (1990).
44. Durdenevskii (1927: 13-16). Suny (1972). Volkogonov (1991: 8).
45. The veteran Esperantists A.P. Andreev and Ernst Drezen gave talks on the international language to the Linguistic Section of the Institute of Language and Literature (RANION) in the late 1920s, from *Uchenye zapiski instituta iazyka i literatura RANIONa* 3 (1928: 205).
46. Iushmanov (1987: 458-459). On *etem*, see Iushmanov (1922b: 33-34), and Iushmanov (1922a: 43-44). N.V. Iushmanov (born in 1896) studied Hebrew, Arabic, Syrian, Georgian, and Armenian at St. Petersburg University in 1913, a student of L.V. Shcherba and N.Ia. Marr. From biographical data in TsGA RSFSR f.4655 o.2 d.785 ll.2-26.
47. Protocols and reports, in AAN f.502 o.3 d.88a ll.2-31; RTsKh f.17 o.60 d.25 ll.3-8; and TsGA RSFSR f. 307 o.1 d.434 ll.140-157; o.2 d.438 ll.2-45,105. *Narodnoe prosveshchenie* 15 (October 1919: 102-103). *Mezhdunarodnyi iazyk* 23/49 (September 1926: 3). See the two publications of the All-Union Society for Cultural Relations Abroad: *Weekly news bulletin* 39-41 (14 October 1927: 9); and *Bulletin d'information* 29 (1927: 10-12).
48. Izgur (1926); and Mikhal'ski (1929). I thank Ralph Dumain, an active Esperantist in Washington, D.C. circles, for sharing these insights with me.
49. Fersman (1928). Varankin (1977). The preface to Bogdanov (1929: 3-5).
50. Ernst Karlovich Drezen (1892-1937) was Latvian by ancestry and an electric engineer by training. He was a Socialist Revolutionary (SR) from his youth in Kronstadt and St. Petersburg, later a Left SR and Bolshevik. He served as a Signal Corps officer in World War I, and with distinction as a Red Army

officer in the Civil War. From biographical data in *Bulteno de Centra Komitato de SEU* 12/3 (1931: 98); a personal letter from Drezen to Lanti (11 September 1921), generously supplied by Dr. Ulrich Lins; and *The British Esperantist* (May 1970: 344). For his views, see Drezen (1925a: 3-5). Modenov (1928: 45). Drezen (1934b).
51. See the assorted works by Drezen and by Vitte & Drezen (1925). A member of the NOT League, Drezen wrote these works as a functionary of the Administrative Technology Section of the Workers' and Peasants' Inspectorate (NKRKI). He also taught the basic correspondence course, "Introduction to Rationalization", offered to adult learners throughout the country by the Scientific-Technological Directorate of the All-Union Exhibition of the Achievements of the National Economy (VDNKh SSSR).
52. Drezen (1925e: 5); Drezen (1926b: 12-14); and Drezen (1926c). *Mezhdunarodnyi iazyk* 1/27 (1925: 4-6); and 3/29 (1925: 3-5). Unlike Bogdanov, Drezen was not a systems thinker. He opposed philosophies that attempted to classify and order "the whole sum of human knowledge into a unified structure, into an all-embracing system". Drezen (1934a: 8).

Chapter 4

1. For views along these lines, see Fierman (1991: 227); and Crisp (1989: 31).
2. For background, see Aarsleff (1982: 91). Nikolai Iakovlevich Marr (1865-1934), the "Stalin of the humanities" as he became known, was born to a Scottish father and Georgian mother in Kutais, Georgia. His academic career began in 1884 at St. Petersburg University, where he studied Georgian, Armenian, Arabic, Persian, Greek, Hebrew, Syrian, Sanskrit, and Turkish, among other languages.
3. For his works before 1917, see Marr (1933-1937, 1). For background, turn to Alpatov (1991); L'Hermitte (1987); and Thomas (1957).
4. See Stankiewicz (1972: 253, 303, 71, 127, 54-55) for Baudouin's criticisms. Thomas (1957: 11-13) offers a sustained critique of Marr's faulty methods.
5. Quotes respectively from Thomas (1957: 2-5, 135, 143-144); and from Mikhanovka (1949: 31).
6. Lunacharskii (1925: 2). Matthews (1950: 2). On the politicization of science, see Graham (1993: 90-98); Vucinich (1984: 82-85, 114); and Weiner (1988).
7. From Marr's resume in AAN f.350 o.3 d.236 l.1. Baziiants (1972: 193-203).
8. On these postulates, see Vucinich (1984: 88, 154-155).
9. See "Iafeticheskii kavkaz i tretii etnicheskii element v sozidanii sredizemnomorskoi kul'tury" (1920), in Marr (1933-1937, 1: 79-124); Marr's "Predislovie", in *Iafeticheskii sbornik* 1 (1922: i-xiii); and his "Indoevropeiskie iazyki sredizemnomor'ria", (1923), in Marr (1933-1937, 1: 185-186).

10. "Postanovka ucheniia ob iazyke v mirovom masshtabe i abkhazskii iazyk" (1928), in Marr (1933-1937, 4: 59). Meshchaninov (1926: 9); Pokrovskii (1928: 4). For background, see the discussion on Engels in Samuelian (1981: 70-71). In preparing these formulas, Marr and his supporters took strongest issue with Bogdanov's theories of early human "sound" consciousness and the principle of the "word-idea". See Marr (1926b: 133-139); and Vainshtein (1925).
11. Lenin (1977, 14: 232, 267). For background, see Joravsky (1961: 17-21); Bakhurst (1991); Sakamoto (1988: 65-74); and Katvan (1978: 87).
12. Laboratory records in TsGA RSFSR f.4655 o.1 d.275 ll.3-4,16-21,113-115. Dobrogaev (1929a: 259-309). Dobrogaev (1929b: 57-130). Derzhavin (1931: 174-192). Rafail (1931: 14).
13. The story is told in Volkogonov (1994: 429). On the methods of speech therapy, see Dobrogaev (1919). On "word signals" as "markers of the varied objects and phenomena of social life", see Dobrogaev (1931: 170-173). On Pavlov's broad appeal, and his linguistic hypotheses, see Tucker (1971: 154, 162-164); and Joravsky (1977: 457-477).
14. As Joravsky (1989: 388) points out: "The laws of higher nervous activity founded on the conditional reflex (Pavlov's doctrine) show how the human brain generates the knowledge that reflects external reality (Lenin's doctrine)."
15. For Marrist critiques of Humboldt's principle of linguistic consciousness, of Saussure's theory of the arbitrary sign, and of the "Bogdanov-Plekhanov theory" of the "word-idea", see Pal'mbakh (1931: 9-33); Iakubinskii (1931: 91-104); and Marr (1931: 6-7). For Marrist attacks on Bogdanov's idealistic preoccupation with consciousness, and a defense of Engels' materialist view of labor and production, see Prezent (1928: 103-121); and Rafail (1931: 7-12).
16. Quoted from *Istorik marksist* 11 (1929: 258-260); and *Vestnik prosveshcheniia* 2 (1929). For recent debate on these broader issues, see Joravsky (1983: 583-586); and Markus (1986).
17. See Friche (1929: 6-7). "Pochemu tak trudno stat' lingvistom-teoretikom" (1928), in Marr (1933-1937, 2: 405). *Prosveshchenie natsional'nostei* 6 (1933: 8-10); and Meshchaninov (1931a: 814).
18. Institute records in TsGA RSFSR f.2307 o.9 d.226; o.10 d.278; f.4655 o.1 d.288 and d.289, o.2 d.60. Iakovlev's remarks in *Stenograficheskii otchet vtorogo* (1929: 103-105); and *Rodnoi iazyk v shkole* 11-12 (1926: 272-278).
19. *Vsesoiuznyi tsentral'nyi komitet* (1936: 20). Marr quoted in *Prosveshchenie natsionalnostei* 9 (1931: 79); and Marr (1930).
20. These arguments were advanced by the leading Marrists (B. Aptekar', I Kusikian, and B. Grande) in *Literatura i isskustvo* 1 (1930: 132); *Russkii iazyk v sovetskoi shkole* 4 (1930: 192-196); *Prosveshchenie i natsional'nostei* 9-10 (1930: 75-77); 7-8 (1931: 86); and *Natsional'naia kniga* 5 (1931: 18-20).

21. For these views, see Marr (1930:19-22); and Derzhavin (1929:1).
22. GAIMK materials, in TsGA RSFSR f.4655 o.1 d.192 ll.2-145,182-188; d.196 ll.20-21. For representative works by the Marr school on "precapitalist historical formations", see Bykovskii (1931, 1934a, and 1934b); Meshchaninov (1931b); and *Ukazatel' rabot GAIMK* (1936).
23. See the 1914 letter from Roman Jakobson to A.E. Kruchenykh, reprinted in Jakobson (1985: 2-3).
24. Institute materials in TsGA RSFSR f.4655 o.1 d.274 ll.7-15; d.275 ll.123,208-210; d.277 ll.7-10; d.278 ll.2,10,15.
25. The passage is in Shpet (1923, 3: 78). See chapter one, "Tool and Sign in Child Development," and chapter eight, "The Prehistory of Written Language," in Vygotskii (1978). Joravsky (1989: chapters nine and thirteen). Prezent (1928: 109) criticized Vygotskii for his suspicions of Pavlovian reductionism and for his defense of an independent human consciousness.
26. Voloshinov (1973: 9-19, 14, 23); and Matejka (1973: 163). Although Voloshinov praised Humboldt and Husserl outright (1973: 32, 48), his references to Shpet were much less explicit, perhaps because Shpet had already been purged by the time this book appeared.
27. Voloshinov (1973: 48); and Marr quoted from Bakhtin & Medvedev (1985). Voloshinov's book was published by Marr's Scientific Research Institute for the Comparative Study of the Literatures and Languages of the West and East, under the direction of N.F. Iakovlev; the highly polemical and militant works under Marr's editorship (1929-1931) were companion volumes. Iakovlev and Voloshinov were remarkably similar in their professional ethics, structural approaches, and timely attractions to Marr.
28. Bernshtein (1989: 77-82). Vyshinskii quoted in Joravsky (1961: 223).
29. Pokrovskii (1928: 4). Derzhavin (1925: 234-235). Deborin (1934: 2).
30. *Istorik marksist* 1 (1926: 322-323); 4 (1927: 271-276); 6 (1927: 297-298). Aptekar's various reports before the Communist Academy and the Society of Marxist Historians, in AAN f.350 o.2 d.234 1.17; d.138 ll.4,35,54; d.380 ll.23,25,44,47. V.B. Aptekar', son of a dentist, was born in 1899, joined the communist party in 1918, and worked as a political commissar during the civil war. A graduate of Moscow State University, during the 1920s he taught party history and historical materialism at workers' faculties and worked as a censor for the State Publishing House and propagandist for the Communist Academy. From biographical materials in TsGA RSFSR f.4655 o.2 d.201 ll.5-10.
31. *Bolshevik* 13-14 (1929: 58-59). RANION documents in TsGA RSFSR f.4655 o.1 d.336 1.18; d.349 1.4; and d.324 ll.14,16,45-47. Debates at the Communist Academy Presidium, in AAN f.350 o.1 d.193 ll.14,48. Polivanov had a reputation for mixing politics with scholarship. In April of 1921, as chair of the communist party cell at the Central Institute of Living Eastern Languages in Petrograd, he had organized a campaign of denunciation and purge against all those stale,

traditionalist "White Guard professors" entrenched there, declaring them unfit for Soviet tasks. See the "Protocol Number Six of the Committee of the RKPb of the Second City Region," in TsGAOR f.1318 o.1 d.706(1) l.3.
32. Polivanov (1931: 338, 336-337, 272, 338-341, 335, 342). Many of these selections are reprinted in Polivanov (1974).
33. See Marr's "Aktual'nye problemy i ocherednye zadachi iafeticheskoi teorii," in Marr (1933-1937, 3). Polivanov (1931: 169-170). Purge documents in TsGA RSFSR f.4655 o.1 d.133 l.26; d.389 l.27; d.394 l.8.
34. Quoted from the transcript of the purge hearings in TsGA RSFSR f.4655 o.1 d.283 ll.28-37,40-48,68-73,81,254-268; d.420 l.1; d.128. See also *Russkii iazyk v sovetskoi shkole* 2 (1930: 3); *Literaturnaia gazeta* 3 (20 January 1930) and 7 (17 February 1930).
35. For background, see Vucinich (1984: chapter 3), and Weiner (1988: chapter 8).
36. Shor's remarks (April 1927), in AAN f.350 o.2 d.139 ll.4-10. Danilov's reports (January and April 1929), in AAN f.350 o.2 d.380 ll.2-47; his comments in *Literatura i marksizma* 6 (1928: 116), and *Rodnoi iazyk v shkole* 11-12 (1926: 272-278); and Nikiforov & Danilov (1928: 6-15). Iakovlev's report (December 1928), in AAN f.350 o.2 d.371 and d.402.
37. Dobrovolskii (1931: 60-67). Bubrikh (1930: 4-17). Roman Jakobson recognized Bubrikh's "structural hierarchy of linguistic constituents" in this essay, from Jakobson (1971: 673).
38. N.S. Trubetskoi wrote to Roman Jakobson on 28 May 1930, "in general structuralism is now on the move among Moscow's linguists", in Trubetskoi (1975: 160, 155, 169). For further testimony as to the dominance of the structural approach to language, also see Chernykh (1929b: 11); Reformatskii (1970: 22); and Gvozdev (1928: 44-66).
39. For example, in February of 1928, A.M. Sukhotin read a paper in N.F. Iakovlev's Linguistics Seminar on Saussure's *Course*, critically applauding its structural insights. TsGALI f.454 o.1 d.45 ll.17-19. T.D. Lomtev was born to a peasant family in 1906, studied at the Linguistics Faculty of Voronezh University between 1925 and 1929, continuing with graduate studies and Komsomol work in Moscow until 1931. In 1933 he began a decade of language work in Belorussia, becoming a full member of the communist party in 1939. P.S. Kuznetsov was born in 1899 to a peasant family, fought with distinction in the Red Army during the civil war, and worked as a librarian, propagandist, and NOTist before continuing with Linguistics studies at Moscow State University in 1926. From biographical material in GBOR f.652 o.34 d.15 l.2.
40. For background on the cultural revolution, see Clark (1978: 193-197); and Fitzpatrick (1978).
41. "Gruppa 'Iazykfront,'" *Revoliutsiia i iazyk* 1 (1930: 77); Lomtev (1931: 115-125). The debates in TsGA RSFSR f.2307 o.17 d.100 ll.1-28; and d.84 ll.37-101.

42. *Kul'tura i pis'mennost' vostoka* 7-8 (1931: 204-209). *Revoliutsiia i pis'mennost'* 3 (1932: 125-132). The reports and debates in TsGALI f.454 o.1 d.47 ll.5-7; TsGA RSFSR f.2307 o.17 d.84 ll.35-48.
43. Quoted from a report before the Presidium of the Communist Academy (11 January 1932), in AAN f.350 o.1 d.582.
44. For example, I have in mind the work of Lefebvre (1966); and Habermas (1973 and 1984).
45. As Zenovia Sochor has already demonstrated by comparing Bogdanov and Lenin, in Sochor (1988: 19).
46. See the course materials in TsGA RSFSR f.4655 o.1 d.389 ll.23,25; d.399 ll.2-11,31; d.400 ll.10-20,25,31-45; d.394 l.6; AAN f.468 o.1 d.29 ll.1-4; and TsGALI f.454 o.1 d.4. Valentin Ferdinandovich Asmus was born in 1894, and studied philosophy, history, and literature at Kiev University, graduating in 1919. He was a leading author of works on dialectical materialism and logic during the 1920s. From biographical material in AAN f.350 o.3 d.280 l.109.
47. On Humboldt's popularity, see Peterson (1929: 3); Shor (1930: 804- 805); Strazhev (1931). *Russkii iazyk v sovetskoi shkole* 4 (1931: 142); and *Prosveshchenie sibiri* 6 (1931: 89-90).
48. Lenin's notebooks were published in 1929 and 1930 as volumes 9 and 12 of the official *Lenin anthology*. As Anderson (1995: 40, 67, 71) explains, the notebooks often directly contradict the vulgar "reflective" materialism which Lenin had raised in *Materialism and empirio-criticism*.
49. Language Front documents in TsGA RSFSR f.2307 o.17 d.84 l.42; f.4655 o.2 d.586 ll.4-58. *Revoliutsiia i iazyk* 1 (1931: 13-14). The Frontists were taking issue with several points - that language was a "ceaseless flow of becoming," and "a continuous generative process" - from Voloshinov (1973: 66, 68, 94, 98).
50. AAN f.468 o.3 d.30 ll.1-4. TsGA RSFSR f.2307 o.16 d.52 ll.1-5. TsGALI f.454 o.1 d.66 l.1. *Revoliutsiia i iazyk* 1 (1931: 77-78).
51. Institutional reports in TsGA RSFSR f.2307 o.17 d.84 ll.8-101; o.16 d.52 ll.1-5. TsGALI f.454 o.1 d.47 ll.5-7. *Russkii iazyk v sovetskoi shkole* 6-7 (1931: 158-159). *Kul'tura i pis'mennost' vostoka* 7-8 (1931: 204-209). *Revoliutsiia i pis'mennost'* 3 (1932: 125-132).
52. R.O. Shor's comments in *Russkii iazyk v sovetskoi shkole* 1 (1931: 29-37); A.N. Savinskii's comments in *Sbornik nauchnogo obshchestva etnografii, iazyka i literatury pri Gorskom pedagogicheskom universitete* 1 (1929: 80-85); Strazhev (1931). Marr (1932: 91, 161); *Sovetskaia etnografiia* 1-2 (1931. 162-164).
53. Debates in the Communist Academy, in AAN f.350 o.2 d.139 l.20, d.234 l.12; d.380 ll.22,44,47. Marrist articles in *Literatura i iskusstvo* 1 and 2 (1930: 131-138, and 131-140); *Prosveshchenie natsional'nostei* 7-8 (1931: 70-79); 9 (1931: 76-80); 11-12 (1931: 97-102); *Narodnyi uchitel'* 4 (1932: 86-91). *Izvestiia GAIMK* 10/8-9 (1931). *Iafeticheskii sbornik* 7 (1932); *Literatura i iskusstvo* 4 (1931: 139); 7-8 (1931: 129-132); *Russkii iazyk v sovetskoi shkole* 6 (1930: 150).

54. See the assorted Language Front materials in TsGA RSFSR f.2307 o.17 d.84 ll.169-170,173; d.99 ll.1-10; TsGALI f.454 o.1 d.46; and *Literatura i iskusstvo* 1 (1931: 3-7). The directive of the Director's Board of the Narkompros RSFSR (21 March 1933), in AAN f.502 o.3 d.82 l.24.

Chapter 5

1. From "Quante forme di grammatica possono esistere?", in Gramsci (1975, 3:2343).
2. For background on the complex method and educational reform, see Fitzpatrick (1979: 7-9, 18-22, 168-170).
3. *Narodnoe prosveshchenie* 1-2 (1918: 56). *Revoliutsiia i pis'mennost'* 1 (1933: 27-32). *Russkii iazyk v sovetskoi shkoly* 5 (1927: 180-189). "On Three Principles of Constructing an Orthography," in Polivanov (1974: 240).
4. Comrie & Stone (1978: 212). *Russkaia shkola za rubezhom* 1 (1923: 2-3, 7).
5. The issue was debated widely in 1919-1920. TsGA RSFSR f.2306 o.19 d.125 ll.7-8; o.2 d.487 ll.7-8. AAN f.502 o.3 d.79 ll.1-17; f.696 o.1 d.155 ll.24-36. The negative comments of leading linguists and philologists, in *Izvestiia. Rossiiskaia Akademiia Nauk* series 6, volume 13, numbers 16-18 (1919). Lenin quoted in *Kul'tura i pis'mennost' vostoka* 6 (1930: 20-26).
6. These quotes are from nearly a dozen articles in the journal, *Rodnoi iazyk v shkole*, between 1927 and 1929; as well as *Na putiakh k novoi shkole* 12 (1927: 8-16); Bogoiavlenskii (1928).
7. Quoted from *Vestnik prosveshcheniia* 1 (1926: 19-28); and Akodis & Dreizin (1929: 40-42). Also see *Rodnoi iazyk v shkole* 1 (1927: 211). On correct spelling as the preferred standard to test one's mastery of Russian, see Lewis (1972b: 247).
8. Remarks from *Rodnoi iazyk v shkole* 8 (1925: 98-105); *Uchitel'skaia gazeta* 130 (10 November 1929: 2); *Na putiakh k novoi shkole* 12 (1927: 8-16).
9. *Poligraficheskoe proizvodstvo* 10 (1928: 19-22); 2 (1929: 25-28). *Uchitel'skaia gazeta* 123 (22 October 1929: 3). Complaints of poligraphy workers to Narkompros (1929), in TsGA RSFSR f.4655 o.1 d.392 l.7. AAN f.502 o.3 d.80 ll.1,2.
10. *Komsomolskaia pravda* 105 (11 May 1929); 117 (25 May 1929). *Prosveshchenie sibiri* 9 (September 1929: 92-98); 11 (November 1929: 60-61); 1 (January 1930: 111-115).
11. *Uchitel'skaia gazeta* 126 (29 October 1929: 3); 127 (31 October 1929: 3); TsGA RSFSR f.4655 o.1 d.409 ll.4-6. The radicals proposed to write all prefixes phonetically; to use the Cyrillic soft sign whenever the writer heard it; and to take out consonants in words when they were not pronounced. Barkhin & Kostenko & Ustinov (1930: 55-58).

12. Kremenskii & Mamonov (1930: 41). *Uchitel'skaia gazeta* 123 (22 October 1929: 3). *Krasnaia gazeta* (12 April 1930: 2). *Russkii iazyk v sovetskoi shkole* 1 (1931: 168-170).
13. *Russkii iazyk v sovetskoi shkole* 1 (1931: 102-106); 4 (1931: 192-193). *Uchitel'skaia gazeta* 131 (12 November 1929: 2). *Molodaia gvardiia* 21 (1930: 91). Avanesov & Sidorov (1930 [1970]: 149-156).
14. Kremenskii & Mamonov (1930: 9-12, 20-26). Barkhin & Kostenko & Ustinov (1930: 6-7, 9-10, 53). *Russkii iazyk v sovetskoi shkole* 6 (1929: 170-171). *Uchitel'skaia gazeta* 122 (19 October 1929: 3); 130 (10 November 1929: 2); 148 (21 December 1929: 3).
15. *Russkii iazyk v sovetskoi shkole* 6 (1929: 170-171); 1 (1931: 168-170).
16. Ushakov's project rests in AAN f.468 o.3 d.18 ll.7-28. His heated arguments with teachers may be found in *Vestnik prosveshcheniia* 7-8 (1923); *Nasha gazeta* 249/552 (30 October 1927); *Rodnoi iazyk v shkole* 10 (1926), and 2 (1928); *Uchitel'skaia gazeta* 97 (23 April 1927), and 131 (12 November 1929). Ushakov's 1933 comments before the Culture and Propaganda Division of the TsK VKPb, in AAN f.502 o.3 d.103 ll.6,20; and in a 1934 debate at the Academy of Sciences, in TsGA RSFSR f.2306 o.69 d.2155 l.3.
17. Project reports, in AAN f. 502 o.3 d.102 ll.14-19; o.1 d.68 l.26. *Uchitel'skaia gazeta* 37 (29 March 1930). *Literaturnaia gazeta* (17 March 1930) and (14 April 1930).
18. Barkhin & Kostenko & Ustinov (1930: 50). *Rodnoi iazyk v shkole* 8 (1925: 96-98); 6 (1927: 146-147). Iapol'skii (1931: 196-199).
19. *Sovetskii iug* 94 (27 April 1927); *Russkii iazyk v sovetskoi shkole* 6 (1929: 170-171). *Ku'ltura i pis'mennosti vostoka* 4 (1929: 69).
20. Protocols in TsGA RSFSR f.2307 o.15 d.4 ll.1-30,52-90. TsGA RSFSR f.4655 o.1 d.421 ll.36-37. AAN f.468 o.3 d.12 l.9. AAN f.502 o.3 d.81 ll.3-5; d.102 l.11. *Kul'tura i pis'mennost' vostoka* 6 (1930: 208-211). *Poligraficheskoe proizvodstvo* 2 (1930: 43-44).
21. Trubetskoi (1975: 212). N.S. Derzhavin's remarks in *Kniga i revoliutsiia* 2 (1920: 8-11); and *Krasnaia gazeta* (12 April 1930). Dimanshtein's views in AAN f.361 o.2 d.5 l.39.
22. For the background, see Gorlov (1924). Bogdanov (1925a). See the curriculum proposals in Narodnyi komissariat po prosveshcheniiu (1921a).
23. *Rodnoi iazyk v shkole* 7 (1917: 307-313); 8-10 (1917: 413-415); 1 (1919-1922: 1-9); 1 (1923: 32-52); 8 (1925: 120-121); 11-12 (1926: 97). Narodnyi komissariat po prosveshcheniiu (1924). Chernykh (1925: 1-4, 9-10).
24. For reviews of these texts, see: *Narodnyi uchitel'* 5 (1924: 65-73); *Pedagogicheskaia mysl'* 3 (1923: 59-62); *Rodnoi iazyk v shkole* 8 (1925: 84-92); 3 (1927: 292-299); 2 (1928: 131-136); 1 (1928: 24-45). Kartsevskii (1928).
25. Quoted from Narodnyi komissariat po prosveshcheniiu (1921b: 1-4, 40-44). Moscow formalists explained the union of formal grammar and the complex

method to teachers in a variety of forums: *Narodnoe prosveshchenie* 1-2 (1918: 44). *Rodnoi iazyk v shkole* 1 (1919-1922: 1-9); 4 (1923: 114-129); and Ushakov (1923).
26. See Afanasiev (1924b: 57-60), and its review in *Rodnoi iazyk v shkole* 5 (1924: 132-133).
27. For the historical background, see Orlova (1961: 71-86). Quoted from Durnovo (1924: 69).
28. Suvorovskii (1926); Smirnov-Kutachevskii's comments in *Russkii iazyk v shkole* 1 (1927: 283); Mirtov (1927: 294); Danilov (1931b: 101); Meromskii (1930); and Selishchev (1932: 120-132).
29. Straten (1929: 39-53). Koporskii (1927: 7). Also see Tonkov (1930).
30. Peterson's and Ushakov's remarks, and commentaries on them, in *Rodnoi iazyk v shkole* 3 (1927: 122-127); 8 (1925: 106-108); 9 (1926: 98-101); 4 (1927: 234-238). *Zhurnalist* 5 (1927: 57-61).
31. Debates between teachers and Ushakov, in *Narodnyi uchitel'* 1 (1927: 39-43). Boianus (1930: 30); Ushakov (1928) came to a similar conclusion.
32. *Rodnoi iazyk v shkole* 4 (1927: 234-238); 2 (1928: 154). *Literatura i iazyk v politekhnicheskoi shkole* 2 (1932: 59-65). In 1928 and 1929, no less than six new school textbooks cultivated higher standards of "speech culture" in these ways, as discussed in *Russkii iazyk v sovetskoi shkole* 1 (1929: 81-90).
33. See especially M.D. Gromova's and A. Mirelova's articles, in Luria (1930). Luria quoted in his own contribution to this publication, later translated into English as, "A child's speech responses and the social environment," in Luria (1978: 45, 77). Also see Luria (1976).
34. *Rodnoi iazyk v shkole* 1 (1919-1922: 9-25); 8 (1925: 76-84). *Na putiakh k novoi shkole* 12 (1927: 11-12). *Rodnoi iazyk i literatura v trudovoi shkole* 2 (1928: 138-142). The debates in *Rodnoi iazyk v shkole* 2 (1923: 95); 3 (1923: 38-42); 4 (1923: 65-75); 6 (1924: 88-97). Nikolai Nikolaevich Durnovo (1876-1936) was a leading specialist in Russian dialect and grammar studies, appointed as a Corresponding Member of the Academy of Sciences in 1924. He lived and worked with N.S. Trubetskoi in Czechoslovakia between 1924 and 1926.
35. Ushakov's 1921 report, in AAN f.502 o.3 d.113 l.2. *Rodnoi iazyk v shkole* 2 (1919-1922: 119-122); 8 (1925: 92); 1 (1927: 147-155); 4 (1927: 246); 1 (1928: 45-49); 2 (1928: 138-139). On the chaotic application of the complex method, see Fitzpatrick (1979: 18-22, 36-37).
36. The 1928 report in TsGA RSFSR f.298 o.1 d.39 ll.50-51. *Russkii iazyk v sovetskoi shkole* 3 (1930: 74).
37. *Rodnoi iazyk v shkole* 1 (1927: 268-278); 2 (1927: 235). *Russkii iazyk v sovetskoi shkole* 7-8, 9 (1928: 56-68, 45-52). *Rodnoi iazyk i literatura v trudovoi shkole* 1-2 (1928: 51-55); 2 (1928: 101-107).
38. For the broad polemics of these years, see *Russkii iazyk v sovetskoi shkole* 3 (1930: 157-158); 4 (1930: 192-196); 2-3 (1931: 107-108, 224-232). *Na putiakh k novoi*

shkole 8-9 (1930: 46-52). *Literatura i iazyk v politekhnicheskoi shkole* 1 (1932: 1-5, 76-80); 2 (1932: 52-55); 4 (1932: 83-86, 107-108). Marr (1933-1937, 2: 374-375). Petrova (1932a: 9-17); and Petrova (1931). *Na putiakh k novoi shkole* 1 (1933: 13-18). Voloshinov, who was often the target of these attacks, also joined in them, namely by criticizing Peshkovskii's empty grammatical formalism, in Voloshinov (1973: 48, 112, 128).
39. *Literatura i iazyk v politekhnicheskoi shkole* 4 (1932: 93-96). TsGA RSFSR f.2307 o.17 d.99 ll.47-73, 74-88; d.84 ll.70-72.
40. Danilov (1921: 26-34, 76-78); and Danilov (1929: 1).
41. See the series edited by Danilov & Degterevskii & Neiman & Pal'mbakh (1930).
42. Ustinov & Mamonov & Nikol'skii (1928). Ustinov (1931: 3, 6-8).
43. TsGA RSFSR f.2307 o.17 d.99 ll.47-88. Alaverdov & Bek & Priannikova & Nechaeva (1932). *Literatura i iazyk v politekhnicheskoi shkole* 1 (1932: 21-24). *Russkii iazyk v sovetskoi shkole* 8 (1931).
44. See Iakovlev's comments in *Russkii iazyk v sovetskoi shkole* 1 (1933: 28-31); and the proposals of Ia.V. Loia and A.V. Shapiro in *Russkii iazyk v sovetskoi shkole* 2-3 (1931: 37-46), and 4 (1931: 48-66).

Chapter 6

1. For background, I have relied on Allworth (1971), Baldauf (1993), Caroe (1953a), Fierman (1991), Imart (1965), Isaev (1979), Kreindler (1985), Musaev (1965), Swietochowski (1991), Wheeler (1974), Winner (1952), and Zenkovsky (1960).
2. These peoples include the Mordvinians, Mari, Komi, Udmurts and Chuvash. The latter survived Latinization with a developed literature and educational system functioning in a modified Russian script. See Krueger (1985: 268).
3. Validov (1923 [1986]: 156-157, 189-192, 206). Allworth (1965: 58, 109-115). Polivanov (1923b: i).
4. Bayturgan (1971: 28); Iskhaki (1933 [1988]: 53-54). Panov (1974) offers a more balanced approach.
5. Documents on these scripts are located in TsGA RSFSR f.296 o.2 d.15 l.5; f.2307 o.9 d.226 ll.93,95. *Revoliutsiia i gorets* 1-2 (1929: 43-44); 3 (1930: 54-55). *Izvestiia pervogo i vtorogo severo-kavkazskikh pedagogicheskikh institutov* 2/11 (1934: 223). Iakovlev (1925: 33-34).
6. TsGAOR f.1318 o.1 d.1700 ll.3-4. *Pervyi vsesoiuznyi tiurkologicheskii siezd* (1926: 219, 269); *Stenograficheskii otchet pervogo* (1927: 20-21); and *Stenograficheskii otchet tret'ego* (1928: 40-41, 60). *Revoliutsiia i gorets* 5 (1929: 22); *Kommunisticheskoe prosveshchenie* 2 (1930: 45). *Za gramotu* 6 (25 March 1935: 16).
7. See the official government newspaper, *Azerbaidzhan* 23 (1 February 1919); and 103 (18 May 1919).

8. Babaeva (1989). GANI f.57 o.1 d.151 1.192; d.23 1.264; f.103 o.1 d.12 ll.1-10. Kirov funded Latinization on 7 March 1922, in GAPPOD f.1 o.74 d.41 1.8.
9. *Zhizn' natsional'nostei* 1 (25 February 1922: 13-14); 5 (1 April 1922: 3); 9 (5 May 1922: 2-3); and 13 (26 June 1922: 5-6).
10. Report on the struggle against Islam before the Orgbiuro of the TsK RKPb (May 1923), in RTsKh f.17 o.112 d.447 1.21.
11. On party support in Baku, see GANI f.57 o.1 d.230 1.2; f.103 o.1 d.12 ll.1-10. Stalin's report (25 September 1922) is summarized in RTsKh f.17 o.112 d.373 1.3. *Izvestiia iugo-vostochnogo biuro TsK RKP* 6/13 (November 1922); RTsKh f.17 0.112 d.566 ll.84-86. Pavlovich (1926: 15-19).
12. Commission documents in TsGAOR f.1318 o.1 d.1699 ll.2,6,8,9. Allworth (1965: 38). On Latin as a blow to the Muslim clergy and "Islamic-Arabic culture" in general, see the theses to the report, "On the religious schools", at the Conference of the Commissariats of Education of the Union Republics (1926-1927), in TsGA RSFSR f.2306 o.69 d.649 1.211.
13. Varied commission documents, in TsGAOR f.1318 o.1 d.1700 ll.2-11.
14. Documents of the Azerbaijani KNTA, in GANI f.103 o.1 d.17 1.645; f.103 o.2 d.4 1.203; and GANI f.379 o.3 d.693 ll.1-5. *Bakinskii rabochii* 144 (9 June 1924).
15. GANI f.103 o.1 d.14 1.221; d.12 ll.1-10; d.9 1.77; d.11 1.60.
16. Correspondence of the AzKNTA and Central Asian Bureau of the TsK RKPb, in GANI f.103 o.1 d.15 ll.100-111,206-227; d.17 1.645. Fierman (1991: 81-82, 238).
17. Quoted from *Kul'tura i pis'mennost' vostoka* 4 (1929: 3-6); *Stenotchet tret'ego plenuma* (1928: 1-5); and Fisher (1978: 141-142, 158).
18. Protocol of the preparatory committee in TsGAOR f.5402 o.1 d.108. TsK RKPb documents in RTsKh f.17 o.113 d.169 ll.5, 182-185. Ciphered Telegram from Stalin (TsK Secretariat in Moscow) to the TsK AKPb (Baku), in GAPPOD f.1 o.235 d.251 1.56. Correspondence between Baku and Moscow, in GAPPOD f.1.o.235 d.251 ll.22-25.
19. TsGAOR f.5402 o.1 d.108 ll.28-69; d.109 ll.26,39,41. *Pervyi vsesoiusnyi tiurkologicheskii siezd* (1926: 242, 320-321). *Bakinskii rabochii* 54 (4 March 1926: 4); 56 (7 March 1926: 4). Sharaf (1926: 15-80).
20. Aliev (1930: 25-26). *Revoliutsiia i gorets* 1-2 (1929: 90). RKPb protocols in TsGAOR f.5402 o.1 ll.33,38,52. AzKNTA correspondence, in GANI f.379 o.3 d.693 ll.1-5; f.103 o.1 d.15 1.111; f.103 o.1 d.17 1.610. Agamalyogly's comments in *Stenograficheskii otchet vtorogo* (1929: 3).
21. *Biulleten' organizatsionnoi komissii po sozyvu pervogo vsesoiuznogo tiurkologicheskogo siezda* 3 (1926: 4). TsGA RSFSR f.296 o.1 d.269 ll.184-186; and d.267 ll.38-39. *Nashi dostizhenie* 4 (1929: 10); Agamalyogly's report to the AzKNTA in GANI f.411 o.4 d.175 1.73.
22. Narkompros protocols and reports, in TsGA RSFSR f.296 o.1 d.268 ll.1-4; d.269 ll.53-57, 187-202; d.272 ll.14-15. *Stenograficheskii otchet pervogo* (1927: 36-38). *Sed'moi siezd sovetov* (1927: 187, 212, 219, 255).

23. Quoted from TsGAOR f.5402 o.1 d.109 l.60. *Izvestiia obshchestva obsledovaniia i izucheniia Azerbaidzhana* 2 (1926: 122-127).
24. TsK RKPb reports (February 1926): in TsGAOR f.5402 o.1 d.108 1.184-185; d.109 1.67; in RTsKh f.17 o.113 d.169 1.5; in GAPPOD f.1 o.235 d.251 ll.56-87. Quotes from *Bakinskii rabochii* 54 (4 March 1926: 4).
25. Protocols of the conference (March 1926), in GANI f.379 o.3 d.626 ll.2-4.
26. The Orgbiuro TsK RKPb approved the organization and funding for the VTsKNTA on 28 February 1927, in RTsKh f.17 o.113 d.268 1.4. Swietochowski (1985: 132-133, 192-193). Blank (1994: 145).
27. *Natsional'naia kniga* 3-4 (1931: 22); *Stenograficheskii otchet nauchno-orfograficheskoi konferentsii* (1930: 171). The TsK RKPb resolution (1929), in TsGA RSFSR f.296 o.1 d.385 1.4.
28. *Pervyi vsesoiuznyi tiurkologicheskii siezd* (1926: 164-167, 178-179, 186-187, 211-214, 276-289, 327-328). *Bakinskii rabochii* 54 (4 March 1926: 4). Proceedings of the First All-Russian Congress on the Education of the Turkic Peoples (September 1927), in TsGA RSFSR f.296 o.1 d.269 ll.184-186.
29. *Pervyi vsesoiuznyi tiurkologicheskii siezd* (1926: 11-13, 195, 329-334). *Nashi dostizhenie* 4 (1929: 13). Chobanzade (1925) is a compelling defense of his positions.
30. *Stenograficheskii otchet pervogo* (1927: 112-120, 135, 82-83). TsGAUz f.86 o.1 d.4488 1.82; f.837 o.3 d.503 1.47; Agazade (1927: 6). For more on the specific linguistic discussions, see *Pervyi vsesoiuznyi tiurkologicheskii siezd* (1926: 86, 225-227); and Shcherba (1957: 45).
31. *Pervyi vsesoiuznyi tiurkologicheskii siezd* (1926: 179, 247, 307). *Stenograficheskii otchet piatogo* (1932: 67, 80).
32. *Stenograficheskii otchet pervogo* (1927: 138, 164-165). *Stenograficheskii otchet tret'ego* (1928: 115-124, 130-138, 141-161, 201-205). *Kul'tura i pis'mennost' vostoka* 1 (1928: 91-95); 3 (1928: 35-43). Fierman (1991: 86-87).
33. *Pervyi vsesoiuznyi tiurkologicheskii siezd* (1926: 175). *Stenograficheskii otchet vtorogo* (1929: 14, 26-27).
34. *Stenograficheskii otchet pervogo* (1927: 45, 73, 75, 81-89). *Stenograficheskii otchet vtorogo* (1929: 46). *Stenograficheskii otchet nauchno-orfograficheskoi konferentsii* (1930: 44-46).
35. See *Revoliutsionnyi vostok* 3 (1928: 217-221). *Stenograficheskii otchet nauchno orfograficheskoi konferentsii* (1930: 105). Polivanov (1926c).
36. *Pervyi vsesoiuznyi tiurkologicheskii siezd* (1926: 216, 225-227, 319-320). Zhirkov's report in TsGA RSFSR f.2307 o.17 d.18 ll.1-6. Polivanov (1928a: 315).
37. *Pervyi vsesoiuznyi tiurkologicheskii siezd* (1926: 179). *Stenograficheskii otchet pervogo* (1927: 57-71, 87); *Stenograficheskii otchet vtorogo* (1929: 10-12, 25-33, 96-110); *Stenograficheskii otchet tret'ego* (1928: 21-28); *Sovetskoe stroitel'stvo* 7 (1927: 60-63). In February of 1927, for example, the idealistic Azerbaijanis sent out circulars asking the other Turkic republics to accept

without condition the authority of Baku's Scientific Council. From TsGAUz f.86 o.1 d.448811.17,23,91,100.
38. *Stenograficheskii otchet pervogo* (1927: 79). The debates and reports in GAPPOD o.1 f.74 d.281 ll.154-156; d.282 ll.126-138. GANI f.1119 o.1 d.482 l.2. GANI f.389 o.1 d.25 l.89. GANI f.57 o.7 d.64; d.32 l.15.
39. *Revoliutsiia i pis'mennost'* 2 (1936: 27). Reports in TsGA RSFSR f.2307 o.17 d.18 ll.1-6; TsGA RSFSR f.296 o.1 d.385 ll.40-46. Grande (1933: 128-137).
40. *Revoliutsiia i gorets* (1928-1933 issues) are a helpful source. *Revoliutsiia i pis'mennost'* 2 (1936: 29-30). TsGA RSFSR f.2307 o.17 d.18 ll.1-6.
41. Crisp (1989: 35-36). Narkompros report (1927), in TsGA RSFSR f.296 o.1 d.412 ll.37-38. Report on literacy work in Kirgizstan (1928), in RTsKh f.62 o.2 d.1607 l.14. For impressive psychological studies on the legibility and efficiency of the Latin script, see Artemov (1933) and (1936).
42. *Vestnik nauchnogo obshchestva Tatarovedeniia* 5 (1926: 12-13). *Biulleten' organizatsionnoi komissii po sozyvu pervogo vsesoiuznogo tiurkologicheskogo siezda* 2 (1926: 7); 3 (1926: 10-15). *Kul'tura i pis'mennost' vostoka* 2 (1928: 160-161).
43. Terminological materials in GANI f.57 o.1 d.708; TsGAUz f.34 o.1 d.1801 ll.58,64; f.94 o.1 d.40 l.28. *Biulleten' organizatsionnoi komissii po sozyvu pervogo vsesoiuznogo tiurkologicheskogo siezda* 1 (1926: 20-22). Fierman (1991: chapter 7).
44. Report of a three month inspection of linguistic work in Azerbaijan (1934), in GANI f.379 o.23 d.2 l.59. Terminology reports in GANI f.57 o.1 d.708. TsGAUz f.94 o.5 d.351 l.11. Report of the Press Section of the Central Asian Bureau of the TsK VKP (1928), in RTsKh f.62 o.1 d.503 l.2.
45. *Stenograficheskii otchet piatogo* (1932: 81). Polivanov (1924: 158). For background, see Allworth (1990: 237-238); and Fierman (1991: 89-95).
46. Report of the Narkompros RSFSR and TsK Agitprop Department (October 1927) to the Orgbiuro TsK, in RTsKh f.17 o.113 d.335 l.1. Resolution of the VTsIK and SNK RSFSR of 23 April 1929, in TsGA RSFSR f.259 o.13 d.38 l.100. The Narkompros report, "Podgotovka kadrov natsmen'shinstv RSFSR" (1929), in TsGA RSFSR f.296 o.1 d.387 ll.63-74. *Narodnoe prosveshchenie* 5 (1929: 52). *Prosveshchenie natsional'nostei* 6 (1930: 47-48). *Na putiakh k novoi shkole* 1 (1933: 52-53).
47. Materials in TsGAUz f.86 o.1 d.5511 ll.498,507. For evidence from other Turkic republics, see TsGA RSFSR f.2306 o.69 d.3500 l.1.14; TsGAOR f.3316 o.26 d.647 l.130; and GANI f.387 o.1 d.341 l.2. *Stenograficheskii otchet piatogo* (1932: 47, 129).
48. Reports on the scientific work of the VTsKNA between 1933 and 1936, in TsGAOR f.3316 o.28 d.769. ll.110-111,152,201,212; o.30 d.830 l.1; o.26 d.647 ll.153-154; d.786(2) ll.124,126; o.25 d.783 l.37. *Stenograficheskii otchet piatogo* (1932: 48, 70, 83, 129, 97, 115). Fierman (1991: 110-116, 118-121).

Notes   215

49. Various government documents and correspondence, in TsGAOR f.7543 o.1 d.59 1.10; d.79 ll.17-24; d.61 1.102; and f.3316 o.30 d.778(2) 1.83; o.28 d.769. ll.110-111, 152,201,212. VTsKNA materials in GANI f.379 o.23 d.2 ll.76,88; d.12 ll.1-2. Letter of the chair of the TsKNA to the Kazakhstan Regional Committee of the RKPb and TsK RKPb, in TsGA RSFSR f.296 o.1 d.516 1.23.
50. VTsKNA reports between 1933 and 1936, in TsGAOR f.3316 o.28 d.769 ll.198-203; and in GANI f.379 o.23 d.2 ll.59.63. Central Asian Bureau report (1933), in RTsKh f.62 o.2 d.3193 1.135. *Kul'tura i pis'mennost' vostoka* 2 (1928: 15-16). *Revoliutsiia i gorets* 2 (1928: 36-46); 11-12 (1929: 50-51).
51. *Stenograficheskii otchet vtorogo* (1929: 4); *Revoliutsiia i pis'mennost'* 1-2 (1932: 150-151). *Stenograficheskii otchet piatogo* (1932: 53, 62, 89-90).
52. See the accusations in RTsKh f.62 o.2 d.2460 1.112; d.2474 1.14. TsGA RSFSR f.296 o.1 d.516 1.23. TsGA RSFSR f.2307 o.1 d.516 1.23. TsGAOR f.3316 o.30 d.778(2) 1.194.
53. Debates from the Communist Academy, in AAN f.361 o.2 d.7 ll.14-16; d.1 ll.20-21. *Stenograficheskii otchet piatogo* (1932: 40-42).
54. *Revoliutsiia i natsional'nost'* 2 (1930: 63). *Sovetskoe stroitel'stvo* 8 (1931: 99-105).
55. The campaign of the Japhetites (Kusikian, Filin, Lytkin, Grande and Iakovlev), was waged in: *Prosveshchenie natsional'nostei* 6 (1930: 137-139); 9-10 (1930: 75-77); 1 (1931: 73-77); 7-8 (1931: 86-91); 11-12 (1931: 72-79, 79-83); 5 (1933: 8-11). *Natsional'naia kniga* 5 (1931: 18-24); 6 (1931: 63-64). *Kul'tura i pis'mennost' vostoka* 7-8 (1931: 217-218). *Pis'mennost' i revoliutsiia* 1 (1933: 130); and *Bolshevik* 6 (1934: 81-96).
56. Dimanshtein in his report, "Stalin as a theoretician of the national question," in AAN f.361 o.2 d.5 1.39. *Prosveshchenie natsional'nostei* 4 (1933: 44-48). Fierman (1991: chapter seven).
57. Marr's comments (October 1928) at the Institute of the Peoples of the East, in TsGA f.4655 o.1 d.289(a). *Stenograficheskii otchet vtorogo* (1929: 170-171). Khashba (1972: 29-37). Brazhba (1987: 98-103).
58. *Kul'turu i pis'mennost vostoka* 3 (1928: 63); *Stenograficheskii otchet vtorogo* (1929: 170-171); *Stenograficheskii otchet tret'ego* (1928. 33, 92 93).
59. *Stenograficheskii otchet vtorogo* (1929: 75-78); *Stenograficheskii otchet piatogo* (1932: 67-68); *Stenograficheskii otchet nauchno-orfograficheskoi konferentsii* (1930: 43); Alaverdov (1933: 54-59, 62-71, 129), *Pechat' i revoliutsiia* 6 (1926: 191-192); Agazade (1927: lxxiv); *Kul'tura i pis'mennost' vostoka* 4 (1929: 21); 7-8 (1931: 207-208); 10 (1931: 43-60); *Revoliutsiia i pis'mennost'* 1-2 (1932: 87-103).
60. *Stenograficheskii otchet piatogo* (1932: 42-43). Alaverdov (1933: 52-63, 66-71, 129). *Russkii iazyk v sovetskoi shkole* 2-3 (1931: 236-241). *Prosveshchenie natsional'nostei* 10 (1931: 72-77). *Kul'tura i pis'mennost' vostoka* 7-8 (1931: 125-130, 165-172); 9 (1931: 20); 10 (1931: 61-64).

61. *Stenograficheskii otchet piatogo* (1932: 53, 79). *Kul'tura i pis'mennost' vostoka* 10 (1931: 93-95).
62. *Revoliutsiia i pis'mennost'* 3 (1932: 99-111, 132-133). *Revoliutsiia i gorets* 1 (1932: 142-146).
63. *Kul'tura i pis'mennost' vostoka* 7-8 (1931: 71-78, 227-229). *Natsional'naia kniga* 3-4 (1931: 26-27). Korkmasov (1933: 5, 137-141).
64. Orgbiuro TsK RKPb reports (1933-1936), in RTsKh f.17 o.114 d.357 l.7; d.571 l.85; d.602 l.55; d.606 l.126. VTsKNA and TsIK SSSR reports (1933-1937), in TsGAOR f.3316 o.28 d.769. ll.87-232; d.814 ll.3-21,66; o.30 d.781 l.6; d.778(1) ll.9,12,57.

Chapter 7

1. For background, see Fitzpatrick (1992: 170-182); and Hoffman (1995).
2. Two representative views are Liber (1991: 15-23); and Slezkine (1994: 438-439).
3. Olivier (1990: 77-98). Fierman (1991: 48, 51). Kaiser (1994: 134).
4. Timasheff (1946). Fitzpatrick (1992: 8-9, 144-145, 240-243). Vucinich (1984: 355).
5. For background, see Dunham (1990: 19-22); Williams (1982: 157-172); van Geldern (1991: 62-77); and Kotkin (1995: 220).
6. See Robin (1990: 36-37) for a discussion of the work of Moshe Lewin and Marc Ferro.
7. *Literatura i iazyk v politekhnicheskoi shkole* 1 (1932: 14-20, 57); 3 (1932: 8-17). Holmes (1991: 137). N.F. Iakovlev's remarks at a linguistics conference (2 June 1948), in TsGA RSFSR f.2306 o.71 d.11.1-6.
8. *Russkii iazyk v sovetskoi shkole* 3 (1930: 152-155). On the "thousanders", see Viola (1987).
9. Reports of these commissions (Narkompros, Academy of Sciences and the Cultural-Propaganda Division of the TsK), in AAN f.502 o.3 d.103; d.105; d.109 ll.43,282; TsGA RSFSR f.2306 o.69 d.2155; d.2235; d.2237. Ushakov (1934).
10. Stenogram of the commission (31 January 1936), in TsGA RSFSR f.2306 o.69 d.2235 l.13.
11. Narkompros documents and curriculums (1932-1938), in TsGA RSFSR f.2306 o.70 d.6256 l.19; d.6379; d.6380 l.33; d.6386 ll.14,17,26; d.6390 ll.34,59; d.6392 l.8; and in GAIaO f.2257 o.5 d.541 ll.99,101,318,326,341,368.
12. *Literatura i iazyk v politekhnicheskoi shkole* 1 (1932: 14-20); 3 (1932: 8-17). On the totalitarian language of the modern era, see Marcuse (1964); Orwell (1949); Young (1991).
13. Quoted from a fine study of the monologic "discursive paradigms" of Soviet ideological speech (syntax and semantics), Seriot (1985: 65). Moskovich (1990: 90-94). Robin (1992: 50).

14. Rosenburg (1988: 69). "Signal" statements of the director of the VTsKNA (1936), in TsGAOR f.3316 o.28 d.769 l.203; and of the Azerbaijani party chief (1938), in GANI f.57 o.1 d.1362 l.17. Thompson (1991: 387-388).
15. Gorkii quoted in Robin (1992: 169), whose chapter eight offers excellent background. Gorkii's statements in *Soviet writers' congress 1934* (1977: 53-54).
16. See the articles by L. Iakubinskii and A. Ivanov in *Literaturnaia ucheba* 1 (1930: 34-43); 2 (1930: 32-47); 3 (1930: 49-64); 4 (1930: 80-92); 6 (1930: 51-66); 7 (1931: 22-33); and the articles by Voloshinov in *Literaturnaia ucheba* 2 (1930: 48-66); 3 (1930: 65-87); 5 (1930: 43-59). Ivanov & Iakubinskii (1932: 28, 63), which is also a review of the Russian national language in its rural and urban varieties. Zhirmunskii (1936); *Krasnaia gazeta* (12 April 1930: 2).
17. Reports in AAN f.468 o.3 d.4 ll.3-6. Selishchev (1932: 120-132). Chistiakov (1935). Karinskii (1936).
18. Kenez (1985: 163-164, 255-257). On the role of party "rhetoric" and official quotations in the sciences, see Krementsov (1997: 49-52, 80-83).
19. Moskovich (1989: 95); Vinokur (1968: 12-100). Von Timroth (1986). Robin (1992: 50). Clark (1981: 12-14). Mikhail Bakhtin's celebrated notions of "dialogism, polyphony, heteroglossia, bivocality, plurilingualism, hybridity", quoted from Robin (1992: 178), seem rather ordinary within this broader context.
20. Reports of party observers in the Iaroslavl region revealed that such institutions were staffed by "poorly literate" and "inexperienced" help, and filled with old, unused books and magazines. See the 1937 and 1948 party and government reports in TsDNIIaO f.272 o.223 d.791 ll.17-60; and f.272 o.225 d.900 l.26. Robin (1991: 253-267). Fitzpatrick (1994: 224-230).
21. Reports before the State Academic Council (1928 and 1931), in TsGA RSFSR f.298 o.1 d.39 l.49; d.43 l.51. *Russkii iazyk v shkole* 1 (1936: 3). Sirotin (1936).
22. Government and party reports (1936 and 1938) for Iaroslavl, Rybinsk, and Kostroma, in TsDNIIaO f.272 o.223 d.1092 ll.179-183; d.1093 ll.21,201,242; and in GAIaO f.2611 o.1 d.1 ll.25-26,41; d.3 l.6; and GAIaO f.2257 o.5 d.465.
23. Records of the Iaroslavl State Pedagogical Institute in GAIaO f.2257 o.5 d.617 ll.16,20,21. *Literatura i iazyk v politekhnicheskoi shkole* 2 (1932: 46-49). The series of articles in *Narodnyi uchitel'* between 1930 and 1934, *Bolshevistskaia pechat'* between 1933 and 1937, and *Russkii iazyk v shkole* in 1936.
24. On the TsK and Orgbiuro policies (1933-1935), RTsKh f.17 o.114 d.566 l.38; d.379 l.4; d.568 l.39; d.578 l.5; d. 365 l.2; d.569 l.13; d.598 ll.3,41. For background, especially on Zhdanov, see Clark (1995: 286).
25. Ushakov and Volin (1934-1938). Ushakov's comments in a debate in the Academy of Sciences, in TsGA RSFSR f.2306 o.69 d.2155 l.5; and his correspondence in AAN f.502 o.3 d.82 ll.4,7. Vinokur's plans and programs in TsGALI f.2164 o.1 d.34 ll.1-2. Kupina (1995: 4), has analyzed Ushakov's dictionary as the perfect "lexigraphical monument of the totalitarian epoch", focusing on the semantic "spheres" of politics, philosophy, religion, and art.

26. On this phenomenon, see Stone (1972: 165-183); and Robin (1991: 253-267).
27. *Russkii iazyk v shkole* 5 (1936: 103, 108); and *Govorit SSSR* 1 (1936: 23); 3 (1936: 37); 6 (1936: 27). Debates in the Academy of Sciences, in TsGA RSFSR f.2306 o.69 d.2155 ll.9,13. On the early impact of radio, see Stites (1992: 81-82).
28. Materials on the committee in AAN f.502 o.3 dd. 125-138.
29. Quotes from the committee materials and listener letters in AAN f.502 o.3 d. 128; d.127 l.44; d.138; dd.129,130,131. *Rabotnik radio* 20-21 (1938). Also see the November and December issues of *Literaturnaia gazeta* (1939).
30. Editorial remarks in *Russkii iazyk v shkole* 5 (1936: 159). Levitt (1989: 162-166). Debreczeny (1993: 47-68).
31. Quoted from *Bolshevistskaia pechat'* 9 (1938: 11-13).
32. See *Revoliutsiia i natsional'nosti* 10-11 (October-November 1931: 28); and *Prosveshchenie natsional'nostei* 4 (1933: 51); and *Revoliutsiia i pis'mennost* 2 (1936: 55).
33. Narkompros and Language Front materials, in AAN f.502 o.3 d.82 l.24. TsGA RSFSR f.296 o.1 d.525 ll.120,169; d.513 ll.7-9. TsGA RSFSR f.2307 o.16 d.52 ll.7-16,17-20; d.69 ll.65-66; o.17 d.18 ll.13-14; d.92 l.1.
34. *Stenograficheskii otchet vtorogo* (1929: 5-6). Debate in the Commission for the Study of the National Question (February 1930), in AAN 361 o.2 d.6 ll.28-29. Azerbaijani report in GAPPOD f.1 o.74 d.319 l.113.
35. Narkompros and NIIaz documents in TsGA RSFSR f.2307 o.17 d.18 ll.15-18; d.42 ll.16-17; o.16 d.52 ll.9-16; and TsGALI f.454 o.1 d.7, d.9 and d.10. *Za kommunisticheskuiu prosveshcheniiu* 72 (1930); 123 (1930). *Kul'tura i pis'mennost' vostoka* 7-8 (1931: 79-92).
36. Korkmasov (1933: 11-12, 26-41). *Revoliutsiia i gorets* 6-7 (1933: 55-65).
37. *Sotsialisticheskaia rekonstruktsiia i nauk* 3 (1932: 139-154); 1 (1936: 103).
38. Orgbiuro TsK RKPb decisions, in RTsKh f.17 o.114 d.365 l.44 (8 October 1933); d.573 l.3 (29 October 1934); d.588 l.3 (9 July 1935); d.599 l.37; d.609 l.2 (5 June 1936); d.631 l.2 (26 October 1937).
39. Decree from A.I. Rykov at the All-Union Commissariat for Communications (16 May 1933), with the protest letter from the Central Asian Commissariat (29 July 1933), sent to the Central Asian Bureau of the TsK, in RTsKh f.62 o.2 d.3203 ll.73,110.
40. Liber (1982: 684). For more on this dynamic, see the works of Allworth (1990), Austin (1973), Bruchis (1982), Crisp (1989), Fierman (1991), Gallagher (1981), Krueger (1985), Kreindler (1985), Shevelov (1989), and Wexler (1974).
41. Marr (1925); and his speech in Alaverdov & Dimanshtein & Korkmasov & Nukhrat (1933: 80-81). Stalin quoted in *Revoliutsiia i pis'mennost'* 2 (1936: 55-65).
42. For background, see Stites (1983: 82-83); and Stites (1990: 80-81).
43. *Front nauki i tekhniki* 6 (1936: 107-111). *Vestnik standardizatsiia* 6/54 (November-December 1933: 8-9).

44. Drezen's reports on the code are stored in TsGANKh f.4460 o.4 d.110 l.183; d.112 ll.4-38. For the historical background, see *Vestnik standardizatsiia* 2/56 (March-April 1934: 8-10); 6/60 (November-December 1934: 19); 1 (1936: 43-48). Jacob (1947: 125-128).
45. TsGAOR f.7543 o.1 d.78 ll.2-8,54,36-39; d.90 l.7. Reports of the TsIK SSSR (1935-1937), in TsGAOR f.3316 o.28 d.814 ll.3-21,66; o.30 d.781 l.6; d.778(1) ll.9,12,57. *Revoliutsiia i pis'mennost'* 2 (1936: 3-4, 8-20). *Bolshevistskaia pechat'* 5-6 (1936: 6-7).
46. "All roads lead to Rome", as quoted from Drezen (1935: 78-81). Delcourt & Amouroux (1987: 197-198). My special thanks to professor Ulrich Lins for supplying photocopies of several Esperanto letters between Drezen and Wüster, and between Drezen and Bastien (15 and 30 March 1936, 30 April 1936, and 8 May 1936).
47. VTsKNA materials (1933-1937), in TsGAOR f.3316 o.28 d.769 ll.198-199,203,233; o.29 d.546 ll.1-35,115-117,187,231; o.30 d.778(1) l.61; d.778(2) ll.141,176; d.786(1) ll.7,9. RTsKh f.17 o.114 d.594 l.15; d.607 ll.2,4. *Revoliutsiia i natsional'nosti* 3 (March 1937: 63, 66).
48. Orgbiuro TsK VKPb documents (11 and 17 August 1937), in RTsKh f.17 o.114 d.629 ll.38,43. Narkompros report to the TsK (October 1937), in TsGA RSFSR f.2306 o.69 d.2322 ll.38-42.
49. Grande (1939: 5). Script materials relating to the Azerbaijani, Tatar, Bashkir, Kazakh, Uzbek and Tajik conversion projects (1939), in GANI f.411 o.44 d.3 ll.17,58. TsIK SSSR reports (1937), in TsGAOR f.3316 o.29 d.549 l.2; o.30 d.778(2) l.160. Materials of the conferences of first, second and third grade schoolteachers held at Baku during August of 1939, in GANI f.411 o.44 d.1 ll.60-62; d.3 l.42.
50. GANI f.57 o.1 d.1293 l.25. TsK VKPb materials in GANI f.411 o.44 d.9 l.153. Report of the conference in GANI f.411 o.44 d.5 ll.48-51. For background, see Musaev (1982), Comrie (1981), and Pool (1976).
51. Stenogram of the Central Asian Bureau of the TsK RKPb education conference (1934), in RTsKh f.62 o.2 d.3366 ll.7-56,94. Narkompros and TsK RKPb materials (1935-1938), in TsGA RSFSR f.2306 o.69 d.2196 ll.7,181; d.2322 ll.38-42; d.2436 l.18.
52. Azerbaijani Narkompros reports (1937-1939), in GANI f.57 o.1 d.1231 ll.2-15; d.1293 l.13; d.1296 ll.1-62; GANI f.411 o.8 d.9 l.42. Uzbek Narkompros reports (1938), in TsGAUz f.94 o.5 d.2651 l.11; d.2532 l.56.
53. Educational reports (1938-1941), in RTsKh f.17 o.126 d.3 l.43; in GANI f.57 o.1 d.1293 l.15; GANI f.411 o.8 d.9 l.45; d.2 ll.77,114,134; and in TsGAUz f.94 o.5 d.3058 l.2.
54. Educational materials and party conference stenograms (1939), in GANI f.57 o.1 d.1292 l.30; d.1293 ll.336-348. TsGAUz f.94 o.5 d.3053 ll.2-15; d.3051 l.116; d.3070 ll.1-12.

55. Documents relating to the 1938 decree in TsGAUz f.94 o.5 d.3150 ll.22,34; f.94 o.5 d.3051 l.1; d.3042 ll.26,115,125; d.3492 ll.61-65.
56. Narkompros RSFSR reports (1948-1952), in TsGA RSFSR f.2306 o.72 d.433 l.68; o.71 d.233 l.299. Reports to the TsK Secretariat (1949), in RTsKh f.17 o.132 d.164 ll.16-19,34-39.

Chapter 8

1. For the historical background, see Tillett (1969); and Allworth (1964: 153-163).
2. Thomas (1957: viii). Vucinich (1984: 186, 244); Fierman (1991: 302).
3. Various documents from the Narkompros in AAN f.468 o.3 d.12 l.13,17; in TsGA RSFSR f.2306 o.70 d.6380 ll.9,33,34; and in TsGALI f.2164 o.1 d.29 l.11. AAN f.502 o.3 d.53 ll.21-22,30-31,52-54,71-75; d.54 ll.3,53,83-86; d.55 ll.21,32.
4. The curriculum for "Introduction to linguistics," approved by the All-Union Committee for Higher Education of the SNK SSSR, in GAIaO f.2257 o.5 d.540 ll.15-16. See References for translations of these works. Vvedenskii (1933: 19-20).
5. N. Chemodanov's and G.O. Vinokur's comments (October 1942), in TsGA RSFSR f.2306 o.70 d.6385 ll.49-50,64,81; and the conference materials in AAN f.502 o.3 d.55 l.56.
6. The work rests in GBOR f.718 o.8 d.7, o.9 d.1; o.4 d.7.
7. Vinogradov (1945). Obnorskii (1947). Levitt (1989: 166-167).
8. Iaroslavl Regional Committee report to the School Division TsK VKPb (1948), in TsDNIIaO f.272 o.225 d.905 ll.1,24. Educational reports from the Iaroslavl region (1949-1950), in GAIaO f.2224 o.1 d.261a l.69; d.250 l.130. For background, see Krementsov (1997: 130-131).
9. Arakcheev was one of Tsar-Emperor Alexander I's generals in the early 1800s who established very severe military colonies in southern Russia under his dictatorship. Quoted from the 1949 report from the TsK Agitation and Propaganda Division to TsK Secretary G.M. Malenkov, in RTsKh f.17 o.132 d.164 ll.34-39. For background, see Phillips (1986), Matthews (1950), and Joravsky (1970).
10. *Russkii iazyk v shkole* 1 (1949: 70). Correspondence from the Academy of Sciences to TsK Secretary Malenkov (1949-1950), in RTsKh f.17 o.132 d.164 ll.16-19; d.336 ll.11-13. Jakobson (1971: 535). Viktor Vladimirovich Vinogradov (1894-1969) was professor of Russian language studies at Leningrad State University (1920-1929) and at Moscow State University (1930-1969), appointed to the Academy of Sciences in 1946. Arnol'd Stepanovch Chikobava (born in 1898) graduated from Tilfis University (Georgia) in 1922 and was appointed profesor of Caucasian languages and linguistics there in 1933.
11. Alpatov (1991: 147-151). The campaign filled the pages of *Literatura i gazeta, Sovetskaia kniga, Kul'tura i zhizn* and *Russkii iazyk v shkole*.

12. Educational circular to all regional and local school districts (1949), in GAIaO f.2224 o.1 d.293 ll.6-7.
13. Party and state reports on secondary and higher education in the Iaroslavl region (1946-1949), in TsDNIIaO f.272 o.225 d.676 ll.13-17; d.897 l.19; d.905 ll.13-15; d.1620 l.8; d.337 ll.23,58. GAIaO f.2224 o.1 d.250 ll.30-38; d.277 l.8; and GAIaO f.2257 o.6 d.20 ll.28-30.
14. The communication from the Council of Ministers of the USSR to Beria, in TsGA RSFSR f.2306 o.71(1) d.113 ll.1-2; and reports of the August 1951 Conference of Russian Language Teachers, in TsGA RSFSR f.2306 o.72 d.433 ll.94-95.
15. Reports of the Ministry of Education and Council of Ministers of the RSFSR (1948-1951), in TsGA RSFSR f.2306 o.71 d.234 l.143; o.71(1) d.126 l.28; d.87 l.39; d.112 ll.138-147; d.119 ll.23-29,44; o.72 d.30 l.3; d.410 ll.25,35. Correspondence about education to TsK Secretary Malenkov (1945-1946), in RTsKh f.17 o.126 d.21 l.177; d.13 ll.18-20; o.125 d.457 l.258.
16. Decree of the Ministry of Education of the RSFSR for the 1949-1950 school year, in GAIaO f.2224 o.1 d.292 ll.234-237. Education materials (reports, teacher's comments, conference proceedings), in TsGA RSFSR f.2306 o.72 d.410 l.50; d.433 ll.14-15,67-68; o.71 t.1 d.118. *Russkii iazyk v shkole* 5 (1950: 9-17).
17. Reports from the TsK Agitation and Propaganda Division to TsK Secretaries G.M. Malenkov and M.A. Suslov (1949-1950), in RTsKh f.17 o.132 d.164 ll.34-42; d.336 ll.4-6. The last report to Suslov is dated 13 April 1950.
18. Alpatov (1991: 182); Gorbanevskii (1991: 114, 129, 135). Ushakov appealed to Stalin to intervene in linguistics in a private letter, in AAN f.502 o.3 d.113 l.2.
19. The complete set of *Pravda* articles and comments, including Stalin's, can be found in Murra & Holling (1951: 2, 6, 21-23). Vucinich (1984: 244) wrote, "it did not matter what Stalin said about linguistics". Shapiro (1971: 536) remarked that "nothing is to be gained from an analysis of the tedious and academically worthless debate". Fitzpatrick (1992: 255) called the essay a "very ambiguous message" which "sank without a trace".
20. These and other direct quotes that follow are drawn from Stalin's pieces in Murra & Holling (1951: 70-76, 96-98).
21. Lomtev (1951: 79-80). For background, see Seyffert (1985: 21, 83).
22. Report of the President of the Academy of Sciences to the TsK (June 1950), in RTsKh f.17 o.132 d.336 l.77. See A. Chikobava's "On certain problems of Soviet linguistics (9 May 1950), and V.V. Vinogradov's "A program of Marxist linguistics" (4 July 1950), both reprinted from *Pravda* in Murra & Holling (1951: 9-13, 88-89). *Russkii iazyk v shkole* 4 (1950: 18).
23. Educational reports (1951), in TsGA RSFSR f.2306 o.72 d.443 ll.1-4; d.437 ll.75-76. Reports of linguists in RTsKh f.17 o.132 d.336 ll.108-118; and in GBOR f.652 o.11 d.17 l.1.
24. Educational materials (1951) in GAIaO f.2224 o.1 d.295 ll.33,94,130,271-334; and in TsGA RSFSR f.2306 o.72 d.438 ll.3,37; d.433 ll.99-100. Letter from the

Vice-President of the Academy of Sciences to TsK Secretary Malenkov (July 1950), in RTsKh f.17 o.132 d.336. Kasilov (1990: 92-94, 132).
25. Educational reports (1950-1951), in TsGA RSFSR f.2306 o.72 d.73 ll.1-3, 7-8; d.433 ll.1-12,60.
26. Ministry of Education instructional statements (1948-1951), in TsGA RSFSR f.2306 o.72 d.449; o.71 d.233 l.2. TsGA RSFSR f.259 o.1 d.366 l.213; d.363 ll.112-113; d.374 l.64. Correspondence from the North Caucasus party secretaries to TsK Secretary Malenkov (1945), in RTsKh f.17 o.126 d.23 ll.17,49.
27. Circular from the Ministry of Education RSFSR (December 1949), in GAIaO f.2224 o.1 d.293 ll.6-7. Mirtov's comments in GAIaO f.2257 o.6 d.80 ll.5-12.
28. Educational reports (1946-1948), in TsGA RSFSR f.2306 o.69 d.3284; o.71 d.233 ll.284-285; TsGA RSFSR f.259 o.1 d.239 l.9. Reports to the TsK in RTsKh f.17 o.132 d.164 ll.16-19,34-39. Serebrennikov (1952: 3-6). A whole series of national dictionaries and grammars were published and republished between the late 1930s and late 1940s: see Ashmarin (1928-1941), Baskakov (1940), Baskakov & Toshchakova (1947), Batmanov (1940 and 1946), Batyrov (1940), Begaliev (1945), Dyrenkova (1940 and 1941), Iakovlev (1940, 1941, 1948), Iudakhin (1940), Sanzheev (1940 and 1941), Shaidanov & Batmanov (1938).
29. Correspondence from Kabardin and Dagestan party secretaries to the TsK VKPb (1945-1946), in RTsKh f.17 o.126 d.23 ll.2-6,26; d.27 l.31. Conference report, in TsGA RSFSR f.2306 o.71(1) d.126 ll.1-4,12,25,32-33,37-50. *Russkii iazyk v shkole* 2 (1950: 73-76).
30. Conference reports (1948), in TsGA RSFSR f.2306 o.71 d.122 ll.3-11,30-48; o.71(1) d.126 ll.17-19,28.
31. Conference report (1948), in TsGA RSFSR f.2306 o.71(1) d.119 ll.23-28,30,46. Sovetkin (1958).
32. For a colorful fictional account, see Solzhenitsyn (1969: chapter 19). The quote is from one such letter, among hundreds, in RTsKh f.17 o.132 d.336 ll.150-337.
33. See the interesting discussion in Rossianov (1993: 728-745).
34. Here I have in mind Anderson's (1985) characterization of twentieth-century linguistics; and Bourdieu's (1991: 106) discussion of the "social institution of symbolic power". The quote is from Bourdieu.

Conclusion

1. "I volgari sono scritti quando il popolo riprende importanza." Gramsci (1975, 1: 354). He was referring to the rise of the communes in early modern Italy, as the vulgate began to take literary shape in a successful challenge to the Latin language.
2. For background, and the contributions of P.S Kuznetsov, I.I. Revzin, and V.V. Ivanov, see Segal (1974: 5).

3. "Protocol of the First Meeting of the Linguistics Section of the Council on Cybernetics of the ANSSSR" (3 July 1959), in GBOR f.652 o.11 d.23 ll.1-3. Toporov quoted from Segal (1974: 18).
4. For the positions of the former Marrists, see *Voprosy iazykoznaniia* 4-6 (1956), and 3-6 (1965). Kuznetsov's report, "On the structural analysis of language" (10 September 1959), in GBOR f.652 o.11 d.25 ll.1-6. For background, see Arutiunova & Klimov (1968: 168). Revzin saw structural linguistics not as a "purely abstract theory", but as a "phenomenon with a history and tradition rooted in a pre-structuralist past", founded by "such names as Fortunatov, Baudouin, Durnovo, Peshkovskii, Peterson, Shcherba, Jakobson, Kartsevskii". Segal (1974: 33-35)
5. For Bakhtin's own writings on the varieties of social discourse, see his "From the Prehistory of Novelistic Discourse," and "Discourse and the Novel," in Bakhtin (1981). For studies of the "political" Bakhtin, see Hirschkop (1986: 92-113); and Gardiner (1992).
6. In a 1920s debate in the Communist Academy, from AAN f.350 o.2 d.156 l.35. For background, see Kaiser (1994: 139-140, 254-264).
7. It would seem then, that the nation is more the stable set of objective conditions (Smith 1986) rather than the shifting range of subjective choices (Anderson 1991) - issues which were discussed in the Introduction.
8. See Lewis (1972b: 311); Lewis (1972a: 16, 293, 133-148); Kaiser (1994: 140); and Clem (1986: 70-97). Anderson & Silver (1990: 95-127); Laitin & Petersen & Slocum (1992); Solchanyk (1982: 23-42).
9. Participant at a linguistics conference, "Contemporary Issues of Teaching Languages in the Higher Schools", Azerbaijani Engineering University (Baku, May 1994), from my personal notes. My thanks to Letif Kerimov for hosting this event.
10. For the recent history, see Fierman (1995).
11. See the remarks by N.M. Shanskii, an administrator of bilingual education, in *Russkii iazyk v natsional'noi shkoly* 6 (1989: 3-7). This journal, renamed *Russkii iazyk v SSSR* in 1990 and edited by M.I. Isaev, devoted much attention to bilingual issues. Also see the remarks by G.A. Yagodin, chair of the USSR State Committee on Public Education and member of the Ideological Commission of the Central Committee of the Communist Party (Soviet Union), in *Current politics of the Soviet Union* 1 (1990: 73).
12. See Trubetskoi (1987) and discussions of his work in *Izvestiia ANSSSR. Literatura i iazyk* 2/49 (1990: 148-151); and 50/2 (1991: 188-191), and *Vestnik Moskovskogo universiteta. Seriia 9. Filologiia* 5 (1990: 83-85).

Archival sources

The archival abbreviations listed below designate the names of the archives at the time of my research work in them (in the case of Moscow, quite often before the collapse of the USSR in 1991 and the subsequent renaming of the archives). I conducted archival research in Iaroslavl, Baku, and Tashkent after 1991 and the foundation of the "newly independent states". The textual abbreviations in the notes designate the following: f. - **fond** (collection); o. - **opis'** (inventory); d. - **delo** (file); l. - **list** (page).

Moscow (Russia)

AAN. Archive of the Academy of Sciences of the USSR

fond 350, Communist Academy
fond 361, Commission to Study the National Question
fond 468, N.M. Karinskii
fond 502, D.N. Ushakov
fond 558, F.E. Korsh
fond 688, V.A. Gordlevskii
fond 696, M.N. Peterson

GBOR. State Library, Manuscript Division (Lenin Library)

fond 38, R.F. Brandt
fond 652, P.S. Kuznetsov
fond 718, G.G. Shpet

RTsKh. Russian Center for the Storage and Study of Documents of Contemporary History (the former Central Archive of the Communist Party of the USSR)

fond 17, Central Committee of the All-Union Communist Party
    o.60, Division of Agitation and Propaganda (1920-1927)
    o.61, Agitation-Propaganda for the National Minorities
    o.112, Orgbiuro and Secretariat, 1922-1925
    o.113, Orgbiuro and Secretariat, 1926-1930
    o.114, Orgbiuro and Secretariat, 1931-1939

o.125, Directorate for Propaganda and Agitation, 1938-1948
o.126, Division of Schools, 1939, 1941-1946
o.132, Division of Propaganda and Agitation, 1948-1956
fond 61, Turkestan Bureau TsK RKP(b), 1920-1922
fond 62, Central Asian Bureau TsK VKP(b)
fond 64, Caucasus Bureau TsK RKP(b)
fond 65, South-West Bureau TsK RKP(b)
fond 122, Turk Commission VTsIK, 1918-1923
fond 544, Council for Propaganda and Activity among the People's of the East
fond 583, Central Bureau for Agitation and Propaganda among the Turkic Peoples TsK RKPb, 1918-1921

TsGALI. Central State Archive of Literature and Art of the USSR (now known as RGALI)

fond 454, A.M. Sukhotin
fond 2808, M.S. Gus
fond 2164, G.O. Vinokur

TsGAOR. Central State Archive of the October Revolution of the USSR (now known as GARF)

fond 1235, Central Executive Committee (RSFSR)
fond 1318, People's Commissariat for the Nationalities (RSFSR), 1917-1924
fond 3316, Central Executive Committee (USSR)
fond 4033, Central Publishing House for the USSR Peoples
fond 5402, M.P. Pavlovich
fond 7543, All-Union Committee for the New Alphabet

TsGA RSFSR. Central State Archive of the Russian Socialist Federated Soviet Republic (now known as GARF)

fond 259, Council of Ministers (RSFSR)
fond 296, Committee for the Education of the National Minorities (Sovnatsmen RSFSR), 1921-1934
fond 298, State Academic Council
fond 1575, Main Committee for Social Education (RSFSR)
fond 2306, People's Commissariat for Education
fond 2307, Main Committee for Scientific-Artistic, Musuem, and Environmental Institutions (Glavnauk)

fond 2313, Main Committee for Political Education (Glavpolitprosvet)
fond 4655, Russian Association of Scientific Research Institutes for Material, Artistic and Speech Culture

TsGANKh. Central State Archive of the National Economy (now known as RGAE)

fond 4460, All-Union Committee for Standardization, 1930-1940
fond 8053, Committee for the Poligraphy Industry, 1926-1931

Iaroslavl (Russia)

GAIaO. State Archive of the Iaroslavl Region and its Filials in the Cities of Rostov, Rybinsk, and Uglich

fond 178, Departments of National Education of the Executive Committees of Provincial Soviets
fond 2224, Department of National Education of the Executive Committee of the Iaroslavl Regional Soviet, 1936-1964
fond 2611, Iaroslavl Regional Institute for the Advancement of Teachers, 1938-1970
fond 2257, Iaroslavl State Pedagogical Institute (named for K.D. Ushinskii)

TsDNIIaO. Center for the Documents of Contemporary History of the Iaroslavl Region (the former Regional Archives of the Communist Party of the USSR)

fond 272, Iaroslavl Regional Committee of the Communist Party of the USSR
fond 372, Communist Party Organizations of the Iaroslavl State Pedagogical Institute (named for K.D. Ushinskii)

Baku (Azerbaijan)

GAPPOD. State Archive of Political Parties and Social Movements of the Azerbaijani Republic (the former Archives of the Communist Party of Azerbaijan)

fond 1, Central Committee of the Azerbaijani Communist Party

GANI. State Archive of Contemporary History of the Azerbaijani Republic

fond 57, People's Commissariat of Education
fond 103, Central Committee for the New Azerbaijani Alphabet
fond 379, Azerbaijani Central Executive Committee of the Soviet of Worker,
    Peasant, and Red Army Deputies
fond 387, Azerbaijani State Scientific Research Institute
fond 389, Society for the Research and Study of Azerbaijan
fond 411, Soviet of People's Commissars and Soviet of Ministers of Azerbaijan
fond 1119, Central Department of the All-Union Professional Union of Education
    Workers

GIA. State Historical Archive of the Azerbaijani Republic

fond 45, Chancellery of the Baku Governor (*gubernator*), 1846-1917
fond 46, Chancellery of the Baku Governor (*gradonachal'nik*), 1906-1918
fond 309, Baku-Dagestan Directorate of National Educational Institutions, 1860-1918

Tashkent (Uzbekistan)

TsGAUZ. Central State Archive of the Uzbek SSR

fond 17, Central Executive Committee of the Soviets of Deputies of the Turkestan
    ASSR, 1917-1924
fond 25, Soviet of People's Commissars of the Turkestan ASSR
fond 34, People's Commissariat of Education of the Turkestan ASSR, 1917-1924
fond 86, Central Executive Committee of the Uzbek SSR
fond 94, People's Commissariat of Education of the Uzbek SSR
fond 368, Central Asian State University
fond 837, Soviet of People's Commissars of the Uzbek SSR

References

Aarsleff, Hans
 1982 *From Locke to Saussure: essays on the study of language and intellectual history.* Minneapolis: University of Minnesota Press.

Aarsleff, Hans & Louis Kelly & Hans-Josef Niederehe (eds.)
 1986 *Papers in the history of linguistics. Proceedings of the third international conference on the history of the language sciences.* Amsterdam-Philadelphia: John Benjamins.

Abakumov, S.I.
 1923 *Uchebnik russkoi grammatiki. Opyt primeneniia printsipov nauchnoi grammatiki k shkol'no-grammaticheskoi praktike.* Moscow: Gosizdat.
 1929 *Russkii iazyk. Rabochaia kniga dlia piatogo goda obucheniia.* Moscow: Gosizdat.
 1936 *Materialy k planirovaniiu uchebnoi raboty po russkomu iazyku v 5-10 klassakh na 1-e polugode 1936-1937 ucheb. goda.* Moscow: Gosizdat.

Adler, Max
 1980 *Marxist linguistic theory and communist practice: a sociological study.* Hamburg: Helmut Buske.

Afanasiev, P.O.
 1922 *Putevoditel' po voprosam prepodavaniia rodnogo iazyka v trudovoi shkole.* Moscow: Gosizdat.
 1923 *Metodika rodnogo iazyka.* Moscow: Gosizdat.
 1924a *Rodnoi iazyk v trudovoi shkole.* Moscow: Gosizdat.
 1924b "Russkii iazyk v kompleksnoi sisteme prepodavaniia," *Narodnyi uchitel'* 6: 57-60.
 1925 *Chitai, pishi, schitai.* Moscow: Gosizdat
 1927 *Kak obuchat' gramote.* Moscow: Rabpros.

Agamalyogly, S.A.
 1925 *Neotlozhny nuzhdy tiursko-tatarskikh narodov.* Baku: AzGiz.
 1927 *V zashchitu novogo tiurkskogo alfavita.* Baku: AzGiz.

Agazade, F.
 1926 *Istoriia vozniknoveniia i proniknoveniia v zhizn' idei novogo tiurkskogo alfavita v ASSR, s 1922 po 1925 god.* Kazan: VTsKNTA.

1927   *Materialy po unifikatsii proektov novogo tiurkskogo alfavita.* Baku: VTsKNTA.

Agazade, F. & K. Karakashly
1928   *Ocherk po istorii razvitiia dvizheniia novogo alfavita i ego dostizheniia.* Kazan: VTsKNTA.

Akiner, Shirin
1986   *Islamic peoples of the Soviet Union.* London: Kegan Paul.
1989   "Uzbekistan: republic of many tongues", in: M. Kirkwood (ed.), 100-122.

Akodis, Ia.L. & E.I. Dreizin (eds.)
1929   *Iz opyta raboty shkol podrostkov.* Moscow-Leningrad: Gosizdat.

Alaverdov, K. & A. Bek & Z. Priannikova & N. Nechaeva (eds.)
1932   *Za proletarskuiu literatura. Uchebnik dlia tekhnikum.* Moscow: Uchpedgiz.

Alaverdov, K. & S. Dimanshtein & D. Korkmasov & A. Nukhrat (eds.)
1933   *Iazyk i pis'mennost' narodov SSSR. Stenograficheskii otchet pervogo vsesoiuznogo plenuma nauchnogo soveta VTsKNA, 15-19 fevralia 1933 g.* Moscow: VTsKNA.

Aliev, U.
1930   "Pobeda latinizatsii: luchshaia pamiat' o tov. Agamalyogly", *Revoliutsiia i natsional'nost'* 7: 17-28.

Allworth, Edward
1964   *Uzbek literary politics.* The Hague: Mouton.
1965   *Central Asian publishing and the rise of nationalism.* New York: New York Public Library.
1971   *Nationalities of the Soviet east: publications and writing systems.* New York: Columbia University Press.
1980   *Ethnic Russia in the USSR.* New York: Pergamon.
1990   *The modern Uzbeks: from the fourteenth century to the present.* Stanford: Hoover Institution Press.

Allworth, Edward (ed.)
1967   *Central Asia: a century of Russian rule.* New York: Columbia University Press.
1973   *The nationality question in Soviet Central Asia.* New York: Praeger.

Alpatov, V.M.
1989   "K istorii sovetskogo iazykoznaniia: Marr i Stalin", *Voprosy istorii* 1: 185-188.
1991   *Istoriia odnogo mifa. Marr i marrizm.* Moscow: Nauka.

Alston, Patrick L.
1969　　　*Education and the state in tsarist Russia*. Stanford: Stanford University Press.

Amirova, T.A. & B.A. Ol'khovnikov & Iu.V. Rozhdestvenskii
1975　　　*Ocherki po istorii lingvistiki*. Moscow: Glavredaktsii vostochnoi literatury.

Anderson, Barbara A. & Brian D. Silver
1990　　　"Some factors in the linguistic and ethnic russification of Soviet nationalities: is everyone becoming Russian?", in: L. Hajda & M. Bessinger (eds.), 95-127.

Anderson, Benedict
1991　　　*Imagined communities: reflections on the origin and spread of nationalism*. London: Verso.

Anderson, Kevin
1995　　　*Lenin, Hegel, and western Marxism: a critical study*. Urbana: University of Illinois Press.

Anderson, Stephen R.
1985　　　*Phonology in the twentieth century: theories of rules and theories of representations*. Chicago: University of Chicago Press.

Andreev, A.P.
1929　　　*Revolucio en la lingvoscienco: jafetida lingvo-teorio de akademiano N. Marr*. Leipzig: SAT.
1930　　　*Iazyk i myshlenie. Opyt issledovanniia na baze materialisticheskoi iafeticheskoi teorii*. Moscow: TsKSESR.

Apresian, Iu.D.
1966　　　*Idei i metody sovremmenoi strukturnoi lingvistiki (kratkii ocherk)*. Moscow.
1973　　　*Principles and methods of contemporary structural linguistics*. Trans. Dina Crockett. The Hague: Mouton.

Arkhincheev, I.
1924　　　"Problema prosveshcheniia otstalykh natsional'nostei s tochki zreniia leninizma", *Zhizn' natsional'nostei* 1: 45-55.

Armstrong, Daniel & C.H. van Schooneveld (eds.)
1977　　　*Roman Jakobson: echoes of his scholarship*. Lisse: De Ridder.

Artemov, B.A.
1933　　　"Tekhnograficheskii analiz summarnykh bukv novogo alfavita", in: D. Korkmasov (ed.), 58-60.
1936　　　"Psikhologiia i novyi latinizirovannyi alfavit", *Revoliutsiia i pis'mennost'* 2: 103-120.

Arutiunova, N.D. & G.A. Klimov
1968　　　"Strukturnaia lingvistika", in: F. Filin (ed.), 155-165.

Arvatov, B.A.
1923 "Iazyk poeticheskii i iazyk prakticheskii", *Pechat' i revoliutsiia* 7: 58-67.

Ashmarin, N.I.
1928-1941 *Slovar' chuvashskogo iayka*. Vols. 1-16. Kazan-Cheboksary.

Asimova, B.S.
1982 *Iazykovoe stroitel'stvo v Tadzhikistane, 1920-1940 gg.* Dushanbe: Izd. Don.

Asmus, V.F.
1927 "Filosofiia iazyka Vil'gelma Gumbol'dta v interpretatsii prof. G. Shpeta", *Vestnik kommunisticheskoi akademii* 23: 250-265.

Aspaturian, Vernon
1968 "The non-Russian nationalities", in: Allen Kassoff (ed.), *Prospects for Soviet society*. New York: Praeger, 159-160.

Atadzhanov, A.R.
1976 *TsKK-RKI Uzbekistana v bor'be za sotsializm*. Tashkent.

Auld, William
1976 *The development of poetic language in Esperanto*. Rotterdam: UEA.

Austin, Paul
1973 "Russian loanwords in the proposed reform of Soviet Turkic alphabets", *General linguistics* 13/1: 16-25.
1992 "Soviet Karelian: the language that failed", *Slavic review* 51/1: 16-35.

Avanesov, R.I.
1949 *Ocherki russkoi dialektologii*. Moscow.

Avanesov, R.I. & V.N. Sidorov
1930 "Reforma orfografii v sviazi s problemoi pis'mennogo iazyka".
[1970] [Reprinted in: A.A. Reformatskii (ed.), *Iz istorii otechestvennoi fonologii*. Moscow: Nauka, 149-156.]
1934 *Russkii iazyk: uchebnik dlia pedagogicheskikh tekhnikumov*. Moscow.
1945 *Ocherk grammatiki russkogo literaturnogo iazyka*. Moscow.

Azrael, Jeremy (ed.)
1978 *Soviet nationality policies and practices*. New York: Praeger.

Babaeva, Sima
1989 "Reforma alfavita", *Molodost'* (Baku). July edition.

Bailes, Kendall
1978 *Technology and society under Lenin and Stalin: origins of the Soviet technical intelligentsia, 1917-1941*. Princeton: Princeton University Press.

Bakhtin, Mikhail & P.N. Medvedev
- 1981 *The dialogic imagination.* Ed. and Trans. Michael Holquist and Caryl Emerson. Austin: University of Texas Press.
- 1985 *The formal method in literary scholarship.* Trans. Albert Wehrle. Baltimore: Johns Hopkins University Press.

Bakhurst, David
- 1991 *Consciousness and revolution in Soviet philosophy.* New York: Cambridge University Press.

Baldauf, Ingebord
- 1993 *Schriftreform und schriftwechsel bei den Muslimischen Russland und Sowjetturken (1850-1937).* Budapest: Kiado.

Banac, Ivo & John Ackerman & Roman Szporluk & Wayne S. Vucinich (eds.)
- 1981 *Nation and ideology: essays in honor of Wayne S. Vucinich.* Boulder, Colorado: East European Monographs.

Barannikov, A.P.
- 1919 "Iz nabliudenii nad razvitiem russkogo iazyka v poslednie gody: vliianie voiny i revoliutsii na razvitie russkogo iazyka", *Uchenye zapiski Samarskogo universiteta* 2: 64-84.

Barkhin, K.B.
- 1933 *Razvitie rechi: metodicheskoe posobie dlia uchitelei.* Moscow: Gosizdat.

Barkhin, K. & G. Kostenko & I. Ustinov (eds.)
- 1930 *Proekt reformy pravopisaniia.* Moscow: Gosizdat.

Barthes, Roland
- 1977 "The death of the author," in: *Images, music, text.* New York: Hill and Wang, 142-148.

Baskakov, N.A.
- 1940 *Nogaiskii iazyk i ego dialekty.* Moscow-Leningrad.

Baskakov, P.A. & G.M. Toshchakova
- 1947 *Oirotsko-russkii slovar'.* Moscow.

Bassin, Mark
- 1991 "Russia between Europe and Asia: the ideological construction of geographical space", *Slavic review* 50/1: 9-17.

Batmanov, I.A.
- 1940 *Grammatika kirgizskovo iazyka.* Frunze.
- 1946 *Foneticheskaia sistema sovremennogo kirgizskogo iazyka.* Frunze.

Batyrov, Sh. (ed.)
- 1940 *Turkmeno-russkii slovar'.* Ashkhabad.

Baudouin de Courtenay, J.I.
- 1908 "Vspomogatel'nyi mezhdunarodnyi iazyk", *Espero* 9: 10-11.

1912   *Ob otnoshenii russkogo pis'ma k russkomu iazyku*. St. Petersburg: Obnovlenie shkoly.
1913   *Natsional'nyi i territorial'nyi priznak v avtonomii*. St. Petersburg: Stasiulevich.
1917   *Lektsii po vvedeniiu v iazykovedenie*. Petrograd: Iudelevich
1963   *Izbrannye trudy po obshchemu iazykoznaniiu*. Moscow: ANSSSR.

Bayturgan, Barasbi
1971   "The North Caucasus", *Studies on the Soviet Union* XI: 12-28.

Baziiants, A.P.
1972   *Lazarevskii institut v istorii otechestvennogo vostokovedeniia*. Moscow: Nauka.

Begaliev, G.B.
1945   *Kazakhsko-russkii slovar'*. Alma-Ata.

Beissinger, Mark
1988   *Scientific management, socialist discipline and Soviet power*. Cambridge, Mass.: Harvard University Press.

Beliaev, M.V.
1928   "K izucheniiu vneshnikh i vnutrennikh form iazyka", *Trudy severo-kavkazskoi assotsiatsii nauchno-issledovatel'skikh institutov* 43/4: 128-135.

Bell, David
1995   "Lingua populi, lingua dei: language, religion, and the origins of French revolutionary nationalism", *American historical review* 100/5: 1403-1437.

Belov, A.M.
1958   *A.M. Peshkovskii kak lingvist i metodist*. Moscow.

Bennigsen, Alexandre
1960   *Les mouvements nationaux chez les musulmans de russe: le "sutangalievisme" au Tatarstan*. Paris: Mouton.
1967   *Islam in the Soviet Union*. New York: Praeger.
1984   "Panturkism and panislamism in history and today", *Central Asian survey* 3/3: 39-50.
1985   "Politics and linguistics in Dagestan," in: I. Kreindler (ed.), 125-142.

Bennigsen, Alexandre & Chantal Lemercier-Quelquejay
1960   "Le probleme linguistique et l'evolution des nationalites musulmanes en URSS," *Cahiers du monde russe et sovietique* I-III: 418-465.
1964   *La presse et le mouvement national chez les musulmans de Russie avant 1920*. Paris-The Hague: Mouton.

Bernshtein, S.
1927 "Zvuchashchaia khudozhestvennaia rech' i ee izuchenie", *Poetika* I: 41-53.

Bernshtein, S.B.
1989 "Tragicheskaia stranitsa iz istorii slavianskoi filologii (30-e gody XX veka)", *Sovetskoe slavianovedenie* 1: 77-82.

Birger S.M. & N.V. Chekhov (eds.)
1928 *Russkii iazyk v shkolakh natsional'nykh men'shinstv RSFSR* Moscow: NKP RSFSR.

Blank, Stephen
1983 "The Struggle for Soviet Bashkiria, 1917-1923", *Nationalities papers* XI/1: 1-26.
1988 "The origins of Soviet language policy, 1917-1921", *Russian history* 15/1: 71-92.
1994 *The sorcerer as apprentice: Stalin as commissar of nationalities, 1917-1924* Westport, Connecticut: Greenwood Press.

Blanke, Detlev
1978 *Sociopolitikaj aspektoj de la esperanto-movado*. Budapest: HEA.

Bodanov, A.A.
1914 *Nauka ob obshchestvennom soznanii*. (3rd edition.) Moscow.
1922 *Nauka i rabochii klass*. Moscow: Bib. Vse. Proletkulta.
1923 *Filosofiia zhivogo opyta*. (3rd edition.) Petrograd-Moscow.
1924 "De la filozofio a la organiza scienco". Trans. N. Nekrasov. *Sennacieca revuo* 1/5-6: 83-86, 99-101.
1925a *O proletarskoi kul'ture, 1904-1924*. Leningrad: Izd. Tov. Kniga.
1925b "Uchenie o refleksakh i zagadki pervobytnogo myshlenniia", *Vestnik kommunisticheskoi akademii* 10: 72-79.
1929 *Ruga stelo*. Trans. N. Nekrasov. Leipzig: SAT.
1980 *Essays in tektology*. Trans. George Gorelik. Seaside, Calif.: Intersystems.

Bogoiavlenskii, L.P.
1928 *Pravopisanie v derevenskoi shkole*. Moscow-Leningrad: Gosizdat.

Bogoroditskii, V.A.
1913 *Obshchii kurs russkoi grammatiki*. (4th edition.) Kazan.
1930 *Fonetika russkogo iazyka v svete eksperimental'nykh dannykh*. Kazan.
1934 *Vvedenie v tatarskoe iazykoznanie v sviazi s drugimi tiurkskimi iazykami*. Kazan: Tatar Gosizdat.

Boianus, S.
1930 "Russkoe proiznoshenie", *Russkii iazyk v sovetskoi shkole* 3: 23-30.
Bokarev, E.A.
1976 *Problemy interlingvistiki*. Moscow: Nauka.
Bokarev, E.A. & Iu.D. (eds.)
1959 *Mladopis'mennye iazyki narodov SSSR*. Moscow: ANSSSR.
Borbe, Tasso.
1974 *Kritik der Marxistichen sprachtheorie N.Ia. Marr's*. Kronberg: Scriptor.
Borovkov, A.K.
1935 *Uchebnik uigurskogo iazyka*. Leningrad.
Bourdieu, Pierre
1991 *Language and symbolic power*. Trans. Gino Raymond & Matthew Adamson. Cambridge, Mass.: Harvard University Press.
Bradley, Joseph
1991 "Voluntary associations, civic culture, and 'obshchestvennost' in Moscow", in: E. Clowes & S. Kassow & J. West (eds.), 131-139.
Brazhba, Kh.S.
1987 *Trudy. Kniga pervaia. Etiudy i issledovaniia*. Sukhumi: Alashara.
Breckenridge, Carol A. & Peter Van der Veer (eds.)
1993 *Orientalism and the postcolonial predicament: perspectives on South Asia*. Philadelphia: University of Pennsylvania Press.
Briusov, Valerii
1973 *Sobranie sochinenii*. Vols. 1-2. Moscow.
Brodskii, N.L. & N.P. Sidorov (eds.)
1924 *Literaturnye manifesty*. Moscow: Novaia Moskva.
Brooks, Jeffrey
1982 "Studies of the reader in the 1920s", *Russian history* 9/2-3: 187-202.
1985a "The breakdown in production and distribution of printed material, 1917-1927", in: A. Gleason & P. Kenez & R. Stites (eds.), 151-174.
1985b *When Russia learned to read*. Princeton: Princeton University Press.
1989 "Public and private values in the Soviet press", *Slavic review* (spring): 16-35.
Brower, Daniel R.
1990 *The Russian city between tradition and modernity, 1850-1900*. Berkeley: University of California Press.

1994 "The penny press and its readers", in: S. Frank & M. Steinberg (eds.), 147-167.
Brower, Daniel & Edward Lazzerini (eds.)
1997 *Russia's orient: imperial borderlands and peoples, 1700-1917.* Bloomington: Indiana University Press.
Brown, JoAnne
1992 *The definition of a profession.* Princeton: Princeton University Press, 1992.
Broz, M. & M. Gus
1928 *Stat'ia i fel'eton. Opyt po gazetnoi publitsistike.* Moscow: Rabpros.
Bruche-Schulz, Gisela.
1984 *Russische sprachwissenschaft: wissenschaft im historisch-politischen prozess des vorsowjetischen und sowjetischen Russland.* Tubingen: Niemayer.
Bruchis, Michael
1982 *One step back, two steps forward: on the language policy of the communist party of the Soviet Union in the national republics.* Boulder: East European Monographs.
1984 "The effect of the USSR's language policies on the national languages of its Turkic population", in: Yaacov Roi (ed.), *The USSR and the Muslim world.* London: Allen and Urwin, 129-132.
Bubrikh, D.V.
1929 "Neobkhodim revoliutsionnyi pochin", *Prosveshchenie natsional'nostei* 1: 73-74.
1930 "Neskol'ko slov o potoke rechi", *Biulleten' LOIKFUN* 5: 4-17.
Budde, E.F.
1913 *Osnovy sintaksisa russkogo iazyka.* Kazan: Golubeva.
1917 *Voprosy metodologii russkogo iazykoznaniia.* Kazan: Golubeva.
Bukharin, N.
1927 "Nauka i SSSR", *Pechat' i revoliutsiia* 7: 12-13.
Bulakhovskii, L.A.
1951 *Uchenie I.V. Stalina o iazyke i zadachi sovetskogo iazykoznaniia.* Kiev: ANUSSR.
Burke, Peter & Roy Porter (eds.)
1987 *The social history of language.* New York: Cambridge University Press.
Burliuk, Nicholas & David Burliuk
1914 "Poetickeskaia nachala", *Futuristy* 1-2: 81-85.

Bushnell, Kristine
1991 Appropriation and denial: formalism's debt to Humboldt and Potebnia. [Unpublished paper presented at the Conference on Linguistics and Politics: the Heritage of Potebnia. School of Slavonic and East European Studies. London, 1-14.]

Bushnell, John
1981 "Peasants in uniform: the tsarist army as a peasant society", *Journal of social history* 13/4: 565-566.

Buzuk, P.A.
1924 *Osnovnye voprosy iazykoznaniia.* (2nd edition.) Moscow: Dumnov.

Bykovskii, S.N.
1931 *Metodika istoricheskogo issledovaniia.* Leningrad: GAIMK.
1933 *N.Ia. Marr i ego teoriia.* Moscow: Lensotsekgiz.
1934a "K voprosu ob odomanshii zhivotnykh", *Sovetskaia etnografiia* 3: 3-27.
1934b "Doklassovoe obshchestvo kak sotsial'no-ekonomicheskaia formatsiia", *Sovetskaia etnografiia* 1-2: 6-39.

Bykovskii, S.N. (ed.)
1932 *Protiv burzhuaznoi kontrabandy v iazykoznanii. Sbornik brigady Instituta iazyka i myshleniia.* Leningrad: GAIMK.

Byrnes, Robert
1968 *Pobedonostsev: his life and thought.* Bloomington: Indiana University Press.

Caroe, Olaf
1953a "The heritage of Chaghatai: language in Russian Central Asia", *Royal Central Asian journal* 40.
1953b *Soviet empire: the Turks of Central Asia and Stalinism.* London: Macmillan.

Carrere d'Encausse, Helene
1978 "Determinants and parameters of Soviet nationality policy", in J. Azrael (ed.), 39-62.

Cassirer, Ernst A.
1945 "Structuralism in modern linguistics", *Word* I/II.

Chemodanov N.S.
1956 *Sravnitel'no iazykoznanie v rossii.* Moscow.

Chernykh, P.Ia.
1925 *Neskol'ko zamechanii otnositel'no tak nazyvaemykh 'nabliudenii nad iazykom' v novoi shkole.* Irkutsk: Vlast' truda.
1929a *Russkii iazyk i revoliutsiia.* Irkutsk: Vlast' truda.
1929b *Sovremennye techeniia v lingvistike.* Irkutsk: Vlast' truda.

Chernyshev, V.I.
1947 "F.F. Fortunatov i A.A. Shakhmatov – reformatory russkogo pravopisaniia", in: S.P. Obnorskii (ed.), *A.A. Shakhmatov, 1864-1920. Sbornik statei i materialov*. Moscow-Leningrad, 167-252.
1970 *Izbrannye trudy*. Vols. 1-2. Moscow: Prosveshchenie.

Chikobava, A.S.
1952 *Vvedenie v iazykoznanie*. Moscow.
1951 *Trudy I.V. Stalina po voprosam iazykoznaniia i ikh znacheniie dlia nauki o iazyke*. Tbilisi.

Chistiakov, V.F.
1935 *K izucheniiu iazyka kolkhoznika*. Smolensk: ZONI.

Chizhevskii, D.I.
1939 *Gegel' v' rossii*. Paris: Dom Knigi.

Chobanzade, B.
1925 *Vvedenie v tiurko-tatarskoe iazykovedenie*. Baku.

Clark Katerina
1978 "Little heroes and big deeds: literature responds to the first five-year plan", in: S. Fitzpatrick (ed.), 193-197.
1981 *The Soviet novel: history as ritual*. Chicago: University of Chicago Press.
1995 *Petersburg: crucible of revolution*. Cambridge, Mass.: Harvard University Press.

Clark, Katerina & Michael Holquist
1984 *Mikhail Bakhtin*. Cambridge, Mass.: Harvard University Press.

Clay, Catherine B.
1995 "Russian ethnographers in the service of empire, 1856-1862", *Slavic review* 54/1: 45.

Clem, Ralph
1986 "The ethnic and language dimensions of Russian and Soviet censuses," in: Ralph Clem (ed.), *Research guide to the Russian and Soviet censuses*. Ithaca: Cornell University Press, 70-97.

Clowes, Edith & Samuel D. Kassow & James L. West (eds.)
1991 *Between Tsar and people: educated society and the quest for public identity in late imperial Russia*. Princeton: Princeton University Press.

Coe, Steven R.
1993 Peasants, the state and the languages of NEP: the rural correspondents movement in the Soviet Union, 1924-1928. [Unpublished Ph.D. dissertation, University of Michigan.]

Cole, Michael (ed.)
1978 *The selected writings of A.R. Luria*. White Plains: M.E. Sharpe.

Comrie, Bernard
    1981   *The languages of the Soviet Union*. Cambridge: Cambridge University Press.

Comrie, Bernard & Gerald Stone
    1978   *The Russian language since the revolution*. Oxford: Clarendon Press.

Connor, Walker
    1984   *The national question in Marxist-Leninst theory and strategy*. Princeton: Princeton University Press.

Consey, Eileen
    1995   Mapping human productivity: the commission for the study of the tribal composition of Russia and neighboring countries and the institute for the study of the peoples of the USSR (KIPS-IPIN), 1917-1932. [Unpublished paper presented at the annual convention of the American Historical Association. Chicago, 1995.]

Cooper, Robert L.
    1989   *Language planning and social change*. New York: Cambridge University Press.

Cracraft, James
    1986   "Empire versus nation", *Harvard Ukrainian studies* 10/3-4: 524-540.

Crisp, Simon
    1984   "Language planning and the orthography of Avar", *Folia slavica* 7/1-2: 91-104.
    1985   "The formation and development of literary Avar", in: I. Kreindler (ed.), 143-162.
    1989   "Soviet language planning since 1917-1953", in: M. Kirkwood (ed.), 23-45.

Daniialov, A.D.
    1972   "Iz istorii bor'by za novuiu pis'mennost' i likvidatsiiu negramotnosti v Dagestane", *Narody Azii i Afriki* 6: 133-137.

Danilov, G.K.
    1921a   "Literaturnaia sektsiia v krasnoarmeiskom klube", *Sputnik kommunista* 12 (May): 26-34.
    1921b   "Iskusstvo proletariat", *Sputnik kommunista* 12 (May): 76-78.
    1929   *Programma po sobiraniiu materialov dlia slovaria russkogo rabochego posleoktiabrskoi epokhi (1917-1929)*. Moscow: RANION.
    1931a   "Metodika slovarnogo issledovaniia (na primere iazyka rabochego)", *Uchenye zapiski instituta literatury i iazyka RANIONa* 4: 3-17.

1931b "Cherty rechevogo stiliia rabochego", *Literatura i marksizma* 4/1: 101.
1931c *Kratkii ocherk istorii nauki o iazyke.* Moscow: MGU.
1931d *Russkii iazyk dlia nerusskikh: rabochaia kniga po russkomu iazyku dlia natsional'nykh komvuzov, sovpartshkol i shkol vzroslykh.* (4th edition.) Moscow: Izd. Narodov Soiuza.

Danilov G.K. & I.I. Ustinov (eds.)
1928 *Voprosy prepodavaniia russkogo iazyka v natsshkole vzroslykh (trudy konferentsii prepodavatelei i slovesnikov shkol politprosveta).* Moscow-Leningrad: Gosizdat.

Danilov, G.K. & I. Degterevskii & B. Neiman & A. Pal'mbakh
1930a *Literaturnaia rech': rabochaia khrestomatiia dlia komvuzov, sovpartshkol i samoobrazovaniia.* (2nd edition.) Moscow: Rabpros.
1930b *Literaturnaia rech': rabota nad gazetoi.* Moscow: Rabpros.
1930c *Literaturnaia rech': tekhnika oratorskoi rech.* Moscow: Rabpros.

Davlet, Shafiga
1989 "The first all Muslim congress of Russia", *Central Asian survey* 8/1: 21-47.

De Mauro, Tullio
1978 "Notizie biografiche e critiche su Ferdinand de Saussure", in: F. de Saussure, *Corso di linguistica generale.* Rome-Bari: Laterza.

Deborin, A.
1934 "Nikolai Iakovlevich Marr: genial'nyi lingvist", *Izvestiia* 297 (21 December): 2.

Debreczeny, Paul
1993 "Pushkin's elevation to sainthood in Soviet culture", in: Thomas Lahusen & Gene Kuperman (eds.), *Late Soviet culture: from perestroika to novostroika.* Durham: Duke University Press, 47-68.

Deeters, Gerhard
1963 *Die Kaukasischen sprachen.* Koln: Leiden.

Delcourt, Marcel & Jean Amouroux
1987 "Wuster kaj Drezen", *Esperanto* (November): 197-198.

Derzhavin, N.S.
1925 "Novoe napravlenie v istorii kul'tury i iazyka", *Zvezda* 4.
1929 "Iaficheskie perezhivaniia v prometeidskoi slavianskoi traditsii", *Iazyk i literatura* 3.
1931 "Slovo-signal i slovo-simvol v protsesse glottogonii", in: N. Marr (ed.). Vol. 2, 174-192.

Desheriev, Iu.D.
1958 *Razvitie mlad'opis'mennykh iazykov narodov SSSR*. Moscow: Gosuchpedgiz.
1968 *Razvitie iazykov narodov SSSR v sovetskuiu epokhu*. Moscow: Prosveshchenie.
1976 *Zakonomernosti razvitiia literaturnykh iazykov narodov SSSR v sovetskuiu epokhu*. Vols. 1-3. Moscow: Nauka.

Deutsch, Karl
1966 *Nationalism and social communication*. Cambridge, Mass.: MIT Press.

Devlet, Nadir
1983 "A Specimen of Russification: the Turks of Kazan", *Central Asian survey* 2/3: 79-88.

Dimanshtein, S.M. (ed.)
1927 *Voprosy natsional'nogo partprosveshcheniia*. Moscow: Doloi Negramotnost'.
1936 *Itogi razresheniia natsional'nogo voprosa v SSSR*. Moscow.

Dmitriev, N.K.
1938 *Stroi turetskogo iazyka*. Leningrad.
1940 *Grammatika kumykskogo iazyka*. Moscow-Leningrad.
1946 "Trudy russkikh uchenykh v oblasti tiurkologii", *Uchenye zapiski MGU* 107/III/2. Moscow. 69-70.
1948 *Grammatika bashkirskogo iazyka*. Moscow-Leningrad.

Dmitriev, S.K.
1960 *Zhizn' i deiatel'nost' S.A. Novgorodova*. Irkutsk.

Dobrogaev, S.M.
1919 "O printsipakh klassifikatsii boleznoi rechi", *Nauchnoi meditsiny* 9.
1929a "Fiziologicheskii i sotsial'nyi elementy v uchenii o rechi cheloveka", *Iazyk i literatura* III: 259-309.
1929b "Fonema, kak fiziologicheskoe i sotsial'noe iavlenie", in: N. Marr (ed.). Vol. 1, 57-130.
1931 "Uchenie o reflekse v problemakh iazykovedeniia", in: N. Marr (ed.). Vol. 2, 105-173.

Dobrovolskii, A.I.
1931 "Voprosy o proiskhozhdenii iazyka (kritika iafeticheskoi teorii)", *Literatura i iskusstvo* 2-3: 60-67.

Dowler, Wayne
1995 "The politics of language in non-Russian elementary schools in the eastern empire, 1865-1914", *The Russian review* 54 (October): 516-538.

Drezen, E.K.
1925a "Esperanto i sviaz", *Mezhdunarodnyi iazyk* 4/30: 3-5.
1925b *Na putiakh ratsionalizatsii gosapparata*. Moscow: NKRKI.
1925c *Organizatsiia promyshlenykh, torgovykh i administrativnykh uchrezhdenii*. Moscow: NKRKI SSSR.
1925d *Osnovy operativnogo deloproizvodstva*. Moscow: NKRKI.
1925e *V poiskakh vseobshchego iazyka*. Moscow-Leningrad.
1926a "Osnovnye printsipy organizatsii sovetskogo gosapparata", *NOT i khoziastvo* 8-9.
1926b "Iazyk -- orudie sviazi," in: *Na putiakh k mezhdunarodnomu iazyku*. Moscow-Leningrad.
1926c "K voprosu o ratsionalizatsii iazyka", *NOT i khoziastvo* 8-9.
1926-1927 "Rossiiskie popytki sozdaniia mezhdunarodnykh iskusstvenykh iazykov", *Mezhdunardnyi iazyk* 9-12.
1928 *Za vseobshchim iazykom*. Moscow: Gosizdat.
1929a "Une explication marxiste de l'origine du langage humain: la theorie japhetique de N. Marr," *L'humanite* (27 June).
1929b *La vojoj de formigo kaj disvastigo de la lingvo internacia*. Leipzig: Eldona Fako Kooperativa.
1929c *Osnovy iazykoznaniia, teorii i istoriia mezhdunarodnogo iazyka*. Moscow: TsKSESR.
1929d *Vvodnye besedy po voprosam ratsionalizatsii promyshlennykh predpriiatii (dlia slushatelei raboche-krest'ianskogo universiteta)*. Moscow: NKPT.
1929e *Zamenhof*. Moscow: Mospoligraf.
1931 *Ocherki teorii esperanto*. Moscow: TsKSESR.
1934a "K voprosu o metodike postroenii i ispolzovaniia klassifikatsii", *Vestnik standardizatsiia* 2/56: 8.
1934b "Mezhdunarodnyi iazyk", *Literaturnaia entsiklopediia*. Vol. 7.
1935 *Pri problemo de internaciigo de scienc-teknika terminaro: historio, nuna stato kaj perspektivoj*. Moscow: Ekrelo.
1936a *Internatsionalizatsiia nauchno-tekhnicheskoi terminologii: istoriia, sovremennoe polozhenie i perspektivy*. Moscow: Standartgiz.
1936b *Nauchno-tekhnicheskie terminy i oboznacheniia i ikh standardizatsiia*. (3rd edition.) Moscow: Standartgiz.
1967 *Historio de la mondolingvo*. Trans. N. Khokhlov & N. Nekrasov. Osaka: Pirato [reprint of the 1931 edition].
no date *Vvedenie v ratsionalizatsiiu*. Moscow: VDNKh SSSR.
Drezen, E.K. (ed.)
1932 *Ni odnoi minuty poterianogo vremeni*. Moscow-Leningrad.

Dunham, Vera
1990 *In Stalin's time: middleclass values in Soviet fiction.* Durham: Duke University Press.
Durdenevskii, V.N.
1927 *Ravnopravie iazykov v sovetskom stroe.* Moscow.
Durnovo, N.N.
1924 *Ocherk istorii russkogo iazyka.* Moscow-Leningrad: Gosizdat.
1924-1929 *Povtoritel'nyi kurs grammatiki russkogo iazyka.* Vols. 1-2. Moscow-Leningrad: Gosizdat.
Dyrenkova, N.P.
1940 *Grammatika oirotskogo iazyka.* Moscow-Leningrad.
1941 *Grammatika shorskogo iazyka.* Moscow-Leningrad.
Edie, James M.
1987 *Edmund Husserl's phenomenology: a critical commentary.* Bloomington: Indiana University Press.
Eklof, Ben
1986 *Russian peasant schools: officialdom, village culture, and popular pedagogy, 1861-1914.* Berkeley: University of California Press.
1990 *The world of the Russian peasant: post-emancipation society and culture.* Boston: Unwin Hyman.
Emerson, Caryl
1996 "New words, new epochs, old thoughts", *The Russian review* 55 (July): 355-364.
Enukidze, A.
1926 "K voprosu o natsional'nykh iazykakh", *Sovetskoe stroitel'stvo* 1: 50-53.
Erberg, Konstantin
1928 "O formakh rechevoi kommunikatsii (k voprosu o iazykovykh funktsiiakh)", *Iazyk i literatura* 3: 163.
Erlich, Victor
1980 *Russian formalism: history-doctrine.* The Hague: Mouton.

Evraziistvo (formulirovka 1927 g.). Moscow: 1927.

Evraziistvo: deklaratsiia, formulirovka, tezisy. Prague: Izd. Evraziistsev: 1932.

Fabian, Johannes
1986 *Language and colonial power. The appropriation of Swahili in the former Belgian Congo, 1880-1938.* Berkeley: University of California Press.

Ferrari-Bravo, Donatella
- 1983 "Il concetto di 'segno' nella linguistica russa (da Potebnja a Saussure)", in Jitka Kresalkova (ed.), *Mondo slavo a cultura Italiana*. Rome: Il Veltro, 122-139.

Fersman, A.E.
- 1928 *La vojo de scienco de estonto*. Trans. S. Rublev. Leipzig: SAT.

Fierman, William
- 1991 *Language planning and national development: the Uzbek experience*. Berlin: Mouton de Gruyter.

Fierman, William (ed.)
- 1995 "Implementing language laws: perestroika and its legacies in five republics", *Nationalities papers* 23/3 (September).

Figes, Orlando
- 1997 "The Russian revolution of 1917 and its language in the village", *The Russian review* 56 (July): 342-344.

Filin, F.P. (ed.)
- 1968 *Teoreticheskie problemy sovetskogo iazykoznaniia*. Moscow: Nauka.

Fisher, Alan
- 1978 *The Crimean Tatars*. Stanford: Hoover Institution Press.

Fishman, Joshua
- 1974 *Advances in language planning*. The Hague: Mouton.

Fishman, Joshua (ed.)
- 1972 *Advances in the sociology of language: selected studies and applications*. The Hague: Mouton.
- 1977 *Advances in the creation and revision of writing systems*. The Hague: Mouton.

Fitzpatrick, Sheila
- 1979 *Education and social mobility in the Soviet Union, 1921-1934*. Cambridge, Eng.: Cambridge University Press.
- 1991 "The problem of class identity in NEP society", in: S. Fitzpatrick & A. Rabinowitch & R. Stites (eds.), 12-24.
- 1992 *The cultural front: power and culture in revolutionary Russia*. Ithaca: Cornell University Press.
- 1994 *Stalin's peasants: resistance and survival in the Russian village after collectivization*. New York: Oxford University Press.

Fitzpatrick, Sheila (ed.)
- 1978 *Cultural revolution in Russia*. Bloomington: Indiana University Press.

Fitzpatrick, Sheila & Alexander Rabinowitch & Richard Stites (eds.)
- 1991b *Russia in the era of NEP: explorations in Soviet society and culture*. Bloomington: Indiana University Press.

Fokkema, D.W.
- 1976   "Continuity and change in Russian formalism, Czech structuralism, and Soviet semiotics", *PTL* 1: 153 -196.

Formigari, Lia
- 1973   *Marxismo e teorie della lingua*. Messina: La libra.
- 1977   *La logica del pensiero vivente: il linguaggio nella filosofia della Romantik*. Bari: Laterza.

Forster, Peter
- 1982   *The Esperanto movement*. The Hague: Mouton.

Fortunatov, F.F.
- 1956   *Izbrannye trudy*. Vols. 1-2. Moscow: ANSSR.

Foucault, Michel
- 1973   *The order of things: an archeology of the human sciences*. New York: Vintage Books.
- 1980   *Power/Knowledge: selected interviews and other writings, 1972-1977*. Ed. Colin Gordon. New York: Pantheon.
- 1982   "The subject and power", *Critical inquiry* 8 (summer): 777-778.

Frank, Stephen P.
- 1994   "Confronting the domestic other: rural popular culture and its enemies in fin-de-siecle Russia", in: S. Frank & M. Steinberg (eds.), 74-76.

Frank, Stephen P. & Mark D. Steinberg
- 1994   *Cultures in flux: lower-class values, practices, and resistance in late imperial Russia*. Princeton: Princeton University Press.

Friche, V.M.
- 1929   "Preface", in: N.Ia. Marr, *Aktualnye problemy i ocherednye zadachi iafetichskoi teorii*. Moscow: GAIMK, 6-7.

Fridliand, F. & E. Shalyt, E.
- 1924   *Prakticheskaia grammatika russkogo iazyka (dlia shkol 1 stupeni)*. Moscow: Rabpros.

Gallagher, Robert J.
- 1981   "On modern terminology in the Turkic languages", *Central Asiatic journal* 25/3-4.

Gamkrelidze, T.V. &V.V. Ivanov & N.I. Tolstoi
- 1987   "Afterword", in N.S. Trubetskoi (1987), 492-519.

Gardiner, Michael
- 1992   *The dialogics of critique: M.M. Bakhtin and the theory of ideology*. New York: Routledge.

Gasilov, G.V. (ed.)
- 1929   *Prosveshschenie natsional'nykh men'shinstv v RSFSR*. Moscow.

Gasparov, B.M.
1970 "Lingvisticheskaia kontspetsiia moskovskoi shkoly i problema strukturnogo opisaniia iazyka," *Trudy po russkoi i slavianskoi filologii, XVI. Seriia lingvisticheskaia: iz istorii russkogo iazykoznaniia. Uchenye zapiski tartuskogo gosudarstvennogo universiteta* 247: 177-207.
1985 "The language situation and the linguistic polemic in mid-nineteenth-century Russia," in: R. Picchio & H. Goldblatt (eds.) *Aspects of the Slavic language question*. Columbus: Slavica, 297-333.

Geiger, Bernard & Tibor Halasi-Kun & Aert H. Kuipers & Karl H. Menges (eds.)
1959 *Peoples and languages of the Caucasus: a synopsis*. 'S-Gravenhage: Mouton.

Girke, Wolfgang, and Jachnow, Helmut
1974 *Sowjetische sotsio-linguistik: probleme und genese*. Kronberg: Scriptor.
1975 *Sprache und gesellschaft in der Sowjetunionen*. Munich: Fink.

Gleason, Abbot & Peter Kenez & Richard Stites (eds.)
1985 *Bolshevik culture: order and experiment in the Russian revolution*. Bloomington: Indiana University Press.

Gofman, V.
1936 "Khlebnikov i interlingvistika", in: *Iazyk literatury: ocherki i etiudy*. Leningrad.

Golanov I. & N.N. Durnovo
1924-1925 "Moskovskaia dialektologicheskaia komissiia (1904-1924)", *Slavia* 3: 749-756.

Goodman, Elliot R.
1956 "The Soviet design for a world language", *Russian review* 5: 85-99.
1960 *Soviet design for a world state*. New York: Columbia University Press.
1968 "World state and world language", in: Joshua Fishman (ed.), *Readings in the sociology of language*. The Hague: Mouton, 717-736.

Gorbanevskii, M.V.
1988 "Konspekt po korifeiu; kakoi vklad vnesli v nauku Stalinskie stat'i o iazykoznanii", *Literaturnaia gazeta* (25 May), 12.
1991 *V nachale bylo slovo: maloizvestnye stranitsy istorii sovetskoi lingvistiki*. Moscow: Izd. Univ. Druzhby Narodov.

Gordlevskii, V.A.
1928 *Grammatika turetskogo iazyka*. Moscow.

Gorham, Michael S.
1994 Speaking in tongues: language culture, literature, and the language of state in early Soviet Russia, 1921-1934. [Unpublished Ph.D. dissertation, Stanford University].

Gorlov, N.P.
1924 *Futurizm i revoliutsiia.* Moscow: Gosizdat.

Gornfeld', A.G.
1922 *Novye slovechki i starye slova.* Petrograd: Kolos.

Gorodenskii, N.
1898 *Polemika Lokka protiv teorii prirozhdennosti i ego sobstvenniia vozzreniia po voprosu o proiskhozhdenii znaniia.* Moscow: Snegireva.

Got'e, I.V.
1988 *Time of troubles: the diary of Iurii Vladimirovich Got'e.* Ed. and Trans. Terrence Emmons. Princeton: Princeton University Press.

Graham, Loren
1993 *Science in Russia and the Soviet Union.* New York: Cambridge University Press.

Gramsci, Antonio
1975 *Quaderni del carcere.* Vol. 1-3. Ed. V. Gerratana. Turin: Giulio Einaudi.

Grande, B.
1933 "Opyt klassifikatsii novogo alfavita s tochki zreniia unifikatsii", in D. Korkmasov (ed.), 128-137.
1939 "Iazykovoe stroitel'stvo narodov SSSR", *Literaturnaia gazeta* (7 November): 5.

Gray, Piers
1993 "Totalitarian logic: Stalin on linguistics", *Critical quarterly* 35/1 (Spring).

Grillo, R.D.
1989 *Dominant languages: language and hierarchy in Britain and France.* Cambridge, Eng.: Cambridge University Press.

Grossman, Joan Delaney
1985 *Valery Briusov and the riddle of Russian decadence.* Berkeley: University of California Press.

Grot, Ia.K.
1885-1912 *Russkoe pravopisanie.* St. Petesburg: Akademii Nauk.

Gukhman, M.M. & V.N. Iartseva (eds.)
1964 *Osnovnye napravleniia strukturalizma.* Moscow: Nauka.

Gunther, Hans (ed.)
1990 *The culture of the Stalin period.* New York: St. Martin's Press.

Gus, M.
1927 "Predmet, zadachi i metody izucheniie gazetnogo iazyka", *Zhurnalist* 5: 57-61.
1930 "Problema izucheniia gazetnogo iazyka", in: M. Gus & D. Bentsman & Iu. Bocharov (eds.), 65-68.

Gus, M. & D. Bentsman & Iu. Bocharov (eds.)
1930 *Problemy gazetovedenie.* Moscow: GIZ.

Gus, M. & Iu. Zagorianskii & N. Kaganovich
1926 *Iazyk gazety.* Moscow: Rabpros.

Gusev, N. & N. Sidorov
1923 *Sintaksis russkogo iazyka. Uchebnoe rukovodstvo dlia shkol vtoroi stupeni.* Moscow: Gosizdat.

Guthier, Steven
1977 "The Belorussians: national identity and assimilation, 1897-1970", *Soviet studies* 29/1: (January), 58-60; and 29/2 (April), 273-274.

Gvozdev, A.N.
1928 "Znachenie izucheniia detskogo iazyka dlia iazykovedeniia", *Russkii iazyk i literatura v trudovoi shkole* 3: 44-66.
1954 *Osnovy russkoi orfografii.* (4th edition.) Moscow: Uchpedgiz.
1963 *Izbrannye raboty po orfografii i fonetike.* Moscow: Akademii Pednauk RSFSR.

Haardt, Alexander
1993 *Husserl in Russland: phanomenologie der sprache und kunst bei Gustav Shpet und Aleksei Losev.* Munich: Wilhelm Fink.

Haarman, Harald
1990 "Language planning in the light of a general theory of language: a methodological framework," *International journal of the sociology of language* 86: 103-126.
1992 "Measures to increase the importance of Russian within and outside the Soviet Union", *International journal of the sociology of language* 95: 118-119.

Habermas, Jurgen
1973 *Theory and practice.* Trans. John Viertel. Boston: Beacon Press.
1984 *The theory of communicative action.* Trans. Thomas McCarthy. Boston: Beacon Press.

Hahn, Werner G.
1982 *Post-war Soviet politics: the fall of Zhdanov and the defeat of moderation, 1946-1953.* Ithaca: Cornell University Press.

Hajda, Lubomyr & Mark Beissinger (eds.)
1990 *The nationalities factor in Soviet politics and society.* Boulder: Westview.

Hans, N.
1964 *History of Russian educational policy.* New York: Russell and Russell.

Henze, Paul
1956 "Politics and alphabets in Inner Asia", *Royal Central Asian journal* 43: 29-51.

Hirsch, Francine
1997 "The Soviet Union as a work in progress: ethnographers and the category *nationality* in the 1926, 1937, and 1939 censuses", *Slavic review* 56/2: 251-278.

Hirschkop Ken
1986 "Bakhtin, discourse and democracy", *New left review* 160: 92-113.

Hjelmslev, Louis
1976 *Principios de gramatica general.* Trans. F.P. Torre. Madrid: Editorial Gredos.

Hoffman, David
1995 *Peasant metropolis: social identities in Moscow, 1929-1941.* Ithaca: Cornell University Press.

Holenstein, Elmar
1976a *Linguistik, semiotik, hermeneutic: playdoyers fur eine strukturale phanemonologie.* Frankfurt/Main: Suhrkamp.
1976b *Roman Jakobson's approach to language: phenomenological structuralism.* Trans. C. and T. Schelbert. Bloomington: Indiana University Press.

Holmes, Larry
1991 *The Kremlin and the schoolhouse: reforming education in Soviet Russia, 1917-1931.* Bloomington: Indiana University Press.

Holquist, Michael
1990a "Introduction," in M.M. Bakhtin, *Art and answerability.* Eds. Michael Holquist and Vadim Liapunov. Austin: University of Texas Press.
1990b *Dialogism. Bakhtin and his world.* London: Routledge.

Hosking, Geoffrey
1997 *Russia: people and empire, 1552-1917.* Cambridge, Mass.: Harvard University Press.

Hroch, Miroslav
1985 *Social preconditions of national revival in Europe.* Trans. Ben Fowkes. New York: Cambridge University Press.

Humboldt, Wilhelm von
1859   *O razlichii organizmov chelovecheskogo iazyka i o vliianii etogo razlichiia na umstvennoe razvitie chelovecheskago roda. Posmertnoe sochinenie Vilgel'ma fon-Gumbol'dta. Vvedenie vo vseobshchee iazykoznanie.* Trans. P. Biliarskii. St. Petersburg: Uchebnoe posobie po teorii iazyka i slovesnosti v voenno-uchebnykh zavedeniiakh.
1984   *Izbrannye trudy po iazykoznaniiu.* Ed. and Trans. G.N. Ramishvili. Moscow: Progress.
1985   *Iazyk i filosofiia kul'tury.* Eds. A.V. Gulygi and G.N. Ramishvili. Trans. M.I. Levin. Moscow: Progress.
1988   *On language: the diversity of human language-structure and its influence on the mental development of mankind.* Intro. Hans Aarsleff and Trans. Peter Heath. New York: Cambridge University Press.

Husserl, Edmund
1977   *Logical investigations.* Vols. I-II. Trans. J.N. Findlay. New York: Humanities Press.

Hyppolite, Jean
1972   "The structure of philosophic language according to the 'Preface' to Hegel's *Phenomenology of the mind*", in: Richard Macksey and Eugenio Donato (eds.), *The structuralist controversy.* Baltimore: Johns Hopkins University Press, 157-169.

Iakovlev, Ia.
1924   "Pechat' i zadachi partii v derevne", *Zhurnalist* 16: 3-4.

Iakovlev, N.F.
1922   "Voprosy natsional'noi gramoty", *Zizhn' natsional'nostei* 18: 4--5.
1923   *Tablitsy fonetiki kabardinskogo iazyka.* Moscow: Institut vostokovedeniia.
1925   *Ingushi.* Moscow.
1927a   *Materialy dlia kabardinskogo slovaria.* Moscow: Tsentrizdat.
1927b   *Voprosy izucheniia chechentsev i ingushei.* Groznyi: Izd. Chechnarobraza.
1928   "Matematicheskaia formula postroeniia alfavita (opyt prakticheskogo prilozheniia linvisticheskoi teorii)."
[1970]   [Reprinted in: A.A. Reformatskii (ed.), *Iz istorii otechestvennoi fonologii.* Moscow: Nauka, 123-148.
1940   *Sintaksis chechenskogo literaturnogo iazyka.* Moscow-Leningrad: 1940.
1941   *Grammatika adygeiskogo literaturnogo iazyka.* Moscow.

1948   *Grammatika literaturnogo kabardino-cherkesskogo iazyka.* Moscow.

Iakovlev, N.F. & D. Ashkhamaf
1930   *Kratkaia grammatika adygeiskogo (kiakhskogo) iazyka dlia shkoly i samoobrazovaniia.* Krasnodar.
1940   *Grammatika Adygeiskogo iazyka.* Moscow-Leningrad.

Iakubinskii, L.P.
1931   "F. de Sossiur o nevozmozhnosti iazykovoi politiki", in: N. Marr (ed.). Vol. 2, 91-104.
1974   "On verbal dialogue". Trans. Jane Knox and Luba Barna. *Dispositio* 4/11-12: 323.
1986   *Izbrannye raboty: iazyk i ego funktsionirovanie.* Moscow: Nauka.

Iapol'skii, M.
1931   "Azbuka ili bukvosvod", *Russkii iazyk v sovetskoi shkole* 2-3: 196-199.

Iazykovednye problemy po chislitel'nym. Leningrad: ILIaZV, 1927.

Ilinskaia, I.S.
1966   *Orfografiia i russkii iazyk.* Moscow: Nauka.

Imart, Guy
1965   "Le mouvement de 'latinisation' en URSS", *Cahiers du monde russe et sovietique* VI/2: 223-239.
1967   "Un intellectuel azerbaijanais face a la revolution de 1917: Samad-aga Agamaly-oglu", *Cahiers du monde russe et sovietique* VIII/4: 528-559.

Ingulov, S.B.
1928   *Kul'turnaia revoliutsiia i pechat'.* Moscow.

Iodko, A.R.
1922   *Rabochii klass i mezhdunarodnye iazyk.* Moscow: SESS.

Isaev, M.I.
1958   "V.I. Abaev kak krupneishii iranist-osetinoved", *Izvestiia iugo-osetinskogo nauchno-issledovatel'skogo instituta ANGSSR* IX: 396-414.
1979   *Iazykovoe stroitel'stvo v SSSR: protsessy sozdaniia pis'mennostei narodov SSSR.* Moscow: Nauka.
1982   *Sotsiolingvisticheskie problemy iazykov narodov SSSR.* Moscow: Vysshaia shkola, 1982.

Isaev, M.I., and Zak, L.M.
1966   "Problemy pis'mennosti narodov SSSR v kul'turnoi revoliutsii", *Voprosy istorii* 2 (1966).

Iskhaki, Aiaz
1933 *Idel'-Ural*. Paris.
[1988] [Reprinted, London: Society for Central Asian Studies.]

Iudakhin, K.K.
1927 *Kirgizsko-russkii slovar'*. Moscow.
1940 *Uzbeksko-russkii slovar'*. Tashkent.

Iushmanov, N.V.
1922a "gramatik psiko-ekonomik", *kosmoglott* 7-8: 43-44.
1922b "tri basis de lingu inter-european", *kosmoglott* 6: 33-34.
1928 *Grammatika literaturnogo arabskogo iazyka*. Ed. I.Iu Krachkovskii. Leningrad: LVI.
1933 *Slovar' inostrannykh slov, voshedshikh v russkii iazyk*. (1st Edition) Moscow.
1939 "Grammatika inostrannykh slov", in: F.N. Petrov (ed.), *Slovar' inostrannykh slov*. Moscow: 1939.
1941 *Kliuch k latinskim pis'mennostiam zemnogo shara*. Moscow-Leningrad: ANSSSR.
1968 *Elementy mezhdunarodnoi terminologii: slovar'-spravochnik*. Moscow: Nauka.
1987 "Vsemirnyi iazyk (1928). (Publikatsiia teksta i kommentarii S.N. Kuznetsova)", *Izvestiia ANSSSR, Seriia literatury i iazyka* 46/5.

Ivanov, A.M. & L.P. Iakubinskii
1932 *Ocherki po iazyku dlia rabotnikov literatury i dlia samoobrazovaniia*. Moscow-Leningrad.

Ivanov, V.V.
1957 "Lingvisticheskie vzgliady E.D. Polivanova", *Voprosy iazykoznaniia* 3.
1962 "Cybernetics and the study of language", *Modern language journal* 46/4.
1976 *Ocherki po istorii semiotiki v SSSR*. Moscow.

Izgur, E.
1926 *Je la nomo de l'vivo*. Leipzig: SAT.

Jacob, H.
1947 *A planned auxiliary language*. London: Dennis Dobson.

Jakobson, R.O.
1962 *Selected writings I: phonological studies*. The Hague: Mouton.
1971 *Selected writings II: word and language*. The Hague: Mouton.
1981 *Selected writings III: poetry of grammar and grammar of poetry*. The Hague: Mouton.

1985	"From Alyagrov's letters," in: R.L. Jackson & Stephen Rudy (eds.), *Russian formalism: a retrospective glance*. Columbus: Slavica, 1-5.
1988	*Selected writings VIII: major works*. The Hague: Mouton.

Jakobson, R.O. & Krystyna Pomorska
1983	*Dialogues*. Cambridge, Mass.: MIT Press.

Jakobson, R.O. & P. Bogatyrev
1922	"Slavianskaia filologiia v Rossii za gg. 1914-1921," *Slavia* I: 457-469.

Janacek, Gerald
1984	*The look of Russian literature: avant-garde visual experiments, 1900-1930*. Princeton: Princeton University Press.

Jensen, Kenneth
1978	*Beyond Marx and Mach: Aleksandr Bogdanov's philosophy of lived experience*. Dordrecht: Reidel.

Jersild, Austin Lee
1996	"Ethnic modernity and the Russian empire: Russian ethnographers and Caucasus mountaineers", *Nationalities papers* 4/24 (1996).

Joravsky, David
1961	*Soviet Marxism and natural science, 1917-1932*. New York: Columbia University Press.
1970	*The Lysenko affair*. Cambridge, Mass.: Harvard University Press.
1977	"The mechanical spirit: the Stalinist marriage of Pavlov to Marx", *Theory and society* 4: 457-477.
1983	"The Stalinist mentality and higher learning", *Slavic review* 42/4: 583-586.
1985	"Cultural revolution and the fortress mentality", in: A.Gleason & P. Kenez & R. Stites (eds.), 94-113.
1989	*Russian psychology: a critical history*. Oxford: Basil Blackwell.

Kaganovich, S.K.
1931	"Bor'ba s velikoderzhavnym shovinizm i mestnym natsionalizmom v oblasti iazykovedeniia", *Literatura iskusstvo* 4: 88-95.

Kaiser, Robert
1994	*The geography of nationalism*. Princeton: Princeton University Press.

Karinskii, N.M.
1936	*Ocherki iazyka russkikh krestian'*. Moscow-Leningrad.

Karpinskii, V.
1923	"O krest'ianskikh gazetakh", *Pravda* 282 (12 December).

Kartsevskii, S.O.
1923 *Iazyk, voina i revoliutsiia*. Berlin: Russ. Univ. Izd.
1927 *Systeme du verbe russe: essai de linguistique synchronique*. Prague: Legiografie.
1928 *Povtoritel'nyi kurs russkogo iazyka: posobiia dlia trudovoi shkoly (s predisloviem A. Peshkovskogo)*. Moscow-Leningrad: Gosizdat.
1937 "Sur la rationalisation de l'orthographe russe", in: *Zbornik lingvistichkikh i filoshkikh rasprava*. Belgrade: Mlada Sriia.

Kasilov, Andrei
1990 Deiatel'nost partiinykh organizatsii Verkhnei Volgi po razvitiiu narodnogo obrazovaniia v 1945-1958 godakh. [Unpublished Ph.D. dissertation, Moscow State Pedagogical Institute.]

Katsnelson, S.D.
1941 *Kratkii ocherk iazykoznaniia*. Leningrad: LGU.

Katvan, Zeev
1978 "Reflection theory and the identity of thinking and being", *Studies in Soviet thought* 18: 87-109.

Kaverin, V.A.
1976 *Petrogradskii student*. Moscow: Sov. Pis.
1981 *Skandalist*. Vol. 1. *Sobranie sochinenii*. Moscow: Khud. Lit.

Kenez, Peter
1985 *The birth of the propaganda state: Soviet methods of mass mobilization, 1917-1929*. New York: Cambridge University Press.

Khansuvarov, I.
1932 *Latinizatsiia - orudie leninskoi natsional'noi politiki*. Moscow: Partizdat.

Khashba, A.K.
1972 *Izbrannye raboty*. Sukhumi: Alashara.

Kim, M.P. (ed.)
1985 *Protokoly soveshchanii narkomov prosveshcheniia soiuznykh i avtonomnykh respublikakh, 1919-1924 gg*. Moscow: Nauka.

Kirkwood, Michael
1991 "'Glasnost', 'the national question' and Soviet language policy", *Soviet studies* 43/1: 61-82.

Kirkwood, Michael (ed.)
1989 *Language planning in the Soviet Union*. London: Macmillan.

Klimov, G.A.
1965 *Kavkazskie iazyki*. Moscow: Nauka.

Koerner, Konrad
1982 "The Schleicherian paradigm in linguistics", *General linguistics* 22/1: 1-39.

Konoplev, N.
   1931   "Shire front internatsional'nogo vospitaniia", *Prosveshchenie natsional'nostei* 2: 46-52.

Koporskii S.
   1927   "Vorovskoi zhargon v srede shkol'nikov", *Vestnik prosveshcheniia* 1: 7.

Korkmasov, D. (ed.)
   1933   *Pis'mennost' i revoliutsiia: sbornik I (k VI plenumu VTsKNA)*. Moscow.

Kotkin, Stephen
   1995   *Magnetic mountain: Stalinism as a civilisation*. Berkeley: University of California Press.

Koutaissof, E.
   1951   "Literacy and the place of Russian in the non-Slav republics of the USSR", *Soviet studies* 111/2: 113-130.

Kozulin, Alex
   1986   "Vygotsky in context", in: Lev Vygotsky, *Thought and language*. Cambridge, Mass.: MIT Press.
   1990   *Vygotsky's psychology: a biography of ideas*. Cambridge, Mass.: Harvard University Press.

Krasovitskaia, T.Iu.
   1986   "Soveshchaniia narkomov prosveshcheniia sovetskikh respublik v 1919-1924 gg.", *Istoricheskie zapiski* 113.
   1988   "Nep i rukovodstvo razvitiem natsional'nykh kul'tur", *Voprosy istorii* 9: 47-50.

Kreindler, Isabelle
   1977   "A neglected source of Lenin's nationality policy", *Slavic review* 36/1 (1977).
   1979   "Nikolai Il'minski and language planning in nineteenth-century Russia", *International journal of the sociology of language* 22: 5-26.
   1982   "Lenin, Russian, and Soviet language policy", *International journal of the sociology of language* 33: 130.
   1983   "Ibrahim Altynsarin, Nikolai Il'minskii and the Kazakh national awakening", *Central Asian survey* 1/4: 109-132.
   1985   "The non-Russian languages and the challenge of Russian: the eastern versus the western tradition", in: I. Kreindler (ed.), 345-368.

Kreindler, Isabelle (ed.)
   1985   *Sociolinguistic perspectives on Soviet national languages: their past, present, and future*. Berlin: Mouton de Gruyter.

Kremenskii, N.E. & V. Mamonov (eds.)
1930   *Proekt glavnauki o novom pravopisanii. Sbornik.* Moscow: Rabpros.
Krementsov, N.
1997   *Stalinist science.* Princeton: Princeton University Press.
Kristoff, Ladis
1967   "The state idea", *Orbis* XI/1 (spring): 238-255.
1968   "The Russian image of Russia: an applied study in geopolitical methodology", in: Charles A. Fisher (ed.), *Essays in political geography.* London: Methuen, 352-373.
Kruchenykh, A.E.
1923a   *Faktura slova.* Moscow: MAF.
1923b   *Fonetika teatra.* Moscow: MAF.
1928   *Priemy Leninskoi rechi: k izucheniiu iazyka Lenina.* Moscow: Izd. Vse. Soiuza Poetov.
Krueger, John R.
1985   "Remarks on the Chuvash language: past, present and future", in: I. Kreindler (ed.), 265-276.
Kruszewskii, N.V.
1883   *Ocherk nauki o iazyke.* Kazan: Tip. Imp. Univ.
Kucera, Jindrich
1954   "Soviet nationality policy: the linguistic controversy", *Problems of communism* 3/2: 24-29.
Kudriavskii, D.
1904   *Psikhologiia i iazykoznanie (po povodu noveishikh rabot Vundta i Del'briuka).* St. Petersburg: Izd. Akad. Nauk.
1905   *Vvedenie v iazykoznanie.* Handwritten copy of 5 January 1910 in the Lenin Library, Moscow.
Kuipers, Aert
1960   *Phoneme and morpheme in Kabardian.* 'S-Gravenhage: Mouton.
Kupina, N.A.
1995   *Totalitarnyi iazyk: slovar' i rechevye reaktsii.* Ekaterinburg-Perm': ZUUNTS.
Kurbangaliev, M. & R. Gazizov
1925   *Opyt kratkoi prakticheskoi grammatiki tatarskogo iazyka.* Kazan.
Kuznetsov, P.S.
1932   *Iafeticheskaia teoriia.* Eds. M.P. Bochacher and G.K. Danilov. Moscow: Uchpedgiz.
1959   "Ob osnovnykh polozheniiakh fonologii", *Voprosy iazykoznaniia* 2.

L'adoption universelle des caracteres latines. Paris: Institut international de co-operation intellectuelle.

Labriola, Antonio
1926 *Istoricheskii materializm*. Moscow-Leningrad.

Laitin, David D. & Roger Petersen & John W. Slocum
1992 "Language and the state: Russia and the Soviet Union in comparative perspective", in: Alexander Motyl (ed.), *Thinking theoretically about Soviet nationalities*. New York: Columbia University Press.

Laitin, David
1988 "Language games", *Comparative politics* 20/3: 289-302.
1992 *Language repertoires and state construction in Africa*. New York: Cambridge University Press.

Lanti, E.
1924 *For la neutralismon*. Leipzig: SAT.
1925 *La langue internationale ce que tout militant ouvrier doit connaitre de la question*. Paris: FEO.
1928 *The Workers' Esperanto movement*. Trans. H. Stay. London: NCLC.
1931 *Vortoj*. Leipzig: SAT.
1935 *Cu socialismo konstruigas en Sovetio?*. Paris: Herezulo.
1940 *Leteroj de E. Lanti*. Paris: SAT.

Lapenna, Ivo
1974 *Esperanto en perspektivo: faktoj kaj analizoj pri la internacia lingvo*. London-Rotterdam: UES.

Large, Andrew
1985 *The artificial language movement*. New York: Basil Blackwell.

Larin, B.A.
1928 "K lingvisticheskoi kharakteristike goroda", *Izvestiia. Leningradskii gosudarstvennyi pedagogicheskii institut* 1: 175-184.

Larson, Megali Sarfatti
1984 "The production of expertise and the constitution of expert power", in: Thomas Haskell (ed.), *The authority of experts*. Bloomington: Indiana University Press, 28-29.

Lartsev, V.
1988 *Evgenii Dmitrievich Polivanov. Stranitsy zhizni i deiatel'nosti*. Moscow: Nauka.

Laurat, Lucien
1951 *Staline: la linguistique et l'imperialisme russe*. Paris: Les Iles d'Or.

Lazzerini, Edward
 1973 Ismail Bey Gasprinskii and Muslim modernism in Russia, 1878-1914. [Unpublished Ph.D. dissertation, University of Washington.]
 1975 "Gadidism at the turn of the twentieth century: a view from within", *Cahiers du mondes russes et sovietiques* XVI/2 (April-June): 245-277.

Lefebvre, Henri
 1966 *Le langage et la societe*. Paris.

Lelyveld, David
 1993 "The fate of Hindustani: colonial knowledge and the project of a national language", in: Carol A. Breckenridge and Peter van der Veer (eds.), *Orientalism and the postcolonial predicament: perspectives on South Asia*. Philadelphia: University of Pennsylvania Press, 192-193.

Lemercier-Quelqejay, Chantal
 1983 "Abdul Kayum Al-Nasyri: a Tatar reformer of the nineteenth century", *Central Asian survey* 1/4: 109-132.

Lenin, V.I.
 1977 *Materialism and empirio-criticism*, in his *Collected works*. Vol. 14. Moscow: Politlit.

Leontiev, A.A.
 1961 "I.A. Boduen de Kurtene i peterburgskaia shkola russkoi lingvistiki", *Voprosy iazykoznaniia* 4.
 1967 *Psikholingvistika*. Leningrad: Nauka.
 1969 *Iazyk, rech', rechevaia deiatel'nost'*. Moscow: Pros.
 1983 *Evgenii Dmitrievich Polivanov i ego vklad v obshchee iazykoznanie*. Moscow: Nauka.

Leopold, Joan
 1987 "Ethnic stereotypes in linguistics: the case of Max Müller", in: H. Aarsleff & L. Kelly & H. Niederehe (eds.), 501-512.

Levi-Strauss, Claude
 1973 *Tristes tropiques*. Trans. by John and Doreen Weightman. New York: Penguin.

Levitt, Marcus C.
 1989 *Russian literary politics and the Pushkin celebration of 1880* Ithaca: Cornell University Press.

Lewin, Moshe
 1985 *The making of the Soviet system: essays in the social history of interwar Russia*. New York: Pantheon.

Lewis, E. Glyn
 1972a "Migration and language in the USSR," in: Fishman (ed.), 311.

1972b   *Multilingualism in the Soviet Union: aspects of language policy and its implementation.* The Hague: Mouton.

L'Hermitte, Rene
1987   *Science et perversion ideologique. Marr, Marrisme, Marristes* Paris.

Liber, George O.
1982   "Language, literacy and book publishing in the Ukrainian SSR, 1923-1928", *Slavic review* 41/4: 673-685.
1991   "Korenizatsiia: restructuring Soviet nationality policy in the 1920s", *Ethnic and racial studies* 14/1 (January): 15-23.
1992   *Soviet nationality policy, urban growth, and identity change in the Ukrainian SSR, 1923-1934.* New York: Cambridge University Press.

Liberman, Anatoli
1991   "Postscript", in: N.S. Trubetskoi, *The legacy of Genghis Khan and other essays on Russia's identity.* Ann Arbor: Michigan Slavic Publications.

Lins, Ulrich
1970   "Lenin kaj esperanto", *Esperanto* 63/7-8: 108-111.
1973   *La dangera lingvo: esperanto en la uragano de persekutoj.* Kioto: Omnibuso.
1987   "Drezen, Lanti kaj la Nova Epoko", *Sennacieca revuo* 115: 35-52.

Litvinova, E.F.
1892   *Dzhon' Lokk': ego zhizn' i filosofskaia deiatel'nost'.* St. Petersburg: Erlikh.

Lo Piparo, Franco
1979   *Lingua, intelletuali, egemonia in Gramsci.* Rome-Bari: Laterza.

Locke, John
1898   *Opyt' o chelovecheskom razume.* Trans. A.N. Savin. Moscow: Kushnerev.

Lomtev, T.P.
1931   "Za marksistskuiu lingvistiku", *Literatura i iskusstvo* 1: 115-125.
1949   "Problemy fonemy v svete novogo ucheniia o iazyke", *Izvestiia ANSSSR OLIa* VIII/4.
1951   "A fighting program for the elaboration of Marxist linguistics", in: J. Murra & F. Hollings (eds.), 79-80.
1958   *Osnovy sintaksisa sovremennogo russkogo iazyka.* Moscow.
1976   *Obshchee russkoe iazykoznanie. Izbrannye raboty.* Moscow: Nauka.

Lotman, Yuri
1976 *Analysis of the poetic text.* Trans. D.B. Johnson. Ann Arbor: Ardis.

Lotte, D.S.
1941 *Nekotorye printsipal'nye voprosy otbora i postroeniia nauchno-tekhnicheskikh terminov.* Moscow-Leningrad: ANSSSR.
1961 *Osnovy postroeniia nauchno-tekhnicheskoi terminologii (voprosy teorii i metodiki).* Moscow: ANSSSR.

Lubrano, Linda & Susan Gross Solomon (eds.)
1980 *The social context of Soviet science.* Boulder: Westview Press.

Luk'ianennko, A.M.
1926 *Russkii iazyk kak predmet prepodavaniia v tiurko-tatarskikh shkolakh.* Baku.

Lunacharskii, A.
1925 "Materializm i filologiia", *Izvestiia* 84 (12 April).

Luria, A.R.
1976 *Cognitive development: its cultural and social foundations.* Cambridge, Mass.: Harvard University Press.
1978 "A child's speech responses and the social environment", in: Michael Cole (ed.), *The selected writings of A.R. Luria.* White Plains, N.Y.: M.E. Sharpe, 45-77.
1979 *The making of mind: a personal account of Soviet psychology.* Eds. Michael and Sheila Cole. Cambridge, Mass.: Harvard University Press.

Luria, A.R. (ed.)
1930 *Rech' i intellekt derevenskogo, gorodskogo i besprizornogo rebenka.* Moscow-Leningrad.

Maguire, Robert A.
1987 *Red virgin soil: Soviet literature in the 1920s.* Ithaca: Cornell University Press.

Maiakovskii, Vladimir
1978 "Domoi", in his *Sobranie sochinenii.* Vol. 3. *Stikhotvoreniia, 1924-1925,* Moscow.

Mallory, J.P.
1989 *In search of the Indo-Europeans: language, archeology and myth.* London: Thames and Hudson.

Mally, Lynn
1990 *Culture of the future.* Berkeley: University of California Press.

Manchester, Martin L.
1985 *The philosophical foundations of Humboldt's linguistic doctrines.* Amsterdam and Philadelphia: John Benjamins.

Manning, C.A.
1931 "Japhetidology", *Language* 7: 143-146.
Mansurov, G.G. & M.S. Epshtein
1927 *Voprosy vseobshchego obucheniia (sredi natsmen)*. Moscow: Gosizdat.
Marcellesi, Jean-Baptiste
1978 "Sul Marrismo", in: *Linguaggio e classi sociale: Marrismo e Stalinismo*. Bari: Daedelo, 81-115.
Marcuse, Herbert
1964 *One-dimensional man*. Boston: Beacon Press.
Markovskii, N.
1926 "Za kul'turu komsomol'skogo iazyka", *Molodoi Bolshevik* 15-16.
Markus, Gyorgy.
1986 *Language and production: a critique of the paradigms* Dordrecht: Reidel.
Marr, N.Ia.
1925 "Pis'mo i iazyk budushchego", *Vestnik znaniia* 15.
1926a *Abkhazskii analiticheskii alfavit (k voprosu o reformakh pisma)*. Leningrad: Gosakadtip.
1926b "K voprosu o pervobytnom myshlenii v sviazi s iazykom v osveshchenii A.A. Bogdanova", *Vestnik kommunisticheskoi akademii* 16: 133-139.
1930 *Rodnaia rech' - moguchii rychag kul'turnogo pod'ema* Leningrad: LVI.
1932 *K bakinskoi diskussi o iafetidologii i marksizme*. Baku.
1933-1937 *Izbrannye raboty*. 5 vols. Moscow: ANSSSR.
1938 *O iazyke i istorii Abkhazov*. Moscow-Leningrad: ANSSSR.
Marr, N.Ia. (ed.)
1929-1931 *Iazykovedenie i materializm*. Vols. 1-2. Leningrad: Priboi and Gossotsekizdat.
Marx, Karl
1977 "The fetishism of the commodity and its secret", in Karl Marx, *Capital: a critique of political economy*. Vol. 1. Trans. Ben Fowkes. New York: Vintage.
Massell, Gregory
1974 *The surrogate proletariat: Moslem women and revolutionary strategy*. Princeton: Princeton University Press.
Matejka, Ladislav
1973 "The first Russian prolegomena to semiotics", in: V.N. Voloshinov, *Marxism and the philosophy of language*. New York: Seminar Press, 161-174.

1978	"The roots of Russian semiotics of art", in: R.W. Bailey & L. Matejka & P. Steiner (eds.), *The sign: semiotics around the world*. Ann Arbor: Michigan Slavic Publications.

Matthews, W.K.

1948	"The Japhetic theory", *Slavic and East European review* 27/68: 172-192.
1950	"The Soviet contribution to linguistic tought", *Archivium linguisticum* 2/1: 1-23; 2/2: 97-121.
1951	*The languages of the USSR*. Cambridge: Cambridge University Press.

McReynolds, Louise

1991	*The news under Russia's old regime*. Princeton: Princeton University Press.

Mekhmedzade, S.

no date	*Samouchitel tiurkskogo iazyka (po novomu tiurkskomu alfavitu)*. Baku (5th edition).

Meillet, A.

1938	*Vvedenie v sravnitel'noe izuchenie indoevropeiskikh iazykov [Introduction a l'etude comparative de la langues indoeuropeenes]*. Trans. D. Kudriavskii and A.M. Sukhotin. Ed. R.O. Shor. Moscow: Sotsekgiz.

Meromskii, A.

1930	*Iazyk selkora*. Moscow: Federatsiia.

Meshchaninov, I.I.

1926	*Osnovnye nachala iafetidologii*. Baku: Izd. Azer.
1931a	"Iaficheskaia teoriia", *Bol'shaia sovetskaia entsiklopedia* 65: 814.
1931b	*Verkhnii paleolit: sotsial'no-ekonomicheskaia sreda, obuslovlivaiushchaia oformlenie chlenorazdelnoi zvukovoi rechi*. Leningrad: GAIMK
1940	*Obshchee iazykoznanie*. Moscow.

Meshchaninov, I.I. (ed.)

1935	*Akademiia nauk SSSR akademiku N. Ia. Marru XLV (Sbornik)*. Moscow: ANSSSR.
1938	*Pamiati akademiku N. Ia Marra (1864-1934)*. Moscow: ANSSSR.

Mikhal'ski, E.

1929	*Prologo: jubilea kolekto de originalaj poemoj, 1918-1928*. Leipzig: SAT.

Mikhanovka, V.A.

1949	*Nikolai Iakovlevich Marr*. (3rd edition.) Moscow: ANSSSR.

Miller, M.
1951 "Marr, Stalin, and the theory of language", *Soviet studies* 2: 364-371.
Mirtov, A.V.
1915 *Russko-nemetskoe pravopisanie Ia.K. Grota.* Petrograd.
1926 *Russkii iazyk v natsional'nykh shkolakh SSSR. Metodika prepodavaniia.* Rostov-na-Donu.
1927 "Ispravlenie rechi uchashchikhsia", *Russkii iazyk v shkole* 1: 294.
Modenov, N.
1928 *Granda en malgranda: Esperanto kaj PTTR.* Paris: Biblioteko de ligilistoj.
Morson, Gary Saul
1990 *Mikhail Bakhtin: creation of a prosaics.* Stanford: Stanford University Press.
Morson, Gary Saul (ed.)
1986 *Bakhtin: essays and dialogues on his work.* Chicago: University of Chicago Press.
Morson, Gary Saul & Carol Emerson (eds.)
1989 *Rethinking Bakhtin: extensions and challenges.* Evanston: Northwestern University Press.
Moskovich, Wolf
1989 "Planned language change in Russian since 1917", in: M. Kirkwood (ed.), 85-99.
Mstislavskii, Sergei
1988 *Five days which transformed Russia.* Trans. Elizabeth K. Zelinsky. Bloomington: Indiana University Press.
Mugdan, Joachim
1984 *Jan Baudouin de Courtenay (1845-1929): leben und werk.* Munich: Fink.
Muller, Max
1865 *Lektsii po nauke o iazyke.* St. Petersburg
1868-1870 *Nauka o iazyke.* Voronezh.
1891 *Nauka o mysli.* St. Petersburg.
Murra, John & Fred Holling (eds.)
1951 *The Soviet linguistic controversy.* New York: King's Crown Press.
Musaev, K.M.
1965 *Alfavity iazykov narodov SSSR.* Moscow.
Musaev, K.M. (ed.)
1975 *Orfografii tiurkskikh literaturnykh iazykov narodov SSSR.* Moscow: Nauka.

1982 *Opyt sovershenstvovanie alfavitov i orfografii iazykov narodov SSSR*. Moscow: Nauka.

Musul'manskaia pechat' rossii v 1910 godu. Oxford: Society for Central Asian Studies, 1987.

Narodnyi kommissariat po prosveshcheniiu. Otdel edinoi trudovoi shkoly
1921a *Primernye programmy i plany zaniatii v shkole gramoty dlia podrostkov*. Moscow: Gosizdat.
1921b *Rodnoi iazyk v shkole 1 stupeni*. Moscow: Gosizdat.
1924 *Novye programmy edinoi trudovoi shkoly pervoi stupeni* Moscow: Gosizdat.

Nemeth, Thomas
1995 "Husserl, Shpet and Losev", *The Slavonic and East European review* 73 (January): 103.

Nenarokov, A.P.
1990 "Iz opyta natsional'no-iazykovoi politiki pervykh let sovetskoi vlasti", *Istoriia SSSR* 2: 4.

Neuberger, Joan
1993 *Hooliganism: crime, culture and power in St. Petersburg, 1900-1914*. Berkeley: University of California Press.

Newman, Fred & Lois Holzman
1993 *Lev Vygotsky: revolutionary scientist*. London: Routledge.

Nikiforov, S.D.
1924 "O nekotorykh iazykovykh problemakh v svete sovremennosti", *Zapiski kommunisticheskogo universiteta imeni Sverdlova* 11: 236.

Nikiforov, S.D. & G.K. Danilov (eds.)
1928 *Rabochaia kniga po iazyku dlia vtoroi stupeni pedtekhnikumov, rabfakov, i komvuzov*. Moscow: Gosizdat.

Novgorodov, S.A.
1977 *Pervye shagi Iakutskoi pis'mennosti. Stati i pis'ma*. Moscow: Nauka.

Nurmakov, N. (ed.)
1934 *Alfavit oktiabr'ia: itogi vvedeniia novogo alfavita sredi narodov RSFSR*. Moscow: Vlast sovetov.

Obnorskii, S.P. (ed.)
1947 *A.A. Shakhmatov, 1864-1920, sbornik statei i materialov*. Moscow: ANSSSR.

Olivier, Bernard V.
1990 "Korenizatsiia", *Central Asian survey* 9/3: 77-98.

Orlova, V.G.
1961 "Razvitie russkoi dialektologii v sovetskoi period, 1918-1959", in: B.V. Gornung (ed.), *Istoriia russkoi dialektologii*. Moscow: ANSSSR, 71-78.

Ornstein, J.
1959 "Soviet language policy: theory and practice", *Slavic and East European journal* 17/1.
1968 "Soviet language policy: continuity and change", in: E. Goldhagen (ed.), *Ethnic minorities in the Soviet Union*. New York: Praeger, 121-146.

Orwell, George
1949 *Nineteen eighty-four: a novel*. New York: Harcourt, Brace, and World.

Otsup, N.A.
1961 *Sovremmeniki*. Paris: Imprimerie Cooperative Etoile.

Pal'mbakh, A.
1931 "K probleme dialektiki iazyka", in: N. Marr (ed.). Vol. 2, 9-33.

Panov, M.V.
1974 "Teoriia fonem N.F. Iakovleva i sozdanie novykh pis'mennostei v SSSR", *Narody Azii i Afriki* 4: 210-223.

Pashkov, N.
1924 *Deklamatsionnaia khrestomatiia*. Moscow: Dumnova.
1925 "O nedostatkakh rechi", *Rodnoi iazyk v shkole* 7: 164-169.

Patenaude, Bertrand
1995 "Peasants into Russians: the utopian essence of war communism", *The Russian review* 54 (October): 552-570.

Pavel, Thomas G.
1989 *The feud of language: a history of structuralist thought*. London: Basil Blackwell.

Pavlovich, M.P. (ed.)
1926 *V borbe za novogo tiurkskogo alfavita*. Moscow: Izd. Nauchno-Assots-Vostok.

Payne, Matthew J.
1995 Turksib: the building of the Turkestano-Siberian railroad. [Unpublished Ph.D. dissertation, University of Chicago.]

Perel'muter, I.S.
1989 "Oppositsiia 'iazyk-iazyki' v lingvisticheskoi kontseptsii F.F. Fortunatova i uchenykh ego shkoly", *Izvestiia ANSSSR. Seriia literatury i iazyka* 48/1:72-82.

Pervyi vsesiouznyi tiurkologicheskii siezd, 26 fevralia - 5 marta 1926 g. Stenograficheskii otchet. Baku: ASSR, 1926.

Peshkovskii, A.M.
1914 *Russkii sintaksis v nauchnom osveshchenii. Populiarnyi ocherk. Posobie dlia samoobrazovaniia i shkoly.* (1st of 7 editions to 1956.) Moscow.
1922 *Kratkie plany urokov po grammatike (obuchenie vzroslykh). Elementy sintaksisa i morfologiia (primenitel'no k programme rabochikh fakultetov).* Moscow: Gosizdat.
1922-1927 *Nash iazyk.* 3 vols. Moscow: Gosizdat.
1925 *Sbornik statei: metodika rodnogo iazyka, lingvistika, stilistika, poetika.* Leningrad: Gosizdat.

Peter, M.
1957 "K teorii moskovskoi fonologicheskoi shkoly", *Studia slavica* III/1-4: 327-348.

Peterson, M.N.
1923 *Ocherk sintaksisa russkogo iazyka.* Moscow.
1925 *Russkii iazyk. Posobie dlia prepodavatelei.* Moscow-Leningrad: Gosizdat.
1928 "Iazykoznanie", in: V.P. Volgin (ed.), *Obshchestvennye nauki SSSR (1917-1927).* Moscow, 206-207.
1928-1929 *Vvedenie v iazykovedenie. Zadaniia 1-16.* Moscow: MGU.
1929 *Sovremmennyi russkii iazyk.* Moscow: MGU.
1956 'Akademik F.F. Fortunatov", in: F.F. Fortunatov, *Izbrannye trudy.* Vol. 1. Moscow: MPRSFSR, 5-20.

Petrova, E.N.
1931 *Iazyk i literatura v politekhnicheskoi shkole povyshennogo tipa.* Moscow.
1932a "Iafetidologiia litsom k shkole", *Iafeticheskii sbornik* 7: 9-17.
1932b "Metodologicheskoe litso zhurnala *Russkii iazyk v sovetskoi shkole*", in: S. Bykovskii (ed.), 153.
1933 "Novaia programma po russkomu iazyku dlia srednei shkoly", *Na putiakh k novoi shkole* 1: 13-18.
1936 *Grammatika v srednei shkole.* Moscow-Leningrad.

Phillips, Katherine
1986 *Language theories of the early Soviet period.* Atlantic Highlands: Humanities Press.

Pipes, Richard
1964 *The formation of the Soviet Union: communism and nationalism, 1917-1923.* Cambridge, Mass.: Harvard University Press.
1989 *Russia observed: collected essays on Russian and Soviet history.* Boulder: Westview Press.

Plotnikov, I.P.
1919   *Psikhologicheskaia shkola v iazykoznaniia i metodika russkogo iazyka.* Kursk.

Pocock, J.G.A.
1984   "Verbalizing a political act: toward a politics of speech", in: Michael Shapiro (ed.), *Language and politics.* New York: New York University Press, 25-43.

Pokrovskii, M.N.
1928   "N.Ia. Marr (K sorokaletiiu nauchnoi deiatel'nosti)", *Izvestiia* 118 (23 May): 4.

Politicheskaia zhizn' russkikh musul'man do fevral'skoi revoliutsii. Oxford: Society for Central Asian Studies, 1987.

Polivanov, E.D.
1917   "Svoevremenna li reforma", *Novaia zhizn'* 44 (9 June): 4.
1922   "O printsipakh postroeniia turetskoi grammatiki", *Nauka i prosveshchenie* [Tashkent] 1: 14-16.
1923a   *Lektsii po vvedeniiu v iazykoznanie i obshchei fonetike.* Berlin: Izd. Grzhebina.
1923b   *Problema latinskogo shrifta v turetskikh pis'mennostiakh (po povodu novogo iakutskogo alfavita, azerbaidzhanskoi azbuki jeni jol, i uzbekskogo alfavita, sanktsionirovannogo 2-ym siezdom uzb. rab. prosveshcheniia).* Moscow: Inst. Vostok.
1924   "Proekt latinskogo shrifta uzbekskoi pis'mennosti", *Biulleten', Sredne-Aziatskii gosudarstvennyi universitet* 6: 158.
1925   *Etnograficheskaia kharakteristika uzbekov.* Vol. 1. Tashkent: Uzgiz.
1925-1926   *Vvedenie v izuchenie uzbekskogo iazyka.* 3 vols. Tashkent: Turkpechati.
1926a   *Kratkaia grammatika uzbekskogo iazyka.* 2 vols. Tashkent-Moscow: Turkpechati.
1926b   *'Mak'. Russkii bukvar dlia uzbekskikh shkol.* Tashkent.
1926c   *Proekty latinizatsii turetskikh pis'mennostei SSSR k turkologicheskomu siezdu II.* Tashkent: Uzgiz.
1926d   *Russko-uzbekskii slovar'.* Tashkent: Turkpechati.
1927   "Rodnoi iazyk v natsional'noi partshkole", in S. Dimanshtein (ed.), 111-122.
1928a   "Osnovnye formy graficheskoi revoliutsii v turetskikh pis'mennostiakh SSSR", *Novyi vostok* 23-24: 314-330.
1928b   "Russkii iazyk sevodniashchnego dnia", *Literatura i marksizm* 4: 168.

1928c   *Vvedenie v iazykoznanie dlia vostokovednykh vuzov.* Vol. 1. Leningrad: Izd. Enukidze.
1931   *Za marksistskoe iazykoznanie.* Moscow: Federatsiia.
1968   *Stat'i po obshchemu iazykoznaniiu.* Moscow: Nauka.
1974   *Selected works: articles on general linguistics.* Compiler A.A. Leontiev. Trans. Daniel Armstrong. The Hague: Mouton.

Pomorska, Krystyna.
1977   "The utopian future of the Russian avant-garde", in: D. Armstrong & C.H. van Schooneveld (eds.), 371-372.

Pool, Jonathan
1976   "Developing the Soviet Turkic tongues: the language of the politics of language", *Slavic review* 35: 425-442.
1978   "Soviet language planning: goals, results, options", in J. Azrael (ed.), 223-249.

Poppe, Nicholas
1983   *Reminiscences.* Ed. Henry G. Schwarz. Bellingham, Washington: Western Washington University.

Potebnia, A.A.
1892   *Mysl' i iazyk.* (2nd edition.) Kharkov: Darre.
1913a   "Iazyk i narodnost", in his *Mysl' i iazyk.* (3rd edition.) Kharkov: Mirnyi trud, 187-220.
1913b   "O natsionalizme", in his *Mysl' i iazyk.* (3rd edition.) Kharkov: Mirnyi trud, 221-225.
1958   *Iz zapisok po russkoi grammatike.* 2 vols. Moscow. [First published in 1873-1874, with a 3rd vol. in 1899.]

Potseluevskii, A.A.
1929   *Rukovodstvo dlia izucheniia turkmenskogo iazyka.* Ashkhabad
1936   *Fonetkia turkmenskogo iazyka.* Ashkhabad.

Prezent, I.
1928   *Proiskhozhdenie rechi i myshleniia.* Leningrad: Priboi.

Programmnye dokumenty musul'manskikh politicheskikh partii 1917-1920 gg. Oxford: Society for Central Asian Studies, 1985.

Rabinowitch, Alexander
1976   *The Bolsheviks come to power: the revolution of 1917 in Petrograd.* New York: W.W. Norton.

Raeff, Marc
1989   "Un empire comme les autres?", *Cahiers du monde russe et sovietiques* 30/3-4: 321-328.

Rafail, Ia.A.
1931　　　*Marksistskaia filosofiia, iafetidologiia i teoriia uslovnykh refleksov.* Leningrad: GAIMK.
Rakowska-Harmstone, Teresa
1974　　　"The dialectics of nationalism in the USSR", *Problems of communism* 23/3 (May-June).
Reformatskii, A.A.
1933a　　　"Lingvistika i poligrafiia", in: D. Korkmasov (ed.), 42-58.
1933b　　　*Tekhnicheskaia redaktsiia knigi: teoriia i metodika raboty.* Ed. D.L. Veis. Moscow: Gizlegprom.
1947　　　*Vvedenie v iazykovedenie: posobie dlia uchitel'skikh institutov.* (1st edition.) Moscow: Uchpedgiz.
1962　　　"Ob odnom izdanii komiteta tekhnicheskoi terminologii ANSSSR", *Voprosy iazykoznaniia* 4: 142-145.
1970　　　"Petr Savvich Kuznetsov (1899-1968)", in: *Iazyk i chelovek: sbornik statei pamiati professora Petra Savvicha Kuznetsova (1899-1968).* Moscow: MGU, 18-30.
1987　　　*Lingvistika i poetika.* Ed. G.V. Stepanov. Moscow: Nauka.
1988　　　*Selected writings: philology, linguistics, semiotics.* Ed. Victor Vinogradov. Moscow: Progress.
Reformatskii, A.A. (ed.)
1970　　　*Iz istorii otechestvennoi fonologii.* Moscow: Nauka.
Renfrew, Colin
1987　　　*Archeology and language: the puzzle of Indo-European origins.* New York: Cape.
Riasanovsky, N.V.
1964　　　"Prince N.S. Trubetskoy's 'Europe and mankind'", *Jarbucher fur geschichte osteuropas* 12/2: 207-220.
1972　　　"Asia through Russian eyes", in: W. Vucinich (ed.), 19-23.
Rice, Martin
1973　　　*Valery Briusov and the rise of Russian symbolism.* Ann Arbor: Ardis.
Richards, Thomas
1993　　　*The imperial archive: knowledge and the fantasy of empire.* London: Verso.
Riddell, John (ed.)
1993　　　*To see the dawn. Baku, 1920 – first congress of the peoples of the east.* New York: Pathfinder.
Rieber, Alfred
1991　　　"The sedimentary society", in: E. Clowes & S. Kassow & J. West (eds.).

Robin, Regine
1990 "Stalinism and popular culture", in: H. Gunther (ed.), 36-37.
1991 "Popular literature of the 1920s: Russian peasants as readers", in: S. Fitzpatrick & A. Rabinowitch & R. Stites (eds.), 253-267.
1992 *Socialist realism: an impossible aesthetic.* Stanford: Stanford University Press.

Rogger, Hans
1960 *National consciousness in eighteenth-century Russia* Cambridge, Mass.: Harvard University Press.

Rorlich, A.A.
1974 *"Which way will Tatar culture go?.* A controversial essay by Galimdzhan Ibragimov", *Cahiers du mondes russe et sovietique* 14/34: 363-371.
1982 "Islam under communist rule: Volga-Ural Muslims", *Central Asian survey* 1/1: 5-42.
1986 *The Volga Tatars: a profile in national resistance.* Stanford: Hoover Institution Press.

Rosenburg, Suzanne
1988 *A Soviet odyssey.* New York: Penguin.

Rossianov, K.O.
1993 "Editing nature: Joseph Stalin and the 'new' Soviet biology", *Isis* 84: 728-745.

Rothstein, Robert A.
1975 "The linguist as dissenter: Jan Baudouin de Courtenay", in: *For Wiktor Wientraub.* The Hague: Mouton, 391-406.

Ruane, Christine & Ben Eklof
1991 "Cultural pioneers and professionals: the teacher in society", in: E. Clowes & S. Kassow & J. West (eds.), 199-211.

Rudolph, Richard & David F. Good (eds.)
1992 *Nationalism and empire: the Hapsburg empire and the Soviet Union.* New York: St. Martin's Press.

Rubakin, N.A.
1924 *Chto takoe bibliologicheskaia psikhologiia.* Leningrad: Kolos.
1929 *Psikhologiia chitatelia i knigi.* Moscow.

Russell, Robert
1982 "Red pinkertonism: an aspect of Soviet literature in the 1920s", *Slavonic and East European review* 60/3 (July): 390-412.

Russkii iazyk v mordovskoi shkole I-i stupeni (metodicheskoe pis'mo). Moscow: 1928.

Rybnikova, M.A.
1931 "Metod proektov", *Russkii iazyk v sovetskoi shkole* 2-3: 84.
Rywkin, Michael
1990 *Moscow's Muslim challenge.* Armonk, N.Y.: M.E. Sharpe.
Safarov, G.
1921 *Kolonial'naia revoliutsiia.* Moscow: Gosizdat
[1985] [Reprinted Oxford: Society for Central Asian Studies.]
Said, Edward
1979 *Orientalism.* New York: Vintage.
Sakamoto, Hiroshi
1988 "Teoriia ieroglifov Plekhanova", *Japanese Slavic and East European studies* 9: 65-74.
Sakulin, P.N.
1917a *Novoe russkoe pravopisanie.* Moscow: Sytin.
1917b *Reforma russkogo pravopisaniia.* Petrograd.
Salamani, Leonardo
1984 "Gramsci and Marxist sociology of language", *International journal of the sociology of language* 32: 28-44.
Samoilovich, A.N.
1925 *Kratkaia uchebnaia grammatika sovremennogo osmansko-turetskogo iazyka.* Leningrad.
Samuelian, Thomas
1981 The search for a Marxist linguistics in the Soviet Union, 1917-1950. [Unpublished Ph.D. dissertation, University of Pennsylvania.]
Samurskii, N.
1925 *Dagestan.* Moscow.
Sanzheev, G.D.
1934 *Sintaksis mongol'skikh iaykov.* Moscow: NIANKP.
1940 *Grammatika kalmytskogo iazyka.* Moscow-Leningrad.
1941 *Grammatike buriat-mongol'skogo iazyka.* Moscow-Leningrad.
Sapir, E.
1934 *Iazyk. Vvedenie v izuchenie rechi [Language].* Trans. A.M. Sukhotin. Ed. R.O. Shor. Moscow: Sotsekgiz.
Saussure, F. de
1933 *Kurs obshchei lingvistiki [Cours de linguistique generale].* Trans. A.M. Sukhotin. Ed. R.O. Shor. Moscow: Sotsekgiz.
Schafer, Daniel
1995 Building nations and building states: the Tatar-Bashkir question in revolutionary Russia, 1917-1920. [Unpublished Ph.D. dissertation, University of Michigan.]

Schogt, Henry G.
1966 "Baudouin de Courtenay and phonological analysis", *La linguistique* 2/2: 15-29.

Sed'moi siezd sovetov avtonomnoi TSSR. Stenograficheskii otchet. Kazan, 1927.

Segal, Dmitri
1974 *Aspects of structuralism in Soviet philology*. Tel Aviv: Papers on Poetics and Semiotics.

Selishchev, A.M.
1925 "Revoliutsiia i iazyk", in: P.O. Afanasiev (ed.), *Rodnoi iazyk vo II-ei stupeni V gruppa. Rabochaia khrestomatiia*. Moscow: Gosizdat: 207.
1928 *Iazyk revoliutsionnoi epokhi. Iz nabliudenii nad russkim iazykom poslednikh let (1917-1926)*. (2nd edition). Moscow.
[1974] [Reprinted Leipzig: Zentral.]
1932 "O iazyke sovremennoi derevni", *Zemlia sovetskaia* 9: 120-132.
1968 *Izbrannye trudy*. Moscow: Prosveshchenie.

Sennacieco Asocio Tutmonda
1924 *Proletaria kantaro*. Dusseldorf: Eldono Fako Kooperativa.
1925 *Petro: Kursa lernlibro por laboristoj*. Leipzig: Eldono Fako Kooperativa.
1937 *Manifesto of non-nationalists*. Paris.

Serdiuchenko, G.P.
1949 *Rol' N.Ia. Marr v razvitii materialisticheskogo ucheniia o iazyke*. Moscow: Pravda.
1955 "Ob alfavitakh na russkoi graficheskoi osnove dlia iazykov zapadnogo kavkaza", in: *Rodnoi i russkii iazyki v shkolakh severnogo kavkaza*. Moscow.

Serebrennikov, B.A.
1952 "Novye zadachi v oblasti izucheniia iazykov narodov SSSR", *Trudy instituta iazykoznaniia ANSSSR* I: 3-6.

Seregny, Scott
1990 *Russian teachers and peasant revolution: the politics of education*. Bloomington: Indiana University Press.

Seriot, Patrick
1985 *Analyse du discours politique Sovietique*. Paris: Institut d'etudes slaves.

Seyffert, Peter
1985 *Soviet literary structuralism*. Columbus: Slavica.

Shafir, Ia.M.
1923　　　*Gazeta i derevnya*. Moscow: Krasnaia nov.
1924　　　"O iazyke massovoi literatury", *Knigonosha* 39.
1926　　　*"Rabochaia gazeta" i ee chitatel'*. Moscow: Raboch. gaz.
1927　　　*Ocherki psikhologii chitatelia*. Moscow.
Shaginian, Marietta
1991　　　*Mess-mend. Yankees in Petrograd*. Trans. Samuel D. Cioran. Ann Arbor: Ardis.
Shaidanov, A. & I.A. Batmanov
1938　　　*Elementarnye osnovy grammatiki kirgizskovo iazyka*. Frunze-Tashkent.
Shakhmatov, A.A.
1941　　　*Sintaksis russkogo iazyka*. (2nd edition) Moscow: NKP RSFSR.
Shapiro, A.B.
1939　　　"Orfografiia", *Bolshaia sovetskaia entsiklopedia*.
Shapiro, Leonard
1971　　　*The communist party of the Soviet Union*. New York: Vintage.
Shaposhnikov, I.N.
1931　　　*Orfograficheskii slovar': s prilozheniem zadanii dlia pis'mennykh uprazhnenii po slovariiu*. (15th edition.) Moscow: Gosuchpedgiz.
Sharaf, G.
1926　　　"K voprosu o priniatii dlia tiurkskikh narodnostei latinskogo shrifta", *Vestnik nauchnogo obshchestva tatarovedeniia* 5: 1-80.
Shaumian, S.K.
1962　　　*Problemy teoreticheskoi fonologii*. Moscow.
1965　　　*Strukturnaia lingvistika*. Moscow.
Shcherba, L.V.
1939　　　"Sovremennyi russkii literaturnyi iazyk", *Russkii iazyk v shkole* 4: 19-26.
1945　　　"Ocherednye problemy iazykovedeniia", *Izvestiia ANSSSR OLIa* IV/5.
1957　　　*Izbrannye raboty po russkomu iazyku*. Moscow: Gosuchpedizdat.
1974　　　*Iazykovaia sistema i rechevaia deiatel'nost*. Eds. L.R. Zinder and M.I. Matusevich. Leningrad: Nauka.
Shevelov, George Y.
1989　　　*The Ukrainian language in the first half of the twentieth century (1900-1941): its state and status*. Cambridge, Mass.: Harvard University Press.

Shklovskii, V.B.
1966   *Zhily-byli.* Moscow: Sov. Pis.
Shor, R.O.
1926   *Iazyk i obshchestvo.* Moscow: Rabpros.
1927   "Krizis sovremmenoi lingvistiki", *Iafeticheskii sbornik* 5: 32-71.
1929   *Obshchee iazykoznanie. Vvedenie v materialisticheskoe iazykoznanie.* Preface by I.I. Meshchaninov. Moscow.
1930   "Gumbol'dt", *Bol'shaia sovetskaia entsiklopedia*: 804-805.
1931   *Na putiakh k marksistskoi lingvistike.* Moscow: Uchpedgiz.
Shor, R.O. & N.S. Chemodanov
1945   *Vvedenie v iazykovedenie.* Ed. I.I. Meshchaninov. Moscow: Uchpedgiz.
Shorish, M. Mobin
1984a   "Islam and nationalism in West Turkestan (Central Asia) on the eve of the October revolution", *Nationalities papers* XII/2 (Fall): 247-264.
1984b   "Planning by decree: the Soviet language policy in Central Asia", *Language problems and language planning* 8/1: 35-49.
Shpet, G.G.
1914   *Iavlenie i mysl'; fenomenologiia kak osnovnaia nauka i eia problemy.* Moscow.
1917   "Predmet i zadachi etnicheskoi psikhologii", *Psikhologicheskoe obozrenie* 1/4.
1922-1923   *Esteticheskie fragmenty.* 3 vols. Petrograd: Kolos
1927a   *Vnutrenniaia forma slova.* Moscow: GAKhN.
1927b   *Vvedenie v etnicheskuiu psikhologiiu.* Moscow: GAKhN.
[1989]   [Reprinted in his *Sochineniia.* Ed. E.V. Pasternak. Moscow: Pravda.]
1989   "Preface", to his *Ocherk razvitiia russkoi filosofii*, in his *Sochineniia.* Ed. E.V. Pasternak. Moscow: 11-19.
Shpilrein, I.N. & D.N Reitenbarg & G.O. Netskii
1928   *Iazyk krasnoarmeitsa. Opyt issledovaniia slovaria krasnoarmeitsa moskovskogo garnizona.* Moscow: Gosizdat.
Sidorov, E. & A. Shapiro & S. Shuvalov
1926   *Delovaia rech'.* Moscow: Rabpros.
Silver, Brian
1978   "Language policy and linguistic russification of Soviet nationalities", in: J. Azrael (ed.), 250-308.
Simon, Gerhard
1991   *Nationalism and policy toward the nationalities in the Soviet Union.* Trans. K. Forster and O. Forster. Boulder: Westview.

Sinel, Allen
   1973   *The classroom and the chancellery: state educational reform in Russia under count Dmitry Tolstoi*. Cambridge, Mass.: Harvard University Press.

Sirotin, V.
   1936   "Nuzhna khoroshaia grammatika", *Pravda* 128 (11 May).

Slezkine, Yuri
   1993   *Arctic mirrors*. Ithaca: Cornell University Press.
   1994   "The U.S.S.R as a communal apartment, or how a Socialist state promoted ethnic particularism", *Slavic review* 53/2: 443-445.

Sliusareva, N.A.
   1974   "Essai de comparaison des conceptions de F. de Saussure et de von Humboldt", in: Rene Amacker & Tullio de Mauro & Luis Prieto (eds.), *Studi saussuriani per Robert Godel*. Bologna: Il Mulino, 265-274.
   1976   *Sovetskoe iazykoznanie (20-30e gody)*. Moscow: Nauka.

Sliusareva N.A. & V.G. Kuznetsov
   1976   "Materialy i soobshcheniia. Iz istorii sovetskogo iazykoznaniia. Rukopisnye materialy S.I. Bernshteina o F. de Sossiure", *Izvestiia ANSSR. Seriia literatury i iazyka* 35/5.

Smith, Anthony D.
   1986   *The ethnic origins of nations*. Oxford: Oxford University Press.

Sochor, Zenovia
   1988   *Revolution and culture: the Bogdanov-Lenin controversy*. Ithaca: Cornell University Press.

Solchanyk, Roman
   1982   "Russian language and Soviet politics", *Soviet studies* XXXIV-1 (January): 23-42.

Solomon, Susan G.
   1980   "Reflections on western studies of Soviet science", in L. Lubrano & S. Solomon (eds.), 4-8.

Solzhenitsyn, Alexander
   1969   *The first circle*. Trans. Thomas P. Whitney. New York: Bantam Books.

Sovetkin, F.F.
   1958   *Natsional'nye shkoly RSFSR za 40 let*. Moscow.

Soviet writers' congress 1934: the debate on socialist realism and modernism in the Soviet Union. London, 1977.

Spiridovich, E.F.
1931   *Iazykoznanie i mezhdunarodnyi iazyk.* Moscow: TsKSESR.

Spravochnik dlia postupaiushchikh v tekhnikumy, profshkoly i fabzavuchi severo-kavkazskogo kraia v 1926-1927 g. Rostov-na-Donu, 1926.

Springer, George P.
1956   *Early Soviet theories in communication.* Cambridge, Mass.: MIT Press.

Stalin, Iosef
1931   *Fundamentoj de Leninismo.* Trans. V. Lebedev and N. Khokhlov. Leipzig: Ekrelo.
1946-1951   *Sochinenie.* Moscow: Politlit.

Stankiewicz, Edward (ed.)
1972   *A Baudouin de Courtenay anthology: the beginnings of structuralism.* Bloomington: Indiana University Press.

Steiner, Peter
1984   *Russian formalism: a metapoetics.* Ithaca: Cornell University Press.
1988   "Gustav Shpet et l'ecole de Prague: cadres conceptuels pour l'etude de la langue", in: *Centres et peripheries.* Brussels.

Stenograficheskii otchet chetvertogo plenuma VTsKNA. Leningrad: VTsKNA, 1931 [Held in Alma-Ata, 6-13 May 1930.]

Stenograficheskii otchet nauchno-orfograficheskoi konferentsii sozvannoi 2-4 iunia 1929 goda nauchno-metodicheskim sovetom NKP i TsKNKA. Kzyl-Orda: Kazizdat, 1930.

Stenograficheskii otchet pervogo plenuma VTsKNTA. Moscow: VTsKNTA, 1927. [Held in Baku, 3-7 June 1927.]

Stenograficheskii otchet piatogo plenuma VTsKNA (Moscow: VTsKNA, 1932. [Held in Tashkent, 2-9 June 1931.]

Stenograficheskii otchet tret'ego plenuma VTsKNTA. Kazan: VTsKNTA, 1928. [Held in Kazan, 18-23 December 1928.]

Stenograficheskii otchet vtorogo plenuma VTsKNTA. Baku: VTsKNTA, 1929. [Held in Tashkent, 7-12 January 1928.]

Stites, Richard
1983 "Stalin: utopian or antiutopian? An indirect look at the cult of personality", in Joseph Held (ed.), *The cult of power: dictators in the twentieth century.* Boulder: East European Monographs.
1989 *Revolutionary dreams: utopian vision and experimental life in the Russian revolution.* New York: Oxford University Press.
1990 "Stalinism and the restructuring of revolutionary utopianism", in: H. Gunther (ed.), 80-81.
1991 "Bolshevik ritual building in the 1920s", in: S. Fitzpatrick & A. Rabinowitch & R. Stites (eds.), 300-301.
1992 *Russian popular culture: entertainment and society since 1900.* New York: Cambridge University Press.

Stoliarenko, M.A.
1931 *Russkii iazyk v turetskoi shkole.* Baku.

Stone, Lawrence
1972 "Language planning and the Russian standard language", *Transactions of the philological society*: 165-183.

Straten, V.
1929 "Ob argo i argotizmakh", *Russkii iazyk v sovetskoi shkole* 5: 39-53.

Strazhev, V.I.
1931 *Ocherk po izucheniiu iazyka.* Moscow: Gosfinizdat.

Suny, Ronald G.
1972 "A journeyman for the revolution: Stalin and the labour movement in Baku, June 1907 - May 1908", *Soviet studies* XXIII/3 (January).
1991 "Beyond psychohistory: the young Stalin in Georgia", *Slavic review* 50/1 (Spring): 56-57.
1994 *Revenge of the past.* Stanford: Stanford University Press.

Suvorovskii, A.M.
1926 "Iazyk truda", *Trudy iaroslavskogo pedagogicheskogo instituta* 1/1-2.

Swietochowski, Tadeusz
1985 *Russian Azerbaijan, 1905-1920.* New York: Cambridge University Press.
1991 "The politics of a literary language and the rise of national identity in Russian Azerbaijan before 1920", *Ethnic and racial studies* 14/1 (January): 55-63.

Taylor, Charles
1975 *Hegel.* New York: Cambridge University Press.

1983 "Hegel and the philosophy of action", in: L.S. Stepelevich and D. Lamb (eds.), *Hegel's philosophy of action*. Atlantic Highlands: Humanities Press.

Taylor, F.W.
1981 "Scientific managment", in: George A. Miller and Oscar Grusky (eds.), *The sociology of organizations*. New York: Free Press, 58-59.

Thaden, Edward C.
1984 *Russia's western borderlands, 1710-1870*. Princeton: Princeton University Press.

Thomas, Lawrence
1957 *The linguistic theories of N.Ia Marr*. Berkeley: University of California Press.

Thompson, Ewa M.
1991 "Nationalist propaganda in the Soviet Russian press, 1939-1941", *Slavic review* 50/2 (Summer): 387-388.

Thurston, Robert
1991 "Social dimensions of Stalinist rule: humor and terror in the USSR, 1935-1941", *Journal of social history* 24/3 (Spring): 541-562.

Tillett, Lowell
1969 *The Great friendship: Soviet historians on the non-Russian nationalities*. Chapel Hill: University of North Carolina Press.

Timasheff, Nicholas
1946 *The great retreat*. New York: E.P. Dutton.

Titunik, I.R.
1976 "M.M. Bakhtin (the Bakhtin school) and Soviet semiotics", *Dispositio* 1/3: 327.
1986 "The Bakhtin problem", *Slavonic and East European journal* 30/1: 91.

Toman, Jindrich
1991 "Nationality as choice: Baudouin de Courtenay's individualistic approach", *Cross currents* 10: 47-50.
1995 *The magic of a common language*. Cambridge, Mass.: MIT Press.

Toman, Jindrich (ed.)
1994 *Letters and other materials from the Moscow and Prague linguistic circles*. Ann Arbor: Michigan Slavic Publications.

Tomsen, A.I.
1910 *Obshchee iazykovedenie*. (2nd edition.) Odessa: Tekhnik.

Tonkov, V.A.
1930 *Opyt issledovaniia vorovskogo iazyka*. Moscow-Leningrad.

Trotskii, Lev
- 1923 "Bor'ba za kul'turnost' rechi", in: his *Voprosy byta: epokha 'kul'turnichestva' i ee zadachi.* Moscow: Kras. nov.
- 1971 *Literature and revolution.* Trans. Rose Strunsky. Ann Arbor: University of Michigan.

Trubetskoi, N.S.
- 1969 *The principles of phonology.* Trans. Christiane A.M. Baltuxe. Berkeley: University of California Press.
- 1975 *N.S. Trubetzkoy's letters and notes.* The Hague: Mouton.
- 1987 *Izbrannye trudy po filologii.* Eds. T.V. Gamkrelidze, V.V. Ivanov, V.P. Neroznak, & N.I. Tolstoi. Moscow: Progress.
- 1991 *The legacy of Genghis Khan and other essays on Russia's identity.* Ann Arbor: Michigan Slavic Publications.

Tsentral'nyi ispol'nitel'nyi komitet
- 1927 *Doklad tsentral'noi komissii po realizatsii tatarskogo iazyka pri TsIK TSSR.* Kazan: Gosizdat.

Tsentral'noe statisticheskoe upravlenie SSSR
- 1928 *Narodnost' i rodnoi iazyk naseleniia SSSR.* Moscow: TSU.

Tucker, Robert C.
- 1971 *The Soviet political mind: Stalin and post-Stalin change.* New York: Norton.

Tugenkhol'd, Ia.
- 1926 "Sovremennyi plakat", *Pechat' i revoliutsiia* 8: 57.

Turchaninov, G. & M. Tsatov
- 1940 *Grammatika Kabardinskogo iazyka.* Moscow-Leningrad.

Ukazatel' rabot gosudarstvennoi akademii istorii material'noi kultury imeni N.Ia Marra izdannykh s 1921-1935 gg. Moscow: Gosotsk, 1936.

Ushakov, D.N.
- 1917 *Russkoe pravopisanie.* Moscow.
- 1922 *Kratkoe vvedenie v nauku o iazyke.* (2nd edition.) Moscow: Gosizdat.
- 1928 "Russkaia orfoepiia i ee zadachi", *Russkaia rech'* 3.
- 1934 *Orfograficheskii slovar' dlia nachal'noi, nepolnoi srednei i srednei shkoly.* (1st edition.) Moscow: Uchpedgiz.

Ushakov, D.N. (ed.)
- 1923 *Russkii iazyk v shkole. Trudy postoiannoi komissii prepodavatelei russkogo iazyka i literatury (pri tsentral'nom gumanitarno-pedagogicheskom institute).* Moscow-Petrograd: Gosizdat.

Ushakov, D.N. & B.M. Volin (eds.)
1934-1938   *Tol'kovyi slovar russkogo iazyka.* Moscow: Sovetskaia Entsiklopedia.
Uspenskii, Lev
1931   "Russkii iazyk posle revoliutsii", *Slavia* X: 273-281.
Ustinov, I.V.
1922   *Razvitie rechi: k voprosu o metodakh zaniatii v shkolakh vzroslykh i na komandnykh kursakh.* Moscow: GIZ.
1923   *Novyi orfograficheskii spravochnik.* Moscow: GIZ.
1931   *Tekhnika razvitie ustnoi i pis'mennoi rechi.* (5th edition.) Moscow: Gosuchpedgiz.
Ustinov, I.V. & V.A. Mamonov & N.N. Nikol'skii (eds.)
1928   *Russkii iazyk: programma kursa i obiasnitel'naia zapiska razrabotannye predmetnoi kommissiei.* Moscow: GIZ.
Vakar, Nicholas
1956   *Belorussia: the making of a nation.* Cambridge, Mass.: Harvard University Press.
Valkenier, Elizabeth
1977   *Russian realist art: the state and society: the peredvizhniki and their tradition.* Ann Arbor: Ardis.
Validov, Dzhamaliutdin
1923   *Ocherk obrazovannosti i literatury Tatar (do revoliutsii 1917 g.).* Moscow: Gosizdat.
[1986]   [Reprinted Oxford: Society for Central Asian Studies.]
Vainshtein, I.
1925   "Myshlenie i rech: k kritike A. Bogdanov", *Pod znamenem Marksizma* 1-2.
van Geldern, James
1991   "The centre and the periphery: cultural and social geography in the mass culture of the 1930s", in: Stephen White (ed.), *New directions in Soviet history.* Cambridge, Eng.: Cambridge University Press, 62-77.
Varankin, V.
1929   *Teorio de esperanto.* Moscow: TsKSEU.
1977   *Metropoliteno.* (Reprint edition.) Copenhagen: TK.
Vareikis, I.
1926   *Zadachi partii v oblasti pechati.* Moscow.
Vendryes, J.
1924   "La theorie japhetique de N. Marr", *Revue celtique* XII: 291-293.
1937   *Iazyk. Lingvisticheskoe vvedenie v istoriiu* [*Language*]. Trans. P.S. Kuznetsov, Ed. R.O. Shor. Moscow: Sotsekgiz.

Vinogradov, V.V.
1922 *Aleksei Aleksandrovich Shakhmatov*. St. Petersburg: Kolos.
1935 *Iazyk Pushkina*. Leningrad.
1938 *Sovremennyi russkii iazyk*. Vol. 2. *Grammaticheskoe uchenie o slove*. Moscow.
1941 *Stil' Pushkina*. Moscow.
1945 *Velikii russkii iazyk*. Moscow.
1953 "Prof. L.P. Iakubinskii kak lingvist i ego *Istoriia drevnerusskogo iazyka*", in: L.P. Iakubinskii, *Istoriia drevnerusskogo iazyka*. Moscow: Uchpedgiz.
1964 "Sintaksicheskaia sistema prof. M.N. Petersona i ee razvitii", *Russkii iazyk v shkole* 5.

Vinogradov, V.V. & B.A. Serebrennikov (eds.)
1951-1952 *Protiv vulgarizatsii i izvrashcheniia marksizma v iazykoznanii*. 2 vols. Moscow: ANSSSR.

Vinokur, G.O.
1923a "Futuristy - stroiteli iazyka", *LEF* 1: 205.
1923b "O revoliutsionnoi frazeologii (odin iz voprosov iazykovoi politiki)", *LEF* 2: 104-106.
1923c "Poetika. Lingvistika. Sotsiologiia (metodologicheskaia spravka)", *LEF* 3: 104-113.
1925 "Poeziia i nauka", *Chet i nechet: al'manakh poezii i kritiki*. Moscow: Avtorsk. Izd.
1929a "Kul'tura rechi v gazete", *Literaturnaia gazeta* 4 (13 May).
1929b *Kul'tura iazyka. Ocherki lingvisticheskoi tekhnologii*. (2nd edition.) Moscow: Federatsiia.
1971 *The Russian language: a brief history*. Trans. Mary A. Forsyth. Cambridge, England: Cambridge University Press.
1988 "O vozmozhnosti vseobshchei grammatiki", *Voprosy iazykoznaniia* 4: 71-90.

Vinokur, T.G.
1968 "Stilisticheskoe razvitie sovremennoi russkoi razgovornoi rechi", in: T.G. Vinokur & D.N. Shmelev (eds.) *Razvitie funktsional'nykh stilei sovremennogo russkogo iazyka*. Moscow: Nauka, 12-100.

Viola, Lynne
1987 *The best sons of the fatherland: workers in the vanguard of Soviet collectivization*. New York: Oxford University Press.

Vitte, Rudolf R. & E.K. Drezen
1925 *Not v sovetskikh uchrezhdeniiakh (iacheiki Not i ekonomkomisii); prakticheskoe rukovodstvo*. Moscow: NKRKI (Otdel administrativnoi tekhniki).

Volgin, V.P. (ed.)
    1928   *Obshchestvennye nauki SSSR, 1917-1927*. Moscow: Rabpros.

Volkogonov, Dmitri
    1991   *Stalin: triumph and tragedy*. New York: Grove Weidenfeld.
    1994   *Lenin: a new biography*. New York: Free Press.

Volkonskii, Sergei and Aleksandr'
    1928   *V zashchitu russkago iazyka*. Berlin.

Voloshinov, V.N.
    1973   *Marxism and the philosophy of language*. Trans. Ladislav Matejka and I.R. Titunik. New York: Seminar Press.

Von Hagen, Mark
    1990   *Soldiers in the proletarian dictatorship: the Red Army and the Soviet socialist state, 1917-1930*. Ithaca: Cornell University Press.

Von Timroth, Wilhelm
    1986   *Russian and Soviet sociolinguistics and taboo varieties of the Russian language (argot, jargon, slang and "mat")*. Transl. Nortrud Gupta. Munich: Sagner.

Vrubel, S.
    1931   *K itogam lingvisticheskoi diskussii*. Tashkent: Uzgiz.

Vse na bor'bu s temnotoi. vyp. 1. Moscow: 1923.

Vsesiouznyi tsentral'nyi komitet novogo alfavit N.Ia. Marru. Sbornik statei. Moscow: Vlast' sovetov, 1936.

Vsevolodskii-Gerngross, V.
    1922   *Teoriia intonatsii*. Petrograd.

Vucinich, Alexander
    1963   *Science in Russian culture*. 2 vols. Stanford: Stanford University Press.
    1976   *Social thought in tsarist Russia*. Chicago: University of Chicago Press.
    1984   *Empire of knowledge: the Academy of Sciences of the USSR, 1917-1970*. Berkeley. University of California Press.

Vucinich, Wayne S.
    1972   "The structure of Soviet orientology: fifty years of change and accomplishment", in: W. Vucinich (ed.), 52-134.

Vucinich, Wayne S. (ed.)
    1972   *Russia and Asia: essays on the influence of Russia on the Asian peoples*. Stanford: Hoover Institution Press.

Vvedenskii, D.
1933 "Ferdinand de Sossiur i ego mesto v lingvistike", in: F. Saussure (1933): 1-20.

Vygotskii, L.S.
1978 *Mind in society: the development of higher psychological processes.* Ed. Michael Cole. Cambridge, Mass.: Harvard University Press.
1986 *Thought and language.* Trans. Alex Kozulin. Cambridge: MIT Press.

Vysotskii, S.S.
1961 "Razvitie russkoi dialektologii v kontse XIX v. i v nachale XX v.", in: B.V. Gornung (ed.), *Istoriia russkoi dialektologii.* Moscow: ANSSSR, 30-66.

Walsh, Henry Hill
1970 The early development of the concept of phonemes in Russian linguistic science. [Unpublished Ph.D. dissertation. University of North Carolina.]

Weber, Eugene
1976 *Peasants into Frenchmen: the modernization of rural France, 1870-1914.* Stanford: Stanford University Press.

Weeks, Theodore R.
1994 "Defining us and them: Poles and Russians in the 'western provinces', 1863-1914", *Slavic review* 53 (Spring).

Weiner, Douglas
1988 *Models of nature: ecology, conservation, and the cultural revolution in Soviet Russia.* Bloomington: Indiana University Press.

Weinrich, Uriel
1953 "The russification of Soviet minority languages", *Problems of communism* 2/6: 46-57.

Weinstein, Brian
1979 "Language strategists: redefining political frontiers on the basis of linguistic choices", *World politics* XXXI/3 (April): 345.

Wertsch, James
1985 *Vygotsky and the social formation of the mind.* Cambridge, Mass.: Harvard University Press.

Wexler, Paul
1974 *Purism and language: a study in modern Ukrainian and Belorussian nationalism (1840-1967).* Bloomington: Indiana University Press.

Wheeler, Geoffrey
1974 "Modernization in the Muslim east: the role of script and language reform", *Asian affairs* LVI/2: 157-164.
1977 "The Turkish languages of Soviet Muslim Asia: Russian linguistic policy", *Middle Eastern studies* 13/2: 208-217.

Whittaker, Cynthia H.
1984 *The origins of modern Russian education: an intellectual biography of count Sergei Uvarov, 1786-1855*. Dekalb: Northern Illinois University Press.

Wildman, Allan K.
1980 *The end of the Russian imperial army*. Princeton: Princeton University Press.

Williams, Robert C.
1982 'The nationalization of early Soviet culture", *Russian history* 9/2-3: 157-172.

Wimbush, S. Enders
1985 "The politics of identity change in Soviet Central Asia", *Central Asian survey* 3/3: 69-78.

Winner, Thomas G.
1952 "Problems of alphabet reform among the Turkic peoples of Soviet Central Asia", *Slavonic and East European review* 31/76: 137-147.

Wixman, Ronald
1980 *Language aspects of ethnic patterns and processes in the North Caucasus*. Chicago: University of Chicago Press.

Wuster, E.
1935 *Mezhdunarodnaia standartizatsiia iazyka v tekhnike*. Trans. O.I. Bogomolov. Eds. E.K. Drezen, L.I. Zhirkov, A.F. Lesokhin, and M.F. Malikov. Leningrad-Moscow: Standartgiz.
1936 *Konturoj de la lingvo-normigo en la tekniko*. Budapest.

Wuster, E. (ed.)
1979 *International bibliography of standardized vocabularies*. New York: Sauer.

Young, John Wesley
1991 *Totalitarian language: Orwell's newspeak and its Nazi and communist antecedents*. Charlottesville: University of Virginia Press.

Zenkovsky, Serge
1955 "*Kulturkampf* in pre-revolutionary Central Asia", *American Slavonic and East European review* (February): 15-41.
1960 *Pan-Turkism and Islam in Russia*. Cambridge, Mass.: Harvard University Press.

Zhirkov, L.I.
 1924 *Grammatika avarskogo iazyka*. Moscow.
 1925 "Iazyki Dagestana i ikh izuchenie", *Izvestiia obshchestva po issledovaniiu i izucheniiu Azerbaidzhana* 1.
 1926 *Grammatika darginskogo iazyka*. Moscow.
 1927 *Persidskii iazyk. Elementarnaia grammatika*. Moscow: Institut vostokovedeniia.
 1930 *Pochemu pobedil iazyk esperanto?*. Moscow: TsKSESR.
 1941 *Grammatika lezginskogo iazyka*. Makhachkala.
Zhirmunskii, V.M.
 1936 *Natsional'nyi iazyk i sotsial'nyi dialekty*. Leningrad: Gosizdat.
Zhitomirskii, K.G.
 1915 *Molokh' XX veka* (pravopisanie). Moscow: Trud'.
Zhuravlev, V.K.
 1990 "F.F. Fortunatov i lingvisticheskaia revoliutsiia XX v.", *Vestnik Moskovskogo universiteta*. Ser. 9. *Filologiia* 1: 22-30.
Zinder, L.R. & Iu.S. Maslov.
 1982 *L.V. Shcherba - lingvist-teoretik i pedagog*. Leningrad: Nauka.
Zvegintsev, V.A.
 1956 *Esteticheskii idealizm v iazykoznanii*. Moscow: MGU.

Index

Aarsfleff, H., 7, 85
ABCD hierarchy, 4,10, 51-58, 71-72, 144, 153, 177-179
Abazin, 50
Abkhaz, 50, 82, 88, 133
Abkhazian Analytical Alphabet (AAA), 82, 107, 140-141
Academy of Pedagogical Studies, 167, 171
Academy of Sciences, 16, 21, 23-26, 82-83, 93, 96, 152, 170, 176
Acronyms, 37
Adygei, 49-50, 53, 122-123, 134, 166
Afanasiev, P.O., 24, 112
Agamalyogly, S.A., 124, 128, 130, 132
Agglutinative languages, 17, 28, 79, 87
Agitation, 43, 67
Alaverdov, K., 118
Aliev, Umar, 125, 138
All-Russian Conference of Scientific Workers, 83
All-Union Association of Orientology, 71
All-Union Committee for the New Alphabet (VTsKNA), 100, 133-137, 152, 156
All-Union Committee for the New Turkic Alphabet (VTsKNTA), 125, 129-141
All-Union Committee for Standardization, 154-155
All-Union Communist Party (VKPb), see Russian Communist Party,
All-Union Conference on Machine Translation, 176
All-Union Radio Committee, 150-151
All-Union Society for Cultural Relations Abroad, 78
Allworth, Edward, 12
Alphabet method, 22, 25, 31-32
Alphabets (see Arabic, Latin, Cyrillic)
Althusser, Louis, 11

Artemov, B.A., 200, 214
Aptekar', V.I., 93, 95, 101, 110, 163
Arabic alphabet, 12, 31, 104, 121-142
Armenian, 44, 47, 49, 82-83, 157, 179
Asmus, V.F., 62, 99
Autonomy, 48-52
Avanesov, R.I., 164
Avar, 28, 47, 82
Azerbaijan, 31, 32, 43, 46-49, 50, 53, 76, 123-124, 133, 135, 152, 159, 171, 178-179
Azerbaijani Committee for the New Turkic Alphabet (AzKNTA), 126-129
Backwardness, 2, 66, 73, 148
Baitursunov, A., 122, 127-128, 135, 139
Bakhtin, Mikhail, 11, 18, 92, 99, 177, 135, 139
Baku, 12, 32, 52, 123, 138, 178
  Turkological congress (1926), 8, 126-127, 129, 131-132, 135, 139
Balkar, 49, 122-123
Baltics, 44
Bashkir, 50, 55, 127, 152-153, 170
Bastien, Louis, 156
Batu, 139
Baudouin de Courtenay, J.I., 9, 19-20, 23-24, 28-30, 50, 59, 64, 70-71, 82-83, 90, 98, 122, 151, 168
Bebel, August, 76
Belorussia, 21, 47, 53
Belyi, Andrei, 27
Beria, L.P., 165-166
Bernshtein, S.I., 150
Bilingualism, 29, 178
  Russian, 35-43
Blok, Aleksandr, 27
Bochacher, M., 97
Bogdanov, Aleksandr, 75, 77-78, 110, 117
Bogoroditskii, V.A., 29

Brandt, R.F., 20
Briusov, Valerii, 1
Bubnov, A.S., 145
Bubrikh, D.V., 68, 71, 96, 139, 163, 165
Bukhara, 49
Bukharin, Nikolai, 36, 88
Buriat, 133, 153, 166
Buslaev, F.F., 22, 24
Bykovskii, S.N., 89, 163
Capital letters, 131-132
Central Asia, 28, 31, 43-44, 47, 49, 158, 170
Central Asian Bureau (TsK RKPb), 49, 126, 158, 170
Central Executive Committee (USSR), 72, 78, 156
Central Committee (TsK RKPb), 7-8, 77, 101, 109, 124-126, 128, 149, 156-160
   Agitation-Propaganda, 124, 129, 164, 167
   Cultural-Propaganda, 101
   School Division, 158-159
Central Institute of Living Eastern Languages, 71
Central Scientific Research Institute of Languages and Alphabets (TsNIIaP), 157-160
Central Union of Press Workers, 66
Chan, 82
Chauvinism (Russian), 44-45, 53, 57, 110, 113, 153
Chechen, 28, 49, 53, 123, 134, 158
Cherkess, 49-50, 53, 122-123, 133-134, 166
Chernykh, P.A., 97
Chikobava, A.S., 164-168
Chinese Dungans, 133
Chobanzade, Bekir, 12, 71, 125, 129-132, 139
Chuvash, 28, 53, 139, 153, 170
Circassian, 49-50, 122, 134
Clark, Katerina, 148
Commissariat of Education, 37, 44, 57, 71, 112, 104, 116, 145-146, 158, 161

Commissariat of Communications, 153
Commissariat of Internal Affairs (NKVD), 44
Commissariat of the Nationalities, 44-58, 124-125
Commission for the Reform of the Arabic Script, 124-125
Commission on Reordering the Orthography, 145
Commission on the Problem of Russian Spelling (Imperial), 23
Committee on Spelling Reform (1929-1930), 107
Committee for Technical Terminology, 153
Communist Academy, 99, 101
   Institute of Language and Literature, 94
   Subsection for Materialist Linguistics, 94, 100, 107
Communist University of the Workers of the East, 71, 162
Comparative method, 31, 72-73, 114, 159-160, 171
Complex method, 105, 111-112
Congress of the Peoples of the East (1920), 127
Consey, Eileen, 50
Constitutional Democrats, 20-21
Convergence (*sblizhenie*), 3, 73, 88, 104, 144, 154-156, 176
Council of Ministers (RSFSR), 170
Council of Ministers (USSR), 199
Council of National Minorities (Sovnatsmen), 45, 51
Criminal jargon, 113
Crossbreeding, 83, 87, 153, 169
Cybernetics, 169, 176
Cyrillic alphabet, 107
   dictation lessons, 22, 25, 106, 115
   illiteracy, 103-110
   letter-configurator, 109
   reform, 103-110, 145
   reordering, 109
   Subcommission on the Latinization of the Russian Alphabet, 110
Dagestan, 46, 133-134, 158

Danilevskii, Nikolai, 27
Danilov, G.K., 2, 73, 75, 95, 97, 107-109, 117-118, 140, 152, 163
Dargin, 47
Darwin, Charles, 101
Davydov, I., 71
Derzhavin, N.S., 110
Dialectology, 162
  Moscow Dialectological Commission, 20, 30, 113, 148
  social, 19, 67, 103, 113-114, 117, 147, 150
  territorial, 19, 21, 147, 150, 164-165
Dictionary of the Russian language, 42, 150
Differential grammar (see Comparative method)
Dimanshtein, S.M., 1, 52, 57, 110, 126, 139, 151-152, 177-178
Discord (*raznoboi*), 105, 131-141
Dmitriev, N.K., 157
Dobrogaev, S.M., 86
Dobrovolskii, A.I., 96
Down with Illiteracy Society, 68, 100, 148
Drezen, E.K., 78-79, 97, 155-156, 161, 163
Dunham, Vera, 144
Durnovo, N.N., 114, 163
Dynik, M.A., 99
Energeia, 17-18, 90, 112
Engels, Friedrich, 85
Enukidze, A., 55
Ergon, 17-18, 90, 112
Esperanto, 20, 74-79, 107, 145, 154-156, 161, 163, 168
Estonian, 53
Ethnic psychology, 62-65
Eurasia, 2, 26-31
  imperative, 57-72, 81
Eurasianists, 68-69
Factory Apprenticeship Schools, 118
Fersman, A.E., 78
Feuerbach, L., 95
Fierman, William, 50
Filin, F.P., 165

Finno-Ugric languages, 28, 49, 90
Fishman, Joshua, 24
Formalism, 9, 20, 61, 144
  bourgeois, 86-87, 101, 139
  grammatical, 20, 24, 67, 111-118
Fortunatov, F.F., 9, 20, 23-24, 43, 64, 98, 151, 168
Foucault, Michel, 11
Friche, V.M., 83
Futurism, 21, 78, 111
Gagauz, 28
Gasprinskii, Ismail Bey, 31-32
Gastev, A.K., 75, 155
Georgian, 44, 46, 47, 49, 54, 82
Gorbachev, M.S., 178-179
Gorkii, M., 42, 55, 147
Grammar, 22, 24, 103, 110-118, 145-146, 170, 172
  teaching of concepts, 112, 170
  teaching of skills, 105, 112, 170
Gramsci, Antonio, 6, 103, 175
Grande, B., 157
Grot, I.K., 22-23, 25, 105
Gus, M.S., 40, 66, 97, 117, 163
Hahn, Werner, 164
Hebrew, 82
Hegel, G.W.F., 17, 19, 41, 61, 99, 163
Hegemony, 6-7
Historical comparativism, 16, 27, 28, 82, 168-170
Historical paleontology (see Japhetic theory)
Hjelmslev, L., 61
Humboldt, Wilhelm von, 7, 17-19, 40-41, 61, 64, 91, 92, 96, 99, 101, 112, 116-118, 166, 168
Husserl, E., 61-63, 92
Iakovlev, N.F., 30, 65, 68, 70-71, 88, 96-97, 110, 118, 131-132, 139, 145, 156
Iakubinskii, L.P., 21, 65-67, 90, 147,
Iakut, 53, 122, 133
Iaroslavl, 68
Ibragimov, Galimdzhan, 12, 122, 127-129
Idel-Ural, 48
Il'minskii, N.I., 28

Indo-Europeanism, 16, 21, 28, 60, 83, 86-90, 93-94, 101, 144, 165, 168
Inflective languages, 16, 28, 87
Ingush, 53, 134
Institute for the Comparative Study of the Languages and Literatures of the West and East (ILIaZV), 84, 90, 92, 147
Institute of Language and Literature (RANION), 99
Institute of Language and Thought, 147, 160, 165
Institute of the Living Word, 41, 90
International Standardizing Association, 155
Isolative languages, 17, 28, 87
Iushmanov, N.V., 77, 110
Ivanov, V.V., 11, 177
Iveria, 54, 82
Izhor, 53
Jadidism, 31, 122-125
Jakobson, R.O., 11, 21, 30, 59, 68, 77, 165, 176
Japhetic theory, 9, 11, 81-102, 107, 116-118, 138-145, 161, 173, 176
Jews, 44, 55, 133
Kabardin, 49, 122-123, 134, 156
Kaganovich, S.K., 73
Kalmyk, 55, 57
Kameneva, O.D., 41
Karachai, 49, 122-123
Karakalpaks, 122, 133
Karelian, 53
Karinskii, N.M., 65
Kartsevskii, S., 61, 111
Katsnelson, S.D., 165
Kautsky, Karl, 76
Kaverin, V.A., 79
Kazakh, 28, 43, 49, 50, 126, 131, 133, 135, 153
Kazan, 12, 28, 32, 43, 48
Kerzhentsev, P.M., 74-75
Khakass, 166
Khiva, 49
Khlebnikov, V., 76, 78
Kirgiz, 28, 43-49, 50, 55, 122, 131, 135, 153

Kirov, S.M., 124, 129
Komi, 28, 53
Korkmasov, D., 125
Kruchenykh, A., 43
Krupskaia, N.K., 54, 86
Kumyk, 47
Kurds, 133
Kuznetsov, P.S., 97, 164, 177
Labriola, Antonio, 99
Lak, 28, 47
Language Front, 81, 97-100, 107, 117-118, 140, 145-146, 152, 161-163, 168
Lanti, E., 78
Latinization,
 of the Arabic script, 12 104, 121-142
 of the Cyrillic script, 104, 110, 155-156, 179
Latvian, 53, 90
Lenin, V.I., 4, 7, 9, 35-36, 42-44, 53-54, 85-86, 105
Leninist epistemology, 84-85
Levi-Strauss, Claude, 11
Lezgin, 46-47
Liber, George, 154
Literacy, 25, 35, 74-75, 105, 166
 political, 35, 151-152
 semiliterate, 144-149
Locke, John, 17-18
Lomtev, T., 97, 163
Lotman, Y., 177
Lunacharskii, Anatoli, 2, 38, 40-42, 54, 98, 104, 105
Luria, A.R., 114-115, 138
Lysenko, T., 165, 172
Maiakovskii, V., 35
Main Directorate of Military Education Institutions, 24
Main Scientific Directorate (Glavnauk), 60, 107
Malenkov, G.M., 165
Mansurov, G.G., 72, 165
Mari, 28, 53, 139, 166, 170-171
Marr, N.Ia., 8-9, 80-102, 107, 116-118, 138-142, 161-163, 168-169, 176

Marx, Karl,
  Capital, 64
  German ideology, 144
Medvedev, P.N., 92
Meillet, Antoine, 162
Mel'nichenko, G.A., 149
Mergence (*sliianie*), 3, 73, 88, 144, 154-156, 176
Meshchaninov, I.I., 165
Mikhal'skii, E., 78
Mikoian, A., 54, 124
Mingrelian, 82
Ministry of Education (RSFSR), 166-167, 170
Ministry of Internal Affairs (Imperial), 21, 25, 104
Ministry of National Education (Imperial), 22, 25
Mirtov, A.V., 170
Molotov, V.M., 149-150
Mordvinian, 90, 139
Morphology, 24, 170
  sound-form principle, 23, 108, 130-131
Moscow Institute of History, Philosophy, and Literature, 162
Moscow Linguistic Circle, 21, 65, 70-71, 90
Moscow Pedagogical Institute, 100, 162
Moscow Pedagogical Institute of Foreign Languages, 162
Moscow school (Fortunatov's), 94, 111-118
Moscow State Institute of Foreign Languages, 162
Moscow State University, 43, 61, 165, 176
Mountain Region (*Gorskii*), see Northern Caucasus
Müller, Max, 17
Nation-making, 3, 9, 11, 22, 64-65, 81
"National in form", 54, 64-65, 129
National question, 1, 3, 4, 8, 24
Nativization, 3, 6, 28, 39, 46-47, 51, 53, 57, 71, 88, 135
Neogrammarians, 17

New Alphabet (NA), 125-134
New Turkic Alphabet (NTA), 125-134
New Economic Policy (NEP), 56, 143
Newspapers, 38-43, 67, 146-147
Nogai, 133
Northern Caucasus, 28, 47-49, 52, 55, 123, 137, 158, 166
Novgorodov, S.A., 122
Oirots, 133, 166
Ordzhonikidze, S., 129
Orgbiuro (TsK RKPb), 7, 68, 126, 149-150, 153, 161
Orientalism, 10, 16
Osman, 31-32
Ossetian, 53, 55, 122-123
Ottoman Turkish (see Osman)
Pan-Caucasianism, 32, 50
Pan-Islamism, 28, 129
Pan-Turkism, 12, 28, 31-32, 49-50, 121, 129-130
Pavlov, I.I., 85-86, 91, 96
Pavlovich-Vel'tman, M.P., 8, 54, 127
Peasant question, 8, 15, 36
Peasants' correspondents, 39-40, 68
Pereverzev, V.M., 83
Peshkovskii, A.M., 24, 61, 111, 116
Peterson, M.N., 60, 67, 95, 110, 113, 165, 139
Petrograd University,
  Faculty of Oriental Languages, 122
Petrova, E.N., 116-118, 167
Phenomenology, 9, 61-63
Philology, 16, 28, 83
Philosophy of praxis, 98-99
Phoneme, 19, 23, 130, 141
Phonetics, 122
  sound-principle, 22-23, 107-108, 130-131
Phonology, 19, 23, 69
Plekhanov, V., 85, 89, 97, 116
Pocock, J.G.A., 7
Pokrovskii, M.N., 45, 61, 83, 93
Politburo (TsK RKPb), 8, 126, 167
Polivanov, E.D., 21, 29-30, 37, 67-68, 70, 76-77, 79, 81, 94-95, 97-98, 100, 104, 121-122, 131-133, 136, 139, 163, 168

Pomorska, Krystyna, 69
Porzhezinskii, V.K., 59
Potebnia, Aleksandr, 18, 23, 25, 40, 64, 91, 99, 151, 168
Prague Linguistic Circle, 11, 69, 104, 165
Promethean languages, 89
"Promoted ones" (*vydvyzhentsy*), 57, 143
Protolanguage, 16
Provisional Government, 26, 35, 48, 103
Pushkin, Aleksandr, 15, 42, 55, 106, 151, 169
Qu'ran, 31, 125
Ramiz, 132
Riasanovsky, Nicholas, 27
Readers, 22
Reciprocal bilingualism, 47-58, 179
Red Army, 37, 43, 48
Reflection theory, 116-144, 172-173
Reflexology, 75, 85-86, 91, 96
Reformatskii, A.A., 67-68, 164-165
Revzin, I.I., 177
Rosenburg, Suzanne, 147
RSFSR (Russian Federation), 1, 3, 46
Rubakin, N.A., 39
Russian Association of Proletarian Writers (RAPP), 97
Russian Association of Scientific Research Institutes of Material, Artistic and Speech Cultures, 100
Russian Association of Scientific Research Institutes of the Social Sciences (RANION), 60, 67, 71, 94
Russian language, 4, 21, 25, 51, 54-57, 73-74, 89, 106, 113-114, 117, 143-160, 161-173, 175-180
   obligatory study, 159
Russification, 6, 23, 28
   imperial, 1, 15-16, 27
   scripts, 157-160
   Soviet, 5, 54, 89, 156-160
Rybnikov, M.A., 75-76
Samarkand, 48, 95
Samurskii, N., 46
Sapir, E., 162

Sarts (Uzbeks), 32, 43
Saussure, Ferdinand de, 11, 17, 19, 21, 60, 70-71, 89, 93, 97, 101, 116, 145, 162, 166
Savitskii, P.N., 69
Schleicher, August, 16, 87
Scientific organization of labor (NOT), 74-75, 103, 107
Scientific Research Association for the Study of National and Colonial Problems, 100
Scientific Research Institute of Linguistics (NIIaz), 100-101, 152
Scientific Research Institute of the Non-Russian Schools, 160, 171
Scientific Research Institute for the Study of the Ethnic and National Cultures of the Peoples of the East, 70-71, 88
Scientific-technical terminological code, 154-156
Secretariat (TsK RKPb), 149-150, 161
Selishchev, A.M., 37
Semantics, 23
Seminar on Mathematical Linguistics, 176
Semiotics, 17-18, 21, 67-68, 89, 90
Serdiuchenko, G.P., 165
Shafir, Ia., 39-40, 117
Shakhmatov, A.S., 21, 26, 29, 151, 168
Sharaf, Galimdzhan, 122, 127-128, 131
Shaumian, S.K., 176
Shcherba, L.V., 29, 114, 160
Shklovskii, Viktor, 21, 30, 59-60
Shor, 53
Shor, R.O., 66, 71, 90, 95-96, 100, 162
Shpet, G.G., 9, 18, 57-65, 72, 89, 90-92, 95, 98-99, 117, 163, 172-173
Siberia, 28, 76
Siberian languages (Khanty, Man'si, Nanai, Nivkhi, Saamy), 157
Signal system, 85-87, 96, 146-147, 165
"Socialist in content", 54, 129
Socialist realism, 147-150
Soloviev, Vladimir, 27
Soviet Esperanto Union (SEU), 77-78
Soviet Union (USSR), 46

Speech Physiology Laboratory, 86
"Speech union" (*sprachbund*), 69
Stadialism, 87, 153, 161-169
Stalin, Iosef, 3, 7, 35, 53-54, 70, 88, 161
    Autonomization, 48
    Commissar of Nationalities, 8, 45-46, 51-52, 124, 127
    Esperanto, 76-77, 154-156
    Marxism and linguistics, 8, 167-173
    Marxism and the national question, 44
State Academic Council (GUS), 60, 106, 115
State Academy of Artistic Studies (GAKhN), 61, 72, 95
State Academy of the History of Material Culture (GAIMK), 84
State-building, 3, 9, 11, 81
State Political Directorate (GPU and OGPU), 128, 137
State Publishing House, 111
Structural approach, 9, 17, 19-20, 30, 62, 65-69, 152, 161-162, 176
Structuralism, 11, 176
Sukhotin, A., 97
Sultangaliev, Mir Said, 44, 48-49, 126, 129
Suslov, M., 167
Svan, 82
Syntax, 115
Tajik, 31, 49, 50, 133, 135-136, 153
Talysh, 133
Tashkent, 48, 72
Tatars, 43, 47-48, 50, 57, 153, 166, 170
    Crimea, 31-32, 126-128
    Volga, 28-32, 44-49, 16-127, 133
Taylor, F.W., 74-75, 103
Teachers, 22-26, 114-116, 158, 169
Technical Code Commission, 154-156
Teleology, 21
Terminology, 134-136, 152, 161
Thousanders, 145, 159, 170
Tiuriakulov, N., 71, 125, 131
Toporov, V., 176
Totalitarian language, 146, 169

Trotskii, Lev, 35-36, 81
Trubetskoi, N.S., 21, 30, 59, 68, 163, 179
Tsarist state, 1, 13, 25, 33, 45
Turkestan, 32, 45-46, 49, 72, 135
Turkic (languages), 17, 28, 43, 50, 73, 90, 129-138
Turkmen, 49, 153
Typewriters, 136-137
Udmurt, 28, 53, 139, 166
Uigur, 133
Ukrainian, 21, 44, 47, 53, 73
Ushakov, D.N., 43, 60, 106, 108-110, 113-115, 150-151, 168
Uslar, P.K., 28
Uspenskii, Boris, 177
Ustinov, I.V., 106-109, 118
Uvarov, Sergei, 27
Uzbekistan (people and language), 43, 47, 49, 50, 56, 57, 73, 95, 122, 126, 131, 135-136, 138, 159, 166, 170-171, 179
Varankin, V.V., 78
Vendryes, Joseph, 162
Veps, 53
Verne, Jules, 78
Vertov, D., 107, 110
Vinogradov, V.V., 164, 168
Vinokur, G.O., 15, 21, 65, 97, 110, 113, 117, 150, 163-164
Volapük, 36
Volga-Urals, 28, 31, 48-49, 52, 158
Voloshinov, V.N., 11, 92-93, 97, 99, 116, 144, 147
Von Hagen, Mark, 39
Vowel harmony, 132, 136
Vygotskii, L.S., 11, 91-92, 138
Vyshinskii, A.Ia., 93
Wells, H.G., 78
Workers' correspondents, 39-40, 68
World Non-Nationalist Association (SAT), 77-78
Wüster, Eugene, 156
Young Communist League, 37
Zamenhof, Ludwig, 20
Zaum (nonsense poetry), 21, 74-76, 90
Zhdanov, A.A., 149-150, 159, 164-165

Zhirkov, L.I., 65, 68, 71, 110
Zhirmunskii, V.M., 147, 165
Zoshchenko, M., 113

Contributions to the Sociology of Language

Edited by Joshua A. Fishman

Mouton de Gruyter · Berlin · New York

41 Dilworth B. Parkinson, *Constructing the Social Context of Communication. Terms of Address in Egyptian Arabic.* 1985.
42 *The Fergusonian Impact. In Honor of Charles A. Ferguson on the Occasion of his 65th Birthday.* Vol. 1: *From Phonology to Society.* Vol. 2: *Sociolinguistics and the Sociology of Language.* Edited by Joshua A. Fishman. 1986.
43 A. D. Evans and William W. Falk, *Learning to be Deaf.* 1986.
44 Harald Haarmann, *Language in Ethnicity. A View of Basic Ecological Relations.* 1986.
45 Bent Preisler, *Linguistic Sex Roles in Conversation. Social Variation in the Expression of Tentativeness in English.* 1986.
46 Einar Haugen, *Blessings of Babel. Bilingualism and Language Planning. Problems and Pleasures.* 1987.
47 Lesley D. Harman, *The Modern Stranger. On Language and Membership.* 1988.
48 *Codeswitching. Anthropological and Sociolinguistic Perspectives.* Edited by Monica Heller. 1988.
49 Jeffra Flaitz, *The Ideology of English. French Perceptions of English as a World Language.* 1988.
50 Friederike Braun, *Terms of Address. Problems of Patterns and Usage in Various Languages and Cultures.* 1988.
51 Harald Haarmann, *Symbolic Values of Foreign Language Use. From the Japanese Case to a General Sociolinguistic Perspective.* 1989.
52 *Working with Language. A Multidisciplinary Consideration of Language Use in Work Contexts.* Edited by Hywel Coleman. 1989.
53 *English across Cultures. Cultures across English. A Reader in Cross-cultural Communication.* Edited by Ofelia García and Ricardo Othcguy. 1989.
54 *The Politics of Language Purism.* Edited by Björn H. Jernudd and Michael J. Shapiro. 1989.
55 *General and Amerindian Ethnolinguistics. In Remembrance of Stanley Newman.* Edited by Mary R. Key and Henry M. Hoenigswald. 1989.
56 Karol Janicki, *Toward Non-Essentialist Sociolinguistics.* 1990.
57 *Perspectives on Official English. The Campaign for English as the Official Language of the USA.* Edited by Karen L. Adams and Daniel T. Brink. 1990.
58 *Languages in School and Society. Policy and Pedagogy.* Edited by Mary E. McGroarty and Christian J. Faltis. 1991.
59 Harald Haarmann, *Basic Aspects of Language in Human Relations. Toward a General Theoretical Framework.* 1991.

60 William Fierman, *Language Planning and National Development. The Uzbek Experience.* 1991.
61 *A Language Policy for the European Community. Prospects and Quandaries.* Edited by Florian Coulmas. 1991.
62 *Pluricentric Languages. Differing Norms in Different Nations.* Edited by Michael Clyne. 1991.
63 Richard J. Watts, *Power in Family Discourse.* 1991.
64 *Language Death. Factual and Theoretical Explorations with Special Reference to East Africa.* Edited by Matthias Brenzinger. 1992.
65 *The Earliest Stage of Language Planning. "The First Congress" Phenomenon.* Edited by Joshua A. Fishman. 1993.
66 Monica Heller, *Crosswords. Language, Education and Ethnicity in French Ontario.* 1994.
67 *Linguistic Human Rights. Overcoming Linguistic Discrimination.* Edited by Tove Skutnabb-Kangas and Robert Phillipson. In collaboration with Mart Rannut. 1994.
68 *When East Met West. Sociolinguistics in the Former Socialist Bloc.* Edited by Jeffrey Harlig and Csaba Pléh. 1995.
69 *Discrimination through Language in Africa? Perspectives on the Namibian Experience.* Edited by Martin Pütz. 1995.
70 Clinton D. Robinson, *Language Use in Rural Development. An African Perspective.* 1996.
71 *Contrastive Sociolinguistics.* Edited by Marlis Hellinger and Ulrich Ammon. 1996.
72 *Post-Imperial English. Status Change in Former British and American Colonies, 1940-1990.* Edited by Joshua A. Fishman, Andrew W. Conrad and Alma Rubal-Lopez. 1996.
73 K. Dallas Kenny, *Language Loss and the Crisis of Cognition. Between Socio- and Psycholinguistics.* 1996.
74 Tara Goldstein, *Two Languages at Work. Bilingual Life on the Production Floor.* 1997.
75 *Indigenous Literacies in the Americas. Language Planning from the Bottom up.* Edited by Nancy H. Hornberger. 1997.
76 Joshua A. Fishman, *In Praise of the Beloved Language. A Comparative View of Positive Ethnolinguistic Consciousness.* 1997.
77 *The Multilingual Apple. Languages in New York City.* Edited by Ofelia García and Joshua A. Fishman. 1997.
78 *Undoing and Redoing Corpus Planning.* Edited by Michael Clyne. 1997.
79 Nirmala Srirekam PuruShotam, *Negotiating Language, Constructing Race. Disciplining Difference in Singapore.* 1997.
80 Michael G. Smith, *Language and Power in the Creation of the USSR, 1917–1953.* 1998.